NEW DIRECTIONS IN POLITICAL SOCIALIZATION

Edited by
David C. Schwartz and Sandra Kenyon Schwartz

THE FREE PRESS
A Division of Macmillan Publishing Co., Inc.
NEW YORK
COLLIER MACMILLAN PUBLISHERS
LONDON

This book is dedicated to Meredith Anne with love

The Free Press
A Division of Macmillan Publishing Co., Inc.
866 Third Avenue, New York, N.Y. 10022

Collier–Macmillan Canada Ltd.

Library of Congress Catalog Card Number: 74–2653

Printed in the United States of America

printing number
1 2 3 4 5 6 7 8 9 10

Library of Congress Cataloging in Publication Data

Schwartz, David C.
    New directions in political socialization
    Includes bibliographical references and index.
    1. Political socialization – essays.
I. Schwartz, Sandra Kenyon, joint editor.   II. Title.
JA76.S36   301.5'92   74-2653
ISBN 0-02-928180-6

Contents

iii

Preface

How do people acquire their basic attitudes toward politics? Why do some individuals adopt orientations toward political behavior different from those of others from very similar social backgrounds or even from the same family? Do the processes by which a political attitude is acquired have significant influence on the stability and/or salience of that attitude, on the probability that the attitude will be acted upon, or on the character of political behavior relevant to the attitude? These questions are clearly fundamental to the study of individual political behavior and mass politics, for they concern the underlying operations by which people evaluate political events and systems and the mechanisms by which they are moved to engage in political activities. Further, these questions are important to the investigation of political systems because mass-level behaviors (for example, supportive–compliant versus revolutionary behavior) are crucial to the stability, integration, and development of political systems (Easton, 1965; Lipset, 1960; Almond and Verba, 1963).

This book represents an effort to provide better answers to these questions than are currently available. More importantly, it is an attempt to help others develop still more satisfactory answers to these questions, by identifying and partially charting some important new perspectives and emphases in theory and research.

We believe that explanations of the causes and consequences of political socialization phenomena can be significantly advanced by making three modifications or additions to present research activities. First, we advocate including in socialization studies a far wider array of variables describing the individual being socialized than are presently considered. We believe that the socializee is not a passive *tabula rasa* (as some socialization studies seem to have assumed) but is rather a very active participant, indeed a partially determining force, in the process of his or her own socialization. In particular, we urge substantially greater attention be paid to personality, life-cycle, and life-crisis variables. We hold that the major personal events that dominate people's lives (life crises) and people's reactions to these events (reactions that are part of personality) are of the essence of both general and political socialization.

Second, we suggest that the study of political socialization can be made more rigorous and effective, our explanations more parsimonious, by appreciably greater use of dynamic modelling. In this, we are not merely echoing the growing call for greater focus on the processes rather than the outcomes of socialization (Sigel, 1966; Merelman, 1972; Dennis, 1968) but reminding our readers and ourselves that the very definition of a process requires more dynamic models and research strategies than commonly employed heretofore. More specifically, a process may be defined as a series of changes over time in the state of an attitudinal or behavioral system, a series of changes moving from a specified initial state through one or more transitional states to an end state, a series wherein the probability and speed of the changes are accounted for by specified transition laws or transition probabilities (Schwartz, 1970). We think that this conception of process will be helpful to students of political socialization in linking early learning experiences and attitudes to later political behavior, in discovering discontinuities in socialization and charting the consequences of these discontinuities, and in adapting and applying certain well-developed theories from the other social sciences—especially learning theories and theories of child development.

Finally, we contend that the study of socialization should be expanded to include populations (agencies and age groups) not now well-studied. Among the agencies we believe to have substantial socialization impacts but to have been underemphasized are: popular culture (e.g., music, literature, drama, television) and the heroes, myths, and moods popular culture can create; political events and experiences (e.g., wars, depressions, political movements, critical elections); and generational membership. Among the age groups we think should be accorded greater attention are the very young and the increasingly numerous elderly.

The reasoning and evidence underlying our advocacy of these changes are presented in Chapter 1. There we also place into context the individual chapters of this book—chapters which not only advocate but begin actually to make these changes.

The teaching, encouragement, and advice of several people proved invaluable to us in developing the perspectives advanced here and in organizing the book. Martin Landau, Frederick W. Frey, and Robert C. Wood, friends and former professors, helped us to fashion our basic aspirations and orientations toward political study. Neal Cutler, Robert Frank, Stanley Renshon, and Peter Shubs have provided important and continuous intellectual stimulation to us—both in their scholarly writings and, at least as importantly, in our warm, supportive professional and personal relationships. We are especially grateful to the senior authors of the chapters of this book: Neal Cutler, John Pollock, Stanley Renshon, Ira Rohter, and the late Norah Rosenau. Their ideas, cooperation, enthusiasm, and—at times—forbearance made the process of editing this book a most rewarding experience for us.

Our joy in doing this book has become mingled with profound sadness due to the tragic death in an automobile accident of our colleague and friend, Norah Rosenau. The rich insights found in her chapter demonstrate that Norah will be missed not only by her family and her many friends but by all scholars and students who share her intellectual concerns.

David C. Schwartz
Sandra Kenyon Schwartz

Acknowledgments

These Acknowledgments are in the order in which the chapters appear.

Stanley Allen Renshon's chapters, "The Role of Personality Development in Political Socialization" and "Birth Order and Political Socialization," were facilitated by and largely written during a National Institute of Mental Health postdoctoral fellowship year in Psychology and Politics in the Department of Political Science, Yale University, 1972-73. He wishes to express his gratitude to NIMH and the Yale Political Science Department for the valuable support afforded him.

David C. Schwartz gratefully acknowledges the generous research support of the H. F. Guggenheim Foundation, the Rutgers Research Council, the National Institute of Health—Rutgers BioMedical Sciences Support Grant Program, and the Rutgers Center for Computer and Information Services, which made possible the study reported by Schwartz, Joseph Garrison, and James Alouf in "Health, Body Images, and Political Socialization." In addition, the authors are pleased to acknowledge the very able and dedicated research assistance of Margaret Gaboury.

Much of the research reported in Ira S. Rohter's chapter, "A Social Learning Approach to Political Socialization," was undertaken while the author was a visiting postdoctoral fellow in the Psychology and Politics Program at Yale University, 1969–1970. Dr. Rohter sincerely appreciates the gracious assistance of the Yale Political Science Department and its then chairman, Robert Lane.

Norah Rosenau's chapter, "The Sources of Children's Political Concepts: An Application of Piaget's Theory," builds upon two of the author's previous papers: "The Political Development of Children," Commissioned Paper No. 1, National Science Foundation Elementary Political Education Project, Mershon Center, Ohio State University, 1972; and "Political Learning in Children and Adults," paper presented to the Third Annual Michigan State University Conference on Social Science and Social Education, East Lansing, May 11–12, 1973.

Sandra Kenyon Schwartz's research on "Patterns of Cynicism: Differential Political Socialization among Adolescents" was supported by the National Science Foundation's Doctoral Dissertation Research Grant Program. She wishes to thank Frederick W. Frey for his advice and encouragement on conducting the original research.

John C. Pollock is grateful to the Foreign Area Fellowship Program and the Stanford University Council on International Studies for their support of the research reported in "Early Socialization and Elite Behavior." Appreciation is also extended to Fernando Cepeda and to Bogotá's University of the Andes for support and invaluable assistance.

Sandra Kenyon Schwartz thanks the members of her graduate seminar in Political Socialization at Rutgers University for interviewing the preschoolers reported on in "Preschoolers and Politics." She is especially grateful to Margaret Gaboury for assistance in the data analysis for that chapter.

Neal E. Cutler's chapter, "Toward a Generational Conception of Political Socialization," was prepared while the author was a Visiting Professor, under the auspices of the Senior Fulbright-Hays Program, at the Institute of Political Science, University of Helsinki.

David C. Schwartz and Charles J. Mannella are very much indebted to Margaret Gaboury for her able assistance in the analysis and interpretation of the data reported in "Popular Music as an Agency of Political Socialization. A Study in Popular Culture and Politics." The senior author also wishes to acknowledge the support of the Rutgers Center for Computer and Information Services.

John C. Pollock, Dan White, and Frank Gold wish to thank Professor Charles Cutter of California State University, San Diego, for his organizing assistance and constructive comments on their study, "When Soldiers Return: Combat and Political Alienation among White Vietnam Veterans."

Biographical Notes

These notes are in the order in which the contributors are represented.

David C. Schwartz (A.B., Brooklyn College; Ph.D., Massachusetts Institute of Technology) is presently Associate Professor of Political Science at Livingston College and the Graduate Faculty of Rutgers, The State University of New Jersey. He is the author of *Political Alienation and Political Behavior* (Chicago: Aldine Publishing Company, 1973) and of scholarly articles on political psychology, alienation, political violence, and changing trends in the social sciences that have appeared in books and scholarly journals. Dr. Schwartz is Associate Editor of *Society* magazine, an Associate of the Danforth Foundation, and a consultant in research to several public foundations and research agencies. At present, he is conducting research on the influence of people's health, personality, and life crises on their political attitudes and behaviors.

Sandra Kenyon Schwartz (A.B., Mount Holyoke College; Ph.D., Massachusetts Institute of Technology) is presently Assistant Professor of Political Science at Douglass College and the Graduate Faculty of Rutgers, The State University of New Jersey. She is the author of scholarly papers on political socialization and political psychology, presented to national meetings of the American Political Science Association and the American Psychological Association. Dr. Schwartz is currently working on a study of the political socialization of preschoolers, which builds upon her study reported in this book, and on studies of women in politics.

Stanley Allen Renshon (A.B., Rutgers, The State University of New Jersey; Ph.D., University of Pennsylvania) is presently Assistant Professor of Political Science, Lehman College, and the Graduate Center, City University of New York. He is the author of *Psychological Needs and Political Behavior* (New York: Free Press, 1974) and of several articles and papers on political psychology published in scholarly journals and presented to regional and national meetings of political science associations. Dr. Renshon is currently at work on a book on mental health and political leadership.

Joseph Garrison and *James Alouf* are both graduate students in the New Brunswick Department of Political Science, Rutgers, The State University of New Jersey. Both are presently teaching in New Jersey high schools.

Ira S. Rohter (B.S., Illinois Institute of Technology; Ph.D., Michigan State University) is presently Associate Professor of Political Science, University of Hawaii. He is the author of several papers on political socialization and political psychology that have been presented to meetings of learned societies and have appeared in scholarly literature. His current research includes studies of the political socialization of American preadults.

Norah Rosenau (A.B., Douglass College, Rutgers, The State University of New Jersey; Ph.D., New York University) was, until her recent death, a Research Associate of the Andrus Gerontology Center, University of Southern California. In addition to her research in social psychology, she was the author of several papers on political socialization which were presented to scholarly conferences. At the time of her death she was conducting research on a broad range of social psychological phenomena.

John C. Pollock (A.B., Swarthmore; Ph.D., Stanford University) is an Assistant Professor of Sociology and Political Science, Livingston College, Rutgers, The State University of New Jersey. Several of his articles on political development and political violence in Latin America have been recently published, as have several others on United States press coverage of Latin American politics. Dr. Pollock is now serving as head of the Committee on U.S. Press Coverage of Latin America of the Latin American Studies Association, and Director of the Latin American Institute of Rutgers University. His current research interests focus on political development and underdevelopment, political elites, and the role of the news media in social change.

Neal E. Cutler (A.B., University of Southern California; Ph.D., Northwestern University) is presently Associate Professor of Political Science and Laboratory Chief, Social Policy Laboratory, Andrus Gerontology Center, University of Southern California. He is the author of a number of scholarly papers and articles on generational analysis in political science and political socialization, on television and political socialization, and on foreign and defense policy attitudes. Dr. Cutler is a member of the Editorial Advisory Board of the Sage Professional Papers in International Politics. At present, he is involved in several international projects on television and political socialization and is directing a large-scale, interdisciplinary research program on aging, politics, and social policy.

Charles J. Mannella was a graduate student in political science at Rutgers, The State University of New Jersey and is currently a high school administrator in New Jersey.

Dan White is a law student at the University of California, Berkeley, and *Frank Gold* is a student at California State University, San Diego. Both are United States Army veterans who served overseas and who have worked closely with John Pollock in studies of returning veterans.

Part One

Introduction

Chapter One

New Directions in the Study of Political Socialization

Sandra Kenyon Schwartz and David C. Schwartz

INTRODUCTION

Over the past fifteen years, political socialization has grown to become a field of study attracting large numbers of students in political science and related fields. Initial theories have been proposed, many small and some large studies have been conducted, and the literature has become sufficiently voluminous for books reviewing the field to have appeared (Dawson and Prewitt, 1969; Jaros, 1973). In the wake of this outpouring of early research, a number of scholars have called for some stocktaking and reevaluation of our research goals to determine, in the light of these initial findings, the most promising avenues of future inquiry. What should we study to build on the foundations laid by socialization research to date, and how should we move to correct the imbalances and inadequacies of our early theories?

This book is an effort to identify and partially chart some important new directions and shifts in emphasis of theory and research that will advance the study of political socialization. We believe that attention to these themes will allow us to develop a more dynamic conceptualization of political socialization, increase the scope and precision of our theories, and locate the political socialization process more firmly in the broad context of human life in which it occurs. These new directions are introduced in this chapter against the background of a brief review of the field. Each subsequent chapter argues the case for a specific approach within these general themes and, in many cases, begins actually to test its utility by presenting preliminary data.

To date, the major research thrust in the study of political socialization has been focused on identifying the political information and orientations among elementary and, to a lesser degree, high school children, especially those who are white, American, middle and working class, and reside in urban areas. The attitudes studied have most often been directly political

3

(rather than indirectly related to politics), selected because of their relevance to one or two overlapping theoretical areas of concern. These areas are: (1) system stability, system persistence, or cultural continuity and (2) values and behavior orientations important to a democratic citizenry. In both cases, considerable attention has been directed to orientations toward political authority figures, but other dependent variables such as national symbols and political efficacy have also been studied.

The identification of socialization as a stabilizing social mechanism can be traced to the early interest of cultural anthropologists in socialization as an instrument for maintaining cultural continuity (e.g., Benedict, 1934). Political scientists interested in structural–functional analysis and in political culture tended to adopt this usage (Almond, 1960; Pye, 1968); and Hyman, who coined the term "political socialization," took a similar view as a sociologist concerned with the perpetuation of political values across generations (Hyman, 1959). A third major influence in this area was the work of Easton on systems theory, in which he argues that political systems are able to persist in large part because they have "diffuse support" on which to draw in coping with the problems engendered by unresolved political demands (Easton, 1965). He and his associates have been guided in their socialization research by a concern with the origins of this diffuse support (e.g., Easton and Dennis, 1965; Hess and Easton, 1960; Easton and Dennis, 1969).

The widespread political science interest in democratic theory has, of course, been much in evidence in research on adult political behavior, and its emphasis in the study of political socialization is a natural outgrowth of a more general interest in assessing the strengths and weaknesses of democratic norms and behavior patterns in mass publics. Socialization research in this area has included work on the psychological and attitudinal underpinnings of a democratic citizenry, such as Greenstein's research on democratic and authoritarian characters (1965a) and Almond and Verba's on trust (1963). Studies have been done on support for democratic values such as civil liberties (e.g., Remmers, 1963) and the rule of law (e.g., Hess and Torney, 1967). Perhaps the most commonly studied socialization topic in this area has been the orientations believed to lead to active political participation by adults (e.g., Easton and Dennis, 1967; Greenstein, 1965b; Hess and Torney, 1967).

Survey research, particularly questionnaires administered in schools, has been by far the most common method of conducting research in political socialization to date. Typically, developmental inferences are drawn from cross-sectional data, that is, inferences regarding change over time are based on comparisons among age (or grade in school) groups of children who are surveyed at one point in time.

The basic model of the socialization process that seems to underlie most research is one in which a socializing agency (such as the family) emits cues (often conceived of as the direct, simple expression of values or information) that are picked up and learned by the "socializee" in varying degrees. "Successful" socialization, in this view, is the extent to which the child comes to resemble the socializing agency. The degree of effect has been conceived of largely as a function of exposure to the agency (and sometimes of agency characteristics) and/or the age or maturation level of the person being socialized. Some of the hypotheses in the latter category are psychological arguments, such as Hess and Torney's suggestion that the young child views authority as benevolent because of his dependent, vulnerable position, and some are based on cognitive development arguments, such as the same authors' explanation for the person-to-institution sequence of political learning observed in elementary school children (Hess and Torney, 1967). This model places great emphasis on socializing agencies and conceptualizes socialization as a one-way interaction between the agencies and a rather passive recipient. In general, the picture that tends to emerge from this research is that of a gradual, continuous process of incremental change through childhood and adolescence during which the new generation acquires the norms prevailing within the adult population.

Recently, some new research directions have become evident. The most common one derives from questioning the universality of earlier findings based on one relatively homogeneous type of population in a particular historical period. Thus, an increasing number of studies involve children from different socioeconomic backgrounds, different subcultures, and other political systems (e.g., Jaros, Hirsch, and Fleron, 1968; Greenberg, 1970a and 1970b; Abramson, 1972; Greenstein and Tarrow, 1969). Some additional studies have been done on a variety of other topics on which research is necessary if we are adequately to test the premises of earlier research and make our theories more precise. These include a few studies applying learning theory (e.g., Froman, 1962; Merelman, 1966) and cognitive development theory (e.g., Merelman, 1971; Adelson and O'Neil, 1966; Connell, 1971), some utilizing different methodologies (e.g., Vaillancourt, 1973; Greenstein and Tarrow, 1971), and some comparative studies of socializing agencies (e.g., Langton and Karns, 1969; Jennings and Niemi, 1971). These and similar modifications and departures from earlier assumptions, topics, and methods are exceedingly useful to the development of a theory of political socialization. However, it is still probably fair to say that the earlier research approaches, except as modified by being based on a more socially heterogeneous population, are still characteristic of much, if not most, contemporary political socialization research.

It is not that earlier research approaches have not been valuable. Among other things, they have taught us that politics and childhood are not incompatible and identified a number of important political orientations, related to areas of widespread theoretical interest, that begin to develop in childhood. They have partially traced the sequence and patterning of changes in these orientations and begun the task of relating childhood patterns to adult micro- and macro-level concerns. However, these approaches need to be modified and complemented by new research directions if we are to develop a more precise and comprehensive theory of political socialization.

A number of scholars have critiqued the field and suggested new emphases and directions (e.g., Sigel, 1966; Merelman, 1972; Schonfeld, 1971; Dennis, 1973; Greenstein, 1970). Among the more common and important criticisms made of the research to date are a tendency to be biased toward stability and continuity rather than conflict and change and a lack of attention to the actual processes of socialization, which not only would yield a more adequate explanation of the dependent variables but also is necessary if we are to establish the link between early learning and later attitudes and behavior. Critics have called for more precise theoretical and operational specification of the independent variables and for further work on establishing the relevance of childhood political socialization to macro-level concerns. They have urged us to employ a broader, more heterogeneous research population and a variety of methodological approaches, two suggestions which (as indicated) have met with some response. Further work on identifying and then exploring the potential of new directions is needed, and it is this task to which this book is addressed.

NEW DIRECTIONS

The thesis of this book is that a considerably more precise and comprehensive explanation of socialization can be attained by focusing research attention on several related themes.

First, we believe that the individual being socialized plays a far more direct, dynamic, and important role in political socialization than has been recognized. The traditional model for the socialization process posits a one-way flow of information and value transfers from the socialization agency to the individual. The "socializee" thus becomes the passive recipient of various socializing stimuli. We argue that this view too largely ignores human motivation, the attitudinal context in which a socialization stimulus is perceived and interpreted, and a wide array of individual characteristics that influence people's willingness and capacity to respond to socialization influences. Further, it neglects feedback processes and other two-way interactions between those at both ends of a socialization relationship.

Second, we are arguing for a greater emphasis on process rather than on what attitudes are learned or what Roberta Sigel has called the "output" of socialization (Sigel, 1966, 3). A process focus concentrates attention on how, when, and under what conditions political attitudes are acquired, and it relates variations in these operative processes to variations in the impact of attitudes. Attention to socialization processes per se is necessary if we are to understand the circumstances under which political learning of various kinds occurs. Furthermore, as these conditions are likely to influence the impact such learning has on the individual's subsequent actions, a process focus should enable us to test propositions about the link between early learning and later behavior. We therefore argue for greater emphasis in socialization research on an array of dynamic models explaining (rather than describing) what attitudes are acquired under what circumstances and with what effects. Further we suggest that our conceptualization of the processes of socialization can, and should, be made more rigorous by applying a variety of well-developed process models from psychology and elsewhere, including a variety of learning theories, human developmental models, and Markov process models.

Third, we urge a broadening of research topics beyond the traditional age groups and socializing agencies. We need to study younger and older age groups to develop a more comprehensive picture of socialization patterns. We need also to move beyond the family and school (and occasionally the press and the peer group) to identify other sources of potential socialization stimuli. Particularly important here are socializing agencies that may be characterized by nonconsensual values. Actions within the political system itself can influence socialization. The various combinations of agencies to which individuals are differentially exposed can produce discontinuities and changes as well as continuities and stability.

Research in political socialization has tended to focus on the "fit" of values, attitudes, and beliefs between socializing agencies—fairly narrowly defined—and those exposed to them and on the degree to which prevailing norms among adult populations are foreshadowed in childhood. The themes articulated here are not designed to search for such matching attitudinal patterns but rather to urge us to adopt a less static conceptualization of political socialization, one in which the sources of socialization stimuli, the recipient, and the processes that link them make up a series of dynamic interactions.

In the remainder of this section we outline the new directions we have suggested, stating a fuller rationale for their adoption and giving specific examples and hypotheses. Clearly, no attempt is made here to be comprehensive, for to suggest all the possible influences on political socialization of salient individual characteristics, complex processes, a heterogeneous array of socializing agencies and the like would require far more space than is appropriate. What we offer here is a broad but brief rationale for the basic changes we advocate in the study of political socialization.

The Role of the Individual

We have noted the implicit assumption in much of the socialization literature that the person being socialized plays only a passive role in the process, absorbing the values of the agency (to the extent that he is able) largely as a function of simple exposure. This view of the individual's role is a natural outgrowth of a definition of socialization as the mechanism of transmitting cultural values to new members of the society, a definition shared by the cultural anthropologists and sociologists who did so much to shape the study of political socialization. Such a definition directs one's attention to the character of socializing agencies and their norms rather than to the individuals who seek out and avoid, perceive and misperceive, accept and reject the agencies' values. Further, when one does consider the individuals being socialized, the tendency of such a definition is to direct one's attention to measuring the extent to which the people resemble the values characteristic of the socializing agencies to which they are exposed. Such a perspective rules out a wide array of individual reactions —interpreting, modifying, rejecting, and attacking those values, to list some important examples.

This tendency to downplay the impact of the "socializee" on the political socialization process was probably reinforced by a perception of politics as essentially an adult prerogative which, coupled with a research focus on children, led to the assumption that adult socialization agencies fed political information and values to the "helpless formless child" (Merelman, 1972, 135) in a one-way transaction.

Yet, clearly, there can be no political socialization without a socializee, a living, breathing individual who, like all others of his kind, seeks, screens, and selectively avoids sensory stimuli (Cofer and Appley, 1964, 269–302). Far from being merely passive recipients of information and cues, most people can be assumed to be actively seeking certain kinds of information from specific kinds of sources under identifiable conditions and to be actively avoiding other kinds. Furthermore, people *evaluate* the messages transmitted by socializing agencies, not always in ways congruent with the views characteristic of those agencies. In general, the individual's affective and cognitive responses to socialization stimuli are, to a substantial degree, functions of his mental capacities, his needs, his motivations, and his prior attitudes. In this sense, we are asserting not only that the individual (child or adult) is an active participant in his political socialization but that his specific salient characteristics operate in identifiable ways to influence his socialization.

Not only does the individual actively process the socialization stimuli to which he is exposed, but, as any parent or teacher knows, the actions and reactions of the socializee can substantially affect the socializing agency itself and the relationship between the two. Thus, the socialization process is not a transactional one but an interactional process in which two-way exchanges and influences can occur. Individually initiated actions as well as feedback on agency behavior can be important factors in what is taught as well as what is learned.

We argue, then, for a greater recognition of the role played by the individual in political socialization. His needs and attitudes are an integral element of the interaction, and attention to them will assist us in developing a more dynamic conceptualization and a more precise explanation of the process of political socialization.

Individual characteristics in the literature are typically age (as an indirect indicator of cognitive development) and socioeconomic status (SES), which tends in this context to be a summary indicator of other, unspecified socialization experiences associated with SES. A few studies have dealt with intelligence as an individual factor influencing the efficiency with which socialization occurs (e.g., Hess and Torney, 1967; White, 1968; Jackman, 1970). A few scholars, most notably Fred Greenstein, have argued for the impact of personality on political socialization (e.g., Greenstein, 1965a; Froman, 1961). Sometimes measures of individual orientations to socializing agencies are included, such as "closeness to parent" or "liking for school" (e.g., Jennings and Langton, 1969; Langton and Jennings, 1968). However, the research effort devoted to these variables has been too limited and the range of individual characteristics and behavior studied has been too narrow to develop adequately our understanding of the role played by the individual in political socialization.

The individual's relationships with the various socializing agencies with which he has contact, his sensitivity and response to the particular socialization messages he encounters, and the conscious and unconscious internal states with which he approaches a socialization interaction all deserve our attention. More specifically, we urge a recognition of the importance of the ways in which the individual responds to and shapes potential socialization situations. We suggest that greater attention, with more precisely defined independent variables, be devoted to the impact of developmental levels and prior attitudes on the capability and willingness of people to accept or reject socialization stimuli. We believe that one of the individual characteristics most important for study is personality, by which we mean to include at least that constellation of the individual's typical and enduring needs, values, and cognitions that seem operative across a wide variety of behavior domains (Schwartz, 1969). We should also investigate the impact of variables, such as birth order, that influence the individual's general relationship to socializing agencies, especially the family. We should recognize the importance of biopsychological variables such as health status, energy level, physical development pattern (especially in puberty and aging), drug, alcohol, and medicine usages, and body image—variables that have been shown to have important impacts on social learning and behavior yet are almost totally ignored in the study of political socialization (e.g., Pless and Roghmann, 1970; Fisher, 1970; Birch and Gussow, 1970; Ferguson et al., 1970). We should be particularly sensitive to those life experiences most people find gripping and fundamental. To ignore the fact that people's attitudes and behaviors are influenced by puberty, getting married, having children, getting a job, or having a health trauma is to allow our studies to remain divorced from the salient, engaging stuff of life that motivates so much of human behavior.

These numerous topics clearly cannot all be dealt with in this volume. However, a number of the following chapters deal in part with this general theme, and the three chapters of Part II focus explicitly on personality, birth order, and health and body images, respectively.

A Process Orientation

Our second general theme, that we should redress the balance between studying the processes of political socialization and studying its output, has received wider recognition in the literature. A number of scholars have called for such a shift in emphasis, pointing out that our present theories make processual assumptions to explain political socialization and to estimate its subsequent impact but that these assumptions remain largely untested (Sigel, 1966; Dennis, 1968; Schonfeld, 1971; Merelman, 1972; Jaros, 1973). Hess and Torney, for example, suggest four learning models (accumulation, generalization, imitation, and cognitive development) (1967, 19–22), but they do not actually test whether these mechanisms are operative.

The most common processual assumption made is that early learning not only influences later learning but is itself lasting in impact. Indeed this assumption is basic to the study of political socialization in that it justifies political science interest in the development of political orientations in childhood. However, despite its importance, this proposition has remained too largely untested. Basically we have asserted that the acquisition of political attitudes is not well-described as a Markov process (i.e., is not a process wherein one's present state is independent of the path by which the present state was reached). Although we have asserted it, we have relied too largely on psychological and psychoanalytic materials, rather than on our own data, to document this assertion. But does early political learning last? Does it influence later learning, or is it replaced or swamped by later learning? Does much early learning simply coexist with later learning, as a result of cognitive compartmentalization processes? More importantly, does the manner and timing in which a political attitude is acquired affect the stability and consequences of the attitude; does the process of learning affect the likelihood of its being acted upon and/or the direction of behavior if it is acted upon?

There are a few notable exceptions to the general dearth of process-focused studies, particularly some studies that apply learning theory (Merelman, 1966; Froman, 1960) and cognitive development theory (Merelman, 1969; Adelson and O'Neil, 1966; Connell, 1971). These are important beginnings. However, despite these exceptions and despite the frequency with which a process orientation has been advocated, students of socialization are in general agreement that considerably greater effort in this direction is needed. At present, the topic is more apt to be recognized as important than it is to be studied.

We believe, with Roberta Sigel, that "future political behavior might vary according to the conditions under which learning [is] acquired" (1966, 3) and argue that if we focus our studies on what children learn rather than how they learn it, our interpretations of our findings must remain conjectural. By contrast, attention to dynamic models of socialization processes can lead to explanations of how and why political socialization of various types occurs and can assist us to test propositions concerning the centrality, stability, and relevance for behavior of acquired political orientations.

We include in our conception of a process focus questions relating to the impact of the conditions under which socialization interaction occurs, actual learning mechanisms, and timing and sequencing in political socialization. Questions of the first type deal with the impact of such variables as the frequency and length of exposure to a socializing agency; the extent to which complementary or competing influences within and among socializing agencies are experienced; whether the socialization stimulus is intended or unintended, repeated or occasional, verbalized or acted out; and the overall attractiveness of the socializing agency to the socializee. We need more attention to such questions and suggest that such research would be advantaged by the systematic application of theories of persuasive communication (e.g., Hovland, 1953).

Questions dealing with actual learning mechanisms focus on the individual's mental processing of socialization stimuli emitted in specified ways and concern what will be learned or concluded as a joint function of the individual's internal states and the properties of the stimulus. Existing theories of this general type, which if applied would allow us to conceptualize the socialization process more rigorously, include cognitive balance theories (e.g., Festinger, 1957) and especially certain learning theories (e.g., Bandura, 1969).

Cognitive balance theories basically assert that the degree of congruity among elements of a cognitive set predicts the individual's likely attention to those stimuli perceived as relevant and, given the relative weights associated with the various elements of the set, also predicts both the degree and direction of attitude change. Applying these theories to the study of political socialization should assist us, for example, in predicting responses to competing socializing stimuli and in evaluating the ways in which a stimulus occurring at one point in time is affected by prior beliefs and values.

Perhaps the most obviously relevant subset of well-developed process models are the major theories of human learning. As we speak of "learning" almost constantly in political socialization, it might be expected that greater attention to theories of learning would improve our studies. Theories of learning offer several advantages. First, they have a fairly unambiguous criterion for determining whether or not something has been learned (really, for describing the degree to which it has been learned) in the notion of response tendency over repeated trials (Cofer and Appley, 1964). Adopting this kind of definition in political study would pull us away from the less reliable, one-shot observation procedures used in most of our socialization studies.

Second, most of the major learning theories are rigorously processual. Despite considerable differences among them, they almost all require a precise delineation of (1) the individual's initial state (arousal level, deprivation, motivation); (2) the amount, type, and frequency of stimulation; (3) the individual's intermediate response; (4) the schedule of reinforcement; and (5) the stable pattern of learned behavior (Cofer and Appley, 1964).

Using these notions would allow us to conduct our studies in a far more focused and comprehensive manner. We would presumably begin with a set of measurements on our respondents at a given point in time, but studies would not end there as they now often do. Rather we would proceed to study the stimuli emitted by the socializing agency; to examine the degree to which the respondents perceived those stimuli (and the ways in which they misperceived and interpreted the stimuli); to observe the behavior of our respondents; to measure the feedback or reinforcement emitted by the agency and received by the socializee; and finally, to assess the degree to which a stable pattern of learning resulted. That stable pattern might then be treated as the starting point for a similar set of operations as our respondents continue the process of learning.

We recognize that such an approach, to be implemented outside the laboratory, requires a great deal of effort. It requires, for example, an effort to observe or retrieve and code the major relevant symbolic emissions from all major socialization agencies for the time period under investigation. Some scholars have suggested that to cope with this requirement we move our socialization studies into the laboratory. Others may want to begin with repeated interviewing of respondents to at least get their perceptions of what the socialization agencies were saying.

Our purpose, however, is not to recommend specific research designs but to assert that the precision and parsimony of explanation likely to be gained from an application of learning theories is likely to be worth considerable effort.

The third category of research topics included in our conception of a process orientation has to do with the importance of timing and sequencing in political socialization. This category includes, of course, arguments based on the psychological proposition that early learning is important to later learning and behavior; but it should also direct our attention more broadly to the impact on socialization of an individual's prior attitudes— to the structure of his attitudes and to the ways in which existing beliefs, values, and orientations shape (or fail to shape) his interpretation, acceptance, and rejection of socialization stimuli. In general, questions regarding the timing and sequencing of socialization involve consideration of both the psychological readiness and the cognitive capacity of the individuals being socialized to respond to socializing influences. Among the topics to be investigated here are theories of cognitive development (e.g., Piaget, 1962; Kohlberg, 1964) and life-cycle phenomena (e.g., Erikson, 1967).

These theories typically state a relatively invariant series of stages through which the physical, cognitive, and affective maturation of the individual is alleged to proceed. Many variants and applications of these theories suggest either that social and political attitudes undergo similar development or that, at least, these stages of physical and intellectual development constitute important influences on the sociopolitical learning taking place during the same periods. Some scholars have even argued that under conditions of stress (presumably including stress induced by sociopolitical phenomena) people can revert to the styles and content of thought typical of earlier stages (Adelson and O'Neil, 1966).

In socialization studies there are more than a few hints that we really believe the acquisition of a political attitude to be an act rather than a process. To be sure, we believe that the act tends to take place with greater or lesser frequency in different age groups, races, sexes, or social classes, and we call those associations "evidence" of some learning or socialization process. We tend to infer from the fact of a survey response that some antecedent process must have produced the response. But we rarely conceive of attitude acquisition in truly processual terms. Efforts to do so are complex and not likely to be successful all at once, but our aim should be to develop our theories of the socialization process to the point where by "process" we mean a series of changes over time in the state of an attitudinal or behavioral system, moving from a specified initial state or stage through one or more specified intermediate states to an end state, where the probability and speed of system–state changes are accounted for by specified transition laws (or probabilities) (Schwartz, 1970).

In general, then, we argue that a greater emphasis on a process focus in the study of political socialization would not only improve our understanding of what is happening and why but also facilitate our testing of propositions about the significance of our findings. Further, the application of well-developed process models from other disciplines should make the study of political socialization more rigorously theoretical. The studies in Part III begin to explore such a process orientation. They include chapters on the applicability of learning theories and cognitive development, an exploration of timing and discontinuities in the development of political cynicism, and an assessment of the relative importance of early versus later socialization among Colombian bureaucrats.

A Broader Look at Age Groups and Agencies

Our third general theme is to argue for a broadening of the number of age groups and agencies studied beyond those traditionally studied in political socialization. The focus on school-age children, especially elementary school pupils, has meant neglect of both the beginning and late phases of socialization. To arrive at a comprehensive picture of the development of political attitudes, we need to study the origins of political and politically relevant orientations among very young children and to trace the additions, modifications, and changes in political socialization among adults—young adults establishing themselves in work and family settings, middle-aged adults coming to terms with reaching the peak of their productivity, and elderly people coping with reduced strength, resources, status, and achievement. Psychological theories such as Erikson's (1968) suggest that such an inclusive view of the life cycle is necessary in view of the salient and critical changes in human experiences that accompany these maturational stages.

We should also pay attention to a variety of socialization agencies whose impact is not likely to be consensual, redundant, and incremental —not just to those that tend to share widespread cultural norms or to which most members of a society are exposed. Some effort in this direction has been noted in recent studies of subcultures and racial and other minorities. But still other types of socialization experiences should be studied if we are to do a better job of exploring nonconsensual political attitudes and behavior. Variations in socialization experience can underlie differential political values and demands and hence political issues and conflicts. Further, they can produce people with differential tendencies to become involved and or influential in politics. Thus they are likely to be particularly relevant to questions of conflict, change, and political elites. Our current neglect of the origins of change and conflict in political systems is especially unfortunate in the modern world, where change is widespread, failure to adapt is often disastrous for both individuals and systems, and political conflicts regularly engage masses of people.

Examples of such socializing agencies include occupational roles (particularly those relatively closely linked to politics), specialized media ranging from an underground press to professional publications, and sociopolitical events themselves, including wars, riots, mass movements, protests, and critical elections. Events in the latter category are likely to be differentially experienced by different generations, and intergenerational discontinuities can be an important source of stress and change within a political system.

The political system itself tends to be a much neglected institutional agency, although a few scholars have recognized its importance in this context (e.g., Sigel, 1970; Merelman, 1966; Wolfenstein and Kliman, 1965). In addition to the illustrations cited, conventional forms of political participation, political traumas such as the assassination of a President and such crises of confidence as Watergate, and the usual flow of symbolic and tangible political goods can, we believe, have important effects on the political socialization of citizens. These interactions can be particularly important for those interested more generally in the relationship between political decision-makers and mass publics. Their study within political science should not be understood to lie outside the interests of students of socialization.

Our list of relevant socializing agencies should also be broadened to include the elements of popular culture. Popular music, television, literature, movies, humor, rumor, and the like—all of these can contain and transmit political messages. In contemporary America, popular music and television are increasingly political in content (as several other elements of popular culture seem to be). The elements of popular culture can be tremendously engaging, involving, glamorous, and romantic, especially to young people. We know, for example, that by the time an American child reaches eighteen years of age today, he has spent more time watching television than he has spent talking to his parents and teachers combined. We reason therefore that elements of the popular culture and the heroes, myths, and moods they create can be important political socialization agencies; we think that more studies of political socialization should include variables drawn from popular culture so that our theories may take into account these widespread experiences.

As Dennis has noted (1968), despite the large number of studies of socialization with an agency focus, there are few systematic comparisons of the socialization impact of several agencies. We suggest the need for more such comparative assessments and particularly call attention to what might be termed "desocialization" experiences, the impact of which is to reverse earlier learning. Intense, concentrated, and traumatic experiences may have such an effect. Would such desocialization be lasting? Would its effect be general or cognitively compartmentalized?

In summary, then, we argue for attention to socialization throughout the life cycle and to a variety of socializing agencies of particular relevance to questions of conflict, change, the political system's own functioning, and the ordinary, appealing aspects of popular culture. The chapters in Part IV begin this task, discussing preschool children, political generations, popular music, and the impact of combat experience in Vietnam.

THE CHAPTERS OF THIS BOOK

The book is organized into three sections, paralleling the major themes introduced in this chapter: Part Two: The Influence of Individual Characteristics, Part Three: Processes of Political Socialization, and Part Four: Beyond the Traditional Age Groups and Agencies. Here we briefly summarize each chapter.

Part Two includes Chapters Two, Three, and Four. In Chapter Two, entitled "The Role of Personality Development in Political Socialization," Renshon addresses three major questions of fundamental importance to the study of political socialization.

1. Is it really true that the child's early learning experiences are significantly linked to later political attitudes and behaviors?

2. If so, which of the many things learned early in life are important in shaping later political attitudes and behaviors?

3. What is the role of personality in political socialization?

Renshon critically analyzes the political socialization literature and indicates that considerable contradictory evidence exists concerning the stability of early-learned political attitudes and orientations (and therefore, on the importance of such attitudes in shaping later learning and behavior). He suggests that personality elements, especially one's basic beliefs about the world and the self's relationship to the world, are learned early in life and importantly shape later political attitudes and behaviors, under the condition that the polity is perceived to be relevant to the individual and/or his level of need satisfaction. In a study of some 300 college students and their parents, Renshon shows that family characteristics and dynamics are the most important determinants of certain basic beliefs (controllability of the world and the self's capability to influence the social world). He also finds that the individual's "score" on these basic beliefs bears regular and significant association with political attitudes and behaviors. These findings are presented as some support for the conclusions that basic beliefs are both early-learned and important to later political attitudes and that at least one set of personality elements, basic beliefs, play a significant role in political socialization processes.

In Chapter Three, "Birth Order and Political Socialization," Renshon expands upon his strategy for studying the influence of family dynamics on political socialization. He notes that the family, although almost universally accepted as an important socialization agency, in many respects is treated as a "black box." Studies of family outputs and parent–child attitude correlations far outnumber in-depth studies of how specific family dynamics influence political learning. To begin to rectify this situation, Renshon reminds us that specific family dynamics are likely to influence the learning of specific sociopolitical orientations and argues, further, that different family members may well have quite different political socialization experiences. This later point suggests that birth order, the sequential arrival into the family, may prove to be a most useful variable—especially in light of evidence from psychology and sociology that parental child rearing practices tend to differ significantly from first-borns to later-borns. Renshon reviews and synthesizes a very large number of studies that tend to show that birth order has significant influence on such personality variables as need achievement, self-esteem, anxiety, need affiliation, autonomy–dependency, and intelligence. The author then offers interpretive and useful speculative commentary on how the "birth-order, child-rearing, personality" constellation might influence political learning.

The thesis of the authors of Chapter Four, "Health, Body Images, and Political Socialization," is that certain biopsychological characteristics of the individual, especially his or her health status and perceptions and evaluations of the body, are likely to influence significantly the political attitudes and behaviors learned by the individual. This is so, it is argued, because: (a) chronic and traumatic health problems influence both the individual's relationships to socializing agencies and his or her basic images of the body and self; (b) basic images of body and self, in turn, influence the individual's interest in, attention to, and predispositions toward the polity and political behavior. A complex model comprised of thirteen linked hypotheses is developed to chart some of the processes by which health and body images influence political learning. This model is tested, and basically confirmed, in a study of some 2,100 American high school students.

Part Three includes Chapters Five through Eight. In Chapter Five, "A Social Learning Approach to Political Socialization," Rohter argues that, as political socialization is almost universally defined to include the processes of political learning, our studies should be informed by an awareness and application of the various types of learning theory. Rohter explicates the central processes in theories of classical conditioning, theories of secondary reinforcement (which cite the frequency and scheduling of rewards as determinative of the speed and stability of learning), and theories of social learning (as in imitative and observational learning). He argues for the special relevance of social learning theories to the study of political socialization and gives several examples.

Chapter Six, "The Sources of Children's Political Concepts: An Application of Piaget's Theory" provides an overview of Piaget's theory and an exposition of several ways in which Piaget's theory might advance the study of political socialization. More specifically, Rosenau shows us how Piaget's type of thinking might (1) direct our attention to the most relevant variables for study at different levels of cognitive development; (2) explain why some things, rather than others, are learned at certain development levels; and (3) explain why the meanings of political symbols may differ for children at different levels.

Rosenau argues that general, politically relevant experiences occur in the daily lives of children (e.g., interactions with authority figures) and that from these experiences basic general attitudes and orientations are learned which will influence later and more specifically political learning. This argument, which is similar to Renshon's discussion in Chapter Two of basic beliefs, is here placed within the context of, and partly explained by, Piaget's emphasis on the young child's use of direct, proximate experiences in forming his cognitive schemata. Like Renshon, Rosenau would direct our attention more toward the young child's general politically relevant learning and somewhat less toward specific political information and attitudes. In a review of relevant psychological and political science applications of Piaget to political socialization, however, the author also suggests that attention to developmental levels may help us to interpret the meaning and significance of specifically political attitudes observed in children. Rosenau also cautions us that, although Piaget's models seem useful in the study of cognitive development, other theories of development and learning will be required to deal with affective development.

In Chapter Seven, "Patterns of Cynicism: Differential Political Socialization among Adolescents," Sandra Kenyon Schwartz attempts to test one of the most basic assumptions on which the study of political socialization has been based, the assumption that the conditions under which a political attitude is learned (including the time at which and the sequence in which it is learned) has significant influence on that attitude's impact on other attitudes and on political behavior. The author indicates the centrality of this assumption to political socialization research and identifies its important implication that studying adults' political attitudes after they are acquired neglects information likely to be crucial in explaining the linkages between political attitudes and behavior.

The research presented in this chapter explores the influence of the time at which a given attitude, political cynicism, is acquired on the causes and consequences of holding that attitude. In a study of 897 urban adolescents (eighth-, tenth-, and twelfth-graders) the author shows that a very different pattern of causes and consequences is associated with early-acquired cynicism than holds true for respondents who acquire that attitude later in adolescence. Her findings indicate that socialization models that assume relatively linear, gradual development toward adult attitude configurations may require substantial modification.

Chapter Eight, "Early Socialization and Elite Behavior," inquires: Can political socialization processes help to explain adult elite role behavior? Are there significant interrelationships among early learning experiences, occupational socialization, and adult, elite policy preferences? These fascinating and important questions are the focus of Pollock's attention, as he begins by noting that too little is known yet about the role of occupational socialization in forming elite policy preferences and that even less is known about the influence of early life experiences on occupational socialization and elite policy preferences. In a study of 82 Colombian urban housing bureaucrats, the author finds regular and significant associations between policy preferences and (a) their occupational experiences and attitudes (years of experience, perceptions of colleagues, optimism about job performance) and (b) their early life experiences (family size, character of education). Pollock shows that two of the three best predictors of policy preferences are also early life experiences (experiences long predating the onset of occupational socialization) and that early life experiences have significant impacts on occupational learning. He traces some specific influences of early experiences, through occupational socialization, on elite attitudes and develops alternative models to explain these influences.

Part Four consists of Chapters Nine through Twelve. Chapter Nine, "Preschoolers and Politics," asks: When does political socialization begin? In political socialization research we typically talk about "early learning," but virtually all our studies are conducted among children seven years old and older. This tendency is somewhat surprising, in that the psychological literature's proposition that early learning influences later learning and behavior, on which much political socialization study is based, includes in "early learning" the very early years of life. In this chapter, Sandra Kenyon Schwartz attempts to show that directly political learning begins much earlier than age seven, in the preschool age period. She hypothesizes that it is in this period from three to six that children come out of a prepolitical stage in which they tend neither to recognize nor to react to political symbols into a state wherein they become increasingly aware of such symbols. Her pilot data on a population of New Jersey preschoolers provide some support for this notion. The central tendencies among these three-, four- and five-year-olds were for the children to be increasingly able to recognize political symbols (pictures and words), to have some information about and affect for these symbols, and to differentiate political symbols from nonpolitical ones. The author finds a coherent pattern of political responses among these preschoolers, consistent with cognitive development theories.

In Chapter Ten, "Toward a Generational Conception of Political Socialization," Cutler suggests a dramatic reorientation of the way political socialization is investigated. He believes that the concept of political generations supplies part of the linkage between early learning and adult political behavior, arguing that successive generational groups of citizens undergo substantially different sets of experiences in their formative years, adopt distinctive political orientations grounded in their particular experiences, and tend to maintain these orientations across the life cycle. Cutler shows us how all socialization agencies are heavily influenced by macro-political events and trends; that the family, school, and peer groups are all cross-cut by generational influences; that these agencies change and are changed by intergenerational "negotiation" or interactions; and that a portion of the impact of all socialization agencies is attributable to a generational component.

This viewpoint usefully allows us to contrast maturational with generational explanations. But more than that, it encourages us to observe and allows us to explain a great variety of change-producing discontinuities and strains within as well as among agencies of political socialization. Cutler demonstrates this in an examination of party identification in the United States. His chapter's conclusion goes beyond the usual pleas for greater attention to the variable of interest (here, generations); it includes a most useful indication of how we might best utilize extant and growing data bases and resources in order to reap the rewards of increased attention to generations.

Schwartz and Manella argue in Chapter Eleven, "Popular Music as an Agency of Political Socialization: A Study in Popular Culture and Politics," that the elements of popular culture—music, literature, drama, television, humor, rumor, cinema—and the heroes, myths, and moods created by popular culture are vehicles or agencies of socialization widely recognized by the other social sciences. To date, however, these popular culture elements have been almost wholly ignored in the study of political socialization. In this chapter, the authors reason that popular music ought to be a significant agency of political socialization for a substantial portion of American teenagers, given the high and increasing salience and politicization of popular music. They present data from a pilot study of some 600 New Jersey high school students that tend to show that teenagers' involvement in popular music, their musical preferences, the use of music to define peer-group relationships, and the recognition of political statements in popular music all do have some predictable and modest but statistically significant influence on teenagers' political attitudes. The chapter concludes with a brief comparison of political socialization processes involving popular music with processes involving other socialization agencies.

In Chapter Twelve, "When Soldiers Return: Combat and Political Alienation among White Vietnam Veterans," Pollock and his co-authors contend that the study of political socialization has tended to neglect the socializing effects of actual political experiences. Their study is on the socializing influence of one such experience, wartime military service. They reason that such service, during a relatively controversial and unpopular war, is likely to lead to political alienation, and they raise two related questions: (a) Do the character and intensity of the individual's wartime experiences (e.g., combat vs. noncombat; involved in killing others vs. not involved) influence alienation? (b) Does the amount of time elapsed since wartime service influence alienation?

Pollock, White, and Gold conducted a survey-based study of nearly 400 returned Vietnam veterans at a large West Coast university. Their data tend to show that the intensity of war experiences does predict political alienation levels. They also found a sharp reversal of this trend among those who had had the most intense combat experiences. Finally, they found that the time elapsed since military service had little influence on political attitudes but that resocialization experiences (education and the like) did have substantial impact. In an interpretive section the authors argue that the observed alienation in their sample should be expected to persist.

REFERENCES

Abramson, Paul R. "Political Efficacy and Political Trust among Black School-children: Two Explanations," *Journal of Politics* 34 (1972), 1243–75.

Adelson, Joseph, and Robert O'Neil. "Growth of Political Ideas in Adolescence: The Sense of Community," *Journal of Personality and Social Psychology* 4 (1966), 295–306.

Almond, Gabriel A. "A Functional Approach to Comparative Politics," in Gabriel A. Almond and James Coleman (eds.), *The Politics of the Developing Areas* (Princeton: Princeton University Press, 1960), 26–33.

————, and Sidney Verba. *The Civic Culture: Political Attitudes and Democracy in Five Nations* (Princeton: Princeton University Press, 1963).

Bandura, A. *Principles of Behavior Modification* (New York: Holt, Rinehart and Winston, 1969).

Benedict, Ruth. *Patterns of Culture* (Boston: Houghton Mifflin, 1934).

Birch, Herbert, and Joan Dye Gussow. *Disadvantaged Children* (New York: Harcourt Brace, 1970).

Cofer, C. N., and M. H. Appley. *Motivation* (New York: John Wiley, 1964).

Connell, R. W. *The Child's Construction of Politics* (Melbourne: Melbourne University Press, 1971).

Dawson, Richard E., and Kenneth Prewitt. *Political Socialization* (Boston: Little, Brown, 1969).

Dennis, Jack. "Major Problems of Political Socialization Research," *Midwest Journal of Political Science* 12 (1968), 85–114.

Easton, David. *A Systems Analysis of Political Life* (New York: Wiley, 1965).

————, and Jack Dennis. *Children in the Political System: Origins of Political Legitimacy* (New York: McGraw-Hill, 1969).

————. "The Child's Acquisition of Regime Norms: Political Efficacy," *American Political Science Review* 61 (1967), 25–38.

————. "The Child's Image of Government," *Annals* 361 (1965), 40–57.

Erikson, Erik. *Childhood and Society*, 2nd ed. (New York: Norton, 1963).

————. *Identity, Youth and Crises* (New York: W. W. Norton and Co., 1968).

Ferguson, Leroy, *et al.* "An Attempt to Correlate Physical Characteristics with Political Attitudes," paper presented at the meeting of the International Political Science Association, March, 1970.

Festinger, Leon. *A Theory of Cognitive Dissonance* (Stanford: Stanford University Press, 1957).

Fisher, Seymour. *Body Experience in Fantasy and Behavior* (New York: Appleton-Century-Crofts, 1970).

Froman, Lewis A., Jr. "Learning Political Attitudes," *Western Political Quarterly* 15 (1962), 304–13.

--———. "Personality and Political Socialization," *Journal of Politics* 23 (1961), 341–52.

Greenberg, Edward S. "Black Children and the Political System," *Public Opinion Quarterly* 34 (1970a), 333–45.

———. "Children and Government: A Comparison Across Racial Lines," *Midwest Journal of Political Science* 14 (1970b), 249–75.

Greenstein, Fred I. "A Note on the Ambiguity of 'Political Socialization': Definitions, Criticisms, and Strategies of Inquiry," *Journal of Politics* 32 (1970), 969–78.

———. *Children and Politics* (New Haven: Yale University Press, 1965b).

———. "Personality and Political Socialization: The Theories of Authoritarian and Democratic Character," *Annals* 361 (1965a), 81–95.

———, and Sidney Tarrow. "Political Orientations of Children: Semiprojective Responses from Three Nations," *Sage Professional Papers in Comparative Politics* 01–009 (1971).

———. "The Study of French Political Socialization: Toward the Revocation of Paradox," *World Politics* 22 (1969), 95–137.

Hess, Robert D., and David Easton. "The Child's Changing Image of the President," *Public Opinion Quarterly* 24 (1960), 632–44.

———, and Judith V. Torney. *The Development of Political Attitudes in Children* (Chicago: Aldine, 1967).

Hovland, Carl I., *et al. Communication and Persuasion: Psychological Studies of Opinion Change* (New Haven: Yale University Press, 1953).

Hyman, Herbert H. *Political Socialization: A Study in the Psychology of Political Behavior* (New York: Free Press, 1959).

Jackson, R. W. "A Note on Intelligence, Social Class, and Political Efficacy in Children," *Journal of Politics* 32 (1970), 984–9.

Jaros, Dean. *Socialization to Politics* (New York: Praeger, 1973).

———, Herbert Hirsch, and Frederick J. Fleron, Jr. "The Malevolent Leader: Political Socialization in an American Sub-Culture," *American Political Science Review* 63 (1968), 564–75.

Jennings, M. Kent, and Richard G. Niemi. "The Division of Political Labor Between Mothers and Fathers," *American Political Science Review* 65 (1971), 69–82.

————, and Kenneth P. Langton. "Mothers vs. Fathers: The Formation of Political Orientations Among Young Americans," *Journal of Politics* 31 (1969), 329–58.

Kohlberg, Laurence. "Development of Moral Character and Moral Ideology," in M. L. Hoffman and L. W. Hoffman (eds.), *Review of Child Development*, Vol. 1 (New York: Russell Sage, 1964).

Langton, Kenneth P., and M. Kent Jennings. "Political Socialization and the High School Civics Curriculum in the United States," *American Political Science Review* 62 (1968), 852–67.

————, and David A. Karns. "The Relative Influence of the Family, Peer Group, and School in the Development of Political Efficacy," *Western Political Quarterly* 22 (1969), 813–26.

Merelman, Richard M. "Learning and Legitimacy," *American Political Science Review* 60 (1966), 548–61.

————. "The Adolescence of Political Socialization," *Sociology of Education* 45 (1972), 134–66.

————. "The Development of Political Ideology," *American Political Science Review* 63 (1969), 750–67.

————. "The Development of Policy Thinking in Adolescence," *American Political Science Review* 65 (1971), 1033–47.

Piaget, Jean. *Play, Dreams and Imitation in Childhood* (New York: Norton, 1962).

Pless, Ivan B., and Klaus J. Roghmann. "Chronic Illness and Its Consequences," paper presented at the Annual Meeting of the American Public Health Service, 1970.

Pye, Lucian. "Political Culture," *International Encyclopedia of the Social Sciences*, Vol. 12 (New York: Macmillan and Free Press, 1968), 218–24.

Remmers, H. H. (ed.), *Anti-Democratic Attitudes in American Schools* (Evanston: Northwestern University Press, 1963).

Schonfeld, William R. "The Forces of Political Socialization Research: An Evaluation," *World Politics* 23 (1971), 544–78.

Schwartz, David C. "A Theory of Revolutionary Behavior," in James C. Davies, *When Men Revolt—and Why* (New York: Free Press, 1970).

————. "Toward A Theory of Political Recruitment," *Western Political Quarterly* 22 (1969), 552–71.

Sigel, Roberta S. (ed.). *Learning About Politics: A Reader in Political Socialization* (New York: Random House, 1970).

————. "Political Socialization: Some Reactions on Current Approaches and Conceptualizations," paper presented at the Annual Meeting of the American Political Science Association, New York, 1966.

Vaillancourt, Pauline Marie. "Stability of Children's Survey Responses," *Public Opinion Quarterly* 37 (1973), 373–87.

White, Elliott S. "Intelligence and Sense of Political Efficacy in Children," *Journal of Politics* 30 (1968), 710–31.

Wolfenstein, Martha, and Gilbert Kliman (eds.). *Children and the Death of a President: Multi-Disciplinary Studies* (New York: Doubleday, 1965).

The Influence of
Individual Characteristics

Chapter Two

The Role of Personality Development in Political Socialization

Stanley Allen Renshon

INTRODUCTION

In the fourteen years since Herbert Hyman first introduced the study of political socialization (Hyman, 1959), a great deal of theoretical and empirical progress has been made. Yet it should not be surprising at this relatively early stage of development that a number of theoretical problems remain. This chapter deals specifically with two of those problems: (1) the relative importance of childhood experiences in the political socialization process and (2) the nature of the linkage between personality and political socialization.

The listing of these two topics as "problem areas" may well come as a surprise to many, for assumptions in these two areas are among the most basic in political socialization theory. Yet, as we hope to suggest in this chapter, there is no small amount of both theoretical confusion and empirical paradox surrounding these areas. The first part of this chapter will be devoted to an examination of some basic assumptions in these areas, along with a critical evaluation of some of the empirical studies that have furnished evidence for particular positions. We will then turn to the explication of a model that makes manifest the linkages between personality, political learning, and the political socialization process, utilizing political efficacy and its basis in the personality orientation of personal control as an illustration.

The basic themes of this chapter can be stated in a straightforward manner. First, that the analysis of the impact of early childhood in the political socialization process and the relationship between personality and political socialization are inexorably linked. Second, that the crucial link between the two is the specification of exactly what it is that is learned in childhood. Third, that the understanding of what is learned during early childhood in the political socialization process cannot proceed without reference to a psychological model of a personality development.

Last, that a personality-oriented model of the political socialization process helps us to deal with political learning throughout the life cycle.

THE IMPACT OF CHILDHOOD IN THE POLITICAL SOCIALIZATION PROCESS

One of the central questions of political socialization theory is the relative importance of childhood experience on adult political orientations and behaviors. At the theoretical level this question has led to considerable disagreement among political socialization scholars. Hyman, for example, takes the position that human beings learn their behavior early and well and that this early learning persists into adulthood (1959; Chaps. 2–5). This position is even more forceably developed by Greenstein:

> My argument can be briefly summarized; that political behavior which *is most important* in the behavior of adults *arise earliest in the learning experience* (Greenstein, 1965, 78) (emphasis added).

The reasons that is so, according to Greenstein, are that early learning takes place during a formative period when the child is malleable and that early learning affects later learning (1965, 79). Empirical evidence does appear to support the contention that "the child's political world begins to take shape well before he enters an elementary school and that it undergoes the most rapid changes during those years" (Hess and Easton, 1962, 235). Of course, to suggest that the political world takes shape at an early age in no way supplies a theoretical or empirical link between early childhood experiences and adult political orientations. *The crucial question is, exactly what is it that is learned in earliest childhood?* This is a question to which we shall return shortly.

The suggestion that childhood learning experiences are the most important in the political socialization process has not won universal acceptance by political scientists. Almond and Verba suggest, for example, that the assumption that significant socialization experiences that will affect later political behavior take place quite early in life was in some respects too simple. They note that:

> One could not make unambiguous connections between early socialization experiences and politics; the gap between the two is so great that it could not be closed by the use of somewhat imprecise analogies and a rather selective approach to the evidence. Non-political experiences in childhood may play an important part in later political attitudes and behaviors, but the impact of these experiences continues throughout the adolescent and adult years. In

fact there is some evidence that *later political experiences have a more direct political implication* (Almond and Verba, 1965, 235) (emphasis added).

As this discussion suggests, at the theoretical level, there is disagreement over the relative importance of early learning experiences for later adult political behavior. Those who defend the importance of early learning base their defense on two related lines of argument: (1) that early learning shapes subsequent learning and (2) that early learning is the most resistant to change. Carried over to the political arena, these assumptions have become associated with two lines of emphasis. The first is the emphasis on the family as the most important agent in the political socialization process, an assumption derived in modified form from Freudian theory; the second is emphasis on a series of empirical studies suggesting that children acquire political attitudes and orientations at a very early age. In the latter case the studies are usually coupled with the attendant implication that political attitudes learned at this age are important to later political behavior. A typical example of this type of reasoning is suggested in the work of Easton and Dennis, who, after discussing the emergence of a norm of political efficacy among seven-year-olds in a national sample, suggests that it:

> has vital implications for the input of support for a democratic regime. This is especially true if we are willing to assume that, like imprinting, *what is learned early in the life cycle is more difficult to displace than that which is learned later* . . . a not unchallengeable proposition . . . (Easton and Dennis, 1967, 38) (emphasis added).

What can be said of these two lines of emphasis in political socialization research after fifteen years of research?

The Family

Turning our attention first to the family as the most important agent in the socialization process, we immediately note the paucity of research attempting to assess the relative impact of the family and other socialization agencies. Empirical studies that have attempted to assess the relative impact of different agencies have not only been few in number but contradictory in results. In a study designed to assess the relative importance of the family, the school, and the peer group in the acquisition of feelings of political efficacy, Langton and Karns measured the degree of politization of each agency by ascertaining the amount of attention paid to politics. They report that:

> *Among the three agencies it is apparent that the family has the greatest impact on the development of political efficacy.* Its combined effects account for the efficacy level of 27 percent of the sample in contrast to 5.4 and 6.5 for the peer group and the school respectively. While the family has the greatest absolute influence on the movement from low to medium efficacy, *it also plays a greater* role at the high efficacy level than either of the other two agencies (Langton and Karns, 1967, 819) (emphasis added).

On the other hand, Almond and Verba, examining the effects of participation in decision-making in the family, the school, and the job on feelings of political efficacy, reached the conclusion that,

> There appears to be a rank order in the strength of connection between non-political types of participation and feelings of political competence: *the connection becomes stronger as one moves from family to school to job participation* . . . (1965, 303–304) (emphasis added).

Unlike the conclusion of Langton and Karns, that of Almond and Verba suggests that more recent experience may be more important than early learning. Indeed, they suggest that influence may be either cumulative or compensatory, depending on the continuities or discontinuities of experience and the degree of correspondence between social structures and political structures.

Unfortunately, these two studies almost exhaust assessments of the relative impact of socialization agencies upon the acquisition of political orientations. Yet, the idea that the family is the most important agency of socialization remains a dominant assumption in political socialization theory. In view of the fact that few studies have sought to demonstrate the relatively greater importance of the family in the socialization process, what, we may ask, is the basis for the retention of this assumption?

As one reviewer of political socialization research over the last two decades has noted, "The most extensive evidence offered in support of the role of the family is found in correlations between parental and off-spring political orientations" (Dawson, 1966, 42). In most of these studies the political orientations of the parent and the children are measured independently of each other, and positive correlations are then used to support the proposition that they are important in the transmission of political orientations to children. Hyman notes, for example, in an early review of socialization studies that,

> These and other studies establish very firmly a family correspondence in views that are relevant to matters of political orientation.

Over a great many such correlations from the different studies, the
median value approximates .5. The signs, almost without exception,
are *never negative* (1959, 72) (emphasis in original).

Interestingly enough, the highest parent–child correlations are found
mainly for party preference and identification. Campbell found that
respondents were more likely to develop strong party preferences congruent with those of their parents if both parents reported having the
same party preference (Campbell *et al.*, 1959, 97–107). Similar findings
were reported for a study of the French electorate by Converse and
Dupeux (1962). In reporting the results of the only nationwide study
of students and their parents, Jennings and Niemi report that the strongest
correlation was obtained for parent–child party identication (Tau B =
.47) (Jennings and Niemi, 1968, 173). The regularity of these results has
led one reviewer to propose that, "In American Society political party
identification is *one of the most basic political orientations* that is acquired
early . . ." (Dawson, 1966, 28) (emphasis added).

Results on other political orientations, however, have proved dis-
appointing. Jennings and Niemi, after examining the full range of parent–
child correlations in their study, come to the conclusion that:

> it is none the less clear that any model of socialization that rests on
> assumptions of pervasive currents of parent to child value transmis-
> sions of the types examined here *is in need of serious modification*
> . . . . Party identification . . . is a prime exception. The data suggest
> that with respect to a range of other attitude objects the corre-
> spondences vary from, at most, moderate support to virtually no
> support (1968, 183) (emphasis added).

If one takes parent–child correspondence as a valid indicator of the
relative strength of the family's impact in the political socialization process,
then the Jennings–Niemi data do not provide strong empirical support
for the assumption. Recent articles by Searing (1973) and Connell (1972)
have also questioned the importance of the family. Moreover, as we have
seen, attempts to assess the relative impact of the family vis-à-vis other
socialiation agencies have also had mixed empirical results. Of course these
studies do not negate the possibility that the family is the most important
agency in the socialization process, but they do suggest that some modification is in order.

The Early Emergence of Political Attitudes

Parent–child correspondence is not the only evidence that has been
advanced for the importance of the early childhood experience. We also

noted that several studies (Easton and Dennis, 1969; Greenstein, 1965; Hess and Torney, 1967) have documented the emergence of political attitudes at a very early age, with the attendant implication that these attitudes are important for later political attitudes and actions. Underlying these and similar studies, of course, is the assumption that children do indeed have political attitudes and definite opinions about politics. Recent work by Vaillancourt (1970a) calls these assumptions into question. Vaillancourt notes two major problems with studies of the political attitudes of children: (1) a failure to explain variations in the independent variable with traditional dependent variables and (2) the tendency for children's answers to become crystallized after filling out the questionnaire, which may indicate the lack of a stable attitude.

The first problem was encountered in the Easton and Dennis study in their attempt to predict cognitions and affect toward authority figures such as the President and policemen. Using ten independent variables they can "explain" only 7 percent of the variance (1969, 370). The authors suggest looking for new and different predictor variables (1969, 378), but Vaillancourt feels that the real problem is that "the results are due to the high percentage of youngsters in a number of different demographic groups that have no stable attitudes at all on the dependent variables" (1970, 6). Niemi has suggested that the limited findings were due in part to the low stability of children's responses (Niemi, 1970, 190).

The second problem was noted by Torney. After examining and comparing the attitude structure of her young respondents on the first and second questionnaires, she wrote, "it appears that answering questions about an attitude object does increase the crystallization of that attitude" (Torney, 1965, 133). Given the general agreement in the psychological literature that, "the concept of attitude is typically reserved for the more enduring, persistent organization of predispositions" (Rokeach, 1960, Ch. 2), the possibility exists that stable orientations did not exist prior to the distribution of the questionnaire and should not therefore be considered attitudes at all.

In addition, even if we overlook these problems, there is an additional problem in using these studies to validate the importance of early learning in the political socialization process. The national study undertaken by Easton and Dennis was fielded in 1962 using children ranging in age from seven through thirteen, while Greenstein's study was fielded in 1958 using children from the fourth through the eighth grades. Both studies noted the uncritical nature of attitudes toward authority, and both studies found that children had overwhelmingly positive attitudes toward authority figures. Yet these are the very same age cohorts that made demonstrations and sit-ins a routinized aspect of American political participation. What we are suggesting is that the cohort of children who demonstrated such uncritical acceptance of authority in both studies, was the same cohort that reached college age by 1968, the start of a period of mass demonstrations and sit-ins almost unparalleled in American history. Clearly something had changed!

To this point our discussion has appeared to suggest that the assumption of the importance of early learning in the study of political socialization is in need of modification. However, modification does not mean abandonment, for as we shall shortly suggest the family is (ceteris paribus) the most important agency in the political socialization process. Moreover we will suggest that early learning is crucial to later political orientations and activity, but not in the way that political scientists have previously conceived of it. Before we turn to these matters, it is first necessary to briefly examine the relation between personality and political socialization theory.

Personality and Political Socialization

Of all of the socialization theorists, only Froman has included personality as a major variable (Froman, 1961). According to Froman's conceptualization of political socialization there are three major sets of variables: (1) the environment (agents of socialization), (2) personality, and (3) politically relevant behavior. In this formulation, personality is an intervening variable. Froman suggests that what is needed are laws that relate the environment to personality and a separate set of laws that deal with the influence that personality has on behavior (1961, 351). Froman's early suggestion has fallen mostly on deaf ears in political science. Those few who do mention personality at all, often do so in the context of minimizing its importance. For example, Almond and Verba admit that:

> *Early socialization experiences significantly affect an individual's basic personality predisposition, and may therefore affect his political behavior* . . . .[but then go on to suggest that] numerous other factors intervene between these earliest experiences and later political behavior that greatly inhibit the impact of the former upon the latter (1965, 324) (emphasis added).

By far the most frequent assumption about personality and political socialization, however, is that the former is relatively unimportant and unrelated to the latter in any meaningful way. This position is perhaps best typified by Dawson, who, after reviewing a decade of political socialization theory and research, concludes that:

> There is now extensive writing about personality and political behavior that reveals disagreement on the utility of personality explanations of political phenomena. The evidence that personality

is a key variable in explaining political behavior or in analyzing the development of political orientations is still not very convincing. Particularly little evidence supports the use of personality as a major independent variable as Froman proposes. *Consequently, we do not use it as a major variable in our conceptualization of political socialization* (1966, 21) (emphasis added).

The theoretical utility of personality as an explanatory variable in political life has been discussed at some length by Greenstein in a seminal work (Greenstein, 1969). We shall not detail here Greenstein's excellent discussion of the set of erroneous assumptions about the impact of personality in political life. Rather we wish to note and build upon Greenstein's suggestion that *what needs to be done is to specify the ways in which particular social characteristics interact with specific personality orientations to produce particular types of political behavior.* It is our contention, as we suggested at the beginning of this paper, that personality is a crucial link in the political socialization process. Indeed, as we will go on to detail, it is the crucial link between the individual and the political socialization process. Yet, following Greenstein's suggestion, it is not enough to suggest that personality plays a role in the political socialization process; rather we must detail what part it plays, and in what specific way(s) it is either influenced by or influences other learning and institutions.

HUMAN NEEDS AND POLITICAL SOCIALIZATION: A MODEL

We have previously suggested that the question about the impact of the family and the importance of personality in the political socialization process were in fact related. *The key link between these two areas is the question, what is learned in childhood?*

As we have seen, several answers to this question have been put forward. One answer has been that the child learns "political orientations," such as attitudes toward authority, or political efficacy. Yet, as we have noted, the assumption that children do indeed have strong, stable political orientations is open to question. Children do apparently develop affective orientations to political objects at an early age, but without any cognitive or behavioral dimensions; it is difficult to conceive of these orientations as attitudes (Fishbein, 1967). Moreover, these uniformly positive orientations to authority seem to disappear with age. Last, the one national study of parents and children we reviewed earlier could find no great degree of parent–child similarities on a number of political attitudes, suggesting that something other than concrete political orientations are learned in the family.

Another answer put forward to the question of what is learned in childhood is that the child learns political party preferences. We have noted that at least one researcher in the field has suggested that party identification is one of the most basic political orientations acquired at an early age. Yet, the focus on party identification seems to us a somewhat narrow conception of childhood political learning. Second and more important, the emphasis on party identification may be culture-bound. In their 1962 study of the French electorate, Converse and Dupeux found that only 45 percent of the electorate had a political party identification and only 25 percent could name the political party preference of one parent (1962, 9–15). Data from the Almond and Verba study suggest that only 5 percent of the Germans and 14 percent of the Italians interviewed reported hearing conversations as children from which they could ascertain their parent's political party preference (reported in Dawson, 1966, 29).

If children do not have stable attitudes toward political objects and if political party identification is too narrow a conception of political learning in children, exactly what is it that children do learn that is politically relevant? We suggest that the *child learns basic beliefs about the world as a result of the interplay between his own basic needs and their satisfaction (or lack thereof) in a social context.* We do not mean to suggest that this is the only set of politically relevant things that are learned, but we shall attempt to make the argument that it is by far the most important.

Our suggestion then, is threefold: (1) that the child acquires basic beliefs about the nature of the world at an early age, (2) that these basic beliefs are acquired in the attempt to satisfy certain basic human needs, and (3) that this process of basic belief acquisition has crucial implications for the political socialization process.

A basic belief is defined as a set of assumptions about the nature of reality and the world in which one lives, the validity of which is rarely if ever challenged. Thus basic beliefs represent a deeper level of psychic organization than do attitudes or opinions. These basic beliefs are hypothesized to be five in number: first, beliefs about the nature of physical reality (e.g., color, form, sound, space, time); second, beliefs about the potential for individual action within this world (personal control); third, beliefs involving evaluations of the world in which one lives (i.e., whether it is a friendly or hostile place); fourth, beliefs about the other people who inhabit the life space of the individual (i.e., whether people are good and can be trusted or whether they are basically evil and cannot be trusted); and fifth, beliefs about self-evaluation (e.g., is the self generally valued or not). These basic beliefs are interrelated in the acquisition process. By that I mean that we might expect several or all of these beliefs to vary together. For example, the belief that the world is a place in which no personal control is possible (belief type 2) would be associated with the belief that the world is essentially a hostile place (belief type 3).

In an earlier work Rokeach has suggested a similar concept, which he called central beliefs (1960). Although he is one of the few social psychologists to talk about central beliefs (basic beliefs), he neglects to discuss the origin of these beliefs. Our answer suggests a way in which personality theory may be fruitfully linked with social psychology and attitude research, namely, *these beliefs are derived from interactions with the environment in the attempt to satisfy human needs.*

The idea of basic beliefs arising out of human needs provides a new perspective on the impact of early learning in the political socialization process. All of the research we have reviewed has concentrated on either attitudes or party preferences. Our model, on the other hand, suggests that the hypothesis that early political learning shapes later political behavior depends on what it is we specify is being learned. It may be entirely correct to argue at one and the same time that (1) a political attitude learned early in life will not shape subsequent attitude acquisition or be particularly resistant to change and (2) that basic beliefs may shape subsequent political orientations and be highly resistant to change. We are suggesting that the emphasis on the importance of early learning in the political socialization process is essentially correct in its general form, provided that one talks about basic beliefs and not political attitudes.

Several observations need to be made about basic beliefs at this point. Although theoretically they represent a deeper level of psychic organization than do attitudes, there are similarities in so far as they do have cognitive, affective, and behavioral components. What differentiates them from attitudes is their generality: they are beliefs about the nature of the world, while attitudes are orientations toward specific objects.

One question that naturally arises at this point is why, if children do not have stable attitudes toward politics, should they be assumed to have stable basic beliefs about the nature of the world? The answer, we suggest, is that there is no reason to assume that children have no stable orientations because they have unstable or no political attitudes. For most children, the political sphere is far removed from their daily existence. If, as Converse suggests (1964), this is true for over half of the adults in our nation, why should we assume it to be less the case for children? Because politics is so far removed from their lives ordinarily, children acquire affective but not cognitive orientations towards political objects. Moreover, there is some evidence that even these affective orientations are a product of generalization from affective orientations to more immediate objects, namely parents. Yet while politics is distant, the world is not. As we shall detail, because children do acquire information about relevant objects in their life space, their basic beliefs do have a cognitive as well as an affective component. Before we turn to detailing that process it is first necessary to take a brief look at another component of the relationship, human needs.

PERSONALITY AND POLITICS: A THEORY OF HUMAN NEEDS[*]

Political scientists interested in personality have had their choice of either Freudian or trait theories of personality. In effect, however, most work in personality and politics have utilized the latter, with less than overwhelming results.[1] There is, however, another possibility, the utilization of a "third force" approach—more specifically, Abraham Maslow's theory of a need hierarchy (Maslow, 1943, 1954). The needs in order of ascendance are (1) physiological needs, (2) safety needs, (3) love needs, (4) self-esteem needs, and (5) self-actualization needs.

Physiological needs refer to the need of the body for food, sleep, or water. These needs, if unfulfilled, become the basic organizing mechanism of human activity. Although it may be true that man does not live by bread alone, caloric deprivation appears to lead to a decreased interest in the surrounding environment and an increased interest, one might say preoccupation, with food (Davies, 1963). Physiological deprivation is not without its implications for political behavior. As Hoffer notes:

> To be engaged in a desperate struggle for food and shelter is to be wholly free from a sense of futility. The goals are concrete and immediate. Every meal is a fulfillment; to go to sleep on a full stomach is a triumph. . . . Where people toil from sunrise to sunset for a bare living they nurse no grievances and dream no dreams (Hoffer, 1951, 27).

Even more directly political is the description by Angelica Balabanoff of the effect of abject poverty on the political concerns of radicals in Moscow during the early days of the Communist revolution. Balabanoff writes that she "saw men and women who had lived all of their lives for ideas, who had voluntarily renounced material advantages, liberty, happiness, and family affection for the realization of their ideals, completely absorbed by the problems of hunger and cold" (Balabanoff, 1938, 204).

The second set of needs to emerge, according to Maslow, are the safety needs. Maslow suggests that they fall into two categories: (1) bodily safety and (2) psychological security. The first refers to the need to be secure from attack or aggression and to live one's life without being the

---

[1] In a forthcoming work (Renshon) I will analyze and compare the various approaches in the personality and politics field.

[*] AUTHOR'S NOTE: This discussion is drawn, in part, on a similar discussion in Renshon, 1974a.

object of physical threat. The second category is somewhat more subtle and refers to the need for an orderly and predictable world. In children this need takes the form of a

> preference for some kind of undisrupted routine or rhythm . . . a preference for a safe, orderly, predictable, organized world which he can count on and in which unexpected, unmanageable, or other dangerous things do not happen (Maslow, 1954, 86).

Nor is this need absent in adults. Goffman, for example, has noted the elaborate staging and other devices utilized to control the interaction context (Goffman, 1959). He has called these normal attempts at control "stage managing" and found that they are a normal occurrence in social interaction. Carried to an extreme, however, the attempt to manipulate the environment for psychological security needs begins to resemble the compulsive personality described clinically by Horney (1937) and in the area of politics by George and George (1964).

When both physiological and safety needs are satisfied, what Maslow calls the higher needs emerge. Love needs refer to the desire and need for human warmth, affection, and inclusion by desired objects. The deleterious effects to growth when these needs are not satisfied have been well documented in animal studies by Harlow and for humans by Davis (1956). Organisms deprived of this satisfaction early in the life cycle grow up emotionally stunted and never seem able to recover. The implications of the deprivation of this need for the political system may appear small at first glance, but a further look reveals its importance. A recently published psychoanalytic study of Adolf Hitler suggests that emotional deprivation had important consequences for his behavior as a political leader (Langer, 1972). Closer to home, the resurgence of strong ethnic and racial self-group identification can be viewed as arising out of the same need.

The next set of needs to emerge are the esteem needs. Maslow describes these needs in two ways. "First, the desire for strength, for achievement, for adequacy, for mastery, and competence, for confidence in the face of the world, and for independence and freedom. Second, the desire for reputation and/or prestige, status, dominance, recognition, attention, importance, appreciation" (1954, 70). The importance of this need in the study of politics has been suggested by a number of writers. In one study a group of political candidates were asked to describe why men sought elective office. What emerged was "a fairly clear picture of self-interest in which the most important elements were personal advancement and prestige" (Rosenzweig, 1957, 166). The mastery of a particular area of endeavor is the basis for a positive evaluation of self by self. When significant others

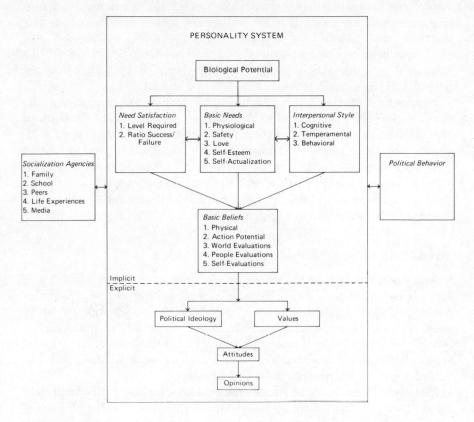

Figure 2–1.

accord legitimacy to the area of mastery, self-esteem and positive evaluation by others coalesce.

Last, when all of these needs have been fulfilled, the need for self-actualization emerges. As Maslow has noted, "what man can be, he must be" (1954, 91). Once the other needs have been met, then men can concentrate on realizing their potential. The relationship between self-actualization and political behavior has been analyzed by Knutson elsewhere in a pathbreaking work (Knutson, 1972). The self-actualizer is found to be more politically concerned, more tolerant, and less likely to join extremist groups.

Maslow's need theory of personality development not only provides an important analytical tool for the analysis of various aspects of political life, but it also provides political scientists with a personality model not linked exclusively with either psychopathology or unconscious motivations.

Elsewhere Greenstein has argued that "one of the great needs of contemporary political analysis is for convenient means of personal characterization that goes beyond political attitudes, but does not focus merely on deeper processes and structures" (Greenstein, 1969, 58). I should like to suggest here that Maslow's theory plus the basic beliefs I have outlined provides the framework for such a model of personality.

Building on Maslow's theory and our discussion we can suggest the outlines of a model of personality be applied to the analysis of the political socialization process. The components of such a personality system include: (1) the biologically transmitted genetic material and potential; (2) basic human needs; (3) interpersonal style in cognitive, temperamental, and behavioral areas; (4) basic beliefs about the world; (5) political ideology and values; and (6) political attitudes and opinions. The basic model is presented in Figure 2–1.

Needs, Political Socialization, and the Social Matrix

Our argument to this point can be briefly summarized as follows. There is within each of us a constellation of needs arising out of a complex biological, psychological, and social interface. In his attempt to satisfy these needs the individual acquires basic beliefs about the nature of his world (life space). These basic beliefs then form the basis of the individual's relation to his world, *which, under conditions of political salience, includes specific political attitudes and values.*

Elsewhere I have spent considerable time examining the important concept of political salience (Renshon, 1974a), and I will not go into considerable detail here. As I have suggested, political salience can best be understood phenomenologically. More specifically, the political system will be salient to the extent that it is felt to have an impact on the individual's social–psychological or physical life space, i.e., his daily existence. Such perceptions arise out of three conditions: (1) the political system may be seen as the only source capable of supplying certain benefits in the form of either goods or services, (2) the decisional outputs of the political system may be viewed as interfering with the pursuit of an individual's values or goals, or (3) salience may derive from a perceived obligation to pay attention to the political system as part of the good citizen role.

Given political salience under one of these three conditions, the individual's level of need satisfaction has its outplay in both political attitudes and political values. The idea that human needs are related to political thinking is not novel. Lane has suggested that human needs are a source of particular political ideologies; in his words, "that human needs are the parents of social thought" (Lane, 1969, 24). Nor is the idea that human needs shape the acquisition of particular attitudes completely new. Over a decade ago, Katz suggested that attitudes serve four functions for the individual, including an "adjustment function," and that "attitudes and habits are formed towards specific objects, people, and symbols as they satisfy specific needs" (Katz, 1960). What has been lacking, however, is a model of the linkage between specific needs, the social experiences that shape these needs, the emerging core beliefs, and the outplay of these factors in the political system.

The problem of linkage has been a serious one in the area of personality and politics. It is not only that there are a variety of approaches to the study of personality within psychological theory (Knutson, 1973) but that in general theories of personality have neglected the detailed analysis of the ongoing interaction between psyche and social context throughout the life cycle. Space limitations preclude our detailing the linkage among all of Maslow's needs and their social shaping and outplay in the political system. What we shall attempt to do is to select one of Maslow's needs, the safety need, and illustrate the ways in which that need is shaped by social experience, the core belief that arises from that experience, and its subsequent outplay in the political system. After such a detailing of these relationships, the model of political socialization we have suggested should emerge in greater clarity.

We noted that Maslow's second need was actually divided into two parts: one, the need to be safe from physical harm, and two, the need for an orderly secure world. Taken together, both of these aspects suggest a need to have control over relevant aspects of one's physical and social life space. Elsewhere I have suggested that evidence for this need, which I have called the need for personal control, may be found in a variety of psychological research, including animal studies, Freudian, neo-Freudian, developmental, and humanistic psychology. Moreover, I have suggested that this need is closely related to that attitude set traditionally known as political efficacy (Renshon, 1974a). Specifically, I have suggested that political efficacy is the belief that one has sufficient control over political processes to satisfy the need for personal control when the political system has become a control-relevant area. Viewed from this perspective, political efficacy is an attitudinal manifestation of the outplay between a basic need for personal control and its subsequent elaboration in the social matrix. Thus, the basic need for personal control is a necessary (but insufficient) component of political efficacy.

The examination of the psychological origins and social shaping of the basic personality characteristic underlying the attitude set known as political efficacy is of major interest to political scientists for several reasons. First, it has been shown that feelings of political efficacy are related to a variety of participatory behaviors in the political system.

Second, because it is a major explanatory variable in the explanation of participation and because participation is an important component of democratic theory, its importance is increased. Last, because many theories of democratic character include the component of feelings of personal control, it is of prime importance to see under what circumstances these feelings are either facilitated or impeded. For these reasons the exact specification of the process through which the need for personal control is shaped by the political socialization experience is the subject of the remainder of this chapter. Additionally, in detailing this process, the relationship among personality, social experience, and political socialization will hopefully emerge in sharper focus.

The Ontological Origins of Personal Control

To propose a need is one thing, but to detail its origin is quite another. One of the problems with need theories is that the number of needs has appeared to some to increase or decrease at the whim of the particular researcher. It is therefore necessary to detail the nature of the origin of the need for personal control. A knowledge of need ontology is also important in another respect; knowledge of the nature and origins of the need also provide important information about the possibilities and nature of the satisfaction of that need.

There has been a controversy in psychology for some time over the nature of the origins of needs. Some, following the work of Freud, have viewed needs as arising out of a deficit, while others have seen the deficit model as too limiting for the variety of human experience. Yet it appears to us that the need for personal control is at base a deficit need arising out of the nature of the child and its relation to the environment.

Unlike other species, the human child is brought into the world totally unprepared to take care of itself, and the period of its dependency is relatively long. This prolonged dependency is indeed one of the few cultural universals that anthropologists have been able to find (Wolfenstein and Mead, 1966), and it has profound implications for human development in general and the need for personal control in particular.

The child arrives in the world with hunger and thirst needs, but no knowledge of how to satisfy them. At a minimum, unsatisfied hunger and thirst needs create physiological discomfort; and the child has few ways to communicate these needs. Typically, the child begins to thrust and cry, until an alert parent (traditionally the mother) interprets the cries correctly and feeds the child. From the child's point of view, there is no connection between his crying and the arrival of food. This means that the child is experiencing *two*, not one, unpleasant experiences. The first is the discomfort of the unmet needs, and the second is the fear (anxiety) that these needs might not be met again in the future. Out of these twin discomforts, the need for personal control is born.

The typical child is hungry seven or eight times a day (Mussen *et al.*, 1969, 184), which means that the same discomfort–crying–feeding ritual is played out more than a hundred times in the first two weeks of life. Gradually, the child begins to connect his crying with the appearance of food. This is, of course, the beginnings of associative learning; but more importantly, it is the child's first experience of being the locus of causality, the initiator of the action that successfully meets biological needs.

At this point, unknown to the child, he is approaching one of life's frequent choice points, although he in effect has no choice. At some point, the parents must decide either on demand feeding or on a feeding schedule. We suggested that there were two discomforts involved in a feeding process; the first was hunger satisfaction, and the second anxiety about the outcomes of future hunger needs. When the child has learned to associate crying with food he has gone some distance toward mastering the first problem; and if the parents decide on demand feeding, in which he is fed whenever he cries, the child will build up a basis of successful reinforcement that should help to alleviate anxiety about future feeding situations.

On the other hand, the use of a schedule means that the child is fed at regular intervals regardless of his immediate needs, and indeed there is some evidence to suggest that children will modify their behavior in accordance to external demands such as feeding schedules (Marquis, 1941). Yet in this situation there is no consummation of the union between self-initiated action and a successful outcome. The child learns not that he is the locus of causality but that compliance to external demands brings with it rewards. He is learning to trust in others but not in himself.

We *do not* mean to suggest that the feeding situation is *the single crucial encounter* for the development of personal control, but it is the earliest social encounter and one of the first chances for the child to master discomfort through his own efforts. Nor do we wish to discount, even at this early stage, individual differences in temperament and spontaneous motor activity. Research has suggested that children are born with different tendencies toward activity, and there is some evidence that early activity levels are precursors of future behavior (Escalona and Heider, 1959). These observations suggest but do not exhaust the possibilities for the beginnings of personal control.

The concept of compensation alerts us to the fact that failure to control one's food availability in the feeding process need not irreparably damage the acquisition of personal control. There is ample research to demonstrate that children are more likely to repeat a *variety of actions* if these actions bring some response, especially from a parent (Mussen, 1969, Ch. 6). In many cases, the knowledge that a certain action has a related result is enough to increase the probability of a repeated action. Piaget has noted that as early as the fourth month, children will engage in play "centered on a result produced in the external environment," which can be described as an exploration of actions that by chance produced a serendipitous effect upon things (Piaget, 1952, 151). What this means is that the child enjoys many opportunities to develop his ability to control his environment, and inability in one area to control may not lead to inability in others.

Generally, however, we would expect that those areas involved with biological satisfaction or rudimentary social needs, such as separation anxiety, would be the most important areas of mastery control. We find ourselves in substantial agreement with Erikson, who suggests that if the child is to develop a meaningful sense of personal control, or to use Erikson's term, autonomy,

> . . . it is necessary that he experience *over and over again* that he is a person who is permitted to make choices. He has the right to choose, for example, whether to approach a visitor or to lean against his mother's knee, whether to accept offered food or reject it. At the same time, he must learn some of the boundaries of self-determination . . . that there are walls he cannot climb . . . objects out of reach, and above all, commands enforced by powerful adults (Erikson, 1953, 108).

Our brief review of the ontological origins of personal control has suggested some of the ways in which a person's basic need is shaped by the social context and human interactions that take place within it. We have suggested that the child's need for personal control grows out of and is shaped by interactions with primary figures associated with the satisfaction of biological necessities. Even at this early stage of development, the basic components of cognitive, affective, and behavioral orientations to environment are already present. In the complex interchange between the child's biological needs, their frequency and the nature of their satisfaction, basic beliefs about the nature of the world are being developed. These basic beliefs are not in themselves political, but I would argue that they have important political implications.

What the child is beginning to learn is a basic belief in controllability of the world in general and his ability to control it in particular. This belief has the most profound implications for political life. Pye, for example, in his discussion of the inability of the Burmese adult to develop stable political identities, traces the origins of this problem to childhood. He notes that the Burmese child is:

brought up to feel that he has no control over the ways in which he is treated by others. . . . Thus from the time of his earliest experiences, the child exists in a world in which there is no rational relationship, no recognizable connection between his powers of action and choice and the things that he most desparately wants. From the beginning the Burmese child comes to feel that unconsciously the world is a fickle place. . . . (He) thus learns the most profound lesson of his life . . . (Pye, 1962, 182).

Our discussion to this point then suggests that basic human needs are shaped by social experience and that basic beliefs about the nature of the world are acquired in social learning. This in turn suggests one way in which personality and social learning theories might be usefully integrated in theories of political socialization. A subsequent article by Rohter in this volume will have more to say about learning theories in political socialization; here we simply note their utility.

THE FAMILY AND PERSONAL CONTROL

As we have seen, it is a standard assumption of political socialization theory and research that the family's impact on the political socialization process is profound. Yet we have suggested that the traditional assumption may need to be modified. The major question then is: *In what specific ways does the family shape the acquisition of personal control?* In examining this question we shall look at a variety of ways ranging from the location of the family in the social structure to the personality and child-rearing patterns of the parents.

Socioeconomic Status

The accident of birth into a particular family structure affects not only the acquisition of personal control, but also life chances. Why this is so will become clearer in a moment. One of the most consistent findings in political science literature is the positive relationship between socioeconomic status (SES) and political efficacy (Milbrath, 1965, Ch. 5) both for adults and for children. The same finding has been reported by Campbell for personal efficacy and SES (Campbell, 1954, 512). Socioeconomic status is usually calculated from occupational, educational, and financial data; and there is usually a high intercorrelation among these three measures in our society, especially between the first two. Thus, SES has usually been taken as a strong indicator of a person's (family) position in the social structure. Certainly, SES *is* a valid indicator of present position, *but it is sometimes overlooked that it is also a shorthand for a whole range of life and developmental experiences, attitudes, and life-styles.* Ignoring these developmental aspects is like being interested only in the outcome of a particular game; it tells us nothing of how or why one produces a winning team. In other words, an emphasis on outcomes or end states obscures important developmental aspects of process.

In a sense then, the difference between being born into a high SES family and a low SES family may be seen as the difference between being in an expanding choice system and a limiting choice system. By "expanding system" we mean that one is more likely to acquire the attitudes, skills, and resources to develop and expand one's personal development and life horizons. By "limiting choice system" we mean that the development of certain attitudes, skills, and resources will not reach that critical level needed to increase both one's life choices and chances. Viewed from another perspective, it is the difference between a homeostatic system and a morphogenic system (Buckley, 1967). Certainly, certain values, skills, and resources have been differentially acquired and rewarded in our society, but we are only now beginning to understand the dynamics of this kind of psychological deprivation.

There is a folk maxim prevalent among the middle and upper classes that money cannot buy happiness, and, although this may be true, money certainly can provide growth potential. For example, poor families are more likely to live in apartments than those who are not poor, and typically they must fit more people into less space (Clausen, 1966, 10). What this means in practical terms is that the child's exploratory behavior is limited because he will always be "getting underfoot" in the limited space available; his world is that much more limited and his motivating curiosity not rewarded (Douglass and Bloomfield, 1968). The middle- or upper-class child typically has fewer siblings or greater amounts of space in which to roam. Exploration is encouraged and rewarded, and the child's horizons and personal control grow accordingly.

The influence of money also works in more direct ways. The ability to take swimming, dancing, and skiing lessons are all areas where practice will produce at least a certain amount of mastery, and the attendant idea of "I can do it if I want to" (personal control). It is not that the higher SES child naturally is a better skier or swimmer than a lower SES child; it is just that his initial possibilities are greater, and therefore he is more likely to find something to master. One look at the number of Blacks in high school swimming or tennis teams should make this clear. The facilities that it takes to master some skills are simply unavailable to those without the requisite wealth.

Finally, wealth provides a certain psychological security against the costs of failure. Banfield has argued that one characteristic of lower-class families is that they live a crisis-oriented existence, wherein even a small loss could be a disaster (1969). Such small margins of error promote habit, not development.

Of course, wealth is not the only benefit that a child who is born into a higher SES family possesses. There is also the matter of differential goals, values, and family socialization routines. In general terms (Kohn, 1959) middle-class parents stress curiosity, happiness, and self-control. The goal of their training is to enable the child to learn to govern himself and make and fulfill his personal control. Working-class parents, on the other hand, are more likely to stress obedience, neatness, and cleanliness, with the emphasis on not transgressing against externally imposed rules. One indication of this tendency was explored by Rosen, who found a significant inverse relationship between mean age at independence training and social class (Rosen, 1956).

The importance of family values and reward structure is difficult to overstress. Many psychologists looking at the need for personal control have arbitrarily limited themselves to such areas as achievement motivation. Yet if we examine these studies as a specific area of socialization for personal control, certain family characteristics stand out. Winterbottom has found that boys who scored high on the need for achievement had received demands for independence of action at an earlier age than those scoring low. Mothers of these children imposed fewer restrictions, but imposed them earlier (Winterbottom, 1958). Another study of mothers of high achievers found that they had rewarded and encouraged attempts at achievement and tried to ignore children's requests for help. Moreover, they were more likely to praise spontaneously their children's efforts, even when the children did not seek approval (Crandall, 1963, 429).

The third dimension of socioeconomic position, occupational status, seems to affect socialization for personal control in two related ways. It seems clear that the attainment of a high status occupation reflects a certain degree of accomplishment and should therefore be associated with higher feelings of personal control. Moreover, the higher the occupational status, the more likely the position is to be located in upper sections of the authority structure, with correspondingly greater personal autonomy and decision-making power that should increase feelings of personal control. Thus, higher occupational status suggests the possibility that the need for personal control has been satisfied to some degree.

Occupational status also influences the acquisition of personal control by children, through the mechanism of identification. Identification refers to the process that leads the child to think, feel, and behave as though the characteristics of another person—for a young child, it is usually a parent—were his. At this early stage, it is not usually a conscious imitative process. The development of identification assumes that the child has some motivation to identify, namely that the model possesses attributes he would like to have. Certainly, parents differ from their children in a multitude of important ways, yet we propose that the most important of these is the area of *personal control.*

It is already established that children tend to attribute great power and control to adults with little discrimination. Apparently, this tendency generalizes to perceptions of political figures like the President (Greenstein, 1965). We believe this attribution will be stronger if the parent is indeed in a position that assumes a high degree of mastery, and there is some empirical evidence to support this finding. For example, Gold found that fathers' influences on their children varied directly with the prestige rank of their occupation (Gold, 1963), while a study by Smelser found that boys from upper-class or upwardly mobile families were rated higher on competence and autonomy and also were more likely to see their fathers the same way (Smelser, 1963). The same process seems to hold true for women. Douvan found that mothers who held jobs connected with personal growth rather than family income addition were more admired and perceived as more competent by their daughters (Douvan, 1963). Thus, there seems to be some evidence that personal control is one of the mechanisms underlying identification with parents and that increased mastery and control as indicated by occupational status should result in greater identification.

The Dynamics of Family Impact

We have already suggested that few political scientists have ignored the theoretical impact of the family in the political socialization process, yet in many respects the family has remained a "black box." That is, although there is agreement about the importance of the family in the political socialization process, there have been few empirical attempts to unravel systematically the exact nature of the impact. Those few studies that have examined the impact of family life have typically examined only one or two dimensions (Middleton and Snell, 1963), such as participation in family decision-making, leaving unexamined other dimensions such as the emotional tone of family life. Moreover, there appears to be no reason to assume that the various dimensions of family life will have equal impact on each orientation to life in general or to the political system in particular. In fact, there is little research available that allows us to examine the differential impact of certain dimensions of family life on different politically relevant orientations. Our major concern here then is to ask the question: What dimensions of family life are associated with facilitating the acquisition of feelings of personal control? Furthermore, we are interested not only in those dimensions which are important, but also will wish to make some evaluation of the relative importance of each dimension. Finally, we shall be interested in examining whether the dimensions shown to be important in facilitating personal control are of equal importance in facilitating another politically important basic orientation, faith in people. These tasks should allow us not only to trace the impact of the family on a particular orientation but also to suggest the ways (if any) that the impact of the family varies on different orientations.

The data reported here are part of an ongoing panel study conducted by the author at a large Eastern university. A random sample of undergraduates (N = 300) were interviewed several times over the course of the 1970–1972 period, and their parents were sent questionnaires. The design allows independent assessment of parents' attitudes and basic orientations, as well as those of their children. The basic dependent variable reported here is the feeling of personal control as measured by the Internal–External Control scale devised by Rotter. According to Rotter:

> . . . a careful reading of the items will make clear that the items deal exclusively with the *subject's belief in the nature of the world*. . . . They are concerned with the subject's expectations about how reinforcement is controlled. Consequently, it is considered to be a *measure of generalized* expectancy (Rotter, 1966) (emphasis added).

In addition, the following dimensions of family life were examined as independent variables:[2]

1. *Degree of autonomy allowed.* The extent to which a child is allowed to direct his (or her) own life while growing up.

2. *The allocation of decision-making authority.* Who makes family decisions; the father only, the mother only, or a sharing of decision-making power.

3. *The nature of rule enforcement.* Given that rules are made, how are they enforced? Are they applied consistently or is there a lack of structure?

4. *Trust in parents.* The degree to which a child would trust his parents with an important personal problem.

---

[2] Data collected about early family life from our respondents are of course recall data and therefore should be interpreted cautiously. However, as a recent study of the reliability of recall data (Yarrow *et al.,* 1970) has made clear, they are a great deal more accurate and reliable than previously suspected.

5. *Parental empathy*. The degree parents were felt to understand the emotional needs and position of the child.

6. *Parents' level of personal control*. The extent to which the parents of the child feel that they have personal control of relevant aspects of their life space.

Thus our independent variables tap both the authority and the emotional structure of family life. In addition our design allows us to assess independently the basic beliefs in personal control that are part of the parents' personality structure. What is then needed at this point is some way to assess the relative importance of each of these independent variables on the dependent variable, beliefs in personal control. Clearly some form of multivariate procedure is called for.

Fortunately there is a technique available, requiring only ordinal-level data, that will allow us to assess the relative contributions of each independent variable on the dependent variable. The program called Multiple Classification Analysis (M.C.A.) was developed at Michigan's Institute for Social Research by Andrews, Morgan, and Sonquist (1967). The program utilizes a technique similar to multiple regression with dummy variables and provides several sets of statistics, including Eta and Beta measures for each independent variable.

Eta is a measure of the ability of the independent variable to predict the value of the dependent variable. When squared, it indicates the total sum of squares "explained" by the coefficient. Beta, on the other hand, provides a measure of the power of the independent variable to explain variation in the dependent variable after adjusting for the effects of all of the other independent variables. Thus, Beta is analogous to the partial regression coefficient. Finally, a third statistic, R^2, is computed by the program. This is a measure of the total effect of the independent variables, taking into effect the degree of freedom, on the attempt to explain variance in the dependent variable. When squared, it indicates how well one could predict the values of the dependent variable, once the values of the independent variables are known. Table 2–1 presents the results of the assessment of the effects of various dimensions of family life on the acquisition of personal control and interpersonal trust.

When we examine the Eta correlations in Table 2–1 for personal control, it appears that at least four of the six independent variables have moderate associations with the dependent variable. Only the level of parental personal control and degree of autonomy allowed have strong correlations in the uncontrolled relationship. When we turn to an examination of the Beta correlations in the second column, however, some interesting changes appear.

Table 2–1. Relative Effects of Dimensions of Family Life on the Acquisition of Personal Control and Interpersonal Trust

PERSONAL CONTROL			INTERPERSONAL TRUST	
ETA	BETA		ETA	BETA
.26	.11	Who made rules?	.27	.26
.25	.31	Rule consistency	.29	.24
.46	.37	Autonomy allowed	.40	.58
.20	.12	Trust in parents	.23	.51
.34	.10	Parental empathy	.30	.11
.41	.84	Parent personal control		
		Parent interpersonal trust	.18	.58

Multiple R (Adjusted) = .597   Multiple R (Adjusted) = .711

Multiple R (Squared) = .356   Multiple R (Squared) = .506

Clearly the best single predictor of our respondent's level of personal control is his parents' level of personal control. This finding suggests that a good deal more attention in political socialization research might profitably turn to the transmission of basic personality orientations from parents to children. *This finding also suggests that one reason for the relatively low level of parent–child correlations of political attitudes might be that the real transmission process takes place at the level of psychic organization we have called core or basic beliefs.*

Some other independent variables, although not as powerful as parents' level of personal control belief, were clearly important. The degree of autonomy allowed while the child was growing up emerges as an important variable in the acquisition of personal control. Apparently, the decision to give the child a great degree of personal autonomy does heighten his belief in his own personal control.

A great deal of attention has been focused on the content of particular rules, but less attention has been paid to the nature of their enforcement. Our data suggest that the inconsistent application of rules is detrimental to the development of personal control, while the consistent application of rules facilitates belief in personal control. Why this should be the case seems clear. One of the mechanisms in the development of personal control beliefs is a form of operant conditioning. That is, behaviors that bring about a desired change in the environment are likely to increase feelings of personal control and to be repeated because having control is rewarding. *Yet there is an important assumption contained within the operant condi-*

tioning model, and that is life-space continuity. In order for an action to bring about the same or similar results, the environment must have remained sufficiently stable to make the action efficacious. In other words, one must have a structure before one can muster and manipulate it.

Lastly, our data suggest that the emotional dimension of family life plays a relatively minor role in the acquisition of personal control beliefs. Such dimensions as trust in parents and perceived parental empathy appear to have a relatively small impact on the development of personal control. Just how different the impact of these dimensions of family life on other orientations can be is suggested by examining the right-hand side of Table 2–1. Here we have data on the impact of the family on another politically important basic belief, trust in people. Rosenberg has already provided some evidence that trust in people is highly associated with political trust (Rosenberg, 1956), an·important ingredient of diffuse support and perceived system legitimacy; and we have already suggested that this is one of the basic beliefs about the world that arises in the attempt to meet biological needs. We have further suggested that there is no reason to assume that the impact of family dynamics is the same for different orientations. The data in Table 2–1 provide support for this interpretation.

Here, as in the case of personal control beliefs, parents' interpersonal trust is one of the best predictors of their child's degree of interpersonal trust. Unlike personal control however, the emotional dimension of family life appears to play an important role in the development of faith in people. The degree of trust in the child's parents is a powerful predictor of trust feelings even with the effects of the other variables taken into account. The same is true for the degree of autonomy allowed. Two other dimensions of family life, democratic rule-making and rule consistency, also appear to play at least a moderately important role in the development of interpersonal trust. It is not within the scope of this paper to analyze extensively the theoretical relationship between dimensions of family life and the acquisition of interpersonal trust. From our brief survey of the effects of the family, however, several points appear to be relevant.

First, our survey suggests that although the family may play an important role in the acquisition of personal control, not all dimensions of family life are salient. For personal control, the most important dimensions appear to be parents' level of personal control, the degree of rule enforcement consistency, and the degree of autonomy allowed while growing up. Second, the data suggest that parental personality traits are important components of the political socialization experience. Indeed, for both personal control and interpersonal trust beliefs, they are among the most influential. Exactly how the links are forged between parents' basic personality orientations and children's basic beliefs remains a largely un-charted area, but a potentially rich avenue of investigation. Last, our data suggest that the family should not be treated as a "black box," as the impact of different dimensions of family life does vary with the particular basic belief under consideration.

The School and Personal Control

Having examined the impact of the family on the acquisition of personal control, the next question to arise is: What is the impact of the second most-frequently mentioned socialization institution, the school? We have already noted that the school has been suggested by some as the crucial agency of socialization. In order to ascertain the effects of different dimensions of school life, we asked each respondent a number of questions about his school experiences including the following:

1. *High school type.* Whether the student attended a public or private high school.

2. *Sports participation.* Whether the student participated in school sports.

3. *Class officer.* Whether the student ever was a class officer.

4. *School club participation.* Whether the student took part in extracurricular activities.

5. *High school politicization.* The degree to which politics were discussed in classes.

6. *Peer group politicization.* The degree to which respondent's peer group discussed politics.

7. *Autonomy in high school.* The degree to which students had a voice in the school decision-making structure.

Again the use of Multiple Classification Analysis will be utilized to assess the relative impact of each of these dimensions of school life. The results are presented in Table 2–2.

As with our data on the impact of the family, many of the variables in the uncontrolled relationship show moderately high association with the dependent variable. In the controlled relationships, however, the degree to which students had a voice in the making of school policies clearly emerges as the most powerful single predictor. This is in accord with findings by Almond and Verba that we discussed earlier. Degree of politicization of both friends and the school also appear to be moderately strong predictors even in the controlled condition. On the other hand,

Table 2–2. The Impact of High School Experiences on the
Acquisition of Personal Control

	ETA	BETA
High school type	.27	.15
Sports participation	.13	.18
Class officer	.23	.16
School clubs	.10	.10
High school politicization	.35	.50
Peer group politicization	.37	.43
High school autonomy	.57	.85

Multiple R (Adjusted) = .471

Multiple R (Squared) = .221

participation in a variety of other school activities such as clubs, sports, and class leadership positions appear to have little impact on the development of personal control.

Of course, important questions arise at this point as to which set of experiences, the family or school experiences, are the most important, and within each set which particular events are the most influential. In order to ascertain the answer to these questions, the family and the school independent variables were run together to assess their impact on the acquisition of personal control. The results are presented in Table 2–3.

Our data in Table 2–3 appear to suggest that, at least as far as the development of personal control beliefs, the family has the most important influence. The two most powerful predictor variables, degree of allowed autonomy (family) and degree of parental personal control beliefs, are both located in the family set. This appears to give some support to the model we have advanced, namely that the hypothesis of the importance of early family experiences is essentially accurate but that what is learned early in the family context is not so much specific political attitudes and identification but basic beliefs about the nature of the world.

This is not to say that no direct political learning takes place. Certainly party identification appears to be part of the child's early learning experience, and as the child grows up more specific political attitudes may be learned. What we are suggesting, however, is that the most important political things that are learned as a child are basic beliefs about the nature of the world, learned in the attempt to satisfy basic human needs. Our data do not appear to support the importance of the high school experience in the acquisition of personal control. Of the several indepen-

Table 2–3. The Impact of Family and School Experiences
on the Acquisition of Personal Control

	ETA	BETA
FAMILY		
Who made rules	.26	.31
Rule consistency	.25	.17
Autonomy allowed	.46	.78
Trust in parents	.20	.10
Parental empathy	.34	.11
Parent personal control	.41	.61
SCHOOL		
High school type	.27	.15
Sports participation	.13	.15
Class officer	.23	.25
School clubs	.10	.10
High school politicization	.35	.10
Peer group politicization	.37	.20
High school autonomy	.57	.32

Multiple R (Adjusted) = .609
Multiple R (Squared) = .370

dent variables in the high school set, only two have moderately strong
correlations with degree of personal control beliefs. Moreover the degree
of autonomy in high school, which when the high school variables were
examined alone was the strongest single predictor, drops to only moderate
predictive power when both family and school sets are examined.

Political Correlates of Personal Control Socialization

As we suggested before, psychological needs become politically relevant
to the extent that the political system is perceived to have an impact on
their satisfaction or deprivation. When politics becomes a control-relevant
sphere, a link is forged between individual needs and the political system.
To this point we have been discussing the socialization process involved
in the satisfaction of the need for personal control, but what are its implications for political life?

Our first step was to ascertain the degree of salience of the political
system. Each respondent was asked about the perceived impact of the

outputs of both the Federal and local governments on his daily life. Over 90 percent of the respondents thought that the government had a great impact on their daily lives, which was not surprising, given the uncertainties about the Armed Services draft and the war in Vietnam. More importantly, for us this finding indicates that for most of our respondents politics was a control-relevant sphere.

Given that an individual perceives politics to be a control-relevant sphere and given the inability to obtain the desired level of personal control satisfaction, what are the implications for the political system? In this section we present some illustrative data on this important question. A more detailed discussion of the relationship between personal control and political life can be found in Renshon (1975).

If the need for personal control in the political arena has not been satisfied, how does the individual evaluate and orient himself to the political system? Each respondent was asked to evaluate the Federal government on a number of dimensions including the following: (1) honest–dishonest, (2) open–closed, and (3) trustworthy–untrustworthy. We then combined the responses to these questions to form a "faith in government" index. The results are presented in Table 2–4.

Table 2–4. Faith in Government by Level of Personal Control

PERSONAL CONTROL	FAITH IN GOVERNMENT			
	LOW	MEDIUM	HIGH	TOTAL N
Low	60.0	18.0	22.0	50
Medium	35.8	51.1	13.1	199
High	20.8	43.8	35.4	50
	Gamma $= .34$; $\chi^2 = 31.41$;			P $= < .001$

The data in Table 2–4 suggest a strong relationship between level of personal control and the degree of faith in government. The overwhelming majority of the respondents with low personal control have little faith in government, while those with high levels of personal control are much more likely to have medium or high levels of faith in government. The large percentage of high personal control respondents in the medium category suggests that they are more likely to hold a balanced view of the government, being neither overly cynical nor overly optimistic.

Another important dimension of political life is the degree of perceived connectedness between the self and the polity. That is, to what extent is the political system seen to encompass those behaviors, values, and assumptions that the individual citizen feels are a part of his identity and aspirations? The degree of difference between the values, behaviors, and assumptions (about the political world) of the citizen and his government may be one way to conceptualize the attitude of political alienation. The operational index of the respondent's level of political alienation was his response to the following three questions: (1) Do you believe the government represents people with your political and social views? (2) Does the government seem unwilling or unable to do the things that you think need to be done? and (3) When you think of your ideas and actions of the Federal government do you feel there is . . . no gap . . . a small gap . . . a fairly wide gap . . . or a very large gap? Table 2–5 presents the relationship between level of personal control and the degree of political alienation.

Table 2–5. Political Alienation by Level of Personal Control

PERSONAL CONTROL	POLITICAL ALIENATION			
	HIGH	MEDIUM	LOW	TOTAL N
Low	55.3	42.6	2.1	47
Medium	28.0	62.5	9.5	200
High	29.8	51.1	19.1	47
	Gamma = .33;	$\chi^2 = 18.86$;		P = < .001

The data in Table 2–5 suggest that respondents with low levels of personal control are significantly more likely to have strong feelings of political alienation, while those respondents with high personal control are more likely to have low levels of political alienation. It is clear that identification with the values and outputs of the political system are part of what Easton has called "diffuse support," which he suggests has important implications for the stability and persistence of the political system (Easton, 1965, 220).

Last, given these data we might ask what the implications are of feelings of personal control in the selection of political behaviors. Each of our respondents was asked to evaluate the efficacy of a range of political behaviors ranging from voting to political assassination. Specifically the question asked was: "There are many different ways to try to influence the government; but people today are often in disagreement about which ones are the most effective. How effective would you say each of the following is in making the government pay attention to what people think?"

Table 2–6 presents both the Pearson correlations and the rank order of the perceived effectiveness of political behaviors, given high or low levels of personal control.

Table 2–6. Correlations and Rank Orders of Efficacy Ratings of Political Behaviors

POLITICAL BEHAVIORS	HIGH PERSONAL CONTROL	RANK	LOW PERSONAL CONTROL	RANK
Voting	.52**	1	.16	4
Being informed citizen	.24*	2	.03	5
Giving money	.20*	3	.14	2
Mass demonstrations	.09	4	.27*	1
Writing to officials	.29*	5	.12	12
Political parties	.23*	6	.08	9
Sit-ins	.13*	7	.23*	7
Personal influence	.10	8	.08	6
Picketing	.08	9	.13	3
Attending meetings	.21*	10	.06	10
Breaking law	−.07	11	.16*	8
Engaging in violence	.08	12	.09	11
Assassination	−.09	13	−.06	13

* = < .05
** = < .01

Briefly stated, the data in Table 2–6 suggest interesting differences between high and low personal control respondents in their perceptions of the efficacy of political behaviors. Generally, respondents with high personal control tend to evaluate more kinds of behaviors as efficacious; respondents with low personal control view fewer political behaviors as efficacious and generally do not support the efficacy of traditional behaviors such as voting or being an informed citizen. This shows up in the rankings, wherein voting is viewed as the most efficacious behavior by the high control respondents; for low control respondents voting drops to fourth place, and mass demonstrations are viewed as the most efficacious. Similar differences can be observed in the perceived efficacy of breaking a law for both groups. It should be noted here that for both groups engaging in political violence is ranked at the bottom of the list.

This brief illustrative data review suggests some ways in which the level of personal control holds important implications for the political system. We again caution that these data are meant to be illustrative and not definitive. Yet they certainly suggest the importance of future research on the relationship between basic beliefs (personality) and orientations to the political system.

Life-Cycle and Continuity Dynamics in the Political Socialization Process

Our model of political socialization to this point has placed great emphasis on the impact of the early development of basic beliefs about the world arising out of the attempt to satisfy psychological needs. Does this mean that political socialization ends after the child has acquired an elaboration of these basic patterns? One way to approach these questions is to focus on two important themes: (1) continuities and (2) life-cycle dynamics.

Although basic beliefs about the nature of the world are acquired at an early age and are resistant to change, they are not impervious to it. That is, to the extent that later life experiences are congruent with and reinforce basic beliefs, we would expect those beliefs to remain stable. However, to the extent that later experiences (including experiences with social institutions such as schools) are dissonant with basic beliefs, the potential for change in these basic beliefs would increase.

As Maslow has noted (1954, Ch. 4), early and prolonged gratification of psychological needs enables an individual to withstand subsequent deprivation for longer periods of time. The individual who always has been given love will feel less need to be loved at any particular time. Transposing this finding to political life, we might suggest that politicians who have satisfied their needs for love might better be able to take unpopular but necessary public stands. On the other hand, individuals whose needs have only infrequently been satisfied would be hypothesized to need extended periods of need satisfaction before they were to withstand some deprivation.

This suggests that individuals with need-deprived childhoods will require longer periods of need satisfaction in order to overcome their previous deprivation. Of course, the person who has not acquired feelings of personal control in early life can do so by a variety of methods. He may learn a skill or otherwise acquire fame in sports or politics that allows him to exercise a greater degree of personal control, or he may attempt to gain control by compensatory compulsive behavior (George and George, 1964). What is important to note here is that in order to overcome early need deprivation and the set of basic beliefs that are a consequence of it, there must be discontinuities between the early family experience and the later school, work, and other life experiences.

Equally important is the change in basic beliefs that can occur with those who have their needs fulfilled in early life. Given early and extended need satisfaction, we would expect these individuals to be less likely to change their basic beliefs, even given life-experience discontinuity. Under certain conditions changes may occur. For example, feelings of personal control can be drastically challenged by the onset of sudden misfortune, such as illness. In political life, feelings of self-esteem can be eroded by a succession of scandalous revelations, for in politics as in life a continuous series of setbacks can cause a reorientation of basic beliefs, with attendant political consequences. That such changes are less likely to happen to need-satisfied individuals provides a strong self-interest rationale for government intervention to insure the minimum need dissatisfaction among its citizenry.

Not only may interpersonal experiences impact upon the political socialization process, but also larger societal dynamics may play a role. The onset of major economic depressions affect basic beliefs about the world, as do wars and other similar disasters. Individuals caught up in these larger social forces may experience a change in their basic beliefs about the world that has direct political implications, especially if the political system is somehow involved (by either action or inaction) in the experience. As an example, one might cite the major realignment of the American political party constituencies after the depression of 1929.

Finally, the pathbreaking work of Erikson (1950; 1968) alerts us to the fact that an individual's path through the life cycle may be viewed from the perspective of a number of different stages. Whether or not one accepts Erikson's eight-stage model[3] it is well to remember that each stage brings with it its own particular problems to be overcome and opportunity for growth. *In fact, it is possible to suggest that one confronts the problems of need gratification (e.g., physiological, safety, love, and self-esteem) at each stage of the life cycle, with attendant potential for changes in the basic belief system.* As Erikson has shown, outplay of these life-cycle dynamics and the attempts to come to grips with them can have revolutionary implications for the political system. The relation between personality development, need satisfaction, and the life cycle

---

[3] These stages include: (1) oral–sensory, (2) muscular–anal, (3) locomotor–genital, (4) latency, (5) adolescence, (6) young adulthood, (7) adulthood, and (8) maturity.

in the political socialization process remains largely uncharted but exciting territory in political socialization theory.

SUMMARY, LIMITATIONS, AND IMPLICATIONS

We started this paper by examining the importance of early childhood learning in political socialization theory and research. We then went on to suggest a model of political socialization based on the role of personality development and, more specifically, on the gratification of basic psychological needs. We suggested that there is within the child a set of needs arising in part out of a biosocial interface, which the child attempts to satisfy. A useful way to order these needs was the need hierarchy developed by Maslow. He suggests that there are five basic needs: (1) physiological, (2) safety, (3) love, (4) self-esteem, and (5) self-actualization needs. We suggested that in the attempt of the child to deal with the satisfaction of the three most basic needs, he develops basic beliefs about the nature of the world. These basic beliefs are concerned with the nature of physical reality, with the basic nature of social reality—whether the world is friendly or hostile, whether people are to be trusted or feared—and with autonomy and dependency.

We suggested that although these beliefs are not "political beliefs" per se, they hold immense implications for political attitudes and political behaviors. What was needed, we suggested, was a model that linked these basic beliefs to human needs, on one hand, and to the social experiences through which they are shaped, on the other.

To illustrate the point, we selected the belief in personal control that arises out of the first two of Maslow's needs. We traced the origins and implications of this need as the basic belief underlying that attitude set known as political efficacy. We then went on to trace the development of the belief in personal control theoretically in the larger social context and empirically in the family and school context. Our data appeared to provide some support for the proposition that the family is the most important context in which belief in personal control is learned.

Our data also suggested, however, that the family is not a "black box" and that different dimensions of family life have differential impacts on different orientations. Our data suggested that the three most important contributors to personal control beliefs in our respondents were: (1) level of parental personal control beliefs, (2) degree of autonomy allowed while growing up, and (3) the degree of consistency of rule enforcement in the family.

At this point it might be useful to present some limitations in what we have tried to do. The first point is the rather limited size and nature of the sample. For this reason the data should be taken as illustrative rather than definitive. The cross-sectional nature of the data is another problem. More research of a longitudinal nature is clearly called for in political socialization research. Indeed, it may be possible for political scientists to tap longitudinal data collected by researchers in other fields, such as the child development studies at Berkeley and Harvard.

Beyond these caveats to our analysis, a number of questions still remain. We have talked about childhood as a rather undifferentiated period. In actuality, we suggest that beliefs arising out of the first two needs begin to form in very early childhood, while beliefs arising out of the satisfaction (or lack thereof) of the next two needs take place in later childhood. We need to know more about the ages at which these basic beliefs become fixed. We also need to know a great deal more about the way that specific family dynamics act on particular belief sets. We have already provided some data to suggest that family dimensions operate in the facilitation of personal control beliefs and interpersonal trust beliefs and that they operate with different strengths.

We also need to trace the effects of life experiences on the development of the basic beliefs, utilizing both personality and learning theories throughout the life cycle. Thus, learning theories might suggest that a certain degree of negative reinforcement will decrease the belief in personal control, but personality theories might suggest what kinds of people would be able to continue to maintain their beliefs in the face of disconfirming stimuli, how long, and under what conditions. We must also begin to trace the effects of other socializing experiences on the acquisition of political beliefs and attitudes—the effects of mass social conditions like the degree of social change in a society as well as more personal experiences such as health or other dramatic changes in life circumstances. In short, political socialization must begin to deal with the variety of human experiences and their impact on the socialization process.

REFERENCES

Almond, Gabriel, and Sidney Verba. *The Civic Culture* (Boston: Little, Brown, 1965).

Andrews, Frank, *et al. Multiple Classification Analysis* (Ann Arbor: ISR, 1967).

Balabanoff, Angelica. *My Life as a Rebel* (New York: Harper and Row, 1938).

Banfield, E. *The Moral Basis of a Backward Society* (New York: Free Press, 1969).

Buckley, Walter. *Sociology and Modern Systems Theory* (Englewood Cliffs, New Jersey: Prentice-Hall, 1967).

Campbell, A., *et al. The Voter Decides* (Evanston, Illinois: Row, Peterson Co., 1954).

Clausen, John. "Family Structure Socialization and Personality," in Hoffman and Hoffman (eds.), *Review of Child Development Research* (New York: Russell Sage Foundation, 1966).

Connell, Richard. "Political Socialization in the American Family: The Evidence Reexamined," *Public Opinion Quarterly* 3 (1972), 323–34.

Converse, Phillip. "The Nature of Belief Systems in Mass Publics," in D. Apter (ed.), *Ideology and Discontent* (New York: The Free Press, 1964).

———, and G. Dupeux. "Politization of the Electorate of France and the United States," *Public Opinion Quarterly* 26 (1962), 1–23.

Crandall, M. J. "Achievement," in H. Stevenson (ed.), *Child Psychology* (Chicago: University of Chicago Press, 1963).

Davies, J. *Human Nature and Politics* (New York: John Wiley and Sons, 1963).

Davis, K. "Final Note on a Case of Extreme Isolation," *American Sociological Review* 4 (1956).

Dawson, Richard. "Political Socialization" in Robinson (ed.), *Annual Political Science Review—1966* (Chicago: Rand McNally, 1966).

Douglass, J. W. B., and J. M. Bloomfield. *Children under Five* (London: Allen and Unwin, 1968).

Douvan, E. "Employment and the Adolescent," in Nye and Hoffman (eds.), *The Employed Mother in America* (Chicago: Rand McNally, 1963).

Easton, D. *Systems Analysis of Political Life* (New York: John Wiley, 1965).

———, and Jack Dennis. "The Child's Acquisition of Regime Norms: Political Efficacy," *American Political Science Review* 6 (1967), 25–38.

———. *Children in the Political System* (New York: McGraw-Hill, 1969).

Erikson, Erik. "A Healthy Personality for Every Child: A Fact Finding Report: A Digest," in J. Seidman (ed.), *The Adolescent: A Book of Readings* (New York: Holt, Rinehart, and Winston, 1953).

———. *Identity: Youth and Crisis* (New York: Norton, 1968).

———. *Childhood and Society* (New York: Norton, 1950).

———. *Young Man Luther* (New York: Norton, 1958).

———. *Gandhi's Truth* (New York: Norton, 1969).

Escalona, S., and G. M. Heider. *Prediction and Outcome* (New York: Basic Books, 1959).

Fishbein, Martin (ed.). *Readings in Attitude Theory and Measurement* (New York: Wiley, 1967), 1–51.

Froman, Lewis. "Personality and Political Socialization," *Journal of Politics* 23 (1961), 341–53.

George, A., and J. George. *Woodrow Wilson and Colonel House: A Personality Study* (New York: Dover, 1964).

Goffman, Erving. *The Presentation of Self in Everyday Life* (New York: Anchor, 1959).

Gold, M. *Status Forces in Delinquent Boys* (Ann Arbor, Michigan: Institute for Social Research, 1963).

Greenstein, Fred. *Children and Politics* (New Haven: Yale Press, 1965).

————. *Personality and Politics* (Chicago: Markham, 1969).

Hess, Robert, and David Easton. "The Child's Political World," *Midwest Journal of Political Science* 6 (1962).

————, and J. Torney. *The Development of Political Attitudes in Children* (New York: Doubleday, 1967).

Hoffer, Eric. *The True Believer* (New York: Harper and Row, 1951).

Horney, K. *The Neurotic Personality of Our Times* (New York: Norton, 1937).

Hyman, Herbert. *Political Socialization* (New York: The Free Press, 1959).

Jennings, M. Kent, and Richard Niemi. "The Transmission of Political Values from Parent to Child," *American Political Science Review* 62 (1968), 169–84.

Katz, Daniel. "The Functional Approach to the Study of Attitudes," *Public Opinion Quarterly* 24 (1960), 163–204.

Knutson, J. "Personality in the Study of Politics," in Knutson (ed.), *Handbook of Political Psychology* (San Francisco: Jossey-Bass, 1973).

————. *The Human Basis of the Polity* (Chicago: Aldine, 1972).

Kohn, M. L. "Social Class and Parental Values," *American Journal of Sociology* 64 (1959), 337–51.

Lane, Robert. *Political Thinking and Consciousness* (Chicago: Markham, 1969).

Langer, Walter. *The Mind of Adolf Hitler* (New York: Basic Books, 1972).

Langton, Kenneth, and David Karns. "The Relative Influence of the Family, the Peer Group and the School in the Development of Political Efficacy," *Western Political Science Quarterly* 22 (1967), 813–26.

Marquis, D. P. "Learning in the Neonate: The Modification of Behavior Under Three Feeding Schedules," *Journal of Experimental Psychology* 29 (1941). 263–87.

Maslow, A. *Motivation and Personality* (New York: Harper & Row, 1954).

————. "A Theory of Human Motivation," *Psychological Review* 50 (1943), 263–87.

Middleton, Russell, and Putney Snell. "Political Expression of Adolescent Rebellion," *American Journal of Sociology* 68 (1963), 757–66.

Milbrath, Lester. *Political Participation* (Chicago: Rand McNally, 1965).

Mussen, Paul, *et al. Child Development and Personality* (New York: Harper & Row, 1969).

Niemi, Richard. "Review of Children in the Political System," *American Political Science Review* 64 (1970).

Piaget, J. *The Origins of Intelligence in Children* (New York: International University Press, 1952).

Pye, Lucian. *Politics, Personality, and Nation Building* (New Haven: Yale Press, 1962).

Renshon, Stanley. *Personality Theories and Political Analyses* (New York: The Free Press, forthcoming).

————. *Psychological Needs and Political Behavior* (New York: The Free Press, 1974a).

————. "Personality, Basic Beliefs, and Political Behavior: A Conceptual Map and Empirical Exploration," paper presented at the Annual Meeting of the Midwestern Political Science Association, Chicago, Illinois, 1974b.

————. "Psychological Needs, Personal Control, and Political Participation," *Canadian Journal of Political Science* 35 (1975).

Rokeach, Milton. *The Open and Closed Mind* (New York: Basic Books, 1960).

Rosen, B. "The Achievement Syndrome," *American Sociological Review* 24 (1956).

Rosenberg, Morris. "Misanthropy and Political Ideology," *American Sociology Review* 21 (1956), 690–5.

Rosenzweig, Robert. "The Politician and the Career in Politics," *Midwest Journal of Political Science* 2 (1957).

Rotter, Julian. "Generalized Expectancies for the Internal vs. External Control of Reinforcements," *Psychological Monographs* 80 (1966).

Searing, David, *et al.* "Political Socialization and Political Belief Systems: An Essay on the Theoretical Relevance of Some Current Research," *American Political Science Review* 28 (1973), 415–32.

Smelser, W. "Adolescent and Adult Occupational Choice as a Function of Family Socio-economic History," *Sociometry* 26 (1963), 393–409.

Torney, Judith. "Structural Dimensions of Children's Political Attitude—Concept Systems: A Study of Developmental and Measurement Aspects" (unpublished Ph.D. dissertation, University of Chicago, 1965).

Vaillancourt, Pauline. "The Political Socialization of Young People: A Panel Survey of Young People in the San Francisco Area" (unpublished Ph.D. dissertation, University of California, 1970a).

————. "The Stability of Children's Political Orientations: A Panel Study," paper presented to the Annual Meeting of the American Political Science Association, Los Angeles, California, 1970b.

Winterbottom, Marion. "The Relation of Need for Achievement to Learning

Experiences in Independence and Mastery," in J. W. Atkinson (ed.), *Motives in Fantasy, Action and Society* (Princeton: Van Nostrand, 1958).

Wolfenstein, M., and M. Mead (eds.). *Child-Rearing in Six Cultures* (Chicago: University of Chicago Press, 1966).

Yarrow, M., *et al.* "Recollections of Childhood: A Study of the Retrospective Method," *Monograph of the Society for Research in Child Development* 35 (1970).

_____

Chapter Three

Birth Order and Political Socialization

_____ *Stanley Allen Renshon*

INTRODUCTION

The major purpose of this essay is to alert political scientists to the concept of birth order and its theoretical and research implications for the socialization experience. The dimension of sequential arrival into the family has almost never appeared as a variable in political socialization research, yet this paper will suggest that it holds important implications for the socialization experience in general and for some dimensions of political socialization in particular.

It has by now become a firmly established tenet in political socialization theory that the family plays an important role in the shaping of politically relevant attitudes and orientations. Although political socialization theorists may differ on the relative impact of the family, none deny that the family does play an important role in the socialization process. This being the case, it is strange to note that in many respects the family has been treated as a "black box" whose outputs are studied (in the form of political attitudes, party identification, and the like) but whose dynamics remain for the most part obscure. One reason for this is that "the most extensive evidence offered in support of the role of the family is to be found in the correlations between parental and offspring political orientations" (Dawson, 1966). Although studies that analyze the degree of concordance between parent and child political orientations provide evidence for the importance of the family, they do not by themselves tell us what it is about the family that is important.

In Chapter Two I suggested a number of potentially relevant dimensions of family life and attempted to assess their relative impact on the acquisition of a basic personality belief underlying the attitude set of political efficacy. The results suggested that both the specific configurations of family dynamics and their relative intensities affect the acquisition of politically relevant orientations in various ways. What I am suggesting is that the family's impact on political socialization might profitably be viewed as a multifaceted, morphogenic process.

If this line of reasoning is followed, two implications present themselves. First, not all dimensions of family life may be salient to each political orientation studied. For example, the degree of role consistency while growing up may be more important to the acquisition of beliefs in personal control (a prerequisite for political efficacy) than to interpersonal trust (a prerequisite for political trust). On the other hand, the degree of parental empathy may be more important for the acquisition of interpersonal trust than it will be for the acquisition of beliefs in personal control. As I suggested in Chapter 2, the empirical demarcation of the impact of these different dimensions on different politically relevant orientations is largely uncharted territory and a potentially rich area of investigation.

The second implication is not only that the various dimensions may differentially affect the acquisition of different orientations but also that the patterns of dimensional salience and potency may differ for each member of the family. Political socialization theorists have recognized this, at least implicitly, for males and females (see Greenstein, 1961; Hess and Torney, 1968). Although little systematic empirical work has been done on just what it is that differentiates socialization experiences for females and for males and the linkage of these experiences to political behavior,[1] the repeated findings of gender differences in political behaviors (Milbrath, 1965, 136) and political orientations (Campbell *et al.*, 1964, 255–61) suggest that political learning is structured differently for males and females.

Although gender differences are the most obvious source of differential socialization experiences, another less obvious dimension to the structuring of socialization experiences is birth order. The importance of birth order, the sequential arrival into the family, may have an impact on socialization experiences, personality development, social learning, and behavioral outcomes.

There is by now in psychology a fairly well-developed body of theory and data dealing with order as a research variable. Some of this theory and data have implications for political socialization theory, although almost no study has attempted directly to link ordinal position with political variables.[2] The purpose of this essay, then, will be fourfold:

1. To introduce the concept of birth order as a research variable and briefly to trace its development.

---

[1] An exception to this statement is the recent work of Iglitizin (1972*a*; 1972*b*).

[2] John Pollock's study, "Early Socialization and Elite Behavior," in this volume, is an exception. See also Knutson (forthcoming) and Forbes (1971).

2. To review over a half century of research findings in the area.

3. Where possible to suggest the implications of these findings for political socialization.

4. To present some data and additional hypotheses that attempt directly to link birth order and politically relevant behaviors and orientations.

In reviewing the many decades of birth order research, we will attempt to stress those areas of potential political importance. For additional reviews, the reader is referred to Sampson (1966) and Clausen (1965).

THE GENERAL FAMILY CONTEXT

Freud, the father of psychoanalytic theory, was among the first to notice the relation between birth order and personality development. However, he limited his observations on the effects of birth order to the context of sibling rivalry. Freud suggested that "there is probably no nursery without violent conflicts between the inhabitants." Such conflict arose in part because the first child "was forced into second place by the birth of another." Accordingly, he might develop a sense of generalized resentment against both the parents and the sibling. Freud then concluded that "Among other things, you will infer from this that a child's position in the sequence of brothers and sisters *is of very great significance for the course of his later life*" (Freud, 1938, 182) (emphasis added).

In spite of his own admonition, Freud's position on the instinctual origins of personality development did not lead him to further study of the effects of birth order on personality development. As Freud's assumptions about the biologically based instinctual origins of personal development began to be modified by some of his disciples, the way was cleared for more detailed study of the effects of birth order and socialization.

In an attempt to study the social, as opposed to the biological, determinants of personality, Alfred Adler, one of Freud's disciples, began to theorize about the differences in personality among older, middle, and younger children (Adler, 1931, 144–154). According to Adler, the first born or older child is given a great deal of attention until the second child arrives. At this point he is suddenly deprived, relative to his former position, of both love and attention, which makes the older child resentful and in many ways insecure. He may, for example, develop a profound distrust of people and take elaborate steps to insure against other sudden reversals of fortune. In short, he is likely to become conservative and cautious in his approach to life. Adler also suggested that such resentment and insecurity might lead to acceptance of deviant social roles such as criminal, drunk, or pervert.

Adler also suggested that the second child was characterized by ambition, constantly attempting to outdo his older sibling. In this case there is also, according to Adler, a degree of resentment. "The attitude of the second born is similar to the envy of the poor classes. There is a dominant note of being slighted, neglected in it" (Adler, 1927, 154). Adler thought that the middle child, however, was generally better adjusted than either the first or the youngest child, whom he characterized as essentially spoiled.

Along with the clinical studies of birth order by Freud and Adler, a number of correlational studies were also extant at the time. These studies for the most part attempted to correlate birth order and innate intelligence and proneness to physical disease. In a review of roughly 250 studies of this type conducted between 1881–1931, Jones (1933, 237) concluded that "birth rank has in itself no explanatory significance." By 1937, however, a review of over 40 studies dealing with socially rather than biologically based outcomes concluded that the child's psychological position in the family "is of the utmost importance for the development of social behavior, yet the psychological position is by no means completely dependent on birth order" (Murphy et al., 1937, 362).

The use of the term *psychological position* alerts us to the fact that the correspondence between sequential arrival and psychological position is itself the object of research interest and not to be taken as a research assumption. In the decades since the first clinical and correlational studies, hundreds of research papers have investigated the relationship between birth order, socialization experiences, personality development, and behavioral outcomes. It is to these studies that we now turn.

Family Size

One of the major dimensions of family life that is hypothesized to account for some of the effects of ordinal position is family size. This dimension has most notably been associated with studies of authority and the child's motivational structure.

Bossard and Boll (1956) have utilized Durkheim's model of the division of labor to account for the changes in family relationships that develop as family size increases. According to Bossard, as family size increases, there is a tendency toward a more centralized family authority structure, which in turn leads to increased parental dominance, decreased parental contact with each child, and increased responsibility by older children for their younger siblings. The tendency toward centralized leadership in large families has also been noted by Elder (Elder, 1962; Elder and Bowerman, 1963). Elder suggests that this centralizing tendency may be the source of adolescent rebellion. Such rebellion may take the form of political deviation from parental political norms and expectations (Middleton and Snell, 1963) when politics is salient to the parents (Lane, 1962).

Not only does authority tend to centralize in larger families, but there may be changes in the locus of decision-making responsibility. Henry (1957) suggests that as family size increases, the mother begins to take on more of the disciplinary responsibility. This means that for the first child, the father is the source of discipline, while for later children, the mother is. Henry suggests that rebellion against the father is more likely than rebellion against the mother because the mother is also a source of affection, while typically the father is less so. This suggests that later children will have to direct their anger inward or displace it outward onto socially approved objects, but first-born children will be able more easily to direct their anger to its instigator, the father as disciplinary figure. As first-born children can more easily achieve catharsis by venting their hostility, we might expect first-born children to be less aggressive; as we shall see when we discuss birth order and aggression, there is some empirical support for this position.

Family size has been related in a number of studies to academic performance and achievement motivation. In general, these studies (Nam and Cowhig, 1962; Clausen, 1966; Schacter, 1963) report an inverse relationship between family size and academic achievement. One of the most impressive studies in this area was conducted by Douglass (1964) who began with a stratified sample of all children born in Britain during one week in 1946. Data on intelligence and academic performance were gathered when the children in the sample reached eight and then again when they reached eleven. Intelligence-test scores were shown to vary inversely with family size. Douglass also found a strong inverse relationship between family size and academic performance, although the relationship was less pronounced for the upper classes than for the working classes. Even in the upper classes, however, it was found that performance decreased in families of more than four children, and that this effect was most pronounced in families of six or more children.

One possible reason for these findings is that the impact of family size has its greatest effect on future academic performance during the child's early cognitive and language-skill development. As the size of the family increases, the parental time spent with each child decreases, with the resultant decrease of assistance in cognitive development by the parents (Nisbet, 1961). Another explanation has been put forward by Douglass (1964), who suggests that at least among working and middle-class families the birth of more children into a family characterized by limited and nonelastic economic resources results in both economic and social deprivation, including poor housing and decreased parental concern.

Several other studies have focused on the relationship between family size and achievement motivation of individuals from large versus small families. In general, these findings suggest that achievement motivation decreases with family size (Rosen, 1961; Elder, 1962). It should be noted here that at least one study has failed to find any relationship between family size and academic performance (Damrin, 1949).

Ordinality and Socialization

One of the most important areas of study in birth order research has to do with the different socialization experiences of first-born and only children as compared to second, third, and later children. Indeed, many studies of the behavioral and attitudinal outcomes we will examine in subsequent sections either assume or relate their findings to supposed differences in socialization experiences (Senn and Hartford, 1968).

One of the clearest theoretical statements on these differences comes from Schacter (1959). Schacter theorizes that although parents give their first-born children a great deal of love and attention, because of their inexperience and anxiety as new parents, they are likely to behave inconsistently with the child. The combination of intense love and anxiety resulting in inconsistent parental behavior is theorized by Schacter to lead to increased dependency for first-born and only children. This increased dependency, according to Schacter, should lead to a greater desire for affiliation, especially under conditions of stress, for first-born and only children.

A number of studies have examined or are related to Schacter's thesis. It appears to be the case that first-born children are given more love and attention. The first-born is more likely to have been planned and wanted and is likely to have been breast-fed for longer periods of time (Sears, Maccoby, and Levin, 1957). Other studies show parents have more affection and pay more attention to the first child (Koch, 1954), spend more time interacting with the first (Bossard and Boll, 1955; Rosen, 1961), and are more likely to call him by an affectionate name or nickname in place of his regular name (Clausen, 1965).

Although the first-born receives more love and attention, he is at the same time the object of parental anxiety and uncertainty about the parent role. Several studies have noted the relative inexperience and anxiety of parents with their first children (Koch, 1956; Phillips, 1956; Sears, 1951). One way in which this anxiety manifests itself is in relative caution in handling first-born children (Koch, 1954; Gewirtz, 1948; Haeberle, 1958). An attendant implication is that this caution produces a degree of fear or timidity in the first-born child. Although parental insecurity may result in caution, it apparently does not limit the use of physical punishment. One of the most consistent findings of parental behavior toward their first-born children is that they are much more likely to use physical than psychological punishment. One study reported that in one fifth grade 44 percent of the last-born children had been physically punished in the last six months, while 88 percent of the first-born children reported being so punished (Clausen, 1966). This finding has been confirmed in other studies (Sears et al., 1957; Clausen, 1965).

Although parents do appear to have anxiety about the parent role, there is evidence that this anxiety is not permanent. Several studies (Lasko, 1954; Stout, 1960) report that parents become more consistent with their child-rearing practices as they gain experience with subsequent children. Along the same lines, others (McArthur, 1956; Sears, 1950) have found that parents report themselves to be more relaxed with later children. Presumably, then, one would find greater latitude and more consistency given to later children.

Although there appears to be some support for Schacter's theory that parents are both more loving toward and more anxious for their first-born children than for their subsequent children, what of his conjecture that first-born children will be more dependent? Schacter hypothesized that first-born children would be more dependent because of parental over-protection, inconsistency, and inexperience (Schacter, 1959). Yet a different theoretical position is possible; certain studies appear to suggest that the firstborn may have the most experience in occupying roles that facilitate independence. For example, the first-born is expected to take a large part in family interactions (Sletto, 1934), is expected in larger families to become an effective role model for younger siblings (Sampson, 1962), and is generally expected to be "adult" at an earlier age (Bakan, 1949; Davis, 1959). Reviewing both theoretical positions, Sampson (1966) suggests that the first-born may have dependency conflict, having a high need for both dependency and independence. Although no study has focused directly on dependency conflict, a number of studies have focused on the relationship between birth order and dependency.

Several studies have found that first-born or only children are more autonomous (Abernathy, 1940; Sampson and Hancock, 1962) than children in other ordinal positions. In a similar vein Masling (Masling et al., 1968) examined the oral-dependent imagery of experimental subjects on Rorschach protocols and found that later-born subjects gave more oral-dependent answers than first-born or only subjects. On the other hand, a number of studies (Stewart, 1967; Alexander, 1968; Bradley, 1968) have found that first-born and only children are more dependent. Sears (1951) reports that mothers tend to rate their first children as dependent and their second as stubborn, while data from Haeberle (1958) utilizing teachers' ratings of a sample of students found that first-born and only children were significantly more likely to be rated as dependent.

Another study (Eisenman and Platt, 1968) examined the relation between birth order and feelings of personal control as measured by the Rotter I–E Scale. Their findings suggest that first-born children are significantly more external than later-borns. Assuming that feelings of personal control are similar to or a component of independence, this study and others dealing with personal control (Renshon, 1972; Marks, 1972) appear to support Schacter's hypothesis.

Our review of the data appears to suggest that first-born children are more dependent in orientation to the world around them. There are several works in political science (Campbell, 1954; Almond and Verba, 1966) suggesting that feelings of independence and autonomy have important implications for political participation. It may be that the learning of political passivity begins earlier than previously thought. Transposing the findings from psychology to political science the hypothesis might be that first-born children are less autonomous and have less well-developed feelings of personal effectiveness in politics than children with later ordinal positions and socialization experiences.

Anxiety, Affiliation, and Birth Order

Another of Schacter's hypotheses was that first-born and only children would be more likely to desire to affiliate under conditions of anxiety. Although there is some evidence that first-born females have higher needs for affiliation (Radloff, 1961; Sarnoff and Zimbardo, 1961) than first-born males, the findings do not support any general differences[3] in the affiliation needs of first-born and later-born children (Waters and Kirk, 1967; Rosenfeld, 1966).

When we turn, however, to an examination of affiliation needs under conditions of stress or anxiety, the findings are both striking and consistent. A number of studies (Suedfeld, 1968; Eisenman, 1968; Jacoby, 1968) have demonstrated that when first-born or only males feel anxious, they will generally attempt to affiliate with those in social and physical proximity. More specifically, first-born males are found to be more likely than later-born males to yield to group pressures (Becker and Caroll, 1962), to be more suggestible (Staples and Walters, 1961), and to be more likely to undergo opinion change under stress (Heimreich et al., 1968). Indeed, a recent study (Collard, 1968) found that first-born infants were much more likely to become upset in a strange situation (i.e., displayed high

---

[3] One exception is a study by Demeber (1964) that found that first-borns did have higher average need-affiliation scores. One potential explanation for these findings comes from a study by Conners (1963) who found that first-borns had less expectations of satisfying their affiliative needs than later-borns. This decreased expectancy might lead to a leveling of the motivating potential of this need (Maslow, 1954).

anxiety) and showed fewer positive social responses to strangers than did children of comparable age with other siblings. Apparently, the anxiety–affiliation syndrome does not apply to females (Sampson, 1962).

The relationship between ordinal position and high need for affiliation under conditions of stress has some interesting implications for the study of political life, especially in conjunction with other findings we have presented.

We have already suggested that first-born and only children are lower in autonomy than later children. Given the combination of low autonomy and high affiliation needs under stress, first-born and only children might be hypothesized to identify with one or another political party or group rather than remain "independent." Other possibilities also suggest themselves. In a time of rapid social change, the pressure to cling to the familiar and the tried is intense (Hoffer, 1959; Toffler, 1971). Under such conditions, first-born and only children might be more likely to support leaders whose programs and symbols stressed inclusion and identity reinforcement.

Finally, another dimension of political significance should be touched upon. A great many discussions of the psychological prerequisites for "democratic man" have stressed autonomy and ego strength (Lasswell, 1951; Greenstein, 1965). *Autonomy* usually refers to the perception of self as a relatively independent agent, an initiator rather than an object of action. *Ego strength*, a related but distinct dimension, refers to the ability of the organism to persist in the face of adversity. Autonomy, then, is the ability to initiate action, while ego strength refers to the ability to persist in that action, despite setbacks. As our review has suggested, the socialization experiences consequent to being a first or only child do not commonly produce characteristics associated with "democratic man." Individuals with high needs for affiliation and conformity in times of stress do not appear to meet the requirements of "democratic man." Even if it were suggested that autonomy, ego strength, and other such requirements characterize only an "ideal type," the dissimilarity between this ideal and the socialization experiences of first-born and only children remains interesting.

Birth Order, Empathy, and Self-Esteem

Another psychological dimension of democratic man involves empathy, the ability to assume the role and feelings of another, which has important implications for political life. For example, in a study of modernization, Lerner (1959) shows the importance of being able to think of oneself in a role other than that of peasant, such as newspaper editor. Those who could not role-empathize were, according to Lerner, "unfinished material for Democracy" (50). Not only is it important to be able to imagine alternative or potential roles, but it is equally important to be able to empathize with the feelings of others. In a study of the psychology of Hitler's dictatorship, Gilbert (1950) was able to show how constricted empathy allowed the German people to select information about the fate of certain groups in Germany, by making their immediate friendship circle and their "empathy circle" coterminous. With these relations in mind, we now turn to the question, how empathetic is the first-born or only child compared to later-born children?

Most of the major work in this area has been done by Stotland and his associates, who have attempted to test the hypothesis that first-born and only children will be less empathetic than later-born children. In a series of experiments designed to test this hypothesis, the hypothesis was generally supported. In one study (Stotland and Cottrell, 1962), it was found that increased interaction with other subjects increased the sense of self–other similarity for later-borns to a greater degree than for first-born or only children. In another set of experiments designed to see if there were any differences in the ability to empathize with subject models after they had failed in a task, it was found (Stotland and Dunn, 1962; Stotland and Dunn, 1963) that later-borns had greater empathy than did first-born or only children.

On the basis of these studies it appears that first-born and only children do not develop the ability to empathize as well as their later-born counterparts. According to Stotland, later-borns react to others "as if they were still in a family of peers, which was their initial experience in life" (Stotland and Walsh, 1963, 614). Apparently, as the first-born or only child does not begin by experiencing peers, when he must, the ability or desire has atrophied. The later-borns arrive in a situation wherein they are one of several and begin by experiencing peers. Here again the experimental evidence suggests that the development of interpersonal empathy, with its attendant political implications, has its origins in early developmental experiences.

Another area of political relevance to both the theories of "democratic man" (Lane, 1962) and the psychology of political belief systems (Sniderman and Citrin, 1971) is the development of self-esteem. Although there are differences in the conceptualization of self-esteem (Coopersmith, 1967; Rosenberg, 1965), at base the concept refers to the individual's evaluation of self along a positive–negative continuum. According to Lane, "The person who is disappointed in himself, . . . is also disappointed by the world who sees him that way" (Lane, 1962, 106–7). A number of other studies in the psychology of political behavior have established the crucial importance of self-esteem in political life. For example, in discussing President Woodrow Wilson's search for power in politics, the authors note that power "was for him a compensatory value, a means of restoring the self-esteem damaged in childhood" (George and George, 1956, 320). Other studies have connected low self-esteem with decreased interest in world affairs (Rosenberg, 1962), recruitment into political roles (Mathews, 1960; Browning and Jacob, 1964), rigid belief systems (Rokeach, 1960), and hostility toward minority groups (Middleton, 1960).

The study of birth order and self-esteem has provided some interesting results. A number of very early studies (Busemann, 1928; Goodenough and Leahy, 1927) found that only children reported themselves to be more dissatisfied with themselves and to feel more introverted and less self-confident. The finding that only children were more introverted has also been established in a later study by Hillinger (1958).

Recent studies utilizing psychometric assessment techniques have provided additional information. One study (Dittes and Capra, 1962) found that the first-born developed lower self-esteem. The authors reasoned that the first-born must relate to parents who are extremely powerful and perhaps viewed as omnipotent, causing a comparative loss of self-esteem. The later child, in comparison, has a sibling close in both age and abilities to relate with, resulting in less of a lowering of self-esteem via social comparison. Some support for this position has come from a study by Zimbardo and Formica (1963) of male undergraduates, which found that first-born students had lower self-esteem than later-born. However, in another study (Stotland and Dunn, 1962), the results failed to indicate any differences in self-esteem levels. Finally, in a previously mentioned study, Rosenberg studied the relationship between birth order and self-esteem. He found that male only children had higher self-esteem than children with siblings (111) and that this tendency was particularly pronounced among Jewish only children. Rosenberg suggests that this may be due in part to the greater amount of attention that only children receive. Rosenberg's study adds an important consideration to the discussion of birth order and self-esteem. Based on the research we have reviewed it might be possible to put forward the following generalizations about birth order and self-esteem: only children have higher self-esteem than children from multisibling families, and first children in multisibling families have lower self-esteem than later-born children from multisibling families.

Birth Order, Intelligence, and Achievement

The relationship between individual intelligence and political life has not been the subject of extended study in political science. Yet among psychologists there is a general recognition that "general intelligence cannot be equated with intellectual ability, but must be regarded as a manifestation of the personality as a whole" (Wechler, 1961, 660). Support for this position has come from a study by Gough (1961) which found that among the psychological correlates of general intelligence were self-confidence, personal autonomy, faith in people, and good general psychological functioning. The relationship of some of these correlates to political life has already been discussed. In one of the few studies that have directly attempted to link I.Q. with political attitudes, White (1968) has found that intelligence as measured by scores on an I.Q. test has great predictive power for ranges of political efficacy in children. In a study based on the same data that White utilized, Hess and Torney (1968) found significant association between I.Q. and the acceleration of the acquisition of political attitudes (148), the evaluation of governmental effectiveness (168), more frequent political discussions (176), and greater acceptance of the possibility of change in the governmental system (181).

As we noted in the beginning of this paper, the study of ordinal position began with the relationship between birth order and intelligence. The review of these studies by Jones (1933) led him to the position that the reported differences in intelligence between only and later-born children were mostly the product of statistical artifact, more specifically the failure to standardize the intelligence scores by age. Later studies have not conclusively demonstrated any relationship between birth order and intelligence. Several studies (Koch, 1954; Altus, 1962) have found an effect favoring first-born males on verbal abilities, but not for mathematical abilities. Although these results might be explained by the increased verbal exchanges and attention that characterize first-born-parent interactions (see the preceding discussion), several studies have failed to find any relationship between intelligence and birth order (Schoonover, 1959; Douglass, 1964). It appears then, that the relationship between birth order and intelligence is problematic and that if it does obtain it is probably for the verbal dimension of intelligence.

Along similar lines a number of studies have attempted to ascertain if first-born or only children have higher achievement motivation. Following the work of Winterbottom (1958) on the relationship between ordinality and autonomy training, several researchers have suggested that there should be a correlation between ordinality and achievement motivation. The reasoning appears to be that the first child is more often put in roles such as sibling model that provide training in independence (but note the contrary evidence we have presented). This training, it is hypothesized, should lead to a higher need for achievement on the part of first-born children (Rosen, 1961; Demeber, 1964).

In an early study designed to test this hypothesis subjects were given a projective test to measure Need Achievement (Sampson, 1962). Results indicated that first-born children had higher need for achievement than the later-born and that this result was especially pronounced for girls. In view of the fact that women receive significantly less training for autonomy, no matter what their ordinal position (Renshon, 1972), the results indicate mixed support for the ordinality-achievement motivation hypothesis. Another researcher using a similar projective test (Rosenfeld, 1964) found that first-born children had *lower* achievement motivation than later-born children. Another experiment (Moore, 1964) utilized self-report measures of achievement motivation for first-born and later-born children and found no differences; nor did a study by Munz (Munz *et al.*, 1969). Finally, a study by Sampson and Hancock (1962) utilized both self-report and projective measures of achievement and found that first-born children were significantly more likely to have high achievement motivation on the self-report measures, but not on the projective measure. The evidence reviewed does not appear to present strong support for the proposition that first-born children have higher achievement motivation than later-born children. Yet in one of the strange paradoxes of the birth-order literature, it turns out that, although first-born do not have higher achievement motivation than later-borns, they do have greater achievement.

One of the most consistent set of findings in the birth-order literature is that first-born and only children are significantly more likely to be high achievers than later-born children. As Schacter notes in a recent study:

> . . . . marked surpluses of first-borns have been reported in samples of prominent American men of letters, of Italian University professors, of starred men in *American Men of Science*, of the biographies in *Who's Who*, of ex-Rhodes scholars and of eminent research biologists, physicists, and social scientists (1963, p. 757).

Along similar lines research has established that first-born males are more likely to be in medical school (Cobb and French, 1964), more likely to be leading American scientists (Visher, 1948), are more likely to hold better jobs (Yasuda, 1964), and are generally more likely to reach a higher level of intellectual attainment (Chen and Cobb, 1960) than later-born children.

Our previous review of intelligence and birth order does not allow us to attribute this showing to any innate advantage in intelligence in first-born and only children. Nor are we able to state that there are consistent differences in achievement motivation between the two groups. *It appears to be the case that the relatively better showing of first-born and only males is a result of pressures put on the child by his parents and the coterminous shaping of the child's personality and values by these socialization experiences.* These pressures are facilitated by the lack of siblings and the attendant increase in parental attention, which results in a high level of verbal and other types of interaction.

The first-born males' academic prominence has been shown in a number of studies. Many studies (Lees and Stewart, 1957; Bradley and Sandborn, 1969; Smelser and Stewart, 1968) have found that first-born or only children have greater academic achievement than later-born children. Not only do first-born and only children achieve more in school, they also tend to go further in their studies (Rossi, 1965; Lees, 1952).

Although a number of studies have suggested that first-born or only males are likely to be prominent in a variety of fields, there has yet be a study of the effects of birth order and political eminence. In order to investigate the hypothesis that first-born and only sons would be more likely to achieve political eminence, the biographies of U.S. Presidents were examined to learn about sibling relationships. As the Presidency is the highest office of the land, if birth order does play a role in the achievement of eminence in American politics, we would expect it to show up in the attainment of this high office. The results are presented in Table 3–1.

Table 3–1. Presidential Ordinality

1.	Washington		20.	Garfield	
2.	Adams	✻ ✻	21.	Arthur	✻ ✻
3.	Jefferson	✻ ✻	22.	Cleveland	
4.	Madison	✻ ✻	23.	Harrison	
5.	Monroe	✻ ✻	24.	Cleveland	
6.	Adams	✻ ✻	25.	McKinley	
7.	Jackson		26.	Roosevelt	✻ ✻
8.	Van Buren		27.	Taft	
9.	Harrison		28.	Wilson	✻ ✻
10.	Tyler		29.	Harding	✻ ✻
11.	Polk	✻ ✻	30.	Coolidge	
12.	Taylor		31.	Hoover	
13.	Fillmore		32.	Roosevelt	✻ ✻
14.	Pierce		33.	Truman	✻ ✻
15.	Buchanan	✻ ✻	34.	Eisenhower	
16.	Lincoln	✻ ✻	35.	Kennedy	+
17.	Johnson		36.	Johnson	✻ ✻
18.	Grant	✻ ✻	37.	Nixon	+
19.	Hayes		38.	Ford	+

A look at Table 3–1 suggests some very interesting results. All Presidents who are the first-born male have a double asterisk (**) after their names. Almost half of all the Presidents of the United States were first-born males. In addition two Presidents not included in this group (Presidents Kennedy and Nixon) had older brothers who died while they were young, in effect making them the first males in the family and subject to all the pressures we have described earlier.[4] If we include these two Presidents in our first male list, then the percentage jumps from 17 of 37 (45%) to 20 of 37 (56%).[5] Of course, these results are merely suggestive.

Birth Order, Aggression, and Psychopathology

We have already suggested that one theoretically possible relationship between birth order and aggression is that first-born and only children would be lower in aggression than later-born children. Henry (1957) reasoned that for the first child the father is the source of discipline, while for later children the mother takes over this role. Because the father is not a source of affection for the first child as is the mother, it should be theoretically easier for the child to express hostility toward the father than toward the mother. Having been able to reduce the hostility by expressing it, the first child should be less aggressive than later children for whom the mother is both the disciplinarian and the affection object.

Of course, it is also possible to suggest that the father is such a powerful figure that even though he stands out as the sole source of discipline it might be perceived to be dangerous to attack him (Freud, 1933). In this condition, hostility would be repressed, not expressed. On this same point we have already suggested that inconsistent behavior characterizes the treatment of the first-born, and such inconsistency might easily lead to a great deal of frustration and thus possibly to aggression. However, we have also noted that restrictiveness and parental control are also characteristics of the socialization process of first-born and only children. The different positions appear to suggest that the first child has more frustration-induced hostility but is less able to directly express it.

Several older studies (Stratton, 1934; Wile and Noetzel, 1931) found no differences with respect to anger levels or loss of temper. Another older study (Goodenough and Leahy, 1927) found that only children were high in aggression and later children were low. On the other hand, Sears (1951)

---

[4] President Gerald Ford was the first born and only male child for two years before his mother remarried.

[5] Percentages are based on 37 rather than 38 Presidents because Cleveland won election twice but not in succession. For purposes of presidential numbering, he is therefore counted twice.

found no differences in aggressive play between only and younger children. In a later study by Koch (1955) it was found that first males who had older sisters were rated as less aggressive by teachers. In addition, he found that first-born females were more aggressive than later-born females or first-born males.

It appears from these studies that the first-born male is not more aggressive than his later-born counterparts, but may be slightly more aggressive if he is an only child. Finally, there is some indication that the sex of siblings plays an important role in the aggressiveness or lack of directed aggressiveness. In general, the results do not at this time permit a strong defense of any particular hypothesis about birth order and aggressiveness.

One might expect that parental inconsistency on matters of autonomy and restrictiveness coupled with the greater demands placed on the first or only child might lead to a deterioration of mental health, and a greater likelihood of neuroses or perhaps even psychoses. There have been a number of attempts to assess the impact of ordinality both on mental and physical health. In a number of early studies there appeared to be some evidence of greater adjustment problems for first-born (Berman, 1933; Rosenow and White, 1931) and for only children (Bellrose, 1927; Campbell, 1933). However, an equal number of early studies (e.g., Stagner and Katzoff, 1936; Witty, 1934) found no differences in neurotic patterns among the three groups.

There does appear to be a consistent pattern of findings that first-born children are more often brought into child guidance centers for treatment (Chombart de Lauwe, 1959; Phillips, 1956; Rosenow, 1930). Phillips (1956) suggests that this may have more to do with parental inexperience in dealing with the problems of their first child than a greater incidence of emotional problems. It is also of interest to note here that Douglass's (1964) longitudinal study of British children found that first-born children were more likely to be taken to welfare centers for medical services in the first five years. Yet later-born children were found to have twice as many infectious diseases by age four than did the first-born. This suggests that as parents become more experienced they are more able to differentiate dangerous from nondangerous situations.

Those later studies that have attempted to assess the relative mental health connected with ordinality have had mixed results. Phillips (1956) and Haeberle (1958) have found some evidence that first-born had more problems of emotional adjustment than later-born children. A somewhat later study (Cushna et al., 1964) found that first-born children had more functional disorders and withdrawal problems. Schacter (1959) however found no relation between ordinal position and scores on a series of instruments designed to assess neurotic problems. Schacter's finding of no relationship between ordinality and neurotic symptoms has been duplicated in a later study by Bennett (1960). Another study has even suggested that first-borns have superior personal adjustment (Lessing and Oberlander, 1967).

At the more serious level of psychic disorder, several studies have failed to turn up any significant relationship between birth order and psychosis, including schizophrenia (Plank, 1953; Patterson and Zeigler, 1941) and obsessive–compulsive character (Kayton and Borge, 1967). One study (Schooler, 1961) has suggested that there is a slightly higher tendency for schizophrenics to be found in the latter half of the family, but also warns that the factor of family size plays an important role. Related to impaired psychic functioning is the issue of physical functioning. It has been known for a long time that physical health is at least partially dependent upon mental health (Miller and Galton, 1971). In a review of the relationship between ordinal position and physical health, Chen and Cobb (1960) found that the incidence of asthma, tuberculosis, and obesity were higher for first-born, while the incidence of peptic ulcers was greater for later children.

SUMMARY AND IMPLICATIONS

At this point it is important to suggest some caution. We have not dealt at length with a number of methodological problems that have affected birth order research. For more detailed discussions of the methodological difficulties encountered with this type of research the reader is referred to Sampson (1966) and Kammeyer (1967). Generally these criticisms are directed toward the sampling procedures, research subjects, and lack of longitudinal research. An equally important caution, but one that has not received much attention, is the problem of the culture-boundness of birth order research. Almost all the research has been done with American samples, and there is some indication that the effects of birth order on socialization experience do not hold for certain national groups (see for example the work with Arabs by Diab and Prothro, 1968). As I suggested previously, the examination of "life path analysis" in political socialization will eventually lead to cross-cultural comparisons of political socialization processes. It is possible that in some countries characterized by remnants of a social system in which primogeniture was or continues to be important (we might expect this to be the case for some countries in Latin America), the impact of birth order on the socialization experience will be dramatically increased. In other countries, we might expect the impact to be small or nonexistent. Last, this chapter represents an attempt to introduce and suggest potential relationships between ordinality and political socialization. As such it is meant to be suggestive rather than inclusive. We began by suggesting that our major purpose was to alert political scientists to the concept of birth order and its theoretical and research implications for the socialization experience. Our review of the literature covering several decades has, we hope, suggested that birth order research has both general and specific implications for political socialization theory.

The most general implication of birth order research we have presented is related to the role of the family in the political socialization process. We have suggested that although most theorists in the area agree that the family plays an important role in the acquisition of politically relevant orientations, it has for the most part not been sufficiently examined. One of the major debates in political socialization research has revolved around the relative importance of the family as one agent of socialization. Investigations into the relative impact of the family on different sets of political orientations has received a good deal less attention. As we have suggested in Chapter 2 there is neither theoretical nor empirical reason to assume that the impact of the family is undifferentiated, either for specific basic politically relevant personality orientations or for more directly political information. That is, we would hypothesize that different dimensions of family life (e.g., emotional and authority dimensions) would have differential impact on the acquisition of specific politically relevant orientations.

Along similar lines, our review of birth order research suggests an additional consideration of some importance in the study of the political socialization process. *That is, not only may different dimensions of family life have differential impact on specific politically relevant orientations, but these patterns of salience and potency may themselves differ for different members of the family.* Future research in political socialization will not only have to specify and deal with multiple dimensions of family life, but will also have to explore the linkages between those effects and specific existential condition and life experience potential of the child. By existential condition, I refer to the particular set of expectancies and potentials that surround different members of any society. These in turn both limit and shape the resultant life experiences of the person with specific implications for political orientations and behavior. Our present analysis suggests that these differences in life experiences may begin as early in life as the arrival into the family. Other forces acting to shape the "life path" that come immediately to mind are gender (Greenstein, 1961) and class (Sennett, 1968). Others will no doubt emerge in future research.

Birth order research suggests that one new and potential useful direction in political socialization research would be a form of comparative research that might be called "political life path analysis." By life path analysis I mean the study of the way in which a person's particular place in the social structure and his own characteristics (both innate and socially ascribed) act to influence the nature of his life experiences and the implications of these interactions for the acquisition of politically relevant orientations and behaviors. The empirical study of the effects of different socialization experiences on the acquisition of political orientations has already begun. There are now studies on the comparative political impact of gender (Renshon, 1974), race (Greenberg, 1969), nationality (Hess, 1963), and the effects of economic deprivation on attitudes toward political authority (Jaros *et. al.*, 1968). Such attempts to trace the effects of life experiences on individual orientations suggest one way in which micro and macro considerations may more profitably be brought together in empirical political socialization research.

Aside from the broader implications of the birth order research we have reviewed, we have suggested a number of more immediate links to political orientations and behaviors. We have suggested that there is a linkage between ordinality and the socialization experiences that influence the acquisition of politically relevant orientations. More specifically we suggested the following politically relevant relationships between ordinality and socialization experiences:

1. A relationship between ordinality and feelings of dependency and autonomy, with attendant implications for feelings of capacity (efficacy) in the political arena.

2. A relationship between ordinality, affiliation needs under conditions of stress, and opinion change with implications for the retention and change of political attitudes and opinions and the support of particular types of political leadership.

3. A relationship between ordinality and affiliation needs under stress conditions with attendant implications for recruitment into political groups and roles.

4. A relation between ordinality and the psychological characteristics of democratic man, including more specifically the relationship between ordinality and self-esteem and between ordinality and empathy.

5. A relation betwen ordinality and achievement, with attendant implications for achievement in political roles.

Although these relationships are only suggestive at this stage, it is hoped that this chapter will serve to stimulate further investigation of the concept and linkages suggested.

REFERENCES

Abernathy, E. "Data on Personality and Family Position," *Journal of Psychology* 10 (1940), 303–7.

Adler, A. *Understanding Human Nature* (New York: Greenberg, 1927).

———. *What Life Should Mean to You* (Boston: Little, 1931).

Alexander, N. "Ordinal Position and Social Mobility," *Sociometry* 31 (1968), 285–93.

Almond, G., and S. Verba. *The Civic Culture* (Boston: Little, Brown, 1966).

Altus, W. D. "Sibling Order and Scholastic Aptitude," *American Psychologist* 17 (1962), 304.

Bakan, D. "The Relationship between Alcoholism and Birth Rank," *Quarterly Journal for the Study of Alcoholism* 10 (1949), 334–40.

Becker, S. W., and Caroll, J. "Ordinal Position and Conformity," *Journal of Abnormal and Social Psychology* 65 (1962), 129–31.

Bellrose, D. "Behavior Problems in Children" (unpublished M.A. thesis, Smith College, 1927).

Bennett, I. *Delinquent and Neurotic Children* (New York: Basic Books, 1960).

Berman, H. H. "Order of Birth in Manic-depression Reactions," *Psychoanalytic Quarterly* 7 (1933), 430–5.

Bossard, J. M. S., and E. S. Boll. "Personality Roles in the Large Family," *Child Development* 26 (1955), 71–8.

———, and ———. *The Large Family System* (Philadelphia: University of Pennsylvania Press, 1956).

Bradley, Richard. "Birth Order and School-related Behavior," *Psychological Bulletin* 70 (1968), 45–51.

———, and M. Sandborn. "Ordinal Position of High School Students Identified by their Teachers as Superior," *Journal of Educational Psychology* 60 (1969), 41–5.

Browning, R., and H. Jacob. "Power Motivation and the Political Personality," *Public Opinion Quarterly* 28 (1964), 75–90.

Bussman, A. "The Family as a Milieu of the Children," Z. *Kinderforch* 34 (1928), 170–82.

Campbell, A. A. "A Study of the Personality Adjustments of Only and Intermediate Children," *Journal of Genetic Psychology* 43 (1933), 197–206.

Campbell, A., *et al. The American Voter* (New York: Wiley and Sons, 1964).

———. *The Voter Decides* (New York: Harper, 1954).

Chen, E., and S. Cobb. "Family Structure in Relation to Health and Disease," *Journal of Chronic Diseases* 12 (1960), 544–67.

Chombart De Lauwe, V. "The Family Group of the Infant," in *Psychopathologie Sociale de L'enfant Inadapté* (Paris, National Center of Scientific Research, 1959), 175–210.

Clausen, J. "Family Size and Birth Order as Influences Upon Socialization and Personality," *Social Science Research Council*, 1965.

——. "Family Structure, Socialization and Personality," in Hoffman and Hoffman (eds.), *Review of Child Development Research* (New York: Russell Sage, 1966).

Cobb, S., and J. French. "Birth Order Among Medical Students" (unpublished manuscript, 1964).

Collard, R. "Social and Play Responses of First-born and Later-born Infants in an Unfamiliar Situation," *Child Development* 39 (1968), 325–35.

Connors, C. K. "Birth Order and Needs for Affiliation," *Journal of Personality* 31 (1963), 408–16.

Coopersmith, S. *The Antecedents of Self Esteem* (London: W. W. Friedman, 1967).

Cushna, B., *et al.* "First Born and Last Born Children in a Child Development Clinic," *Journal of Individual Psychology* 20 (1964), 179–82.

Damrin, D. "Family Size and Sibling Age, Sex and Position as Related to Certain Aspects of Adjustment," *Journal of Social Psychology* 29 (1949), 93–102.

Davis, A. "American Status Systems and the Socialization of the Child," in C. Cluckhohn and H. Murray (eds.), *Personality in Nature, Culture, and Society* (New York: Knopf, 1959), 567–76.

Dawson, R. "Political Socialization" in Robinson (ed.), *Annual Political Science Review* (Chicago: Rand McNally, 1966).

Demeber, W. M. "Birth Order and Need Affiliation," *Journal of Abnormal and Social Psychology* 68 (1964), 555–7.

Diab, L. M., and E. T. Prothro. "Cross-cultural Study of Some Correlates of Birth Order," *Psychological Reports* 22 (1968), 1137–42.

Dittes, J., and P. Capra. "Affiliation: Comparability or Compatibility," *American Psychologist* 17 (1962), 329–35.

Douglass, J. W. B. *The Home and the School* (London: MacGibbon & Key, 1964).

Eisenman, R., and J. Platt. "Birth Order and Sex Differences in Academic Achievement and Internal-External Control," *Journal of General Psychology* 78 (1968), 279–85.

Elder, G. H. "Structural Variations in Child Rearing Relationships," *Sociometry* 25 (1962), 241–62.

——, and C. E. Bowerman. "Family-Structure and Child Rearing Patterns:

The Effects of Family Size and Sex Composition," *American Sociological Review* 28 (1963), 891–905.

Forbes, G. "Birth Order and Political Success," *Psychological Reports* 29 (1971), 1239–42.

Freud, S. *A General Introduction to Psycho-Analysis* (New York: Archer, 1938).

————. *New Introductory Lectures on Psycho-Analysis* (New York: Norton, 1933).

George, A., and J. George. *Woodrow Wilson and Colonel House* (New York: Dover, 1956).

Gewirtz, J. L. "Dependent and Aggressive Interaction Among Young Children" (unpublished Ph.D. dissertation, State University of Iowa, 1948).

Gilbert, G. M. *The Psychology of Dictatorship* (New York: Ronald, 1950).

Goodenough, F. L., and A. M. Leahy. "The Effects of Certain Family Relationships upon the Development of Personality," *Journal of Genetic Psychology* 34 (1927), 45–72.

Gough, D. "Cognitive and Non-Intellective Intelligence," in Jenkins and Peterson (eds.), *Studies in Individual Differences* (New York: Appleton-Crofts, 1961).

Greenberg, E. "Children and the Political Community: A Comparison Across Racial Lines," *Canadian Journal of Political Science* 4 (1969), 471–92.

Greenstein, F. "Sex Related Differences in Childhood," *Journal of Politics* 23 (1961), 353–71.

————. "Personality and Political Socialization: Theories of Authoritarian and Democratic Character," *Annals* 361 (1965), 81–95.

————. *Children and Politics* (New Haven: Yale University Press, 1965).

Gregory, I. "An Analysis of Familial Data on Psychiatric Patients: Parental Age, Family Size, Birth Order and Ordinal Position," *British Journal of Preventive and Social Medicine* 12 (1958), 42–59.

Haeberle, A. "Interactions of Sex, Birth Order, and Dependency with Behavior Problems and Symptoms in Emotionally Disturbed Pre-School Children" (paper read at the Annual Meeting of the Eastern Psychological Association, Philadelphia, 1958).

Heimreich, R., D. Kuiken, and B. Collins. "Effects of Stress and Birth Order on Attitude Change," *Journal of Personality* 36 (1968), 466–73.

Henry, A. F. "Sibling Structure and Perception of Disciplinary Roles of Parents," *Sociometry* 20 (1957), 67–74.

Hess, R. D. "Socialization of Attitudes towards Political Authority: Some Cross-national Comparisons," *International Social Science Journal* 15 (1963), 542–59.

————, and J. Torney. *The Development of Political Attitudes in Children* (New York: Anchor, 1968).

Hillinger, F. "Introversion and Rank Position Among Siblings," Z. Exp. Angen. Psychology 5 (1958), 268–76.

Hoffer, E. The Ordeal of Change (New York: Harper, 1959).

Iglitizin, L. "Political Education and Sexual Liberation," Politics and Society, Winter (1972a).

———. "Sex-typing and Politization in Children's Attitudes: Reflections on Studies Done and Undone" (paper presented to the Annual Meeting of the American Political Science Association, Washington, D.C., 1972b).

Jacoby, J. "Birth Rank and Pre-Experimental Anxiety," Journal of Social Psychology 76 (1968), 9–11.

Jaros, D., et al. "The Malevolent Leader: Political Socialization in an American Sub-Culture," American Political Science Review 62 (1968), 564–75.

Jones, H. E. "Order of Birth," in C. Murchison (ed.), A Handbook of Child Psychology (Worcester, Mass.: Clark University Press, 1933), 551–89.

Kammeyer, K. "Birth Order as a Research Variable," Social Forces 46 (1967), 71–80.

Kayton, L., and G. Borge. "Birth Order and Obsessive-Compulsive Character," Archives of General Psychiatry 17 (1967), 751–54.

Knutson, J. Personality Stability and Political Belief (San Francisco: Jossey-Bass, forthcoming).

Koch, H. L. "Attitudes of Young Children Towards their Peers as Related to Certain Characteristics of their Siblings," Psychological Monographs 70 (1956b), 1–41.

———. "The Relation of Certain Family Constellation Characteristics in Relation to Sibling Characteristics," Child Development 26 (1955), 13–40.

———. "The Relation of Primary Mental Abilities in Five and Six Year Olds to Sex of Child and Characteristics of his Sibling," Child Development 25 (1954), 209–23.

———. "Sibling Influence on Children's Speech," Journal of Speech Disorders 21 (1956a), 322–8.

Lane, R. Political Ideology (New York: The Free Press, 1962).

Lasko, J. K. "Parent Behavior Towards First and Second Children," Genetic Psychological Monographs 49 (1954), 96–127.

Lasswell, H. "Democratic Character," in Political Writings of Harold Lasswell (New York: Free Press, 1951).

Lees, J., and A. Stewart. "Family or Sibling Position and Scholastic Ability," Sociological Review 5 (1957), 85–106.

Lees, J. P. "The Social Mobility of a Group of Eldest-born and Intermediate Adult Males," British Journal of Psychology 43 (1952), 210–21.

Lerner, D. The Passing of Traditional Society (New York: The Free Press, 1959).

Lessing, E. E., and M. Oberlander. "Developmental Study of Ordinal Position and Personality Adjustment of the Child as Measured by the California Test of Personality," *Journal of Personality* 35 (1967), 487–97.

Marks, E. "Sex, Birth Order, and Beliefs about Personal Power," *Developmental Psychology* 6 (1972).

Masling, J. L., Weiss, and B. Rothschild. "Relationships of Oral Imagery to Yielding Behavior and Birth Order," *Journal of Consulting and Clinical Psychology* 32 (1968), 89–91.

Maslow, A. *Motivation and Personality* (New York: Harper, 1954).

Mathews, D. *U.S. Senators and Their World* (New York: Vantage, 1960).

McArthur, C. "Personalities of First and Second Children," *Psychiatry* 19 (1956), 47–54.

Middleton, R. "Ethnic Prejudice and Susceptibility to Persuasion," *American Sociological Review* 25 (1960), 679–86.

———, and P. Snell. "Political Expression of Adolescent Rebellion," *American Journal of Sociology* 68 (1963), 527–35.

Milbrath, L. *Political Participation* (Chicago: Rand McNally, 1965).

Miller, B., and L. Galton. *The Book of Preventive Medicine* (New York: Simon and Schuster, 1971).

Moore, R. K. "Susceptibility to Hypnosis and Susceptibility to Social Influence," *Journal of Abnormal and Social Psychology* 68 (1964), 282–94.

Munz, D., *et al.* "Achievement Motivation and Ordinal Position by Birth," *Psychological Reports* 23 (1969), 175–80.

Murphy, G., *et al.* "Birth Order," *Experimental Social Psychology* (New York: Harper and Row, 1937).

Nam, C. B., and J. Cowhig. *Factors Related to College Attending of Farm and Non-Farm High School Graduates: 1960* (Washington, D.C.: U.S. Government Printing Office, 1962).

Nisbet, J. "Family Environment and Intelligence," in A. H. Halsey *et al.* (eds.), *Education, Economy, and Society* (New York: The Free Press, 1961).

Patterson, R., and T. Zeigler. "Ordinal Position and Schizophrenia," *American Journal of Psychiatry* 98 (1941), 455–6.

Phillips, E. L. "Cultural vs. Intropsychic Factors in Childhood Behavior Problem Referrals," *Journal of Clinical Psychology* 12 (1956), 400–1.

Plank, R. "The Family Constellation of a Group of Schizophrenic Patients," *American Journal of Orthopsychiatry* 23 (1953), 817–25.

Radloff, R. "Opinion Evaluation and Affiliation," *Journal of Abnormal and Social Psychology* 62 (1961), 578–85.

Renshon, S. *Psychological Needs and Political Behavior: A Theory of Personality and Political Efficacy* (New York: The Free Press, 1974).

————. "The Psychological Origins of Political Efficacy: The Need for Personal Control" (unpublished Ph.D. dissertation, University of Pennsylvania, 1972).

Rokeach, M. *The Open and Closed Mind* (New York: Basic Books, 1960).

Rosen, B. C. "Family Structure and Achievement Motivation," *American Sociological Review* 26 (1961), 574–85.

Rosenberg, M. "Self-esteem and Concern with Public Affairs," *Public Opinion Quarterly* 36 (1962), 201–11.

————. *Society and the Adolescent Self-Image* (Princeton: Princeton Press, 1965).

Rosenfeld, H. "Relation of Ordinal Position to Affiliation and Achievement Motives," *Journal of Personality* 34 (1966), 467–79.

————. "Relation of Ordinal Position to Affiliation and Achievement Motives" (unpublished paper, 1964).

Rosenow, C. "The Incidence of First-born among Problem Children" *Journal of Genetic Psychology* 37 (1930), 145–51.

————, and A. White. "The Ordinal Position of Problem Children," *American Journal of Orthopsychiatry* (1931), 430–4.

Rossi, A. "Naming Children in Middle Class Families," *American Sociological Review* 30 (1965), 499–513.

Saburo, S. "A Methodological Inquiry into Social Mobility," *American Sociological Review* 29 (1964), 16–23.

Sampson, E. "Birth Order, Need, Achievement, and Conformity," *Journal of Abnormal and Social Psychology* 64 (1962), 155–59.

————. "The Study of Ordinal Position: Antecedents and Outcomes," in B. Maher (ed.), *Progress in Experimental Personality Research* (New York: Academic Press, 1966).

————, and P. Hancock. "Ordinal Position, Socialization, Personality Development, and Conformity" (unpublished paper, 1962).

Sarnoff, I., and P. Zimbardo. "Anxiety, Fear and Social Affiliation," *Journal of Abnormal and Social Psychology* 62 (1961), 353–63.

Schacter, S. "Birth Order, Eminence, and Higher Education," *American Sociological Review* 28 (1963), 757–68.

————. *The Psychology of Affiliation* (Stanford, Cal.: Stanford University Press, 1959).

Schooler, C. "British Order and Schizophrenia," *Archives of General Psychology* 4 (1961), 91–7.

Schoonover, S. M. "The Relationship of Intelligence and Achievement to Birth Order, Sex of Sibling and Age Interval," *Journal of Educational Psychology* 50 (1959), 143–6.

Sears, P. S. "Doll Play Aggression in Normal Young Children: Influence of Sex, Age, Sibling Status, Father's Absence," *Psychological Monographs* 65 (1951).

Sears, R. R. "Ordinal Position in the Family as a Psychological Variable," *American Sociological Review* 15 (1950), 397–401.

————, E. E. Maccoby, and H. Levin. *Patterns of Child Rearing* (Evanston, Illinois: Row & Patterson, 1957).

Senn, M. J. E., and C. Hartford (eds.). *The Firstborn* (Cambridge, Mass.: Harvard Press, 1968).

Sennett, R. *The Hidden Injuries of Class* (New York: Alfred Knopf, 1972).

Sletto, R. F. "Sibling Position and Juvenile Delinquency," *American Journal of Sociology* 39 (1934), 657–69.

Smelser, W. T., and H. L. Stewart. "Where Are the Siblings: A Re-Evaluation of the Relationship between Birth Order and College Attendance," *Sociometry* 31 (1968), 294–303.

Sniderman, P., and J. Citrin. "Psychological Sources of Political Belief: Self-esteem and Isolationist Attitudes," *American Political Science Review* 65 (1971), 401–17.

Stagner, R., and E. T. Katzoff. "The Personality as Related to Birth Order and Family Size," *Journal of Applied Psychology* 20 (1936), 340–6.

Staples, F. R., and R. H. Walters. "Anxiety, Birth Order and Susceptibility to Social Influence," *Journal of Abnormal and Social Psychology* 62 (1961), 716–9.

Stewart, R. "Birth Order and Dependency," *Journal of Personality and Social Psychology* (1967), 192–4.

Stotland, E., and N. B. Cottrell. "Similarity of Performance as Influenced by Interaction, Self-esteem and Birth Order," *Journal of Abnormal and Social Psychology* 64 (1962), 183–91.

————, and R. Dunn. "Empathy, Self-esteem and Birth Order," *Psychological Monographs* 76 (1962).

————, and ————. "Identification, Opposition, Authority, Self-esteem and Birth Order," *Journal of Abnormal and Social Psychology* 66 (1963), 532–40.

————, and J. Walsh. "Birth Order and an Experimental Study of Empathy," *Journal of Abnormal and Social Psychology* 66 (1963), 610–14.

Stout, A. "Parent Behavior Towards Children of Different Ordinal Position" (unpublished Ph.D. dissertation, University of California, Berkeley, 1960).

Stratton, G. M. "The Relation of Emotion to Sex, Primogeniture and Disease," *American Journal of Psychology* 46 (1934), 590–5.

Suedfeld, P. "Anticipated and Experienced Stress in Sensory Deprivation as a

Function of Orientation and Ordinal Position," *Journal of Social Psychology* 76 (1968), 9–11.

Toffler, A. *Future Shock* (New York: Bantam, 1971).

Visher, S. "Environmental Backgrounds of Leading American Scientists," *American Sociological Review* 13 (1948), 66–72.

Waters, L. K., and W. E. Kirk. "Birth Order and PPS Affiliation," *Journal of Psychology* 67 (1967), 241–3.

Wechler, D. "Cognitive and Non-Intellective Intelligence," in Jenkins and Peterson (eds.), *Studies in Individual Differences: The Search for Intelligence* (New York: Appleton-Crofts, 1961), 651–61.

White, E. "Intelligence and the Sense of Political Efficacy of Children," *Journal of Politics* 30 (1968), 710–31.

Wile, I. S., and E. Noetzel. "A Study of Birth Order and Behavior," *Journal of Social Psychology* 2 (1931), 52–71.

Winterbottom, M. R. "The Relation of Need for Achievement to Learning Experiences in Independence and Mastery," in Atkinson (ed.), *Motives in Fantasy, Action and Society* (Princeton: Van Nostrand, 1958).

Witty, P. A. "'Only' and 'Intermediate' Children of High School Ages," *Psychological Bulletin* 31 (1934), 734.

Yasuda, S. "A Methodological Inquiry into Social Mobility," *American Sociological Review* 29 (1964), 16–23.

Zimbardo, P., and R. Formica. "Emotional Comparison and Self-Esteem as Determinants of Affiliation," *Journal of Personality* 31 (1963), 141–62.

Chapter Four

Health, Body Images, and Political Socialization
David C. Schwartz, Joseph Garrison, and James Alouf

INTRODUCTION

The thesis advanced and tested in this chapter is that we can significantly improve our understanding of political socialization by including in our studies two related sets of variables that heretofore have been almost wholly ignored in political study: health processes and body images. We advance this thesis because recent empirical findings indicate that people's health experiences and body images bear regular, significant, and apparently causal association with some very basic social and political attitudes, behaviors, and processes. More specifically, the degree of one's physical well-being (especially freedom from chronic illness) has been found to be significantly and positively associated with personality structure and adjustment, satisfactory family dynamics, level of general social participation, relationships with teachers and peers, and learning capabilities and school achievement (Birch and Gussow, 1970; Pless and Roghmann, 1970; Pless and Douglas, no date; Mechanic, 1959). Similarly, people who have clear, positive perceptions and evaluations of their own bodies (i.e., body images) have been shown to have significantly different orientations to learning, group interaction patterns, sociopolitical values, and social influence from those of individuals with more ambiguous and/or negative body images (Fisher and Cleveland, 1968; Fisher, 1970, 6–50). From the recent literature, then, it appears that certain characteristic health experiences and body images influence people's motivation toward social learning, their capability to learn, the content of their learning, and the relationships they have with various agencies of socialization.

If such relationships obtain in the processes of political socialization, as is our hypothesis, then including health and body images as variables in studies of political learning should yield two advantages. First, the strength of the significant direct relationship of health and body image to political attitudes should allow us to account for a greater proportion of the variance in attitudes. Second, if health and body image factors are also important intervening variables that mediate the relationships between socialization agencies and political attitudes, we should achieve greater precision and parsimony in our explanations of the processes of political learning.

In this chapter we: (1) offer a brief review of recent relevant literature, (2) develop several alternative models relating health experiences and body images to political attitudes and behaviors, (3) describe the procedures used to test these models in a study of some 2,100 American high school students, (4) summarize the relationships that obtained in our data, and (5) discuss some of the implications of our findings for future studies of political socialization.

A BRIEF REVIEW OF RECENT LITERATURE ON HEALTH PROCESSES, BODY IMAGES, AND SOCIAL ATTITUDES AND BEHAVIORS

Health Processes

There seem to be at least three separable strands of research on the psychological and social consequences of health processes.

First, there are a few important studies comparing people (usually children or teenagers) diagnosed as having one or more chronic illnesses (e.g., asthma, epilepsy, cerebral palsy) to a control or "healthy" population (i.e., one which has been designed to be comparable to the chronically ill sample by random selection or by matching but wherein all persons have been assessed to be free of chronic illness) (Pless and Roghmann, 1970, 6–12).

Second, there is a somewhat larger number of studies comparing the psychological characteristics and social attitudes of people at very different health status levels. In these studies, health status has been variously defined. Sometimes it has been conceived of as the individual's general level of physical well-being, measured, for example, by the number of days of incapacity or reduced personal functioning due to health conditions over a standardized time period. In other studies, health status has been operationally defined as the incidence or frequency of a given set of health conditions (physical underdevelopment, vision problems, malnutrition) in the individual's health history or current health report (Birch and Gussow, 1970).

Finally, there is some research that compares patients with one given health condition (such as hypertension or limb amputation) to a designedly comparable population of healthy individuals (Fisher and Cleveland, 1968, 11–12; Jaros, 1970; Stauffer, 1970; Ferguson et al., 1970).

The results of these three strands of research are quite compatible: by whatever measure health is defined, people who are "healthy" are found to be very different in their psychological reactions and social attitudes from those who are less healthy. We will discuss the findings of each strand separately here in order that the reader can identify the specific pattern of linkages between given health processes and psychosocial characteristics.

In the first category, Pless and Roghmann summarize three major studies on the psychosocial consequences of chronic illness among children: (1) A fourteen-year longitudinal study of more than 5,000 children, all of the children born in England, Scotland, and Wales during the first week of March 1946; (2) A comparative study of the educational, emotional, and physical disabilities in a total sample of nine- to eleven-year-old children on the Isle of Wight, England (wherein the chronically ill population was contrasted with "a small random sample of healthy children"); (3) The Rochester Health Survey in which a group of 350 chronically ill children (6 to 16 years of age) and a matched control group were drawn from a 1 percent probability sample of all children under 18 living in Monroe County, New York (Pless and Roghmann, 1970, 6–12).

The results of these three studies are strikingly similar. In each study, the sickly children are found to have significantly more limited and unsatisfactory participation in school, family, and peer group settings than their healthier counterparts, a pattern of diminished social functioning that may have potentially profound effects on the amount and content of sociopolitical learning among chronically ill young people. In all of the studies, the chronically ill children scored significantly lower on school achievement measures (controlling for age and I.Q.) and on personal adjustment or mental health ratings than did the healthier population. The sick children in the English national survey were significantly more likely to experience social isolation, coupled with troublesome conflicts in school, findings consistent with the Rochester study in which the sickly children were found to receive significantly less peer attention and friendship than did those in the healthy group.

Chronic illness, then, tends to influence one's relationship to major agencies of socialization: In the national survey, teachers rated the sickly youngsters as significantly more nervous and/or aggressive than their healthier students; in the Isle of Wight study both teachers and parents perceived roughly twice as many sick children to be "psychiatrically deviant" as they had among the control group. These ratings, moreover, are not merely the perceptual biases of mothers and fathers or teachers who have had their family lives or classrooms profoundly disturbed, although we know that certain illness patterns can be quite disruptive of family relationships. In these studies, independent psychiatric evaluation tended to confirm parental and teacher ratings. The chronically ill population exhibited from about half again as many to nearly 3 times the proportion of children with behavior disorders compared to the healthier control group. In light of the fact that the chronically ill tend to constitute 5 percent to 20 percent of all children in developed countries, and perhaps even more in less developed nations, these relationships seem especially important (Pless and Roghmann, 1970, 6–12).

Birch and Gussow summarize the results of a larger series of investigations on the psychosocial consequences of health processes. In these studies, malnutrition, gross physical underdevelopment, vision problems, neurological disorders, and a wide variety of other health difficulties were consistently shown to be significantly associated with poor performance on tests purporting to measure mental abilities and learning (I.Q.; D.Q.; Sentence Completion; Reading; Vocabulary; Arithmetic; Picture Intelligence; Similarities; Object Assembly, and the like) (Birch and Gussow, 1970).

More important to our interests, Birch and Gussow document the existence of a coherent, fundamental personality syndrome associated with low (poor) health status (here including chronic illness and physical underdevelopment). They and other researchers find that the effects of this low health status typically include a high degree of anxiety, an excessively dependent personality orientation, a high degree of self-concern, social withdrawal and depression, a low sense of self-esteem, low or diminished capability to handle stress, and, as indicated, severe learning difficulties (Birch and Gussow, 1970).

The findings of studies that focus on one specific health condition and its psychosocial consequences tend to be broadly similar, as most of them tend to show that specific illnesses or health conditions limit social or political participation. Thus Fisher and Cleveland (1968, 11–12) show that patients with recent limb amputations tend to focus inward on body and self rather than outward on society and polity; Jaros (1970) indicates a similar biochemical "desocialization" under the conditions of a tranquilization regimen; Stauffer (1970) demonstrates that nutritional deficiencies are significantly associated with low levels of political participation; and Ferguson, Ferguson, and Young, in a cross-national study of political socialization (1970), find that the respondent's age at the onset of puberty was a significant predictor of his political attitudes (the later the onset of puberty, the less interested/efficacious the respondent).

As indicated, most of these health conditions appear to limit or inhibit sociopolitical participation. This impedance may be due to sheer physical limitations imposed by the health condition or to the fact that the health condition functions to focus the individual's attention and psychic energy inward on body or self rather than outward on society and politics. Consistent with this latter interpretation are studies by Sapira *et al.* (1970)

and by Schwartz (1970). Sapira *et al.* suggest, from experimental evidence, that hypertensive patients tend to screen out (i.e., perceptually block) arousing stimuli, as a defense against their cardiovascular hyperreactivity, with no such tendency among normotensive patients. This suggestion, if it proves generalizable, would indicate why certain body or health states tend to be associated with diminished social participation. Schwartz studied the orientations toward political behavior adopted by a sample of American college students and found that students who perceived themselves to be low in personal energy tended to adopt relatively withdrawn or passive behavior orientations, whereas those who perceived themselves as higher in physical energy took up more active (reformist and even revolutionary) orientations. Similarly, persons experiencing health problems or exhibiting low general health statuses, who may perceive energy drain and a high anxiety level, may both reduce the amount of sociopolitical stimuli they allow to pass through their perceptual screen and react more passively to such stimuli as they do admit.

We should note, of course, that it is entirely conceivable for persons with, say, moderate degrees of health difficulty to block or redirect their health-related anxieties out onto the society and polity: one can offer at least some *prima facie* justification for an hypothesis suggesting that low-to-moderate degrees of health problems should lead to increased sociopolitical interest and participation.

Virtually all of the research literature, however, posits that health difficulty should lead to low or diminished sociopolitical interest and participation.

Body Images

Body image, the individual's set of characteristic perceptions and evaluations of his or her body, is also expected to have profound influence on political socialization phenomena. These images are learned very early in life, in a very direct manner. They are strongly related to, but conceptually different from, self-concept and identity—such that people who perceive and evaluate their bodies positively tend to have positive self-images, high self-acceptance, and high self-esteem. As such, body images are tremendously salient to the individual and important to his behavior. In more than one hundred post-World War II studies, for example, body images have been found to be significantly related to an enormous range of the individual's most basic psychological, social, and even political characteristics. Among these are personality structure (e.g., need achievement), anxiety or personal insecurity, sex-role learning, ability to cope with stress, classroom achievement, behavior and social influence in small group settings, adjustment to physical illness or disability, and relationships with authority. In addition, body images have been related to a wide variety of political and social values (Fisher and Cleveland, 1968; Fisher, 1970).

Essentially, then, body images appear to be fundamental, personality-related, psychological elements. They are expected to exert profound socialization influence because they are so early-learned and so self-defining as to condition a good deal of later social learning. In addition, a person's body image tends to influence his relationship to such socializing agencies as schools and peer groups.

Also, we believe that a child's fundamental perception and evaluation of his or her own body often gets generalized to, or projected onto, the sociopolitical world. In other words, we expect that youngsters who perceive their bodies as unpredictable, immovable, or weak will tend to see their world in similar ways, will attribute the felt qualities of unpredictability, weakness, and the like to the society and polity as well. If this hypothesis proves as generally true as it appears from our data, then body images will be shown to be direct influences on political socialization.

BODY IMAGE DIMENSIONS

The set of characteristic perceptions and evaluations of the body that comprise the individual's body image includes, but is not limited to, the following dimensions.

1. The degree of body satisfaction: the tendency to evaluate one's body positively (e.g., as good, attractive, a source of pleasure).

2. The degree of body concern or awareness: the degree to which the body occupies a prominent place in the individual's consciousness.

3. The degree of perceived definiteness of body boundaries: the extent to which the individual perceives sharp, clear, fixed boundaries between the body and its environment.

4. Basic perceptions of the body's physical characteristics: the perceived size, strength, activism, predictability, and so on of one's body.

5. The degree to which the individual uses his or her body as a basis for perceiving non-body space or objects: the extent to which the individual generalizes perceptions of body to social objects. This dimension of body image prompts such questions as: Do people who perceive their bodies as basically unpredictable or immovable or weak attribute these qualities (unpredictability, immovability, weakness) to society and polity as well?

Several excellent general reviews of the large and rapidly growing literature on these dimensions are available elsewhere. We offer here only a very brief indication of the social, psychological, and political correlates of body images, and some thoughts on their probable significance to students of political socialization.

BODY SATISFACTION

The overwhelming weight of accumulated evidence on this body image dimension shows significant positive association between body satisfaction and self-acceptance (self cathexis, confidence, well-being, self-esteem) (Jourard and Secord, 1955; Johnson, 1956; Weinberg, 1960; Gunderson and Johnson, 1965; Zion, 1965; Fisher, 1970, 19–20). As self-esteem has already been shown to be a significant predictor of political participation, we believe that positive evaluations of the body will predict to high levels of political interest, learning, and participation—operating both directly on these variables and through self-esteem or self-confidence. We would expect, also, that people who express high degrees of body satisfaction will express significantly higher degrees of satisfaction with the sociopolitical system than do persons who are less positive about their bodies (and selves).

BODY CONCERN AND AWARENESS

The degree to which the body typically occupies a prominent place in a given individual's consciousness has been shown to be associated with several interesting patterns of thinking and behavior. When measured projectively, by a word-association technique, body concern seems to indicate some dissatisfaction or insecurity about the body and is significantly and negatively associated with personal adjustment to stressful situations (Secord, 1953; Weinberg, 1960; Landau, 1960). Conceptualized in this manner, body concern might be expected to be negatively related to sociopolitical interest and participation.

PERCEIVED DEFINITENESS OF BODY BOUNDARIES

This body image dimension has probably received most attention in recent years. Fisher and Cleveland, who first recognized the importance of this variable, conceive of the individual who perceives highly definite body boundaries as likely to engage in "self-steering behavior." Proceeding from a stable, secure, well-articulated body base of operations, such individuals were hypothesized to engage in forceful, confident, effective striving in pursuit of their life goals.

This conception has generally been confirmed in scores of relevant studies. "Boundary definiteness" has been found to be significantly and positively associated with the following personality and behavioral traits.

1. A value on political activity (high power orientations).
2. Need achievement.
3. Ability to cope with life stress.
4. Effectiveness as leader of small groups.
5. Social successes in small group settings.
6. Resistance to suggestibility.
7. High degrees of energy-activism.
8. Classroom achievement.
9. Preference for social participation values.
10. Preference for occupational roles involving influence, and many others (Fisher and Cleveland, 1968).

BASIC PERCEPTIONS OF THE BODY'S PHYSICAL CHARACTERISTICS

Interestingly, there has been rather little systematic work on people's perceptions of the strength, activism, predictability, mobility, or health of their bodies—or on the sociopolitical correlates of such perceptions. There has been some work showing that such perceptions change as body-relevant circumstances change (e.g., during pregnancy) (McConnell and Daston, 1961). There has been a bit more work on people's perception of their body size. This work suggests that one's perceived body size affects the degree of one's body satisfaction and, further, that people's body size perceptions are related to the stress levels they are experiencing (Jourard and Secord, 1955; Magnussen, 1958; Calden, 1959; Singer and Lamb, 1966; Arkoff and Weaver, 1966; McFarland et al., 1960; Wagner, 1960). In children, body-size perceptions have been related to intelligence, maturation, and independence as a personality attribute, such that less intelligent, younger, and less independent children tend to underestimate body size (Schaffer, 1962; Beller and Turner, 1964; Nash, 1951; Stauffieri, 1967).

Although we also study perceived body size, our research on the psychological, social, and political correlates of basic body perceptions (other than size) seems to constitute a rather new line of research. As will be developed in our discussion of hypotheses, we expect people's fundamental perceptions of their own bodies to influence their sociopolitical orientations in two ways. Individuals who perceive their bodies as inactive, weak, or unpredictable will tend to be less interested, less knowledgeable, and less participant in sociopolitical affairs (perhaps because such body images lead to greater concern with body or self and less concern with society or politics); and individuals will tend to generalize or project their basic perceptions of their body out onto the sociopolitical system.

This latter hypothesis derives from research on our final body-image dimension.

THE USE OF BODY PERCEPTIONS AS A BASIS FOR PERCEIVING NON-BODY OBJECTS

In a long, fascinating, and important series of investigations Werner and Wapner (1965, 1956, 1949) and Witkin (1954) have shown that the mature individual tends to use his or her body as a perceptual landmark or standard by which to orient toward other objects in the perceptual field. These studies provide unequivocal evidence that individuals differ systematically in the manner in which they perceive non-body space and that these perceptual differences are significantly related to the individual's perceptions and orientations to the body.

In our studies, we have extended this reasoning by applying it to the individual's perceptions of the sociopolitical space around him. We hypothesize that individuals tend to generalize their perceptions of their own bodies to their perceptions of sociopolitical systems. People who learn that their bodies are unpredictable, weak, immovable or whatever —and learn it both early in life and with high salience—are, we think, very likely to see the world in similar terms.

All this, of course, is not intended to deny the obvious fact that the characteristics of political systems condition how people perceive and evaluate politics; rather it is intended to affirm the perhaps equally obvious fact that the characteristics of people also condition their perceptions and evaluations.

HYPOTHESES

Working with the variables identified above, we have developed four patterns, or models, of hypothesized relationships which link people's health experiences and body images to their political attitudes and behaviors. For the purposes of this paper, we state the hypotheses concerning health experiences in terms of illness patterns rather than general health status (degree of physical well-being). Our hypotheses are stated in this manner because the measures of health available in this study permit us to assess the relative frequency and severity of significant illnesses but do not include assessments of more general health states (e.g., level of individual incapacity or reduced functioning due to less severe health conditions or to frequent but short-term illnesses).

We believe that the sociopolitical influence here attributed to a person's gross illness pattern will also be found to be attributable to general health status. Indeed, we are presently engaged in several efforts to test this notion.[1] In this chapter, however, we are examining the sociopolitical impacts of the individual's health experiences, defined as the average frequency and severity of illnesses experienced over a standardized time period.

Pattern 1: A Basic Model Linking Health to Political Attitudes and Behaviors

Hypothesis 1. The individual's level of health (i.e., the average frequency and severity of recent illnesses) will tend to be significantly associated with his or her participation in social and political settings, such that relatively healthier individuals will tend to be more participant in election campaigns, school activities, church, and community organizations.

Hypothesis 2. Level of health will also tend to be significantly associated with vicarious sociopolitical participation, such that young healthier people will tend to report themselves as willing to be politically active to a significantly greater degree than will less healthy individuals. In this hypothesis, we are postulating that health level influences a process of anticipatory socialization.

Hypothesis 3. Health level will tend to bear significant positive association with interest in sociopolitical affairs (e.g., self-reported political interest or involvement with news media).

Hypothesis 4. As we are hypothesizing that illness patterns influence the individual's interest, media involvement, and firsthand participation in social and political affairs, we also reason that healthier individuals will tend to be more knowledgeable about sociopolitical events. As the individual's level of sociopolitical knowledge may well have its own independent influence on the extent of his participation in public affairs, this linkage

---

[1] The senior author is presently engaged in three large-scale efforts to investigate the sociopolitical consequences of health status, in which variation in health status is defined in terms of day-to-day physical functioning. They are:

1. An investigation of 300 adults using health status materials derived from 2–20 years of physicians' records.

2. An investigation of 400 adults in two cities, using a battery of health history and symptom checklists.

3. A study of health status in a national probability sample of American adults using five to ten different health status assessment routines.

between health and politics may operate to reinforce the basic "health → political activity" relationship indicated above.

Hypothesis 6. In general, we would expect the individual's health characteristics (and the body image characteristics discussed hereafter) to be equally or more powerful predictors of his or her sociopolitical behavior as are the more typically studied age, sex, and SES characteristics.

Hypothesis 7. We would also expect the relationships between health levels and political attitudes to be sufficiently general and basic to be observed in most if not all age, sex, and social-class categories. In other words, we would not expect that these relationships would be significantly attenuated by the introduction of age, sex, or social-class controls.

Pattern 2: A "Health ⟶ Body and Self Images ⟶ Political Attitudes" Model

Hypothesis 8. The relationships between an individual's health and his political attitudes and behaviors will tend to be significantly mediated by body-image variables. Less healthy individuals who do not learn negative perceptions and evaluations of their bodies and/or who do not express unusually high body concern, will tend not to exhibit low degrees of political interest, participation, and knowledge. Such individuals will evince significantly greater political interest, participation, and knowledge than do sickly people who also have negative body images.

Hypothesis 9. The relationships between an individual's health level and his political interest–participation will also tend to be significantly mediated by his degree of self-doubt. Less healthy people with high self-confidence will tend to be significantly more interested and participant in politics than those less healthy people who have strong self-doubt.

Pattern 3: Some Linkages Between Body Images and Political Attitudes and Behaviors

Hypothesis 10. There will be a significant and positive relationship between an individual's body image and his degree of political interest and participation, such that individuals who tend to perceive and evaluate their bodies positively will tend to be significantly more politically interested and participant than persons with negative body images. More specifically, individuals who tend to perceive their bodies as predictable, active, strong, healthy, and satisfactory will tend to be significantly more interested and active in social and political processes than are people with the opposite set of body images. Individuals who express high body concern will tend to be significantly less socially and politically interested and participant than their less body-concerned counterparts.

Hypothesis 11. We would expect the relationships between body images and political attitudes and behaviors stated in Hypothesis 10 to be sufficiently general and basic to be observed in most if not all age, sex, and social-class categories. The introduction of age, sex, and SES "controls" should not attenuate the relationships between body images and political attitudes and behaviors.

Hypothesis 12. We would expect the relationships between an individual's body image and his degree of political interest and participation to be significantly mediated by the degree of his self-doubt. Individuals with negative body images who do not exhibit strong feelings of self-doubt will tend to be significantly more politically interested and active than people who experience both negative body images and strong self-doubt.

Pattern 4: A Linkage Between Body Images and Political Images

Hypothesis 13. As stated at several earlier points in this chapter, we expect there to be a significant, positive association between an individual's perceptions and evaluations of his own body and his perceptions and evaluations of the political system of which he is a part.

Working with these variables, several more complex causal models could be elaborated. We believe, however, that these four patterns of associations are sufficient to indicate some of the major alternative ways in which health experiences and body images may influence people's political attitudes and behaviors.

PROCEDURES

We tested these hypotheses in a respondent population of 2,130 American high school students who completed a self-administered questionnaire on their body images, political attitudes, and behaviors in the winter of 1972. More specifically, these students represented 100 percent of the student body of a suburban New Jersey parochial high school and more than 90 percent of the students at a nearby public high school of similar size and social composition. The respondents participated in the study on a volunteer basis, completing, in class, a 9-page instrument composed of 106 largely closed-ended items. In addition, students' health records and I.Q. scores were made available to us on a confidential basis.

We selected these schools as research sites purposively because of outstanding access to these schools—as witness the high response rates and unusual cooperation—and because of the fascinating extant demographic diversity within these schools.[2] If our hypotheses relating health and body images to people's political attitudes were sustained across the range of age, SES, and life-styles represented in these schools, we felt that we could repose considerable confidence in the generality of the hypothesized relationships. For the purposes of this introductory investigation, no effort was made to secure a more representative sample of American high school students.

MEASURES

Virtually all our measures of the variables of interest were multi-item indices. These were constructed by aggregating individual scores across specified sets of items, after assuring ourselves of index homogeneity by inspection of the inter-item correlations.

Here, we provide the text of one item for each of our attitudinal indices to give the reader some idea of the character of our measures.[3] It may be useful, however, to provide the reader with some greater detail on our health measures.

HEALTH VARIABLES

The school health records made available to us contained the following information: First, there was a notation of all illnesses and/or health conditions that had necessitated a continuous absence from school of three days or longer. Health problems of such duration must be included in

[2] Approximately 86 percent of the population completed the demographic portion of the instrument. Of the total population:

(a) 41.4 percent were male and 45.4 percent female

(b) 16 percent were freshmen, 27 percent sophomores, 26 percent juniors, 18 percent seniors

(c) 12 percent upper middle class, 27 percent middle class, and 48 percent working class

(d) 22 percent were urban residents and 64 percent suburban

We think that the diversity on the latter two dimensions is quite unusual, given the still prevalent pattern of neighborhood schools and relatively homogeneous neighborhoods.

[3] A complete description of all items and indexes, including the inter-item correlations used to assess index homogeneity, is available from the senior author.

school health records as a matter of State policy. This requirement provided some standardization of the severity of health problems in our data. The notation of these health problems yielded one component of our basic "level of health" measure.

Second, the school health records contained data on the incidence of other illnesses and health conditions that, in the opinion of the student's physician or of the school nurse, might have a material bearing on the child's performance and/or behavior in school. These tended to be continuing, chronic sorts of health conditions. They were added to the health problems noted from the absentee data and used in forming our basic health level measure, the average annual number of recorded illnesses experienced during the high school years. Typically, we aggregated together those students who had an annual average of one or more serious health problems and compared them with the healthier groupings.

To the illnesses and health conditions in our measure, we applied a standardized "seriousness of illness" ranking. This ranking was derived from a delphi panel of physicians asked to rank order the typical seriousness of some 200 diseases (Wyler et al., 1968). We used the resulting severity scores to compose a second measure of health level. In this index, students who had only a moderate frequency of illness score but who had a high severity of illness ranking were combined with more frequently sick students; this group was then compared with their healthier counterparts.

The school health records also included an indication of the place of treatment—hospital, clinic, home—for each regularly noted health problem. At first, we thought that this would be highly useful to us, because hospitalization has been widely used as an indicator of the severity of an illness in the medical science and health care literatures (Patrick et al., 1972). Accordingly, we tried many combinations of this indicator with our basic measure (and tried, too, many other combinations and weightings of the indicators in our basic measures). These combinations, however, all failed to achieve a meaningful level of intercorrelation with the individual's perceived health treated as a criterion measure (Patrick et al., 1972). Accordingly, we restricted ourselves to two measures of the individual's level of health:

Variable 1. The first measure of level of health was the average annual number of health problems experienced during the high school years. Because we were primarily interested in comparing those individuals who tend to be consistently unhealthy with those who are regularly quite healthy, we tended to exclude those who were only very occasionally ill. In analysis, then, we typically trichotomized this measure between those students with no annual illnesses (the healthiest group), those with an average of one illness (the relatively less healthy), and those with an average of two illnesses (the "unhealthy"). As indicated, this measure excludes persons with only a very modest illness average (.25–.99).

The students who averaged one or more illnesses per year, and hence were considered as low in health level, composed about 4 percent of our population. This seems quite appropriate to us, as it is similar to the national estimates which suggest that 5 to 10 percent of our teenage population is chronically ill. The fact that our figure is somewhat below the national estimates also seems to lend some face validity to our measure, because our population was somewhat more affluent, better nourished, and therefore probably somewhat healthier than a national sample of teenagers would be.

Variable 2. The second measure of level of health was intended to recapture some of those who were only occasionally ill but whose occasional sickness was quite severe, in order to add them to our relatively less healthy group. Operationally, we selected those individuals who had health problems at an annual rate of .50 to .90 and who also had high rankings on the "seriousness of illness" variable and added them to our relatively less healthy group. This brought our low health level group up to 5.5 percent of our population.

POLITICAL, BODY IMAGE, AND DEMOGRAPHIC VARIABLES

The political and demographic measures will be quite familiar to our readers. The body image indices, although probably not familiar, are measured by semantic differential or word-association techniques which will also be reasonably familiar to most readers. Therefore, we merely present a list of these next eighteen variables with a brief example of each measure.

VARIABLE	DEFINITION OR SAMPLE ITEM
3. Political interest	"Do you think of yourself as being not at all interested in American politics, somewhat interested, or very interested?"
4. School involvement	A three-option ranking of the respondent's degree of participation in school activities (including clubs and sports activity).
5. Political participation	A seven-item campaign and general political activity index.
6. Civic involvement	A five-item index of the respondent's participation in community, church, and other civic activities.

7. Political cynicism; alienation

"Do you think that public officials are concerned with the interests of the average man?"

8. Political knowledge

A six-item political information score.

9. Print media involvement

"How often do you read news-papers and news magazines?"

10. News media involvement

"Do you listen to news broadcasts on radio or TV?"

11. Political images

Variables 11a through 11h are defined as multi-item semantic differential measures.

   a. perceived health of political system:

well ——————— ill

   b. perceived size of political system:

big ——————— small

   c. perceived strength of political system:

sturdy ——————— fragile

   d. perceived predictability of political system:

orderly ——————— chaotic

   e. perceived satisfaction with political system:

good ——————— bad

   f. perceived mobility of political system:

agile ——————— clumsy

   g. perceived activism of political system:

energetic ——————— tired

   h. perceived definiteness vs. permeability of political system's boundaries:

having fixed boundaries ——————— having indefinite boundaries

12. Hypothetical political involvement

"Would you vote in the next presidential election, provided you were old enough to vote?"

13. Body images

Variables 13a through 13h are defined as multi-item semantic differential measures. The same word pairs were used as for Variable 11.

   a. perceived health of respondent's body
   b. perceived size of respondent's body
   c. perceived strength of respondent's body
   d. perceived predictability of respondent's body
   e. perceived satisfaction with respondent's body
   f. perceived mobility of respondent's body
   g. perceived activism of respondent's body
   h. perceived definiteness vs. permeability of body boundaries

14. Body concern	The number of body references given by the respondent in a twelve-item word association test (adapted from Secord, 1953).
15. Self-doubt	"Compared to people my own age, I often feel less sure of myself."
16. Age	In years.
17. Sex	
18. SES	Principally, father's occupational status.
19. Neighborhood type	Urban vs. suburban.
20. Respondent's after-school life-style	Part-time job vs. no job; number of hours worked.

FINDINGS

Our findings support our general conceptualization, and most of our specific hypotheses, linking people's health experiences and body images to their sociopolitical attitudes and behaviors. More specifically, eight basic relationships obtained in our data. These are first stated here and then documented and discussed at length.

1. Students low in health level tended to be significantly less involved in school affairs, less vicariously participant in politics, and less knowledgeable about politics than relatively healthier students. Less healthy students also tended to have lower overall political participation scores, but this relationship was weak and not statistically significant.

2. The apparent degree of influence exerted by health level on one's sociopolitical participation tends to be as strong or stronger than that exerted by social-class variables. The influence of health on sociopolitical participation tends to be mediated by social-class variables only to a quite limited degree (and in an inconsistent manner).

3. On the other hand, health experiences seem to have more of their impact on sociopolitical participation through the mediation of body image variables (including body concern).

4. Body image variables also tend to have regular and significant independent influence on sociopolitical participation, such that students who perceive their bodies as predictable, active, and satisfying tend to be highly participant in social and political settings.

5. These relationships tend to be as strong as or stronger than any between social class and sociopolitical participation. In addition, the relationship of body image to participation is not substantially attenuated by the operation of social class or other social background factors.

6. Body images also seem to serve as basic standards by which people perceive and evaluate their political worlds. We find a significant positive association between each and every body image dimension investigated here and the individual's perceptions and evaluations of the polity.

Two of our findings ran counter to our expectations:

7. Low health levels did not predict to low levels of political interest. Surprisingly, the less healthy students tended to be significantly more interested in politics than were the healthier respondents. It is important to note, however, that low health levels significantly attenuate the typically strong relationship between political interest and participation. Poor health, in our population, tended to increase one's interest but decrease one's activity in politics. We should also note that the relationship between health level and interest in politics is very much mediated by body image factors, factors which we think explain the association between poor health and political interest.

8. As hypothesized, the individual's level of self-confidence did bear some significant relationships to sociopolitical participation—as both an independent and an intervening variable. In general, however, self-confidence was very weak and very limited in its explanatory power.

Pattern 1

Our first pattern of hypothesized relationships posited the following points:

1. Healthier individuals will tend to be significantly more participant, knowledgeable, and interested in sociopolitical affairs than will less healthy people.

2. This relationship will compare favorably with more typically emphasized relationships between social background factors and sociopolitical participation.

3. The relationship between health and participation will not be attenuated by controlling for social background factors.

Tables 4–1, 4–2, and 4–3 document the considerable support for these hypotheses in our data. Table 4–1 indicates that the healthier students were significantly more active in school, willing to be more active in politics, and more knowledgeable about political affairs than were less healthy respondents. Health problems, in this population, do dampen social participation and sociopolitical learning.

Table 4–1 also shows a significant tendency for less healthy students to be appreciably more satisfied with American politics than their healthier colleagues, to evaluate the polity more positively. This difference might be attributable to any of several factors. It might be linked to a greater social dependence, leading to acquiescence, or to a preference for low stress found in more sickly populations (Mechanic, 1959). Alternatively, it might be due to the lower levels of political information or to the higher level of political interest that we found among our less healthy respondents. But whatever its causes, it is clear that this greater satisfaction with the American political system is not a factor in the low levels of political participation evinced by our less healthy students. We know this because political evaluation proved to be essentially unrelated to any of the sociopolitical participation variables (mean association = .03, not significant).

The fundamental relationship revealed in Table 4–1, however, should not be obscured: Health level is significantly associated with the individual's sociopolitical participation and with the extent of his political learning (information).

More evidence on this point is presented in Table 4–2. We observe that the ordinarily strong relationship between political interest and political participation is attenuated to insignificance among less healthy students. Interestingly, relatively low health levels predict to greater political interest in this population (Table 4–1), but low health levels also block the ordinary impact of political interest (Table 4–2).

Our final hypothesis in Pattern 1 is also supported in these data. Inspection of Table 4–1 indicates that the strength of the influence of health levels on political participation is generally as strong or stronger than the much more frequently emphasized relationships between social background factors and participation. Table 4–3 depicts the relationships between health level and political participation, controlling for social class. There we find that the impact of health on school involvement and political interest tends to be strongest in the upper SES populations, whereas the impact of health on political knowledge and hypothetical political involvement tends to be weakest in precisely the same upper SES group. This inconsistent impact of SES on the linkage between health and participation and the relatively modest quantitative difference SES makes in several of these cases suggest that the basic causal process through which health levels influence political participation is not through social class.

Table 4–4 also indicates that the link between people's health experiences and their political attitudes and behaviors is not an artifact of social background factors. In that table, we note that sex and grade in school seem to have some mediatory impacts but that these impacts are quite inconsistent. We find, for example, that the influence of health level on both hypothetical involvement and political evaluation is strongest among boys, while health influences school involvement and political interest most powerfully among girls. Another inconsistency can be seen in the fact that health level is most highly correlated with political interest and hypothetical political participation among freshmen but bears its strongest association with political knowledge and political evaluation among sophomores.

From these disparate directions in which sex and grade (and social class) influence the linkage between health and political attitudes, we conclude that social background factors tend not to have consistent, systematic influence on this fundamental relationship.

Table 4–1. The Relationship of Health Levels and Social Background Factors to Sociopolitical Participation Variables (Gamma Values)

	HEALTH LEVEL[1]	HEALTH LEVEL[2]	SOCIAL CLASS	URBAN-SUBURBAN	AGE	SEX
SOCIOPOLITICAL VARIABLES						
School involvement	.22[1]	.13	.06	.05[2]	−.02	.04[1]
Civic involvement	−.08	−.02	.05[1]	.02	−.14	.14[1]
Hypothetical political involvement	.30[2]	.15	.08	−.03	.00	.35[1]
Political participation	.05	.08	.04	−.18	.07[1]	−.04[1]
Political knowledge	.46[2]	.38[2]	.08[1]	.006	.28[1]	−.17[1]
Political interest	−.36[2]	−.27[2]	−.04	.10	−.15[1]	.07[1]
Print media involvement	−.16	−.15	−.06	.04	.01	.12[1]
News media involvement	.13	.09	.06	.03[1]	.06[1]	.17[1]
Evaluation of the American polity	−.26[1]	.12	−.03	−.10[1]	−.03	−.01

[1] Significance = .05.

[2] Significance = .01 or better.

Table 4–2. The Relationship of Political Interest to Sociopolitical Participation, Controlling for Health Level[1]* (Gamma Values and Significance Levels)

	UNCONTROLLED RELATIONSHIP	GOOD HEALTH SAMPLE	RELATIVELY POOR HEALTH SAMPLE
Political participation	.40	.41 (.01)	.22 (N.S.)
Hypothetical involvement	.39	.39 (.01)	.16 (N.S.)
Civic involvement	.20 (.0001)	.35 (.03)	−.20 (.05)

* Control variable showed no significant influence on the relationship of school involvement and political interest.

N.S. = Not significant.

Table 4–3. The Relationship of Health Level to its Sociopolitical Correlates, Controlling for Social Class (Gamma Values and Significance Levels)

	WORKING-CLASS POPULATION	MIDDLE-CLASS	UPPER MIDDLE-CLASS
School involvement	.13 (N.S.)	.37 (N.S.)	.32 (.09)
Hypothetical involvement	.33 (.10)	.42 (.14)	−.18 (.15)
Political interest	−.25 (.06)	−.44 (.07)	−.60 (.10)
Political knowledge	.41 (.008)	.52 (.09)	.36 (.05)
Political evaluation	.29 (.05)	.18 (N.S.)	.20 (N.S.)

N.S. = Not significant.

Table 4–4. The Relationship of Health Level to Sociopolitical Variables, Controlling for Sex and Grade* (Gamma Values and Significance Levels)

	MALE	FEMALE	FRESHMAN	SOPHOMORE
Political evaluation	−.38 (.03)	−.12 (.10)	−.10 (N.S.)	−.56 (.01)
Political interest	.31 (.02)	.44 (.03)	.29 (.007)	.02 (N.S.)
Hypothetical involvement	.34 (.09)	.21 (N.S.)	.42 (.004)	−.42 (N.S.)
School involvement	.09 (N.S.)	.35 (.004)	no significant difference	
Political knowledge	No significant difference		.16 (.08)	.44 (N.S.)

* The control variables made no significant differences to civic involvement or the media involvement variables.

N.S. = Not significant.

Pattern 2

In our second pattern of hypotheses, we posit that health levels tend to influence people's political attitudes and behaviors through the operation of body images, i.e., that body images are significant intervening variables tending to mediate the relationship between health levels and political variables. More specifically, we hypothesize that less healthy individuals who do not learn negative perceptions and evaluations of their bodies will tend not to exhibit the low degrees of political participation, knowledge, and the like that other less healthy people do.

Abundant and striking confirmation of this hypothesis is presented in Table 4–5. The findings displayed there are clear and consistent, illustrating that the impact of health experiences upon people's political orientations depends to a significant degree on the individual's body image.

In our data, poor health generally tends to diminish one's political knowledge, but Table 4–5 shows that this impact is least strong for those sickly individuals who perceive their bodies as most predictable, active, strong, and clearly bounded. Similarly, the typical influence of poor health is to increase one's satisfaction with politics. Table 4–5 illustrates that it is those sickly individuals who perceive their bodies as strongest, most predictable, most active, clearly bounded, and healthy—those people who are best able to cope with their illness pattern—who adopt favorable evaluations of the polity.

Consistent with this pattern is our finding that poor health tends to dampen hypothetical participation most strongly among those less healthy individuals who perceive their bodies as most unpredictable (Table 4–5).

The relationship between low health level and high political interest, a seemingly anomalous finding, may also be rendered more explicable by considering the mediation of body image variables. In Table 4–5, we note that this relationship is strongest among less healthy people who see their bodies as least predictable, least active, weakest, and smallest. It may be that persons with this pervasively negative view of their own bodies tend to focus out on politics in an attempt to shift their attention away from the self. People who have such unsatisfying perceptions of their own bodies may well find that increased attention paid to society and politics shields them from the anxieties and emotional pain of thinking about the self. A wide array of compensation, avoidance, and denial processes may be operative here.

The interpretation placed on specific findings in Table 4–5 must be tentative, pending future research. When the findings are considered together, however, we think that no scholar will disagree with our conclusion that body images are a consistently significant component of the processes by which health levels influence people's political orientations.

Table 4–5. The Relationship of Health Level to Sociopolitical Variables, Controlling for Body Images*

	LOWEST VALUE OF BODY IMAGE	MIDDLE VALUE	HIGHEST VALUE
POLITICAL EVALUATION			
a. Body predictability	.20 (N.S.)	.21 (N.S.)	.34 (.04)
b. Body strength	.20 (N.S.)	.22 (N.S.)	.38 (.05)
c. Body activism	.16 (N.S.)	.37 (.05)	.42 (.20)
d. Body boundary	.15 (N.S.)	.29 (.14)	.26 (.12)
e. Body health	.30 (.15)	.46 (.03)	.17 (.14)
f. Body evaluation	.32 (.06)	.21 (N.S.)	.36 (.02)
POLITICAL KNOWLEDGE			
a. Body predictability	−.48 (N.S.)	−.68 (.003)	−.29 (.01)
b. Body strength	−.45 (N.S.)	−.55 (.03)	−.37 (.02)
c. Body activism	−.52 (.05)	−.60 (.13)	−.22 (.03)
d. Body boundary	−.71 (N.S.)	−.51 (.12)	−.27 (.008)
e. Body evaluation	−.45 (.05)	−.56 (.13)	−.41 (.03)
POLITICAL INTEREST			
a. Body predictability	−.52 (.06)	.50 (.07)	−.19 (.16)
b. Body strength	−.25 (N.S.)	−.57 (.003)	−.19 (.07)
c. Body activism	−.49 (.02)	−.24 (.19)	−.26 (.15)
d. Body size	−.80 (.0002)	−.08 (N.S.)	−.30 (.04)
HYPOTHETICAL INVOLVEMENT			
a. Body predictability	−.60 (.02)	−.14 (N.S.)	−.19 (N.S.)
SCHOOL INVOLVEMENT			
a. Body boundary	.11 (N.S.)	−.20 (N.S.)	−.35 (.09)
CIVIC INVOLVEMENT			
a. Body activism	−.11 (N.S.)	.20 (N.S.)	.46 (.09)
b. Body evaluation	.22 (.09)	−.24 (N.S.)	.14 (N.S.)

* Body images not shown under a given political variable were found not to have a significant intervening influence on the relationship between health level and that political variable.

N.S. = Not significant.

We also hypothesized in Pattern 2 that a person's degree of body concern and degree of self-confidence would mediate the linkage between health level and political orientation. We reasoned that poor health would lead to even lower levels of political involvement among people who typically focussed a great amount of their attention on their bodies (or who were especially low in self-confidence). The data in Table 4–6 indicate that there is some modest tendency for body concern to operate as we hypothesized but that our measure of self-doubt was rather weak and inconsistent in its functioning.

Table 4–6. The Relationship of Health Level to Selected Sociopolitical Correlates, Controlling for Body Concern and Self-Doubt (Gamma Values and Significance Levels)

	LOWEST LEVEL OF CONTROL VARIABLE	MIDDLE LEVEL OF CONTROL VARIABLE	HIGHEST LEVEL OF CONTROL VARIABLE
POLITICAL KNOWLEDGE			
a. Body concern	.03 (.17)	.23 (.001)	.18 (.05)
b. Self-doubt	.59 (N.S.)	.51 (.04)	.38 (.11)
POLITICAL INTEREST			
a. Body concern	.02 (N.S.)	−.29 (.002)	−.14 (.23)
b. Self-doubt	.60 (.07)	.27 (N.S.)	.48 (.15)
HYPOTHETICAL INVOLVEMENT			
a. Body concern	−.08 (N.S.)	.08 (N.S.)	.02 (N.S.)
b. Self-doubt	.02 (N.S.)	.51 (.03)	.18 (N.S.)
POLITICAL EVALUATION			
a. Body concern	−.13 (N.S.)	−.05 (N.S.)	.004 (N.S.)
b. Self-doubt	.09 (N.S.)	−.27 (N.S.)	−.26 (.06)

N.S. = Not significant.

Pattern 3

In the data just reported, we have seen evidence that body images influence political socialization by serving as significant intervening variables between the individual's health levels and his participation and learning in social and political settings. In Pattern 3 of our hypotheses, we postulated that body images also tend to have independent influence on political socialization. We believe that students who tend to perceive and evaluate their bodies positively will tend to be significantly more involved and participant in politics than students with negative body images. Additionally, we expect that the influence of body image on political orientations will compare favorably in explanatory power with that exerted by social background factors (and will be stable when these factors are controlled).

These hypotheses receive some support in our data. Students who perceive their bodies as active, strong, healthy, and satisfying tend to be significantly more civically involved and active in school. A subset of these body images also predicts significantly to the individual's self-reported levels of political participation and vicarious political involvement.

These four sets of relationships linking body images to political orientations are all quite modest in strength (gamma values in the .10 to .30 range; significance at the .05 to .001 levels). Still, the strength of these associations is in the same order of magnitude as those linking political orientations to age, sex, and social-class variables (i.e., the influence of body image on politics seems as strong as or stronger than the influence of other factors generally accepted as basic socialization influences). All these relationships are expressed in Table 4–7.

Table 4–7. The Relationship of Body Images and Social Background Factors to Political Interest and Participation

	SCHOOL INVOLVEMENT	CIVIC INVOLVE-MENT	HYPOTHETICAL INVOLVEMENT	POLITICAL PARTICIPA-TION
Body Activism	.30[3]	.24[1]	.14[1]	.12[1]
Body evaluation	.20[3]	−.16[1]	.11[1]	.17
Body strength	.17[3]	−.12[1]	.01	.06
Body health	.15[3]	.08[1]	.04	.02
Body predictability	.10[2]	.10[1]	0	−.03
Body mobility	.12[2]	.07	0	0
Age	−.02	−.14[1]	0	−.04[1]
Sex	.04[1]	.14[1]	.35[1]	.07[1]
Social class	.06	.05[1]	.08	−.04
Urban-rural	.05[2]	.02	−.03	−.18[1]

[1] Significance = .05.

[2] Significance = .01.

[3] Significance = .001.

Our hypothesis that the influence of body images on political orientations tends to be unmediated by social background factors is also broadly confirmed. If we require that an intervening variable produce a change of at least .10 in the strength of the basic association from its original uncontrolled value in order to be judged significant: (1) Sex fails to significantly mediate the link between body images and political orientations in 15 of 22 relevant instances. (2) Social class is a significant intervening variable in a majority of instances but mediates the basic relationship in a highly inconsistent fashion (i.e., the impact of people's body images on their politics is not systematically enhanced or depressed at any given status level).

These inconsistencies in the relationships among body images, social background factors, and political orientations raise basic questions about the relative importance of body image and social background as predictors of political attitudes and behaviors. To answer these questions, a stepwise multiple regression analysis was performed on our data. In this analysis, we were able to compare the respective contributions of five body images (activism, predictability, strength, evaluation, and health) and four social background factors (age, sex, urban–suburban residence, and social class) on eight of our basic political orientations (political participation, civic involvement, and so on).[4] The stepwise regression analysis ranks the independent variables in descending order of their influence on the independent variable after assessing the independent contribution of each independent variable, holding all others constant. From these rank orders, we computed a mean rank order of the nine independent variables (averaged over the eight dependent variables). That rank order (Table 4–8) shows that body images tended to have consistently more influence on the political variables than did the social background factors.

Pattern 3 also included the hypothesis that the influence of body images on people's political orientations would be significantly mediated by the degree of one's body concern and self-doubt. These hypotheses, however, were disconfirmed by our data. Again, requiring that an intervening variable produce at least a gross change of .10 in the strength of the basic

---

[4] We restricted ourselves to these five body images because:

1. As the regression analysis may be sensitive to the intercorrelation of independent variables, using all of our highly intercorrelated body images might have artificially inflated the resulting regression coefficients.

2. These five were of greatest theoretical interest and had also been found to be empirically related to sociopolitical variables in our earlier analyses.

Table 4-8. Mean Rank Order of the Importance of Body Image and Social Background Factors to Eight Basic Political Orientations

1. Body activism
2. Sex
3. Body predictability
4. Body strength
5. Body evaluations
6. Age
7. Urban-suburban residence
8. Body health
9. Social class

association from its uncontrolled value to be judged significant: (1) Body concern failed to mediate the link between body image and political orientations in at least 13 of 22 relevant instances. (2) Self-doubt failed in at least 16 of 22 cases. In those instances in which body concern was a significant intervening variable, the impact of body images on political orientations was consistently greatest at low levels of body concern. No consistent relationships emerged in the few cases in which self-doubt proved to be important.

Pattern 4

Our final hypothesis is that the individual tends to use his perceptions and evaluations of his own body as a basis for perceiving and evaluating the social and political world. In other words, we think that the fundamental ways in which people view themselves has direct impact on the ways in which they conceive of the political system, that people tend to generalize from their basic ideas about the body to their basic notions about their political environment. Table 4-9 indicates that this hypothesis tended to be true in our respondent population. There is a positive and statistically significant relationship between each and every body image we studied and the corresponding image of the American political system.

CONCLUSION

In our respondent population, an individual's level of health and body images predict significantly to his or her participation in politics, knowledge about public affairs, and evaluation of the political system. These health and body image variables also predict to the individual's degree of

Table 4-9. The Relationship of Body Images to People's Fundamental Perceptions and Evaluations of the Political System[*]

	POLITICAL PREDICT- ABILITY	POLITICAL EVAL- UATION	POLITICAL MOBILITY	POLITICAL ACTIVISM	POLITICAL BOUNDARY DEFINITE- NESS	POLITICAL HEALTH	POLITICAL STRENGTH	POLITICAL SIZE
Body predictability	**.29**	.21	.22	.20	.23	.21	.18	.68
Body evaluation	.20	**.23**	.21	.24	.22	.20	.22	.22
Body mobility	.21	.17	**.29**	.18	.30	.18	.17	.15
Body activism	.13	.16	.15	**.22**	.17	.15	.16	.18
Body boundary	.15	.20	.28	.16	**.33**	.19	.06	.04
Body health	.12	.11	.08	.15	.19	**.18**	.17	.20
Body strength	.13	.11	.17	.13	.22	.16	**.20**	.15
Body size	.08	.12	.13	.08	.15	.12	.14	**.15**

[*] Relationships on the diagonal are emphasized for clarity of presentation. All relationships printed in bold face type are significant at .05 or better.

involvement with a major agency of political socialization, the school. Using the strength of association as a measure of relative influence, health level and body images seem to have at least as strong an impact on people's political orientations as age, sex, and social class. In addition, we find that the linkages between people's health and their political attitudes and behaviors are not consistently mediated or attenuated by social background factors.

These findings suggest that health factors and body images—two sets of variables wholly ignored in previous studies—may be quite important to our understanding of political socialization. Certainly these findings seem to warrant replication of this study and expanded work on a greater number of health and body image factors. If successful, such expanded work may well lead us to the regular incorporation of biopsychological variables—health, body image, energy levels, and the like—in our studies of political socialization.

We believe that such a turn of events is quite likely and will be most useful. Human beings do have bodies; variations in body states, and in perceptions of body states, can have powerful influences on social and political behavior. The sooner we recognize and explore the implications of these fundamental facts, the better, for biopsychological variables may well prove to have basic influence on processes of political socialization. If so, the study of these variables will be a vital, as well as almost wholly new, direction in which political study should move.

REFERENCES

Arkoff, A., and H. B. Weaver. "Body Image and Body Dissatisfaction in Japanese Americans," *Journal of Social Psychology* 68 (1966), 323–30.

Beller, K., and J. Turner. "Personality Correlates of Children's Perceptions of Human Size," *Child Development* 35 (1964).

Birch, Herbert G., and Joan Dye Gussow. *Disadvantaged Children: Health, Nutrition, and School Failure* (New York: Harcourt, Brace and World, 1970).

Calder, G., *et al.* "Sex Differences in Body Concepts," *Journal of Consulting Psychology* 23 (1959).

Ferguson, Leroy, *et al.* "An Attempt to Correlate Physical Maturation with Attitudes Toward Politics" (paper read to the 1970 Meeting of the International Political Science Association, Munich, Germany).

Fisher, S. *Body Experience in Fantasy and Behavior* (New York: Appleton-Century-Crofts, 1970).

———, and Sidney E. Cleveland. *Body Image and Personality* (New York: Dover Publications, 1968).

Gunderson, F. K., and L. C. Johnson. "Past Experience, Self-Evaluation and Present Adjustment," *Journal of Social Psychology* 66 (1965), 311–21.

Jaros, Dean. "Bio-Chemical Desocialization" (paper presented to the 1970 Annual Meeting of the American Political Science Association, Los Angeles, California).

Johnson, L. "Body Cathexis as a Factor in Somatic Complaints," *Journal of Consulting Psychology* 20 (1956), 145–9.

Jourard, S. M., and P. F. Secord. "Body-Cathexis and the Ideal Female Figure," *Journal of Abnormal and Social Psychology* 50 (1955), 243–46.

Landau, M. F. *Body Image—as a Variable in Adjustment to Physical Handicap* (unpublished Ph.D. dissertation, Columbia University, 1960).

Magnussen, M. G. "Body Size and Body Cathexis Replicated," *Psychological Newsletter* 10 (1958), 33–4.

McConnell, O. L., and P. G. Daston. "Body Image Changes in Pregnancy," *Journal of Projective Techniques* 25 (1961), 451–56.

McFarland, J. H., *et al.* "Factors Affecting Body Image as Measured by Perceived Arm Length" (paper presented to the Annual Meeting of the American Psychological Association, 1960).

Mechanic, David B. *Medical Sociology* (New York: The Free Press, 1959).

Nash, H. "The Estimation of Body Size in Relation to Actual Body Size, Personal Ethos and Developmental Status" (Ph.D. dissertation, University of California, 1951).

Patrick, Donald L., *et al.* "Toward an Operational Definition of Health" (Department of Community Medicine, University of California at San Diego, 1972).

Pless, Ivan B., and James W. B. Douglas. "Chronic Illness in Childhood," (University of Rochester School of Medicine and Dentistry, n.d.).

———, and Klaus J. Roghmann. "Chronic Illness and Its Consequences" (paper presented to the 1970 Annual Meeting of the American Public Health Service).

Sapira, Joseph D., *et al.* "Differences in Perception Between Hypertensive and Normotensive Populations," *PsychoSomatic Medicine* 33 (1970), 239–55.

Schaffer, Juliet P. "Social and Personality Correlates of Children's Estimates of Height," *Genetic Psychology Monographs* 70 (1964), 97–134.

Schwartz, David C. "Perceptions of Personal Energy and the Adoption of Basic Behavioral Orientations to Politics" (paper read to the 1970 Meeting of the International Political Science Association, Munich, Germany).

Secord, P. F. "Objectification of World Association Procedures by the Use of Homonyms: A measure of body Cathexis," *Journal of Personality* 21 (1953), 479–95.

Singer, J. E., and Patricia Lamb. "Social Concern, Body Size and Birth Order," *Journal of Social Psychology* 68 (1966), 143–51.

Staffieri, J. H. "A Study of Body Image in Children," *Journal of Personality and Social Psychology* 7 (1967), 101–04.

Stauffer, Robert B. "The Bio-Politics of Underdevelopment," *Comparative Political Studies* 2 (1970).

Wapner, S. "An Experimental and Theoretical Approach to Body Image" (paper presented to the 16th International Congress of Psychology, 1960).

———, and H. Werner (eds.). *The Body Percept* (New York: Random House, 1965).

Weinberg, J. R. "A Further Investigation of Body Cathexis and the Self," *Journal of Consulting Psychology* 24 (1960).

Werner, H., and S. Wapner. "Sensory-Tonic Field Theory of Perception," *Journal of Personality* 18 (1949), 88–107.

Werner, H., and S. Wapner. "Toward a General Theory of Perception," *Psychological Review* 59 (1956), 324–38.

Witkin, H. A., *et al. Personality Through Perception* (New York: Harper and Row, 1954).

Wyler, Allen R., *et al.* "Seriousness of Illness Rating Scale," *Journal of Psychosomatic Research* 31 (1968), 363–74.

Zion, L. E. "Body Concept as Related to Self-Concept," *Research Quarterly* 36 (1965).

Part Three

Processes of Political Socialization

Chapter Five

A Social-Learning Approach to Political Socialization

Ira S. Rohter

INTRODUCTION

Although *political socialization* has a diversity of meanings (Dawson, 1966; Dawson and Prewitt, 1969), its fundamental concern is with the *functional relationships between the antecedent conditions that individuals experience and their subsequent political behavior.* Political scientists have, by and large, conceptualized how the individual's past experiences affect his current behavior by adopting from psychology the state-trait approach to personality functioning. In this approach attitudes, values, and personality traits are viewed as the stable, enduring effects of socialization that account for an actor's behavioral consistencies across varying situations and over time. Liberalism, conservatism, authoritarianism, alienation, self-esteem, and aggressiveness are just a few of the many dispositional concepts we employ as independent variables in trying to account for political behaviors. The genesis or *acquisition* of politically relevant dispositions thus becomes the focus of study for students of political socialization (Langton, 1969; Greenstein, 1965; Jaros, 1967).

I am convinced that the state-trait approach to political socialization should be abandoned. In its place I propose a social-learning theory approach that consciously utilizes the most recent theorizing and experimental findings of learning and developmental psychology. In this chapter I argue that the mode of theory construction, the methodology, and the substantive principles of modern social-learning theory can provide us with powerful explanatory schemes for establishing the lawful relationships between prior personal experiences and current political behaviors.

My purpose in writing this chapter is to introduce the student of political socialization to a conceptual framework radically different from the approaches commonly employed in the political science literature. I hope to convince the reader that modern social-learning theory is sufficiently rich to organize and guide our research, or if unconvinced, at least I hope he will read further in a field which is undergoing rapid changes

129

from the simple concepts of learning we associated with the early psychological behaviorists. As this is only a brief survey of some of the more important principles, I have noted in the bibliography those works I have found most valuable in studying socialization from this perspective.

Prevailing Conceptions of the Socialization Process

The process of political socialization has been conceptualized in at least three major ways, but all commonly view the outcome of socializing experiences as enduring dispositional personal traits.

One approach, associated with Easton, which has drawn its inspiration from system and role theories, is concerned with the transmission of norms, expectations, beliefs, and orientations from one generation to another. Considerable emphasis is placed on the consequences the resulting orientations have for the political system (Easton and Dennis, 1969; Almond and Verba, 1963; Sigel, 1965). While the research of Easton, Hess, Torney, Greenstein, and Dennis has been pathbreaking in providing a preliminary mapping of the attitudes and orientations of young children toward politics, it has left largely unexplored the exact nature of the acquisition process itself. Although the authors have freely suggested some mechanisms from psychoanalytic, cognitive, and learning theories, little if any direct empirical evidence has been produced supporting or disconfirming their hypothesis about causal processes (Sigel, 1965; Greenstein, 1968).

This early research leaves us with what might be called the "osmosis" theory of political socialization: Somehow, through unclearly specified processes, the family, schools, churches, peers, and other agents *transmit, expose,* or *inculcate* children with their own political views. The result is that these basic orientations are *absorbed, acquired, incorporated,* or *internalized,* to function as influential determinants of later political behavior.

Efforts to explain the specific mechanisms involved in the formation and development of politically relevant dispositions have most frequently drawn on psychoanalytic principles (Easton and Hess, 1962, 243–4; Greenstein, 1965, 45–51; Pye, 1962; Langton, 1969, Ch. 2 esp.; Wolfenstein and Kliman, 1965; Jaros 1967). This probably reflects to some extent the seminal influences of Lasswell's *Psychopathology and Politics* (1930) and *Power and Personality* (1948), *The Authoritarian Personality* (Adorno, 1950), and the more recent writings of Lane, Greenstein, and Davies, all of whom view political psychology from a decidedly psychoanalytic perspective. A second likely contributor to the popularity of the psychoanalytic approach is its connection to trait psychology, for both positions commonly assume that underlying inferred states (whether called psychodynamics, defense mechanisms, motives, or drives) exert generalized and enduring effects on all behavior (see Maddi, 1968, for example). Thus we find in the recent sophisticated research of Langton (1969) and Jaros (1967) into socialization processes the use of dispositional traits and personality dynamics such as ego-strength, authoritarianism, dependency, efficacy, identification, dogmatism, democratic orientation, rebelliousness–conformity, and anxiety.

It is to their credit that political scientists such as Jaros and Langton are beginning to explore specific processes involved in political socialization. Unfortunately, the utility of the state-trait approach they employ is being seriously questioned and abandoned by an increasing number of personality and developmental psychologists (Mischel, 1968; Vernon, 1964; Berlyne, 1968; Baldwin, 1968; Gewirtz, 1969). First, psychoanalytic principles have been under substantial attack for many years by academic psychologists for failing to yield testable or empirically supported propositions (Jenness, 1962; Zeigler, 1963). While harsh critics have judged the psychoanalytic approach as misleading and empirically "barren" (Sewell, 1963; Bandura, 1969), even sympathetic reviewers admit the problematic nature of Freudian-inspired formulations (Child, 1954; Zeigler and Child, 1969) for the study of socialization.

Probably less recognized by many political scientists is the fact that contemporary personality theory and research is moving away from a trait conception of human functioning. Traditional personality theory assumes an hierarchic-dynamic system, in which hypothetical and covert emotional, cognitive, and motivational processes determine the individual's observable behaviors (Maddi, 1968; Sanford, 1963). Central to the trait concept of personality is the belief that characteristic behaviors will be displayed in widely varied situations and account for most of the individual's acts.

The actual empirical data lend little support to the assumption central to a viable trait theory, that individuals display broad behavioral consistencies (Mischel, 1968). In fact, the evidence suggests that behavioral specificity across varying situations and not generalization, is the better rule (Hunt, 1965). Considerable specificity has been found regularly for even such basic dispositions as authoritarianism, aggressiveness, and dependency (Mischel, 1968), although their cross-situational generality has been commonly assumed by many psychological formulations (Zeigler and Child, 1969).

Social Behavior Theory: An Introduction

The inability of the trait theory approach typically to do more than modestly predict actual behavior in specific circumstances, even after years of intensive efforts at developing sophisticated measuring instruments (see Cattell, 1965; Hase and Goldberg, 1967), is increasingly leading psychologists to reject the entire conception of energized global traits and concealed motivational states that impel behavior. An alternative formulation, most often called social behavior theory, interprets the diversity of behavior across situations as predictable, expected results, and not as inconsistencies that must be explained away. The essential hypothesis is that behavior is linked to specific stimuli. The fact that an individual may display one form of behavior in one situation, and perhaps its opposite form in another, can be accounted for by differences in the situational cues and reinforcement contingencies. A major principle of social behavior theory is that the consequences of behavior affect responses. Thus we should not expect a person to act similarly across situations if the reward or punishment consequences produced by the same behavior are different. (We therefore should not be surprised that the Langton and Jaros studies produced only weak relationships between their measures of general traits and political variables.) The facts of behavioral specificity therefore lead us to consider a formulation that includes specific situational conditions and reinforcement contingencies in the prediction and control of behavior.

This emphasis on stimulus conditions and reinforcements does not mean that the individual is ignored. Quite the contrary. For it is the individual's prior experience with similar stimuli that determines his subsequent reactions. As we shall see below, his experience with similar stimuli affects the later meaning of new stimuli, and his prior reinforcement history alters the probability that particular response patterns will be evoked. In sum, the antecedent conditions to which the individual has been exposed, together with current situational stimuli, affect his performance in new environments.

We thus come full circle, back to the notion that as students of political socialization we are interested in the functional relationships between antecedent experiences and later behaviors. But now we approach things differently. For the *trait theorist*, who views behavior as the manifestation of broad dispositions, socialization means seeking out how politically relevant global traits are acquired through mechanisms contained in state-dynamic formulations. For the *social-learning theorist*, behavior is determined by a number of principles that carefully tie together prior experiences and later behavior as a function of reinforcement contingencies. A number of other important principles, based on careful experimental research, are also involved in any complete explanation of behavior. This view of the connection between past and present environmental events leads us to consider the body of learning literature, in which such relationships have been systematically studied.

This chapter will next survey some of the substantive principles, concepts, and formulations of contemporary neo-behavioral psychology and social-learning theory that seem relevant in generating useful explanatory schemes for the study of political learning.

CHANGES IN LEARNING THEORY, FROM PAVLOV TO NEO-BEHAVIORISM AND SOCIAL-LEARNING THEORY

Most political scientists equate learning theory with the basic principles of classical and instrumental conditioning associated with Pavlov and Skinner. But stimulus–response (S–R) theory has undergone radical changes, especially during the last 20 years, and has followed many new lines of inquiry.

As Berlyne (1969) has outlined, the early behaviorism of J. B. Watson, Pavlov, and Thorndike gave way in the early 1930s to a somewhat different conception of learning. Hull, Tolman, and Spence, influenced by the logical-positivists in philosophy, devoted considerable attention to the construction of rigorous and systematic processes, and in general established the need for a stimulus–organism–response (S–O–R) conception of the learning process. They also devoted considerable attention to motivational problems.

This enriched conception of functioning was even further broadened by such people as Miller, Dollard, Sears, Mowrer, and Osgood, all of whom began to tackle human behavior from a learning theory perspective. This was particularly evident in the joint efforts of Miller and Dollard to integrate Freudian notions with learning principles (Miller and Dollard, 1941; Dollard and Miller, 1950; Miller, 1959).

Since the 1950s, S–R theory has undergone profound changes as behavioral theorists have begun to attack more complex phenomena. These changes, presented in the following discussion against the background of early learning theories, should be of considerable interest to students of political socialization.

Conditioning and Reinforcement

Many textbooks on learning begin their discussion of learning mechanisms with what were traditionally viewed as two distinctive processes. *Classical or Pavlovian conditioning* involves, at the descriptive level, the repeated pairing of a neutral stimulus (a bell, for example), with an unconditioned stimulus (food), which evokes an unconditioned response (salivation). Eventually, the ringing of the bell alone elicits the unconditioned response. The Pavlovian model is the prototypical example of the *contiguity principle* of learning, which states that the contiguity of two stimuli tends to give one of them the ability to elicit responses previously made to the other. The second kind of learning is *instrumental conditioning*, which occurs when a particular response to a specific stimulus is reinforced. The

Law of Effect holds that when a given response is followed by a positive reinforcing consequence, it increases the likelihood that that response will be repeated on subsequent occasions. Thus, any action can be put under control of any stimulus, by rewarding the action consistently when it is performed in the presence of the stimulus.

Reinforcers, From Drives to Secondary Motivational Systems

A significant trend in S–R theory is the change in the conception of what constitutes a reinforcer. Early learning theorists viewed the effects of reinforcements as produced by some sort of physiological drive–reduction (needs for food, water, and so on) (Kimble, 1961; Brown, 1961). Subsequent research led many theorists to seriously question this homeostatic conception of the reinforcement process, and some have even recommended it be dropped (Cofer and Appley, 1965).

A number of alternative conditions have been found to have reinforcing qualities (see Appley, 1970, for an excellent review of theoretical positions). Perhaps most important for students of socialization is the notion of *secondary reinforcer,* for most of the occurrences that regulate post-infant behavior are not directly punishing or rewarding but imply social consequences. (Staats and Staats, 1963; Gewirtz, 1969). The general principle underlying this phenomenon is that any neutral stimulus paired with a stimulus having reinforcement value will, through repeated pairing, acquire reinforcing value itself (Brown and Farber, 1968; Brown, 1961). In the early learning experiences of an individual, with his dependency upon others, social stimuli acquire positive or negative reinforcing values because they are initially associated with a variety of primary reinforcers (such as food, water, or removal of aversive conditions). Through secondary and even higher-order conditioning, social stimuli such as attention, approval, affection, praise, criticism, and tokens (money, honors, grades, medals) acquire the capacity to control behavior. In fact, as Premark (1965) has shown, any event valued by the individual can be employed as an effective reinforcer. Thus the experimental findings indicate that a wider range of reinforcers than is often thought possible can be employed in socialization research and behavior modification.

Examples of Positive Reinforcement Controls

The Law of Effect states that when a given response is followed by a positively reinforcing consequence, there arises an increased probability that the response will be repeated in the same or a similar situation. If, for example, parents respond to a child's tantrum with prompt solicitous attention, it is likely that the child will perform similarly in the future. Nonattention leads to a lessening of the crying (Williams, 1959, discussed in Bandura, 1969a, 368). One of the major principles of social-learning theory is that behavior is extensively determined by reinforcement conditions. In the most comprehensive review of this literature, Bandura (1969a, Ch. 4 esp.) describes a number of studies that demonstrate the potency of systematically applied rewards on the modification of behavior. Gross behavior disorders of psychotics have been substantially modified by positive responses to desired behaviors on their parts and by ignoring undesired ones. Many forms of deviant behaviors in children have been altered by changing the social reinforcers administered by adults, and reinforcement–contingency methods have been applied to developing social and self-management skills in severely retarded children.

Similar reinforcement–contingency techniques have produced extensive modifications in the behavior of large groups in educational, rehabilitative, and other social institutions. "Token society" methods particularly have produced exciting results. Behaviors such as self-management, appropriate social behavior, or satisfactory work performance are designated as responses to be reinforced. The mental patient or delinquent youth earns a number of points or is paid a simulated currency (tokens) for the performance of a desired response; he can in turn exchange his earnings for a variety of valued objects, activities, and special privileges. That these group reinforcement procedures exert powerful controls over the institutional population has been shown by employing as a validation procedure an experimental design involving presentation and withdrawal of reward contingencies. The performance of desired behaviors varies directly with the experimental manipulations of reinforcements.

The theoretical argument is that the same kinds of reinforcement–contingencies are involved in shaping behavior in natural environments. One example of systematic group-based reinforcement practices adopted on a society-wide basis is the Soviet Union. Bronfenbrenner (1962) reports a number of conscious practices followed by Soviet authorities to explicitly develop a strong sense of group or collective responsibility. The primary method is to administer rewards and punishments on a group basis, so that each individual's behavior is carefully monitored and regulated by his peers.

Negative Reinforcement

Not all behaviors lead to rewarding consequences. *Negative* reinforcement actually involves two very different sets of learning consequences. The *removal of positive reinforcers* tends to have an extinction effect on responses and turns out to be an effective technique for eliminating behavior, especially when the individual possesses responses within his repertoire that can result in positive rewards (Bandura, 1969*a*). A second kind of negative reinforcer involves *aversive* stimuli, such as physical punishment, or secondary social ones, such as disapproval. Aversive reinforcers suppress rather than eliminate behavior, and strong punishments often produce conditioned fear–emotional reactions and undesired avoidance behaviors. Such response patterns are exceedingly difficult to change (Solomon, 1964; Church, 1963; Brown and Farber, 1968; Bandura, 1969*a*). Under some circumstances, however, aversive stimuli can be efficient modifiers of behavior, particularly if alternative modes of behavior are strengthened (Bandura, 1969*a*, Chs. 5 and 8).

Parameters of Reinforcement

There is a considerable literature describing how the amount and scheduling of reinforcement differentially affects learning performance (Kimble, 1961; Logan and Wagner, 1965). Any attempt to apply a social learning analysis to some socialization problem would require that these parameters of reinforcement be considered.

Amount of Reinforcement. In general, one ought to expect to find a simple positive relationship between the amount of effective reinforcement and the speed and diversity of learning. However, while some research on the quantity and quality of various reinforcers (mostly primary) has been done on animals (Kimble, 1961, 137–140), it appears that little empirical work has been done on human subjects. In many studies the value of the employed reinforcer seems fairly obvious but, given the nature of secondary and other conditioned reinforcers, it seems unlikely that any *a priori* scaling scheme for human beings can be established. However, the work on utility theory in economics and psychology (Edwards, 1961) does suggest some techniques for assessing subjective valuations.

In addition, the *contrast effect* should be considered, that is, the incentive value of any particular reward or punishment is dependent upon other reinforcers the organism has received (Logan and Wagner, 1965; Gewirtz, 1969, 86–92; Black, 1968; Appley, 1970). When several reinforcers occur either together or in sequence, they *contrast* with one another, modifying what their reinforcing value would be if presented in isolation. Thus, any analysis of the reinforcers involved in a situation must consider contextual and antecedent learning effects. For example, when an infant receives only a limited amount of affection, scolding, which might normally be considered an aversive stimulus, may act as a positive reinforcer, especially if he is otherwise ignored. Thus the child may repeat his behavior, because even negative attention is rewarding in contrast to what he normally experiences.

Schedules of Reinforcement

Reinforcing consequences need not always occur after the performance of a response in order to affect learning. In fact, while *continuous* reinforcement results in the more rapid acquisition of responses, behavior that is most stable and resistant to extinction occurs under a schedule of *intermittent* reinforcements (Ferster and Skinner, 1957; Kimble, 1961). In most real social situations, reinforcements are characteristically dispensed on variable schedules (the number of unreinforced responses and the time interval between the reinforcers tend to vary). Thus behavioral control or influence is established without requiring constant surveillance and reinforcements.

Intermittently reinforced individuals tend to emit strong responses and to work persistently, even when not rewarded for some time. In motivational terms we would say such an individual is "hard-working" and "ambitious." A social-learning theory analysis, however, would address itself to both the net value of reinforcements present in the environment and the schedules of reinforcement the individual has previously experienced (Staats and Staats, 1963). "Poor" or "inadequate" motivation, that is, the display of little work or tenacity, would then be attributed to a lack of sufficient positive incentives in the situation as mediated by the individual's expectations (Logan and Wagner, 1965). The schedule whereby reinforcements are administered has a significant impact on the emission of responses and their extinction in subsequent nonreinforcing situations.

In summary, contemporary social-learning theory takes a much broader view of what constitutes a reinforcing event than simple physiological need reduction. An extension of the schema of reward and punishment to encompass socially derived incentive systems and learned secondary reinforcers, plus a better understanding of the effects of schedules and contrast, provide modern behavior theorists with an enriched set of basic conditioning principles with which to study complex social behavior. However, even more principles must be posited, as we shall see before we can really do an adequate job.

OBSERVATIONAL, VICARIOUS, AND MODELING LEARNING PROCESSES

The instrumental training mechanism, even if extended through secondary and higher-order conditioning processes, seems grossly inadequate in accounting for the complex behavioral patterns (such as language) that all members of society exhibit. One of the most prominent characteristics of the social-learning approach to socialization is its emphasis on the fact that virtually all learning phenomena resulting from direct experiences can occur on a vicarious basis through observations of other persons and the environment (Bandura, 1969a; Bandura and Walters, 1963). Observational learning processes (or its functional equivalent, including modeling, imitation, identification, copying, and contagion) (Bandura, 1969b; Gewirtz, 1969) are used to describe some important mechanisms through which people learn new behavior patterns and change older ones, without engaging in direct trial and error acts.

One of the basic principles of social-learning theory is that a great deal of human learning is mediated by perceptual and higher-order processes and depends on observations of environmental contingencies rather than on direct reinforcements of the person's own behavior. For example, suppose we asked a child to engage in a relatively simple learning activity, working with a puzzle box. He could eventually learn how to open it by simple trial and error. Alternatively, he could observe it, making his explorations visually. Or he might watch another person go through certain steps to open it and later imitate them. Observing someone else's mistakes and correct response may, on the other hand, teach him about the harmful or rewarding objects available in the environment. He may note for instance that holding the box gives a shock. Thus he may acquire an avoidance response based not on his own direct experiences but on observation. Symbolic mediation can also affect learning: Verbal or written instructions can communicate expected consequences or behavior or convey information about the rewarding or punishing power of objects (Campbell, 1960). Some experimental studies have demonstrated that verbal or written information about response–reinforcement relationships can greatly shorten the learning processes (Mischel and Grusec, 1967; Bandura and Mischel, 1965; Lovaas, 1964).

People can learn entire behavior patterns merely by watching others perform the sequences (Bandura, 1969a; Walters, 1963). Observing the rewards and punishments administered to others can also reinforce and inhibit the observer's own acts as well. A behavior, for example, may not be performed because it does not exist in the actor's repertoire, or it may be potentially available but inhibited by the situation's incentive conditions. Observing the reinforcement administered to a model can also elicit responses previously inhibited. Studies done by Bandura and his associates on the effects of models on aggressive behavior show that whether or not models are rewarded or punished for such behavior significantly affects the performance of aggressive acts among observers in subsequent situations. In one experiment the introduction of highly attractive incentives demonstrated that all the children had learned the same responses (that is, they could reproduce them when sufficiently rewarded) but that those who had observed the model being punished had learned to inhibit performing these acts (Bandura, 1965). A general disinhibition effect has also been observed in modeling studies. The aggressive behavior of children exposed to an aggressive model includes not only the specific acts demonstrated by the model, but other sorts of hostile and belligerent responses already in the child's repertoire.

Vicarious Conditioning of Emotional Reactions

One of the most intriguing instances of vicarious learning is the process whereby people acquire conditioned emotional responses to stimuli that accompany a painful stimulus experienced by another person, or to symbolic mediators. The basic principle underlying these processes is that of higher-order conditioning: Neutral stimuli associated contiguously with aversively conditioned stimuli become aversive themselves. Through contiguous association with actual aversive experiences, words and other symbols can become conditioned stimuli with the capacity to elicit fear and strong avoidance reactions (Miller, 1948). Another person's reactions can likewise act as the stimulus setting off aversive and autonomic responses in the observer.

Vicarious conditioning helps to account for the development of emotional reactions towards people and objects that were never directly associated with either noxious or positive outcomes in the individual's own personal experiences. Thus an individual may come to fear dogs even though he has never personally been harmed by them; his fear results from observing the emotional turmoil and strong fear reaction of others when they directly or symbolically encounter canines. Behavior modification techniques based on understanding this process, and the use of counterconditioning models, have been highly successful in eliminating such fear-based phobias (Bandura, 1969a).

Susceptibility to Models

Several classes of variables are associated with an individual's susceptibility to models. The general rule is that a previous history of being rewarded for imitative behavior increases the probability of imitation in the future. The most direct example is the case in which the observer has been directly rewarded for matching the model's behavior. The underlying mechanism here is straightforward instrumental conditioning, as well as the principle of anticipatory responses (see Logan and Wagner, 1965, Ch. 2).

A model's example is often followed even though direct reinforcements do not occur on every occasion. Several mechanisms may be involved in such instances.

Generalized imitation is an often-employed concept that refers to the fact that individuals imitate both reinforced and nonreinforced responses of a particular model. While different reasons have been proposed to account for such behavior (such as a trait of dependency or identification), the phenomena can be parsimoniously interpreted by social-learning theory. As Gewirtz (1969) has argued, the key factor is the observer's failure to discriminate between the reinforced and nonreinforced responses exhibited by the model. Because extrinsic reinforcements from socializing agents are administered on an *intermittent schedule,* the individual continues to perform imitative responses on even nonrewarded trials. If reinforcers come from a variety of sources, on an over-all intermittent schedule and for diverse imitative responses, the phenomenon we call *generalized imitation* will result.

Identification has been frequently employed in the socialization literature to explain the intergenerational transmission of basic values and orientations from parents to their children. Although psychoanalytically oriented researchers have viewed identification as a special mechanism, social-learning theorists have more parsimoniously considered it another manifestation of imitative behavior (Bandura, 1969b; Gewirtz, 1969). There are some new features of imitative behavior that this concept does require us to consider, however.

During their life history children are exposed to many different models. The influence on the child depends upon their availability, the homogeneity or heterogeneity of behaviors they display, and the extent to which their being imitated results in reinforcement. The child's family, particularly in the early years, constitutes a crucial influence, since the range of models is restricted to family members, especially the parents, who serve as sources of biological and conditioned rewards for the child's behavior. The child's imitative behavior thus becomes focused because of frequent or exclusive contact with one or two models. The behavior of these models will therefore acquire special discriminant value for the child, as imitating them produces a higher probability of being reinforced than does the imitation of other models.

The child thus comes to copy diverse responses performed by his parents because he is consistently and potently reinforced for such behavior. Through a process of differential reinforcement for a range of behaviors, the child may develop an abstract schema of certain common elements and apply it to situations in which he may not have actually seen the models perform. Thus the child may be said to have acquired the parents' "values" (see Hill, 1960; Aronfreed, 1969). This class of copying responses (Millenson, 1967, Ch. 8) is highly likely to elicit extrinsic reinforcers in a variety of settings and from many sources. Because the intermittent schedule of reinforcers administered for performing these responses are acquired at such an early age, they are likely to be strongly resistant to change as long as an occasional reward is available from any source.

The degree to which a child "identifies" with one particular model over another is determined by the greater rewards to be derived from the imitation of one model's behavior rather than another's. Identification is thus not a process that calls for a special set of constructs, but an example of learning, which means we can study it according to well-established laws of behavior.

A somewhat different approach to imitative learning posits that, on the basis of the model's personal attributes, the observer hypothesized that similar consequences will accrue to him if he matches the model's behavior. The ability of a model to elicit matching behavior should, therefore, be a function of information conveyed to the observer that the model has amassed rewarding resources (prestige, power, competence, high status), or has been generally unrewarded during his life. Two lines of empirical evidence are generally offered in support of this interpretation. One set of findings comes from research on persuasion and social conformity (see McGuire, 1969, for a detailed review of this literature): Variables such as prestige, power, expertise, and status attributes (possession, money, style of speech) are found to significantly affect susceptibility to social influences (Bandura and Walters, 1963, 84). The literature on hypothesis testing and decision-making (discussed below in the mediational processes section) is also invoked by these theorists (Bandura, 1969a; Bandura and Walters, 1963). They believe that higher-order thinking and concept formation processes that include hypothesizing and making inferences are necessary adjuncts to more traditional learning mechanisms.

Both these approaches agree that a significant portion of a child's socialization experiences do not take place through direct training but rather are acquired through the active process of the child imitating parents and other models. It seems quite simplistic to assume that children acquire most of their politically relevant learnings as a result of the direct conditioning of parents with clear goals and disciplined differential training procedures. The child need not be hit over the head when he says he is a Republican and given candy when he says he is a Democrat, to acquire a party identification. Modeling and generalized imitation processes seem more likely mechanisms to account for the acquisition of party identification and other political orientations.

MEDIATIONAL PROCESSES

To many, learning theory primarily involves causal explanations of behavior rigorously couched in terms of variables that may be *externally manipulated*. The methodological arguments of the early behavioralists are still represented today, at least in the popular view, by the hardline approach of Skinner. The strict behaviorist position rests on the basic assumption that covert processes are lawfully determined by externally occurring events and that internal states therefore can be bypassed in the prediction and control of behavior.

To a considerable extent modern social-learning theorists are also wary of invoking inner psychic agents or states as determiners of behavior. Particularly unsatisfactory to them are personality theories assuming that energizing traits and complex dynamic motivations impel most behavior. As we noted in the beginning of this chapter, trait theories based on hypothetical internal conditions that are autonomous of situational stimuli have not distinguished themselves when put to the empirical test of actually predicting and controlling behavior (see Bandura, 1969a).

Nevertheless, considerable experimental evidence exists to indicate that human behavior in particular cannot be satisfactorily accounted for without entertaining mediating and higher-level cognitive processes. As we have already seen in the preceding discussion of observational learning and modeling, a great deal of human learning falls beyond the kind of relatively simple trial-and-error learning studied in the classical laboratory experiment. Interest in imitating learning processes is one of the outstanding characteristics of the contemporary social-learning approach to socialization; another major feature is a concern with mediational and symbolic higher-level processes.

Here we trace some recent psychological thinking and research on these matters.

S–R Associational Theorists

As Bourne (1966) has noted in his recent review of human conceptual behavior, the more traditional position tends to picture the organism as a passive recipient of environmental information. In its simplest form this type of theory attributes nothing to the organism but a memory for previous conditions. Activities or conditions internal to the organism make little or no difference in learning the correct stimulus pattern to respond to. The subject does not operate on incoming information in any essential way; he is viewed as a passive system on which the environment inscribes its information. Learning the correct stimulus discrimination is viewed simply as an automatic process wherein stimuli become gradually connected with some response, through differential reinforcements. (See Riley, 1968, esp. Ch. 4, for a discussion of continuity models of discrimination learning, which are prototypes of this approach.)

In more modern interpretations, however, learning seldom represents a single S–R association. Even simple acts involve a series of interconnected stimulus–response sequences. Learning theorists, particularly Skinner and his associates, delineate and emphasize the process by which each response acts as a discriminative stimulus for responses that follow it (Millerson, 1967, Ch. 12). The underlying mechanism is higher-order conditioning. Day-to-day behavior is made up of *behavioral chains*, involved not in just motor skills like walking, driving a car, or playing a piano but in the evoking of conditioned emotional reactions that influence subsequent behavior in complex ways (Brown, 1961; Brown and Farber, 1968; Appley, 1970). Cues that have become aversive stimuli through conditioning are capable of eliciting autonomic reactions (fear, anxiety), which in turn set in motion a long string of responses and avoidance behaviors. As these avoidance behaviors eventually become conditioned to autonomically produced stimulation, they both instigate and direct the performance of what are frequently labelled psychopathological reactions. Dollard and Miller (1950) have suggested a similar learning theory explanation for the acquisition of "neurotic" defensive behaviors; such behavior patterns are acquired and maintained because of their ability to reduce fear, a powerful reinforcer. Counterconditioning and desensitization behavior modification techniques are based on these same learning principles (Wolpe, 1961; Bandura, 1969a, Ch. 7), that is, they are designed to disrupt aversively conditioned emotional chains.

Individuals normally bring to a new situation a repertoire of possible responses rather than a single response. The particular response or chain of responses elicited in the individual's *response-hierarchy* has been conceptualized by Hull and other experimental learning theorists as a function of past conditioning (Hull, 1943; Dollard and Miller, 1950; Spence, 1956). Each response in the hierarchy can be thought of as having a certain strength, based on its past history of reinforcement. The flexibility and variability exhibited by an individual in his everyday behavior can be conceptualized as a statement about his response-hierarchy; if one response is inhibited or not elicited in a particular situation, the next strongest one may be exhibited. Thus the analysis of behavior in any situation must consider all the stimuli in the environment capable of evoking alternative responses in the individual's behavior repertoire. Behavior modification often involves not only the extinguishing of undesired responses, but the establishment of alternative responses which are desired (Bandura, 1969a).

Many learning theorists have come to accept the notion that internal processes mediate between external stimuli and overt responses. S–R associational theorists have extended the notion of behavior chains to explain these internal mediating responses, speaking of external stimuli

(S) evoking internal responses (r), which in turn act as stimulation (s) for further overt responses (R):

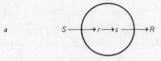

An extension of this simple example is the principle that a number of perceptually different stimuli may, through conditioning, evoke the same internal mediator response:

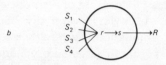

This model can, of course, be expanded by bringing in several mediator-chains (multiple r's) and adding more internal implicit stimuli (s's).

For the S–R theorists the basic laws that govern single-stage S–R processes apply equally well to mediational models (Osgood, 1953, 1956; Kendler and Kendler, 1968). Osgood (1953), for example, offers a simple additive conditioning rule to describe the central integration between external stimuli, internal response–stimuli, and overt responses.

In a somewhat later paper Osgood (1956) describes the first internal mediating stage as the *decoding* of external stimuli into internal symbolic responses, and a similar outputing process as *encoding* a multiplicity of internal stimulations into an external response. It should be made clear that his model is not a decision-making or information-processing one; each stage is itself an S–R process associational chain. Osgood's research with the semantic differential may be viewed as an attempt to establish empirically how mediators are attached to verbal stimuli.

Let me illustrate the mediational approach through a behavioral model of attitude formation and change based on the notions of concept formation, mediated generalization, and response chains. Lott (1955), following an earlier theoretical discussion of Doob (1947), viewed *attitudes* as mediators of responses. Her well-controlled laboratory study of the principle of *mediated generalization* showed that two stimuli that differ from one another in all relevant ways can evoke the same response when children are taught to attach the same *verbal* label to them.

Arthur Staats and his associates (1967) have carried out research on attitudes acquired through higher-order conditioning. Their research demonstrates that words can act as mediators. The meanings of words are, of course, themselves conditioned responses (Staats and Staats, 1963).

This body of research shows that the emotional meanings evoked by these words can be attached to formally neutral stimuli.

The studies mentioned deal with relatively simple attitudes. Fishbein (1967) recently has presented a suggestive theoretical model of complex "belief-attitude" systems based on the notion of the habit-family or hierarchy of responses. Influenced by Rhine's (1958) interpretation of Osgood's schema of attitudes, Fishbein's model of an attitude-system involves a hierarchy of concepts and affective reactions. Figure 5.1(a) represents several stimuli conditioned to a common mediating response. This system of associations between the stimuli and the common mediating process is called a "concept."

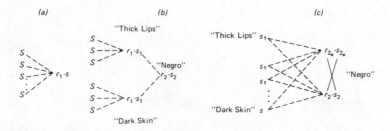

Figure 5–1.

A more complex, or second-order, "concept" is represented by Figure 5–1(b). Each set of stimuli produces first-order concepts. The stimuli produced by the first-order mediators are themselves associated with still another common mediator.

One set of first-order stimuli might be different skin shades leading to a mediator representing "dark skin." The second set of first-order stimuli might be various lip thicknesses associated with the mediator "thick lips." Each of these mediators might, in turn, be associated with the second-order mediator, "Negro."

Concepts alone do not constitute an attitude system; evaluative as well as cognitive elements are also necessary (Fishbein, 1962). In Figure 5–1(a), then, each first-order stimulus of various skin shades evoking the concept "dark skin" also elicits an *evaluative* reaction. It is these affective elements (often measured as pro–con, like–dislike, favor–oppose) that give an emotional quality to attitudes. For a prejudiced person the concept NEGRO may be associated through learning with beliefs that those signified by this term are dirty, evil, or violent, and these beliefs in turn arouse a host of anxiety and fear reactions. Thus a more complete representation of the attitude system associated with these original stimuli is Figure 5–1(c), in which the concept NEGRO contains two components—the cognitive mediator (r_2–s_2) and an evaluative mediator (r_{2_e}–s_{2_e}) made up of the summated product of evaluators from the first-order concepts. So far we have included in the attitude-system only those mediators evoked by the original external input stimuli. Through conditioning, however, an individual has many mediators (beliefs) associated with a concept, and the evaluations linked to these beliefs also become attached to the concept, even though they are not part of the current external stimuli input. This set of added mediators is represented by Figure 5–2(a). An individual's total attitudinal system, then, contains both mediated concepts resulting from external stimuli and those associated with the mediators because of previous conditioning. This is represented by Figure 5–2(b), in which the mediators are analytically separated into their cognitive and evaluative components.

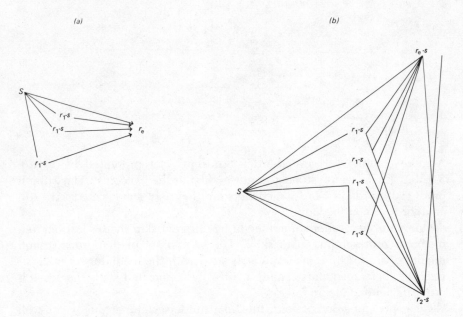

Figure 5–2. A Model of the Relation Between Belief About and Attitude Toward an Object (S = the stimulus, i.e., attitude object; r_1 = first-order mediators elicited by S, indicating belief r, about S; r_e = an evaluative mediator; r_2 = a second-order mediator.)

Fishbein has developed a quantitative set of rules for algebraically predicting an individual's evaluative response to any object. The equation involves summing all his beliefs about the object and the evaluative aspects of these beliefs.

To summarize, attitude formation may be viewed as a conceptual mediating process. Once the concept has been formed, however, different objects, values, beliefs, and other concepts become associated with the object of the attitude. Each of these associated responses also evokes still other mediators. This entire set of implicit responses associated with the attitude-object may be viewed as a complex habit-family or hierarchy of responses. According to this model, attitude change can occur by the addition or subtraction of mediators or by a change in the evaluative responses of existing mediators.

Personality traits may also be interpreted in behavioral terms as examples of mediators that render classes of situations and behaviors equivalent. When we say, for example, that a person has an "inferiority complex," we mean that he perceives any competitive situation as a threat, which he then responds to by such characteristic classes of behavior as avoidance, talking "big," compensating with some other activity, and so on.

The problem with this conception is that it is too simple. Most individuals possess response-hierarchies that are much more responsive to situational cues than trait theory assumes. Also, the reinforcement conditions within each situation vary widely and thus determine which one of the several available responses will be elicited. In sum, trait theory posits a much less complex organism than does social learning theory, in spite of the current popular contrary conception.

Hypothesis-Testing Theories

Associational theories picture learning as a passive, somewhat automatic stamping in of connections between stimulus events and responses through differential reinforcements and contiguity. In contrast, a second line of mediational theorizing pictures the individual as an active participant in the learning process. In this type of theory the learner does much more than merely register incoming information. Instead, it is assumed that he is constantly entertaining some hypothesis about what stimuli in the situation are reinforcing. Consequently he may not respond to all available stimuli in the situation, but instead attend only to those stimuli that are relevant to his hypothesis. Nor does he emit responses only on the basis of previous conditioning. Instead he executes a response which best serves as a test of a hypothesis's adequacy. Each learning trial thus provides an opportunity to test a current hypothesis. Eventually he hits on the correct hypothesis and solves the problem confronting him. These procedures allow the quick, sometimes single-trial development of a learning solution if the hypothesis can be "proved" at once. From this theoretical perspective, learning does not involve merely S–R associations, but rather acquisition of knowledge, recognition, and the "understanding" of a prin ciple required by a task (Bruner, Goodnow, and Austin, 1965; Hovland and Hunt, 1960; Restle, 1962; Bourne, 1966).

SYMBOLIC MEDIATION PROCESSES

Human beings continually engage in self-evaluation and self-reinforcing behaviors. In social-learning language, the individual's own reactions become stimuli in behavior chains or response hierarchies. People set themselves certain standards and self-administer rewarding or punishing consequences depending on whether their performance meets their self-prescribed demands. The reinforcers may be tangible or secondary, such as self-praise or depreciation.

Although there are important interpretative differences in the mechanisms involved (see Bandura, 1969a; 1969b, 32–38; Gewirtz, 1969; Aronfreed, 1969), it seems clear that self-reinforcing responses are to some extent first directly established through selective reinforcements administered initially by socialization agents. In this learning process an agent adopts a criterion of what constitutes a worthy performance and consistently rewards persons for matching or exceeding the adopted standard, while performances that fall short of it are non-rewarded or punished.

Through selective reinforcement, differential achievement levels assume positive and negative values. Eventually, through the process of concept formation (Bourne, 1966), the performance standards common to the various activities are abstracted and applied to new endeavors.

At this stage the whole process becomes relatively independent of external reinforcements and the specific contingencies of the original training situation. Internal stimuli can be self-generated that in turn evoke varieties of emotional reactions, such as anxiety or pleasure.

A substantial body of evidence (see Bandura, 1969a, 32–38) demonstrates that modeling processes are influential in the transmission of self-reinforcement patterns. These studies show that people adopt the standards for self-reinforcement exhibited by exemplary models and employ these standards in judging and reinforceing their own subsequent behavior.

These findings illustrate how self-evaluative processes such as self-esteem and self-concept can be conceptualized within a social-learning framework. From this perspective, a negative self-concept may be attributed to a high frequency of negative self-reinforcements: conversely, a relatively high incidence of positive self-reinforcement will result in a favorable self-concept (Marston, 1965).

In summary, we now see that a modern conception of learning involves much more than the simple external stimulus control models advocated by the early behaviorists. It is clear that if we extend our notion of reinforcers to encompass higher-order conditioned stimuli and incentives, and our notion of learning to include vicarious as well as direct experiences, that many responses fall under external stimulus control. Enriched conceptions of learning go beyond the S–R associational mechanisms, however, and place a great deal of attention on higher-order cognitive processes. What differentiates these formulations from earlier state-trait approaches is their emphasis on systematic theory and rigorous empirical testing through experimentation.

Stimulus Generalization and Discrimination

Stimulus generalization refers to the phenomenon whereby a response conditioned to one particular stimulus is also emitted in the presence of similar stimuli. (See Riley, 1968; Kimble, 1961; and Terrace, 1966, for reviews of the more traditional learning literature.)

Stimulus generalization plays an important role in human behavior because, in a strict sense, we seldom experience the same stimuli in exactly the same way. It is assumed that the response is emitted because the new stimulus contains some feature in common with the stimulus that acquired control over the response in the original acquisition process. Thus, through primary and higher-order conditioning, many so-called "neurotic" behavior patterns characterized by aversive emotional reactions and avoidance responses come to be associated with diverse stimuli that were previously neutral. Likewise, other stimuli that share components of the conditioned stimuli may, through generalization, come to evoke similar reactions.

The key question, of course, is what defines *similarity*. A considerable amount of laboratory research has been done on this issue. Research on physical similarities usually produce roughly bell-shaped *gradients of generalization*. The shape of the curve can be modified by *discrimination learning,* which occurs when responses to particular stimuli are selectively reinforced. Discrimination learning can occur when the organism is not reinforced for responses in the absence of the original stimulus, in the presence of stimuli that vary in salient features from the original cue stimulus, or when he is reinforced for *not* responding to these different stimuli.

Generalization also takes place along nonphysical dimensions. A substantial research literature shows that *mediated* generalization occurs along semantically related dimensions (Feather, 1965; Staats and Staats, 1963).

The concepts of generalization and discriminations are of major importance in any analysis of social behavior. A basic principle of social-learning theory is stimulus control, which assumes that specific responses are associated with discriminative stimuli and certain reinforcers. If behavior depends on specific situational stimuli, as trait proponents have come to acknowledge (Borgatta, 1968), then the factors that affect discrimination and generalization must be considered when we attempt to explain and predict behavior on the basis of previous socialization. That is, it is not enough to know that an individual was socialized to perform a certain way in certain situations. We must also know whether he was exposed to conditions that maximize, minimize, or otherwise affect how these learnings generalize to other situations (Terrace, 1966).

AGGRESSIVE BEHAVIOR, A SOCIAL-LEARNING INTERPRETATION

Up to now we have examined a number of basic principles that a social-learning theorist would employ in his analysis of socialization. It seems useful to review in somewhat greater depth how these principles govern the social behavior of human beings in complex social settings. The determinants of aggressive behavior seem an appropriate example, as it is a topic directly germane to the interests of political scientists that has been well researched by learning theorists. As political scientists we devote a large amount of attention to problems related to war and conflict, thus our conception of the fundamental determinants of aggressive behavior can profoundly affect our theorizing about political structures and processes. This topic also provides a nice example of a behavior area in which state-trait theory conceptions have been supplanted (or substantially modified) by the research findings of social-learning theorists.

Until recently most theorizing about aggression has been heavily influenced by the frustration–aggression hypothesis (Berkowitz, 1962; Yates, 1962). Formalizing to some extent Freud's early views on the psychodynamics of pleasure-seeking or pain-avoiding behavior that is thwarted, this hypothesis in its initial form depicts frustration as the inevitable antecedent of aggression, regarding aggression as the dominant unlearned response to frustration. Many researchers have pursued this hypothesis by searching for the roots of aggressive behavior in a wide range of personally and socially frustrating circumstances such as broken homes, adverse socioeconomic conditions, urbanization, and frustrated mobility strivings (Berkowitz, 1962, 1969).

Drive theories of aggression assume that frustration arouses an aggressive impulse or drive that can be reduced only through some form of aggressive behavior. From a social-learning perspective, however, frustration is regarded as a facilitative rather than a necessary condition for aggression. That is, frustration produces a general state of emotional arousal that may lead to a variety of responses depending upon (1) the type of frustration reactions that have been previously learned, and (2) the reinforcing consequences typically associated with different courses of action (Bandura, 1969a, 381).

As Lawson (1965) has sketched out, the concept of *frustration* has undergone substantial changes in recent years as it has been translated from the vernacular to a scientific construct. This redefinition and refinement occurred under the impetus of a wide variety of experimental work. Frustration was reconceptualized by modern learning theorists as they recognized that the independent conditions and resultant actions associated with frustration could be well-integrated into general behavior theory (Brown and Farber, 1951; Brown, 1961; Brown and Farber, 1968; Amsel, 1962).

For present purposes we can employ Brown's common-language definition (1961) that "frustration" occurs "when stimuli normally capable of eliciting a response are present, but the response is prevented from running its usual course." The consequence of this delay or frustration is a state of emotional arousal, which acts as a facilitator or energizer of other responses. (See Brown, 1961, Ch. 2, and Brown and Farber, 1968, for the necessary operational definitions of what "energize" means when rigorously specified by experimental psychologists.)

Although theories of personality and psychotherapy generally differentiate among types of emotional states, as if the states represent distinct forms of physiological arousal, recent research fails to support this belief. Physiological studies show that although people may report varied emotional conditions, their phenomenological experiences are not accompanied by corresponding distinctive physiological reactions.

Reviewing these findings, in which there seems to be at best only small differences in physiological indicators, Bandura (1969a) concludes

> Results of both physiological and psychological studies support the conclusion that a common diffuse state of physiological arousal mediates diverse forms of emotional behavior and that different emotional states are identified and discriminated primarily in terms of external stimuli rather than internal somatic cues (488).

Research by Schachter (1964) and his associates (Schachter and Singer, 1962; Schachter and Wheeler, 1962; Nisbett and Schachter, 1966) demonstrates that emotional states are partly a function of the degree of physiological arousal but that social and cognitive variables may play a crucial role in determining both the nature and intensity of emotions experienced, especially when individuals cannot accurately label the source of their aroused condition. It has been shown that the same state of physiological arousal can be experienced as euphoria, anger, or some other type of emotional condition depending upon an individual's own defining cognitions and the affective reactions of others around him (modeling effect).

Perhaps the most persuasive demonstration of the powerful interrelationships between external conditions and physiologically based reactions is the experiment by Delgado (1967) employing electrical stimulation of a primate's hypothalamus to induce emotional arousal. When a monkey who occupies a dominant role in the colony receives thalamic stimulation, he is instigated to attack subordinate male members. But when the same monkey is placed in a colony in which he is of low rank, the same thalamic stimulation produces cowering and submissive behavior. Thus, the electrical stimulation of the same cerebral mechanism evokes radically different behavior in the same animal as his social rank changes.

Over-all, it seems clear, there is little evidence for one distinctive state of physiological arousal corresponding to "frustration." Thus we would be well advised to characterize emotional states associated with frustrations as *energizers* rather than *channelizers* of behavior (Brown and Farber, 1968).

The type of response to any particular arousal state depends on the prior social training of the aroused subject, and the reinforcement consequences of response patterns currently dominant in the subject's response-hierarchy.

Learning response patterns. In the course of development a child can acquire responses and skills under nonfrustrating circumstances that could be labelled aggressive when directed against someone. A father encourages his son to use a large stick to hit a baseball with vigor; military recruits acquire and perfect combat skills in training camp; hunters acquire shooting skills by target practice. Much of what is characterized as aggression thus involves the execution of learned response patterns.

Positive reinforcement of aggression. A study by Walters and Brown (1963) showed that boys who were earlier reinforced intermittently for punching a doll exhibited later, in a natural-life situation, more physically aggressive behavior toward other children than did control subjects. Field studies summarized in Bandura and Walters (1963), found that the parents of boys who are normally aggressive outside the home are inclined to encourage this kind of behavior and condone aggression. The positive and negative reinforcers contained in peer responses have also been found to affect the incidence of aggressive acts in children.

Experimental studies have also shown that the *schedule of reinforcement* affects the performance of aggressive responses in natural environments, as well as a *generalization effect* from verbal to nonverbal behaviors (Bandura and Walters, 1963, Ch. 3).

To summarize, the influence of positive reinforcements on the acquisition and maintenance of aggressive behavior has been investigated in a number of studies. It has been demonstrated that positive reinforcements in the form of verbal approval or material rewards will increase the frequency of children's aggressive responses; that reinforcement of one class of aggressive responses may result in an increment in another class of aggressive responses; and that the effects of rewarding aggression in relatively impersonal play situations are transferred to new social situations in which interpersonal aggression may be displayed.

It should not be forgotten that aggressive acts often have a utilitarian value that reinforces their performance. Through dominance by physical or verbal means the individual can obtain material resources, gain control over others, terminate provocation, and remove barriers that block the attainment of desired goals.

Thus aggressive behavior patterns can be acquired and maintained simply because they are instrumental in obtaining rewards and not only because of some aroused emotional state.

Modeling of aggression. A substantial body of evidence shows that novel modes of aggressive behavior are readily acquired through observation of aggressive models. Models have also been shown to have inhibitory and disinhibitory effects on the performance of previously learned behavior patterns, including aggressive acts (Bandura, 1969a; Bandura and Walters, 1963). The parent, for example, who uses physical punishment as a disciplinary technique thereby models for his children the appropriateness of striking someone when angry.

Punishment and inhibition. A considerable amount of theoretical and experimental efforts has been devoted to exploring the effects of punishment as a reinforcer for learning (Millenson, 1967, Ch. 17; Church, 1963; Solomon, 1964; Bandura, 1969a, 295–317). The effects of punishment are quite complex, with the degree of control over behavior in any particular case highly dependent upon a host of other operant variables, in addition to the situational punishment contingencies (Logan and Wagner, 1965). It is clear that aversive reinforcers may inhibit a particular response, although even there the permanence is a function of other factors (see Bandura, 1969a).

Punishment by an authority figure has a significant effect on child development. Direct aggression in the presence of the punitive agent is inhibited, but highly aggressive responses are channelled toward other possible targets (Bandura and Walters, 1963, 182–203). The psychoanalytically oriented literature on scapegoating and prejudice (such as *The Authoritarian Personality*) has often explained this kind of phenomenon through the mechanism of displacement. An alternative learning interpretation has been proposed by Neal Miller, based on his general approach–avoidance conflict model (Miller, 1948, 1959; Dollard and

Miller, 1950), which is used to predict toward whom an individual will aggress.

The basic variables determining whether an individual will be aggressed against are the negative and positive consequences that will follow the aggression. In this formulation, *displacement* results from counteracting forces of excitation and inhibition. While the parent may, through his actions, spur an aggressive response in the child (*excitation*), the parent's punishment of expressions of aggression directed towards him forces the child to inhibit these responses. Because the net inhibitory forces are likely to be greater than the excitation forces, the child will not exhibit his anger towards the parent.

The concept of excitatory and inhibitory forces has often been employed in traditional learning psychology and has even been quantified in performance equations (Hull, 1943; Spence, 1963). A second key learning principle Miller introduced into his model is the principle of *stimulus generalization*. We thus would postulate that both the inhibitory fear or anxiety responses and the aggressive excitation responses with which they compete, *generalize* to other people who share characteristics with the parent. We therefore can generate *gradients of generalization* for excitatory and inhibitory forces as a function of the extent to which that particular individual stimulates such reactions for the child.

The key assumption of Miller's model is that inhibitory tendencies have a narrower range of generalization than the responses they inhibit (Miller has confirmed this in a number of experiments). Consequently, at some point on the stimulus dissimilarity continuum the ratio of excitation to aggression over inhibitory tendencies is greatest. This is the individual ("Boy") toward whom aggression is directed (see Figure 5–3).

Although suggestive, this model is theoretically inadequate because it does not include a number of factors that substantially influence social

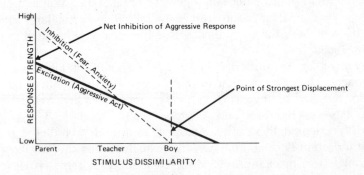

Figure 5–3. Displacement Model of Aggression (After Miller)

behavior. According to Miller's model, the objects and the strengths of displaced aggressive responses are a function of only three variables: strength of instigation, severity of punishment, and a stimulus-similarity dimension.

From a social-learning perspective the formulation must also consider the following:

1. Specifications of the extent of frustration-arousal, and the punitiveness of the primary socialization agents.

2. The hierarchy of frustration responses besides aggression: Some people when thwarted become dependent, others withdraw and resign themselves to their fate, some engage in drinking, and some intensively labor to overcome the obstacles they face.

3. The model effects of parents, teachers, peers, and relevant others when they both aggress against others and find alternative models of reaction to displace aggression.

4. The reward-punishment contingencies of the situation, that is, the likely consequences of engaging in aggressive behavior against different objects.

Again, this is not the place to argue the advantages and disadvantages of the Miller model in comparison with some alternative formulation. It should be clear, however, that the simple trait notion that people can be easily classified as aggressive or nonaggressive is terribly inadequate. The aggressive behavior that a person exhibits is determined by an interaction between situational stimuli, reinforcement contingencies, and their own response-hierarchies. Furthermore, the extent to which aggressive behavior is determined by learning variables rather than the inevitable consequence of frustration should also lead us to examine more closely those cultural and structural factors in our society that serve to model and reinforce aggression.

CONCLUDING REMARKS

In this chapter we have examined a number of basic learning principles. The process of social influence can be conceptualized as a special case of learning wherein all the relevant conditioning stimuli emanate from the behavior of other persons. The section on susceptibility to models contains the basic ingredients to account for group influence. The capacity of a group to elicit conformity is primarily determined by this ability to reinforce desired behaviors, compared to rewards available from alternative sources. The degree of influence parents exert over their children is simply a reflection of the almost exclusive control they have in dispensing reward and punishment. As the child grows older, however, alternative sources of reinforcement from peers and other associates become increasing available and thus the influence of the parents decreases.

A *stimulus sampling model,* taken from discriminant learning, should be mentioned as a way to operationalize the estimation of significant social-influence sources. This model, derived from the mathematical formulation of Trabasso and Bower (1963), posits that the individual is most likely to be influenced by messages that are noticeable and associated with important positive and negative reinforcers.

I believe that most of the basic findings in recent political socialization studies can be interpreted by social-learning theory and that social-learning processes can provide important guidance to our future research.

In closing, then, I would like to reiterate the goal of this chapter: The study of political socialization can be enhanced by consciously adopting a social-learning theory approach utilizing the latest theorizing and research findings of academic psychology. Modern learning theory has much more to offer the student of human behavior than the basic principles of classical and instrumental conditioning. As we have seen, contemporary behavior theory employs more numerous and varied principles, such as higher-order conditioning, complex S–R chains, socially derived incentives and secondary reinforcers, and mediational processes. Furthermore, new response patterns can be acquired and existing ones strengthened or weakened, not only by direct personal experiences but also through observation and written or verbal instructions. In sum, the methodology and substantive principles of modern social-learning theory seem capable of generating forceful explanatory schemes for studying the functional relationships between the antecedent conditions to which an individual has been exposed and his subsequent political behavior.

REFERENCES

Adorno, T. W., E. Frankel-Brunswik, D. J. Levinson, and T. N. Sanford. *The Authoritarian Personality* (New York: Harper, 1950).

Almond, C., and S. Verba. *The Civic Culture* (Princeton: Princeton University Press, 1963).

Amsel, A. "Frustrated nonreward in partial reinforcement and discrimination Learning: Some recent history and theoretical extension," *Psychological Review* 69 (1962), 306–28.

Appley, M. R. "Derived motives," *Annual Review of Psychology* 21 (1970), 485–518.

Aronfreed, J. "The concept of internalization," in D. A. Goslin (ed.), *Handbook of Socialization Theory and Research* (Chicago: Rand McNally, 1969).

Aronson, E., and J. M. Carlsmith. "Experimentation in social psychology," in G. Lindzey and E. Aronson (eds.), *The Handbook of Social Psychology,* second ed. (Reading, Massachusetts: Addison-Wesley, 1969).

Atkinson, G. H., G. H. Bower, and J. Crothers. *An Introduction to Mathematical Learning Theory* (New York: Wiley, 1965).

Baldwin, A. L. *Theories of Child Development* (New York: Wiley, 1968).

Bandura, A. "Influence of models' reinforcement contingencies on the acquisition of imitative responses," *Journal of Personality and Social Psychology* 1 (1965), 589–95.

―――. *Principles of Behavior Modification* (New York: Holt, Rinehart, Winston: 1969*a*).

―――. "Social-learning theory of identificatory processes," in D. A. Goslin (ed.), *Handbook of Socialization Theory and Research* (Chicago: Rand McNally, 1969*b*).

―――, and W. Miscel. "Modification of self-imposed delay of reward through exposure to live and symbolic models," *Journal of Personality and Social Psychology* 2 (1965), 698–705.

―――, and R. H. Walters. *Social Learning and Personality Development* (New York: Holt, Rinehart, and Winston, 1963).

Berger, S. M., and W. W. Lambert. "Stimulus-response theory in contemporary social psychology," in G. Lindzey and E. Aronson (eds.), *The Handbook of Social Psychology,* second ed. (Reading, Mass.: Addison-Wesley, 1969).

Berkowitz, L. *Aggression: A Social Psychological Analysis* (New York: McGraw-Hill, 1962).

―――. "Control of aggression," in B. M. Caldwell and H. Ricciuti (eds.), *Review of Child Development Research* 3 (New York: Russell Sage Foundation, 1969).

Berlyne, D. W. *Structure and Direction in Thinking* (New York: Wiley, 1965).

―――. "Behavior theory as personality theory," in E. F. Borgatta and W. W. Lambert (eds.), *Handbook of Personality Theory and Research* (Chicago: Rand McNally, 1968).

Bijou, S. W., and D. M. Baer. *Child Development, Vol. 1; A Systematic and Empirical Theory* (New York: Appleton-Century-Crofts, 1961).

Black, R. W. "Shifts in magnitude of reward and contrast effects in instrumental and selective learning: A reinterpretation," *Psychological Review* 75 (1968), 114–26.

Borgatta, E. G. "Traits and persons," in E. F. Borgatta and W. W. Lambert (eds.), *Handbook of Personality Theory and Research* (Chicago: Rand McNally, 1968).

Bourne, L. E. *Human Conceptual Behavior* (Boston: Allyn & Bacon, 1966).

Brim, O. G., and S. Wheeler. *Socialization After Childhood* (New York: Wiley, 1966).

Bronfenbrenner, U. "Soviet methods of character education: Some implications for research," *American Psychologist* 17 (1962), 550–64.

Brown, J. S. *The Motivation of Behavior* (New York: McGraw-Hill, 1961).

————, and I. E. Farber. "Emotions conceptualized as intervening variables with suggestions toward a theory of frustration," *Psychological Bulletin* 48 (1951), 456–95.

————. "Secondary motivational systems," *Annual Review of Psychology* 19 (1968), 99–134.

Bruner, J. S., J. J. Goodnow, and G. A. Austin. *A Study of Thinking* (New York: Wiley, 1956).

Campbell, D. T. "Social attitudes and other acquired behavioral dispositions," in S. Koch (ed.), *Psychology: A Study of a Science, Vol. 6* (New York: McGraw-Hill, 1960).

Cattell, R. B. *The Scientific Analysis of Personality* (Chicago: Aldine, 1965).

Child, I. L. "Socialization," in G. Lindzey (ed.), *The Handbook of Social Psychology* (Cambridge, Massachusetts: Addison-Wesley, 1954).

Church, R. M. "Varied effects of punishment on behavior," *Psychological Review* 70 (1963), 369–402.

Cofer, C. N., and H. M. Appley. *Motivation: Theory and Research* (New York: Wiley, 1964).

Cronbach, L. J. *Essentials of Psychological Testing,* third ed. (New York: Harper & Row, 1969).

Dawson, R. E. "Political socialization," in J. A. Robinson (ed.), *Political Science Annual: Vol. 1* (Indianapolis: Bobbs-Merrill, 1966).

————, and K. Prewitt. *Political Socialization* (Boston: Little, Brown, 1969).

Delgado, J. M. "Social rank and radio-stimulated aggression in monkeys," *Journal of Nervous and Mental Disease* 144 (1967), 383–90.

Dollard, J., and N. E. Miller. *Personality and Psychotherapy* (New York: McGraw-Hill, 1950).

Doob, L. W. "The behavior of attitudes," *Psychological Review* 54 (1947), 135–56.

Easton, D., and J. Dennis. *Children in the Political System* (New York: McGraw-Hill, 1969).

Edwards, W. "Behavioral decision theory," *Annual Review of Psychology* 12 (1961), 473–98.

Feather, B. W. "Semantic generalization of classically conditional responses: A review," *Psychological Bulletin* 63 (1965), 425–41.

Ferster, C. B., and B. F. Skinner. *Schedules of Reinforcement* (New York: Appleton-Century, 1957).

Fishbein, M. "A behavior theory approach to the relations between beliefs about an object and the attitude toward the object," in M. Fishbein (ed.), *Readings in Attitude Theory and Measurement* (New York: Wilcy, 1967).

Greene, J. B. *Elementary Theoretical Psychology* (Reading, Massachusetts: Addison-Wesley, 1968).

Gewirtz, J. L. "Mechanisms of social learning: some roles of stimulation and behavior in early development," in D. A. Goslin (ed.), *Handbook of Socialization Theory and Research* (Chicago: Rand McNally, 1969).

Greenstein, F. I. *Children and Politics* (New Haven: Yale University Press, 1965).

———. "Political Socialization," in *International Encyclopedia of the Social Sciences* (New York: Crowell Collier, 1968).

Hase, H. D., and L. R. Goldberg. "Comparative validity of different strategies of constructing personality inventory scales," *Psychological Bulletin* 67 (1967), 231–48.

Hill, W. F. "Learning theory and the acquisition of values," *Psychological Review* 67 (1960), 317–31.

Hovland, C. I., and E. B. Hunt. "Computer simulation of concept attainment," *Behavioral Science* 5 (1960), 265–67.

Hull, C. S. *Principles of Behavior* (New York: Appleton-Century-Crofts, 1943).

Hunt, J. McV. "Traditional personality theory in the light of recent evidence," *American Scientist* 53 (1965), 80–96.

Jaros, D. "Children's orientation toward the President: Some additional theoretical considerations and data," *Journal of Politics* 29 (1967), 368–87.

Jenness, A. "Personality dynamics," *Annual Review of Psychology* 13 (1962), 295–322.

Kendler, H. H., and T. Kendler. "Mediation and conceptual behavior," in K. W. Spence and J. T. Spence (eds.), *The Psychology of Learning and Motivation: Advances in Research and Theory, Vol. II* (New York: Academic Press, 1968).

Kimble, C. A. *Hilgard and Marquis Conditioning and Learning* (New York: Appleton-Century-Crofts, 1961).

Langton, K. P. *Political Socialization* (New York: Oxford University Press, 1969).

Lasswell, H. *Psychopathology and Politics* (Chicago: University of Chicago Press, 1930).

———. *Power and Personality* (New York: Norton, 1948).

Lawson, R. *Frustration: The Development of a Scientific Concept* (New York: Macmillan, 1965).

Logan, F. A., and A. R. Wagner. *Reward and Punishment* (Boston: Allyn & Bacon, 1965).

Lott, B. E. "Attitude formation: The development of color-preference responses through mediated generalization," *Journal of Abnormal and Social Psychology* 50 (1955), 321–26.

Lovaas, O. I. "Cue properties of words: The control of operant responding by rate and content of verbal operants," *Child Development* 35 (1964), 245–56.

Maddi, S. R. *Personality Theories: A Comparative Analysis* (Homewood, Ill.: Dorsey, 1968).

Marston, A. R. "Self-reinforcement: The relevance of a concept in analogue research in psychotheraphy," *Psychotherapy: Theory, Research and Practice* 2 (1965), 1–5.

McGuire, W. J. "The nature of attitudes and attitude change," in G. Lindzey and E. Aronson (eds.), *The Handbook of Social Psychology*, second ed. (Reading, Massachusetts: Addison-Wesley, 1969).

Millenson, J. R. *Principles of Behavioral Analysis* (New York: Macmillan, 1967).

Miller, N. E. "Liberalization of basic S-R concepts: Extensions to conflict behavior, motivation, and social learning," in S. Koch (ed.), *Psychology: A Study of a Science, Vol. 2* (New York: McGraw-Hill, 1959).

————. "Studies of fear as an acquirable drive: I. Fear as motivation and fear-reduction as reinforcement in the learning of new responses," *Journal of Experimental Psychology* 38 (1948a), 89–101.

————. "Theory and experiment relating psychoanalytic displacement to stimulus-response generalization," *Journal of Abnormal and Social Psychology* 43 (1948b), 155–78.

————, and J. Dollard. *Social Learning and Imitation* (New Haven: Yale University Press, 1941).

Mischel, W. *Personality and Assessment* (New York: Wiley, 1968).

————, and J. Grusec. "Waiting for rewards and punishments: Effects of time and probability on choice," *Journal of Personality and Social Psychology* 5 (1967), 24–31.

Mussen, P. H. *Handbook of Research Methods in Child Development* (New York: Wiley, 1960).

Nisbett, R. E., and S. Schachter. "Cognitive manipulation of pain," *Journal of Experimental Social Psychology* 2 (1966), 227–36.

Osgood, C. E. "Behavior theory and the social sciences," *Behavioral Science* 1 (1956), 167–85.

————. *Method and Theory in Experimental Psychology* (New York: Oxford, 1953).

Premack, D. "Reinforcement theory," in D. Levin (ed.), *Nebraska Symposium on Motivation* (Lincoln: University of Nebraska Press, 1965).

Pye, L. W. *Politics, Personality, and Nation Building* (New Haven: Yale University Press, 1962).

Restle, F. "The selection of strategies in cue learning," *Psychological Review* 69 (1962), 329–43.

————, and J. G. Greene. *Introduction to Mathematical Psychology* (Reading, Massachusetts: Addison-Wesley, 1970).

Rhine, R. J. "A concept-formation approach to attitude acquisition," *Psychological Review* 65 (1958), 362–70.

Riley, D. A. *Discrimination Learning* (Boston: Allyn & Bacon, 1968).

Rosenthal, R., and R. L. Rosnow (eds.). *Artifacts in Behavioral Research* (New York: Academic Press, 1969).

Rosnow, R. L. "When he lends a helping hand, bite it," *Psychology Today* 4 (1970), 26–30.

Sanford, N. "Personality: Its place in psychology," in S. Koch (ed.), *Psychology: A Study of a Science.* Vol. 5 (New York: McGraw-Hill, 1963).

Schachter, S. "The interaction of cognitive and physiological determinants of emotional states," in L. Berkowitz (ed.), *Advances in Experimental Social Psychology, Vol. I* (New York: Academic Press, 1964).

————, and J. E. Singer. "Cognitive, social, and physiological determinants of emotional states," *Psychological Review* 69 (1962), 379–99.

————, and L. Wheeler. "Epinephrine, chlorpromazine, and amusement," *Journal of Abnormal and Social Psychology* 65 (1962), 121–28.

Scott, W. A. "Attitude measurement," in G. Lindzey and E. Aronson (eds.), *The Handbook of Social Psychology,* second ed. (Reading, Massachusetts: Addison-Wesley, 1969).

Sewell, W. H. "Some recent developments in socialization theory and research," *The Annals* 349 (1963), 163–81.

Sigel, R. "Assumptions about the learning of political values," *The Annals* 361 (1967), 1–9.

Solomon, R. L. "Punishment," *American Psychologist* 19 (1964), 239–53.

Spence, K. W. *Behavior Theory and Conditioning* (New Haven: Yale University Press, 1956).

Spiker, C. C. "Verbal factors in the discrimination learning of children," in J. C. Wright and J. Kagan (eds.), *Basic Cognitive Processes in Children* (Monograph, Society of Research in Child Development 2, 1963, 2b, whole No. 86).

Staats, A. W. "An outline of an integrated learning theory at attitude formation and function," in M. Fishbein (ed.), *Readings in Attitude Theory and Measurement* (New York: Wiley, 1967).

————, and C. K. Staats. *Complex Human Behavior* (New York: Holt, Rinehart, Winston, 1963).

Terrace, H. S. "Stimulus control," in W. K. Honig (ed.), *Operant Behavior: Areas of Research and Application* (New York: Appleton-Century-Crofts, 1966).

Trabasso, T., and G. H. Bower. *Attention in Learning* (New York: Wiley, 1964).

Vernon, P. E. *Personality Assessment: A Critical Survey* (New York: Wiley, 1964).

Walters, R. H., and M. Brown. "Studies of reinforcement of aggression: III. Transfer of responses to an interpersonal situation," *Child Development* 34 (1963), 563–72.

Weiss, R. F. "An extension of Hullian learning theory to persuasive communication," in A. G. Greenwall, T. B. Block, and T. M. Ostrom (eds.), *Psychological Foundations of Attitudes* (New York: Academic Press, 1968).

Wolfenstein, M., and G. Kliman (eds.). *Children and the Death of a President: Multi-Disciplinary Studies* (New York: Doubleday, 1965).

Wolpe, J. "The systematic desensitization treatment of neuroses," *Journal of Nervous and Mental Disease* 132 (1961), 189–203.

Yates, A. J. *Frustration and Conflict* (New York: Wiley, 1962).

Zeigler, E. "Metatheoretical issues in developmental psychology," in M. Marx (ed.), *Theories in Contemporary Psychology* (New York: Macmillan, 1963).

————, and I. L. Child. "Socialization," in G. Lindzey and E. Aronson (eds.), *The Handbook of Social Psychology*, second ed. (Reading, Massachusetts: Addison-Wesley, 1969).

Chapter Six

The Sources of Children's Political Concepts: An Application of Piaget's Theory

Norah Rosenau

INTRODUCTION

One of the major premises underlying this volume is that students of political socialization need to pay more attention to the processes by which socialization outcomes are generated in order to balance the almost exclusive concern to date with the outcomes themselves. As the editors suggest in Chapter One, we know a good deal by now about what is learned in the course of political socialization but not enough about how this learning occurs. To improve our understanding of the latter, they argue for the systematic application of well-developed psychological theories to the study of political socialization. This essay agrees with their premise and suggests in particular that Piaget's theory of cognitive development can be of substantial utility in understanding political socialization processes. This chapter argues for using a broad conceptualization of "political," summarizes some of the main points of Piaget's theory, and then examines some of the ways in which they have been and might be usefully applied to political socialization.

The political socialization literature generally views as political any learning that is concerned with the processes and institutions of government at any level. Some researchers take a broader view that includes learning about more general processes that underlie the institutional ones, such as authority, compliance, and loyalty. My position agrees with this broader view and treats such phenomena as leadership, influence, conflict, and conflict resolution as political, whether they occur in governmental settings or in families, classrooms, peer groups, and the like. It follows that the individual is encountering political phenomena virtually constantly at all ages and that the phenomena related to government and institutions are only a small and specialized aspect of the total political experience of any individual.

Learning can be considered to be the outcome of the interaction between two events, an environmental event and the individual's response to that event, including as response both overt and easily observable behavior and more covert or internal responses such as perception, cognition, and emotion. Political learning is the outcome of the interaction between a political event and the individual's responses to that event. Using this perspective, this essay identifies and discusses two major sources of political learning in the interactions of the growing individual with his environment: his interpersonal relationships developed in his daily experience in the family, peer group, classroom, and other social situations, and the information about the larger world of formal politics transmitted to him by adults. I attempt to show how, from the point of view of Piagetian theory, certain basic aspects of political learning are inherent in the child's adaptation to his social world, and how learning about the more formal and remote aspects of politics builds on this more basic learning. But first, it is necessary to provide a brief and selective overview of Piaget's concepts and generalizations about learning.

PIAGET'S THEORY OF INTELLECTUAL DEVELOPMENT

Piaget's interest in intellectual development grows out of his concern with how organisms adapt to their environments.[1] He considers all the activity of any organism as an aspect of its adaptation and views intelligence and intellectual functioning in this context (Piaget, 1952c). His stage theory of cognitive development is his answer to the question of how the simple reflexes of the newborn human individual eventually become the complex intellectual processes of the adolescent and adult. In order to survive and function, the individual must adapt to the environment, that is, he must both mold himself to the environment and mold the environment to his needs, and he must keep these two processes in some sort of equilibrium. Animals adapt through physical means. Human beings start out the same way, but their adaptation soon becomes primarily cognitive.

Cognitive processes, according to Piaget, are representations of events and experiences. These representations, which he calls schemas, enable the individual to organize the environment and his relationship to it and thus to deal with it, to adapt. Therefore, the nature of the individual's adaptation is determined by his experience with the environment, and it is only through such experience that cognitive development can occur. Cognitive development is a continuous cumulative process in which every step builds on what has come before. What the individual learns from a given

---

[1] The Piagetian concepts and theoretical statements that I draw on in the discussion that follows are spread over many of Piaget's separate works. For analyses and summaries of the Piagetian framework, see Flavell (1963), Piaget (1970), Piaget and Inhelder (1969).

experience is partly determined by how he represents and organizes that experience cognitively, but this depends on the schemas he has available to apply to the experience, which schemas are the products of prior experience. Piaget's theory of cognitive development deals with the systematic changes that cognitive structures, or schemas, undergo from birth to adulthood. Its major thesis is that they go through a fixed sequence of stages that are qualitatively different from each other but each of which is a restructuring of the prior one.

As I have indicated, Piaget sees intellectual functioning as an integral aspect of biological adaptation that encompasses three interrelated processes: assimilation, accommodation, and equilibration (Piaget, 1952c). Given a new input from the environment, the organism can react in either of two ways. It can change the input to fit existing schemas, or it can alter existing schemas to fit the input. The first process is assimilation, the second, accommodation. When the young child points to a cow and says "dog," he is assimilating the novel stimulus to his single existing schema for four-legged animals. Later, after accumulating experience with other varieties of four-legged animals, he incorporates variation into his cognitive structures; his schema for four-legged animals becomes elaborated and refined and differentiates among them. In other words, he accommodates his schema to experienced reality. According to Piaget, all learning, all cognitive change, occurs and can only occur through assimilation and accommodation. The goal is always assimilation, as after accommodation is completed there exists a new schema into which similar inputs will subsequently be assimilated. But a balance is maintained between the two processes so that neither dominates, and this balancing process is equilibration. The movement toward equilibrium between the two processes is not a static adjustment, not merely a balance of forces, but an active process of self-regulation that is an inherent part of adaptation.

In terms of Piaget's concepts, cognitive development occurs somewhat as follows. The newborn brings into the world two basic schemas that are his only tools for organizing environmental events and adapting to them, the reflexes of grasping and sucking. All stimuli encountered are indiscriminately assimilated to these two schemas. Gradually, as discrimination begins to develop, not everything that touches the infant's hand is grasped and only food stimuli are sucked. These are the first rudimentary accommodations, and through them new schemas develop. As maturation and experience proceed, and gradually language emerges, schemas become more complex, less physical, and intellectual adaptation becomes an internal process. But later cognitive structures are the cumulative products of earlier ones, having been produced by the continuing interaction between assimilation and accommodation. "If the child partly explains the adult, it can also be said that each period of his development partly explains the periods that follow. . . . Mental development during the first eighteen months of life is particularly important, for it is during this time that the child constructs all the cognitive substructures that will serve as a point of departure for his later perceptive and intellectual development . . ." (Piaget and Inhelder, 1969, 3).

Thus, the origins of cognition are in sensorimotor experience. Before he can represent the environment symbolically, the individual develops modes of adapting to it that are purely physical. These physical adaptations, or sensorimotor schemas, gradually become internalized as the organism's capacities evolve, so that they do not need to be acted out in full to accomplish their adaptive function. The ability to represent events and interactions symbolically takes a giant leap with the emergence of language around age two, and from that point on adaptation is primarily cognitive. The path from the toddler's rudimentary symbolizations and internalizations to mature thinking must still be traversed step by step. Piaget's stages of cognitive development are crystallizations of major distinctions in the quality, process, and content of thinking as it evolves through the individual's continuing adaptation.

Piaget has varied in his classification of the stages of cognitive development, but his work distinguishes among four periods, however they are classified: the sensorimotor stage, the preoperational stage, the stage of concrete operations, and the stage of formal operations (Piaget, 1950). Broadly and briefly summarized, the defining characteristics of these stages are as follows. During the sensorimotor stage, which lasts until about age two, behavior and adaptation, as already indicated, are primarily motor and there is not yet any ability for conceptual thought. During the preoperational stage, roughly from age two to age seven, language appears and develops rapidly, but the child's thought is still prelogical and dominated by egocentrism (discussed later). The stage of concrete operations lasts from about age seven to about age eleven, during which time the child develops the ability to use logic in relation to concrete problems. Finally, during the stage of formal operations, which lasts from about age eleven to age fifteen or so, the individual becomes capable of thinking logically about all kinds of problems, of reasoning from a hypothesis to its conclusions, and of thinking about thought itself and about abstract processes, not only about concrete phenomena.

Piaget considers the stages to be qualitatively distinct, but he sees development as continuous and the transitions from one stage to the next as gradual. The ages he indicates as the boundaries of the stages are offered only as general averages and the theory allows for considerable individual variation in the attainment of each stage. The invariant aspect of development, according to the Piagetian view, is the *sequence* of stages, so that an individual cannot attain one stage until he has traversed the prior one. The stage notion has been criticized on many grounds, a major one being that a single child may exhibit the characteristics of several different stages when his thinking is examined across different kinds of problems. For the purpose of drawing on Piaget's theory for its applicability to political learning, it seems unnecessary to take a position on this issue, as it is the logic of development represented in Piaget's theory that seems most relevant, which can be plotted without accepting or rejecting the stage notion in itself.

Cognitive development thus begins with sensorimotor adaptations that build on the simple responses of the newborn and gradually become increasingly internal and symbolic. As is true at any age, the child can directly experience only himself and his interactions with the environment. It is only after considerable development has occurred that the individual becomes capable of representing events that he has not experienced directly. Thus, early cognitive structures are limited to what the child experiences directly.

This quality of early thought is captured in part in Piaget's concept of egocentrism, by which he refers to the relative inability to anticipate, recognize, or understand experiences other than one's own. Illustrating this phenomenon in the physical realm, an experiment (Flavell, 1968) compared the ability of children of different ages, ranging from four to eleven, to predict how a scale model of three mountains would look from positions other than their own. There was a clear relationship between this ability and age. The young child sees his world and only his world and is not capable of mentally representing to himself how the world would look to someone else or from somewhere else. He is in a sense trapped by his perceptions, and reality is only and totally what he perceives.

A set of experiments (Flavell, 1968) demonstrated the nature of social egocentrism by asking second-grade and eighth-grade children to explain to a blindfolded experimenter, who listened without responding, how to play a simple two-person game that they had learned nonverbally. The younger children's descriptions were full of "these" and "here" and other such verbal references, which they often supported with physical gestures, but which could not be understood if these were not seen. This occurred even though the experimenter's inability to understand such references was made clear and salient for them. In contrast, the older children seemed able to imagine what it would be like not to see what they saw and to bridge the gap with words, their statements clearly reflecting an awareness "that [they are] talking to someone and that [they know] full well the *kind* of someone who is listening" (100). What is involved is the ability to take the perspective of another, to role-play, and the absence of this ability pervades the young child's attempts to communicate.

Piaget (1951) has pointed out that there is a vast difference between the ability to speak, which the child acquires about age two, and the ability to use language as either a vehicle of thought or a vehicle for communicating thought and experience, which the child acquires only gradually for several years after he learns to speak. Thus, although if one observes three- and four-year-old children at play together, one will hear them talking, often continuously, the content of their talk is not communicative but consists of what Piaget has labeled "collective monologues" (Piaget, 1952b). Children can talk by about age two, but they are incapable of social communication until perhaps four years later. At the beginning, the talk is egocentric. There is no attempt to obtain or provide information. Speech is occurring concurrently with other behaviors but bears no necessary relationship to these, their motives, their content, or their goals. To the extent that Piaget's view of the nature of egocentrism is correct, at the earliest stages there is no desire or intent to communicate, because such a desire can arise only after there is at least some awareness that other individuals are different and do not share all one's thoughts, feelings, and perceptions. As this awareness develops, the three-, four-, and five-year-old child begins to try to communicate; but for a long time, his efforts are inadequate, still dominated as they are by egocentrism.

Gradually, the child's experience comes to include the concepts and perceptions of others. He must, always through assimilation and accommodation, integrate these into his developing schemas. As the child's experiences come to include conflict between his thoughts and those of his peers, egocentrism begins to yield. Indeed, Piaget (1932) considers peer interaction to be the single most important factor accounting for the decline of egocentrism.[2] Implicit in his formulation, however, is the fact that egocentrism will persist in areas where the individual does not have occasion to encounter the perhaps different concepts of others, and it is

[2] In a discussion of Piaget's view of moral development, Kohlberg (1969) questions whether the evidence supports the causal role of peer participation. Although moral development turns out to be correlated with peer-group participation, he considers that a better inference from the data would be that peer-group participation is important in that it provides "general role-taking opportunities," rather than that it is a specific determinant. A bit of evidence in support of Piaget, however, is provided by the results of an experiment (Weinheimer, 1972) in which five- and eight-year-old children were exposed to situations in which their responses reflected their ability to take another's perspective in relation to a perceptual task. The children more often "reconciled" perspectives—verbally acknowledged that others had different perspectives—when the other was a child than when he was an adult.

likely to recur at any point in the life span when the individual deals with an area which is entirely unfamiliar to him.

The social forms and consequences of egocentrism are reflected particularly clearly in children's understanding and application of rules in their games. Piaget used children's games of marbles as a setting for the study of the development of moral judgment (Piaget, 1932) in this context, and he offers the fullest exploration of the nature of egocentrism, the manner in which it is in part rooted in the relationships between children and adults, its forms and consequences in children's perception of rules and of violations, and in the nature of children's relationships.[3]

Closely related to egocentrism are a cluster of other qualities of thought that also constitute a necessary developmental phase. They are all derivatives of the limitation of the child's cognitive structure to what he experiences directly; and they reveal, by contrast, the tremendous complexity that mature thought involves. Moreover, these limitations have important consequences. Thus, for example, the child's thinking about a situation will be influenced by whatever aspect of that situation is most salient perceptually—the brightest, loudest, biggest, nearest, or last seen. Whatever intrinsic organization may exist in the situation will not affect how the child organizes it as much as the more evident features of its perceptual organization. This characteristic of the child's thinking limits the depth of his understanding and also can seriously distort his causal reasoning. For example, the young child tends to attribute a causal relationship to events that occur together: "It is afternoon because I'm going to take a nap." "It's the leaves moving that make the wind." The child at this stage reasons from percept to percept and not with concepts.

Even after age six or seven or eight (depending on the individual child), when the child has considerable ability to manipulate symbols and concepts, his logical capacities are still very much tied to his perceptions. A child of this age might not be able to solve a geometrical problem presented to him verbally, for example, but could manage it with ease if he could manipulate sticks and shapes to represent the problem and its solution.

Another expression of the limitations of the child's thought to the here and now until late childhood is what is referred to as the attitude of

[3] There is another approach to moral development, which is too extensive and complex to be presented here, that largely derives from Piaget's theory but expands on it greatly. This is the work done by Lawrence Kohlberg. His classification of moral judgment into levels and stages of development suggests the possibility of a parallel classification and investigation of the development of at least certain aspects of political thought and judgment. For comprehensive expositions of his point of view see Kohlberg (1963, 1964, and 1969).

realism (Piaget, 1952b). The child cannot distinguish well—not at all at the outset—among different levels of reality such as words, thoughts, observed events, dreams, or feelings. What he sees, says, or thinks are equally real and objective to him. His name is him. He has no concept of words as arbitrary man-made conveniences. They are as much parts of the objects they denote as are physical characteristics. Thus, it is very difficult for him to understand the meaning of words that do not refer to specific concrete objects. He learns to use words such as time, love, life, and other abstract labels with considerable appropriateness; but if his own understanding of these words is probed, specific objects, events, or actions will be revealed as carrying the meaning. He can understand who the President is, because he can see him and hear him and read about him; but he cannot really grasp what the Presidency is. He is aware of the nation having many people, all of whom do certain things relevant to politics and government, such as vote, read the newspaper, write letters, protest, and picket. But he cannot understand, beyond those concrete acts, what is meant by citizenship, or the citizenry, or public opinion.

Another limitation of the child's thought that is also related to the dominance of what is perceptually salient is his inability to perform what is called multiple classification (Piaget, 1952a). Children can classify objects according to common characteristics at quite an early age. If given some blue and some red chips and asked to put all the ones that are alike together, they will readily sort them into two color piles. But if the young child is given red and blue chips some of which are circles and some of which are squares, with the same instructions, his classification will be more erratic. He may pick up three red squares and put them together, and then see a red circle and put it in the same pile, and then continue adding circles of either color, and so on. What is revealed is that he cannot maintain more than one dimension at a time as his sorting basis; the dimension he uses is likely to be determined by what is perceptually most salient at each point. The ability to deal with multiple classification develops gradually through the childhood years, different children attaining it at different ages, but it is often not a stable ability until the later elementary years.

The relevance of multiple classification for more general aspects of learning is that, beyond the ability to categorize in terms of multiple criteria, it involves the ability to deal with a single object or event in terms of its membership in two different classes. In the sorting example, the child was being asked to deal with a chip as both "red" and "a square" at the same time, seeing the dimensions both together and individually, or to see that the class "squares" included both red and blue squares. It does not seem hard to think of analogues of these problems both in everyday social situations and in aspects of the larger social and political world that we gradually come to understand. Here are some examples of familiar situations and relationships whose understanding requires the ability to deal with multiple classes: The teacher, who has authority over the classroom, is under the authority of the principal, who is under the authority of the superintendent; one's parents are sister and brother to one's aunts and uncles who are mothers and fathers to one's cousins; one lives in Los Angeles, but one also lives in California, and one also lives in the United States; thus one is a citizen of Los Angeles, a Californian, and an American.[4] It is evident that all the qualities of children's thought, such as realism, egocentrism, perception-boundedness, are together relevant to the development of the ability to deal with multiple dimensions simultaneously or to deal with classes and subclasses. It is also evident that this deceptively simple ability is central to understanding much of social and political life.

As a result of both maturation and experience, but in ways that Piaget's theory does not fully explain, the developing individual's thought is gradually freed from the concreteness just described and he moves toward the higher levels of human thought that can function without any reference to observed events. That is, the continued interaction of the individual with the events of the environment and the patterning of these events, together with the continuing assimilation of these into his working schemes and their modification to adapt to novelty, gradually produces mental representations of these events and patterns that are sufficiently stable and autonomous that the individual can manipulate them as substitutes for the reality without the need to refer to that reality. This transition, which occurs at the very end of childhood and beginning of adolescence, is the transition from concrete to formal operations, and it represents in Piaget's scheme the final step in the development of thought. The individual who has attained the stage of formal operations can reason deductively, has a true understanding of causality, and can think without dependence on concrete objects (Inhelder and Piaget, 1958). Thus,

> The great novelty of this stage is that by means of a differentiation
> of form and content the subject becomes capable of reasoning cor-

---

[4] The development of this ability with respect to geographical and political units has been studied by Piaget and others and is discussed more fully below in the context of the applicability of Piaget's theory to political learning and socialization. In one of these studies, the author questions Piaget's view that young children cannot classify phenomena into classes and subclasses (Jahoda, 1964). He suggests that very young children can accurately classify say, men and women as people, as well as understand that potatoes are vegetables, apples are fruit, and fruit and vegetables are food. Piaget has recognized that this is the case, but denies that these examples represent conceptual thinking in the sense that they indicate the child's ability to perform mental operations with the concepts (Inhelder and Piaget, 1964).

rectly about propositions he does not believe, or at least not yet; that is, propositions that he considers pure hypotheses. He becomes capable of drawing the necessary conclusions from truths which are merely possible, which constitutes the beginning of hypothetico-deductive or formal thought (Piaget and Inhelder, 1969, 132).

From this point on, change continues to occur, but it is not change in the basic structure of schemas but rather in their content, refinement, elaboration, and complexity.[5]

POLITICAL LEARNING IN THE LIGHT OF PIAGET'S THEORY

The broad definition of politics that underlies this discussion and the assumption that political phenomena are embedded in the interpersonal worlds of all individuals at all ages together make it possible to draw some rather clear connections between the Piagetian framework and political learning. The individual is assimilating and accommodating to political phenomena all the time, that is, developing political schemas and elaborating and modifying them in light of his continuing experience. At early ages, these schemas (ways of organizing and dealing with the environment) are probably mostly behavioral; and they become increasingly verbal and abstract with age. Thus, even the very young child has patterned and stable ways of adapting to the demands of authority, to attempts to influence him, to cooperative and competitive situations, and so on. He may not be able to verbalize his adaptations or describe the phenomena to which he adapts, but observation will nonetheless reveal the kind of structure and stability characteristic of schemas. In this sense, it may not be meaningful to ask whether the child at such an early age "understands" political phenomena, unless it is clearly specified whether by understanding one refers to the ability to verbally articulate the events or to the ability to deal with the events in a patterned and effective manner.

As the individual's cognitive capacities evolve through experience with the political and nonpolitical aspects of his world, the ability to abstract from experience, to discern regularities, to derive implications from events and apply them to other events all increase. Thus, with development, the individual becomes able not only to adapt to political phenomena but

[5] In a recent paper, Riegel (1974) argues that Piaget's theory does not account for the highest levels of human thought (e.g., creative scientific thought) and that formal operations do not describe the thinking of mature adults. He offers an extended and modified model of cognitive development founded on a "creative, dialectic basis" that he considers capable of dealing with the implicit contradictions that characterize both modern scientific thinking and common thought.

to observe them; he learns not only how to deal with them more and more effectively and maturely but also how to perceive and anticipate political phenomena in the experiences of others as well as in his own. It is in this context that the growing individual's learning about government and formal political institutions and processes can be best understood. As the child learns from an early age to adapt to authority, power, influence, leadership, and so on in his immediate world, he also from a relatively early age hears about and observes—on TV, in newspapers, and through the conversations and explanations of adults—comparable phenomena in the remote world of the formal political system. Sometimes the parallels are obvious to him, depending on his age, and sometimes they are drawn by adults in their attempts to explain a political event in the news. Thus, for example, in explaining a matter related to law enforcement to a young child, an adult may liken it to rules with which the child is familar in the home, the peer group, and the school. In effect, the adult in such a case is facilitating the processes of accommodation and assimilation by evoking the relevant existing schema from the child's own experiences and guiding him in making the connection to the more remote situation.

The child's adaptation to and his learnings from his interpersonal experiences, in short, constitute the basis for the development of his understanding of the larger system. The Piagetian view of the child's development of concepts about the physical world is that it is a gradual process based on the child's direct manipulation of physical objects. The child works inductively from the outcomes of his sensorimotor experiences toward the construction of increasingly abstract concepts to represent these experiences and manipulate them symbolically. From this direct manipulation of physical reality he develops, among others, concepts of object permanence, of number, of mass and volume. It is only in terms of these directly developed concepts that he learns more remote and complex physical relationships that he might be taught formally.

With respect to the development of social and political concepts, it would seem that the child's experiences with the phenomena of his interpersonal world constitute the parallel to the child's manipulations of physical objects. His understanding of the more remote political world thus builds on and is shaped by the schemas he has derived from his interpersonal experiences. The process of learning about the political phenomena of the interpersonal world is a slow and gradual one. As has already been suggested, learning about it behaviorally occurs first, and cognitive understanding of what has already been dealt with in action follows later. Thus, just as there is a logical sequence in the learning of certain physical concepts so that certain aspects of understanding cannot occur until others have preceded, so might there be some such sequence in the development of concepts about political phenomena.

Whatever such a sequence might be, this application of the logic of Piaget's views to political concepts leads to the hypothesis that *each individual's development of an understanding of political phenomena will follow a natural progression whose sequence and content will be dictated by the experience that his interpersonal world provides him as this experience is organized by his evolving cognitive capacities.* This will be true with respect to the politics of his immediate world as well as of the more remote institutional world, but I am hypothesizing in addition that development with respect to the former underlies, and therefore precedes, development with respect to the latter.

Stated differently, the argument just presented implies that learning about the formal political system can only be cognitive, because the child has no way of directly experiencing and manipulating the events of that world to develop behavioral adaptations to it. It follows from this that such learning, as distinguished from the direct political learning from interpersonal relations, is not likely to be extensive or stable until relatively late in childhood.

For very different reasons, many political socialization researchers, who have studied primarily children's perceptions and understanding of the formal and institutionalized aspects of politics, have reached a similar conclusion. Such researchers argue that it is not fruitful to study young children. Gallatin and Adelson, for example, having raised some questions about how a child's "grasp of political principles matures," go on to say that, "Insofar as it provides a basis for inference, previous research indicates that the answers to such questions should be sought among adolescents rather than children. . . . Indeed, studies already conducted by the present authors and associates confirm the impression that the preadolescent youngster is in many respects unable to comprehend political principles" (Gallatin and Adelson, 1971, 94). If the political principles considered relate only to the formal political system, then such a conclusion follows from the application of Piagetian analysis presented here.

Related empirical support for this point is provided by a study by Pauline Vaillancourt, who surveyed 1,000 young people ranging in age from nine to fifteen on their party identification, their estimate of the importance of party identification for adults, their level of political participation, their level of political interest, and their image of the President, as well as on background characteristics and mass media consumption habits. Vaillancourt's major finding is that these children's attitudes had very low stability across three waves of a questionnaire administered over a six-month period. Vaillancourt concludes that

> . . . as far as attitude questions are concerned, this may be due to
> the fact that many children do not have political attitudes on the
> topics about which they are questioned.

She then goes on to say,

> We should re-examine closely what in this field has been so care-
> lessly labelled an "attitude." If an attitude is a "relatively enduring
> predisposition," then the implications of observed low levels of
> stability are that it may be presumptuous to discuss the "attitudes"
> of children. It would perhaps be better only to discuss what might
> be called embryonic forms of attitudes. On many topics, political
> predispositions are probably not "enduring" as is the case with valid
> attitudes, but rather quite transient (Vaillancourt, 1972, 22).

Such verbal responses with respect to the larger political system would
be transient, in terms of the line of reasoning presented here, because
they would reflect only rote verbal learnings of what children have heard,
read, or been taught, instead of reflecting a concept which the child is
able to use to think about politics. Stable attitudes might be uncovered
at relatively early ages if the political attitude objects were drawn from
the more immediate political systems of the family, peer group, and school
in which the child functions. Predispositions with respect to these do not
require that the child deal with abstractions that are remote from events
that he experiences concretely. Thus, even the preadolescent might be
found to have structured judgments and attitudes about political phenomena, although not yet about governmental and other formal institutional
phenomena.

SOME APPLICATIONS OF PIAGETIAN THEORY TO POLITICAL LEARNING AND SOCIALIZATION

A number of researchers interested in political socialization and in the
development of understanding of politics have attempted to link Piagetian
theory to their reasoning and/or their findings. At the theoretical level,
one of the most thoroughgoing attempts is that of Merelman (1969), who
asserts that we cannot understand the development of political ideology
without understanding the course of cognitive and moral development.
He then spells out what he considers to be the cognitive prerequisites of
ideological thought and relates these to the levels of cognitive capacity
that children and adolescents attain in accordance with Piagetian evidence.
In his empirical work too, Merelman has drawn his expectations of
children's and adolescents' understanding and level of reasoning about
political issues or phenomena from Piaget and some of his followers
(Merelman, 1971a, 1971b, 1973). Over-all, his data show that some of
the basic Piagetian notions about the course of cognitive development
are relevant and applicable to the course of development of political
thinking, but with some important qualifications. In order to account for

intra-individual variations in political thinking across different aspects and issues and for inter-individual variations in level of reasoning, he finds it necessary to invoke other variables, to which in one instance he gives the general label of "politically related environmental factors" (Merelman, 1971*a*). As he states at another point, "Political socialization is too complex a process to be encompassed by any single developmental model, even one as sophisticated and subtle as Piaget's" (Merelman, 1971*b*, 89).

Focussing primarily on adolescents, Adelson and his colleagues (Adelson, Green, and O'Neil, 1969; Adelson and O'Neil, 1966; Adelson, 1971), have found the Piagetian generalizations about the changes in the nature of the reasoning process during adolescence to relate quite usefully to observed changes in political reasoning during that period. Thus, they find that the major accomplishments that occur during adolescence in the nature of political thought are the achievement of abstractness, the extension of time perspective beyond the present, an increased understanding of human complexity and motivation, the emergence of hypothetico-deductive reasoning, the decline of authoritarianism, and the growth of a sense of principle (Adelson, 1971). These changes are illustrated with rich detail with respect to the adolescent's development of a sense of community and of the idea of law and are linked quite directly to the changes that Piaget attributes to the shift from concrete to formal operations. Adelson and his associates did not set out to test the validity of Piagetian notions as applied to the development of political thought, but rather they draw on these notions in their interpretations of their findings, and it is clear that, as in the case of Merelman's research, the developmental patterns they report gain in both clarity and general validity when considered in the context of the course of cognitive and moral development as detailed by Piaget and Kohlberg.

Piaget himself has examined the development of a political concept (Piaget and Weil, 1951), that of the homeland or nationality. He sees his findings as showing that the development of the child's understanding of his own country and of other countries reflects progress from egocentrism to reciprocity. The child starts out without any concept of his country as a larger unit encompassing his own village, city, or state, as well as others, and gradually achieves an understanding of this "invisible whole" at the same time that he develops affective allegiance to this larger unit as his own. Piaget summarizes the transition as occurring in three stages. In the first stage, the child has no geographical or logical concept of the country as containing the village or canton, or of the latter as being inside the country. He attributes this to the child's inability to deal with part–whole relations. In the second stage, the spatial relations are understood, so that the children draw the circle representing their canton within the circle representing the country; but they cannot yet deal with the logical relationships that their spatial understanding implies. Thus, they deny that one can be both Genevese and Swiss, although they recognize that Geneva is totally contained within Switzerland. In the third stage, "their ideas are finally synthesized correctly" (Piaget and Weil, 1951, 565).

With respect to the concept of other countries and of a foreigner, the children show a progression from egocentrism to reciprocity (understanding, for example, that they would be foreigners in another country), except that in some cases egocentrism is replaced not by reciprocity but by "sociocentricity" (the perception of the larger group or the nation as special and different from others) before it finally yields.[6]

Jahoda (1963a, 1963b, 1964) attempted to replicate Piaget and Weil's findings on Scottish children, and found the Piaget formulation inadequate. He had, to begin with, a great deal of trouble discerning whether or not he was accurately paralleling Piaget's criteria in categorizing responses according to stages. He found further that his sample did not show the necessary progression from understanding of spatial to understanding of nationality relations. In addition to his useful criticisms of Piaget's analysis and procedures, Jahoda makes a closely related point that has general relevance to the issue of the relationships between cognitive development and the development of political understanding. He suggests that the children's difficulty in handling nationality relations has not to do with their inability to deal with logical class inclusion but with the nature of "nationality" as a logical class.

> Nationality . . . is a highly abstract class whose boundaries are not directly related to any physical cues, therefore remaining vague and uncertain. It must be emphasized that no one, however mature intellectually, can be expected to cope adequately with logical relations between classes whose extent is not clearly defined; for instance, a virus would be hard to allocate to the classes "animal" or "plant" respectively. If this is true, then the difficulty would seem to lie in the children's lack of familiarity with the characteristics of "nationality" classes and their limits, rather than with their incomplete mental equipment as far as the operations are concerned; and Piaget's error would be to argue from relatively concrete classes, such as types of beads, to highly abstract ones.
>
> This kind of difficulty is not confined to nationality. It applies to all the different and often rather subtle social categories children gradually learn to master. This is particularly important where the

---

[6] In a relatively recent study of children's national attitudes, Middleton *et al.* (1970) find that children do not achieve reciprocity equally with respect to all nations but that their feelings for particular countries strongly influence their ability to reason logically with respect to them. They suggest that this constitutes "an important limitation on the generality of the findings of Piaget and Weil" (133).

categories are not even indirectly tied to physical units, as nationalities mostly are. Thus children cannot easily gain insight into the incompatibility of various categories, e.g., that one cannot be a Christian and a Jew at the same time, for there is no conceivable operation whereby they could discover this in the way Piaget's subjects found out relations among beads. There is some evidence that children remain confused about such social categories long after physical class inclusions have become self-evident to them (Jahoda, 1964, 1090–1091).

In another study, Jahoda (1962) investigated the development of children's concepts of foreign countries and found a developmental progression between ages six and eleven not incompatible with Piagetian notions (which Jahoda was not attempting to test in this case), but which could not be specifically derived from them. He found the course of development to be strongly affected by social class, and to show great individual variation. Particularly among the older children, the content of their answers reflected the impact of prevalent political notions in their environment (e.g., the Cold War) and also of recent events involving other countries and their own country's relationship to these.

Another line of research on political orientations that has drawn on Piaget to different extents has focused on the development of children's concepts and attitudes toward war, peace, and other aspects of international politics. Cooper (1965) and later Alvik (1968) studied the development of children's concepts of war and peace. Cooper studied English children of ages seven to eight, ten to twelve, and fourteen to sixteen, and Japanese children of ages seven to eight and thirteen to fourteen. Alvik studied Norwegian children of ages eight, ten, and twelve. Taken together, these studies indicate that children develop more elaborate conceptions of war earlier than they do of peace, and that, at the ages studied, the conceptions of war focus primarily on the concrete aspects of war (fighting, killing, dying, weapons). Children's conceptions of peace largely define it as an inner state of tranquility; particularly lacking are conceptions of peace as a condition among groups that can be achieved through concerted intergroup efforts. Pursuing Cooper's and Alvik's own suggestions in interpreting this result, it makes sense if one considers the nature of the personal experiences that children have on which they can base concepts of war and peace. Conflicts are pervasive and have concrete aspects that can be perceived, discussed, and about which one can receive information. Peace, on the other hand, is a much less concrete and tangible phenomenon in interpersonal experience, one that is not likely to be discussed as such nearly so much as its violation, and one which does not have easily evident concrete dimensions in terms of which a cognitive structure can be developed. Thus, a Piagetian analysis of how children learn about these larger social and political phenomena might well anticipate the observed difference between the developing conceptions of war and peace.

Cooper interprets his results as showing that his subjects progress through a series of stages in the development of the concept of war, seeing these stages as "broadly consistent with Piaget's notions" (Cooper, 1965, 10). Thus egocentrism prevails at earlier ages, and application of logical reasoning is evident at later ones. On the basis of his findings, he constructs a model of the various factors he sees as contributing to the formation of a schema of conflict that cuts across the personal, social, and international levels. He hypothesizes one major contributing factor to be the experience of conflicts and fights in games and play during the early years. War then becomes identified with fighting and an identification occurs between the rules of fighting and the rules of war. Information from adults, from school, and from the media feed into these developing concepts, and, together with continuing social and interpersonal conflict experience, shape a schema of conflict that is at a particular level of equilibrium at any particular point.

Cooper does much more in linking his pattern of development to Piagetian notions, but of particular interest here is the clear association he makes between a concept about an aspect of the remote political world and the interpersonal experience of the child in his earliest years. This is the most explicit connection of the sort that I have found in the political socialization literature, and it implicitly assumes the kind of link between interpersonal experience and understanding of the more remote and more formal world that I hypothesize above.[7] Cooper and the other students of children's learning of international orientations have incorporated the Piagetian scheme much more integrally into the formulation of their research. Moreover, whether as a result or as an unrelated concurrent aspect, they seem to view their findings about development more in terms of the underlying logic of Piaget's theory than narrowly in terms of the specific acquisitions and changes that characterize the various stages.

[7] In their study of the development of the concept of law among adolescents, Adelson et al. (1969) make passing reference to a similar connection without integrating it in a major way into their interpretation. In attempting to explain the change from early to late adolescence, from a view of law as constraining to a view of it as enhancing, they say:

> For one thing, the young adolescent is locked, matter of factly, into benignly authoritarian relationships to his milieu, both at home and at school. He takes it for granted that authority exercises its dominion over its subjects—teacher over student, parent over child—and almost casually he generalizes this direction of ordinance to the domain of government. With the easing of control that accompanies adolescence, with the adolescent's sharp surge toward autonomy, there is a gradual yielding of this way of looking at the politics of household and schoolroom, and ultimately of politics at large (Adelson, Green, and O'Neil, 1969, 329).

Also of interest in this connection is another study on children's conceptions of international phenomena done by Targ (1970). Although he does not build his formulation around a Piagetian framework, he sees his study as continuing the line of research pursued by Cooper and Alvik. His findings, too extensive to summarize here, relate to the development of orientations to national and international institutions, decision-making processes, and interactions. Of particular relevance to this discussion, however, are some of his interpretative statements:

> Second, as with Cooper's findings, there tended to be a relationship between children's belief acquisition and the kinds of social interactions that children were likely to be part of. Whereas children had difficulty identifying the foreign secretary as opposed to other political figures as the chief foreign policy adviser to the head of state, they tended to understand the advisory capacity of a foreign secretary when juxtaposed with other kinds of behaviors. Giving advice might relate to the personal advice-giving functions that friends provided in a group. Similarly, children were better able to understand the function of the United Nations than to identify its members. It might be hypothesized that advice-giving, discussion, bargaining, and negotiation are part of the child's social world and generalizable for the child's political understanding (Targ, 1970, 94).

A seemingly different interpretation of the relevance of Piagetian concepts to the child's understanding of politics is offered by Connell in his book *The Child's Construction of Politics* (1971). He believes there are important differences between learning about politics and learning about other aspects of the world, and he considers that these differences necessitate a more complex theory to account for cognitive development in the realm of politics. It is useful to quote from Connell at some length to appreciate his reasoning fully:

> We must distinguish thought about immediate social relationships, intimate personal contacts, from thought about society on the large scale. Politics is part of the latter; and here is the first main difference we must allow for. The children's political thought differs from their thought about such well-studied features of the physical world as number, weight and volume, spatial relationships, etc., in that the objects of thought are at a distance from the child rather than immediately accessible to him (Connell, 1971, 228).

By distance he means both "subjective distance, a consciousness of being remote from the subject matter," and "objective social distance," the fact that "children learn about politicians and political events through other people, their contact with politics is indirect."

The children can exert no influence on politics themselves. Now a child learns about the physical world in large measure by operating on it, by holding, biting, and moving toys, by walking around a playground, by squashing plasticine, by dismantling a car engine. He learns about his intimate social environment also, in large measure, through the reactions of others to his own advances and enterprises. But the child cannot do this to his political environment, which is as much outside his control as the weather. This means that he cannot test his political conceptions against the reactions of their objects to his actions. Direct feedback effects which seem to play a large part in the control of learning about the familiar reality, and the persistence of gross misconceptions (e.g. about the Queen's power) and implausible myths (e.g. about the Viet Cong invading Australia) is made possible. There is, however, a shorter feedback loop which does operate in political questions, that from the child to familiar adults to the child; we have seen some examples of this, and I suspect that it is more important than the interviews actually prove.

The distance between the child and politics, and the intermediary role of adults, make this learning situation substantially different from the child's basic learning about his physical environment. The object of the child's political thought, the thing we have called "the political world," is itself part of society. Ideas other men have conceived and expressed, relationships other men have set up and changed, actions other men have taken, are the subject-matter of the children's political thought.

In this sense all of the children's ideas about politics are derivative, and in this sense their political thought is entirely a social product. It is clear that we are a long way indeed from the paradigm situation in Piaget's researches, the direct construction by the child of interpretations of his environment independent of adults and their thought. Here we are dealing with a situation where the child's basic task is to master certain forms and realizations of adult thought and where the materials for doing so are manufactured and supplied by adults. Clearly, the stages in the development of children's thinking identified by Piaget and others will be inapplicable in detail, because of the constant intrusions of adult thought-forms into the child's thinking, because in fact adult thought is here the stuff of the children's construction (Connell, 1971, 229–30).

Because Connell distinguishes sharply between learning about the formal institutionalized processes of government and learning from politically relevant experiences in the child's own world, it is necessary for him to hypothesize about how the cognitive links to that remote world can be established. In so doing, Connell makes a valuable contribution by calling attention to, first, the important role of adult-mediated information in the development of cognitive structures about politics and, second, the extent to which "politics" is a social construction that can be transmitted only symbolically, making the symbols themselves the material on which the child works cognitively to develop his own schemas. It does not seem necessary, however, to postulate such a discontinuity between the two realms of learning. Rather it seems plausible to say, as in the formulation presented here, that the cognitive base on which children's learning about political institutions builds is composed of two major elements. One consists of the specific information and affect transmitted to him by the adult world, in deliberate explanations, in conversations that the child hears, and through the mass media. The other encompasses those experiences in the child's immediate interpersonal world that are essentially political. The two elements—those directly induced from experience and those mediated by adults—undoubtedly combine in a complex manner that needs to be analyzed and studied empirically, but to see them as joint contributors to political learning seems to provide a more coherent model of the process.

Connell himself reasons in a very similar manner with respect to what he calls the "threat schema" in children's views of war. He found that the children consistently expressed the fear that their country (Australia) was threatened by war, and in many cases this was the justification for the country engaging in war itself, to ward off the threat. Connell says,

> The evidence of such passages is that children develop a sense of some external menace before they have much concrete detail about Vietnam, sometimes before they have heard of this war, certainly before they know much about those participating. As we argued in chapter 1, the young children do not draw a boundary between the political world and other spheres of life and imagination; we can see this in Adam's fantasy about shooting one of the invaders with his father's gun, and Susan's drift from soldiers and bad men to Captain Cook, knights, dragons, and dinosaurs. Stories of soldiers are assimilated to other dangers; and the military threat, and details about Vietnam when they are acquired, are assimilated to the primitive, diffuse fears of early childhood.
>
> The idea of an external threat to the country thus becomes charged at an early age with personal emotion, with fears of violent intrusion into the "nice and safe" places of the child's own life. We will not be far out if we trace the affect-laden threat schemata of later childhood and adolescence to these roots. At later ages, naturally, as the children construct an image of the political order, the threat is placed more firmly in a political context. Where the young children talk of "baddies" coming to the land, the older children, as we have seen, speak of the Vietnamese and the Viet Cong coming to take over; later again it becomes the communists (Connell, 1971, 102).

Although Connell sees the origins of the threat schema as lying in early emotions and not in experiences with the immediate world, the logic by which he links the later conceptions to early origins is similar to Cooper's in explaining the origins of the concept of war, and to mine in the formulation presented here. If this line of reasoning is valid it should be possible to identify a number of such basic schemas with respect to politics and to trace their development as they become more specified and at the same time more extended to the remote world of political institutions and events.

Another aspect of Connell's analysis provides some guidance in this direction. In analyzing children's understanding of political roles, Connell finds that younger children confuse the "tasks, titles, recruitment rules" and even jurisdictions of various political figures (24). The children seem to have only one encompassing conception of a political role, and they impose it on all the roles they hear about. Connell says about these confusions, "To speak of them as the confusion of things originally distinct is to see them from an adult standpoint only. To the child, the problem is not to bring together what is distinct, but to distinguish what seems to be the same" (24). To such a single conception that many children hold Connell gives the label "task pool." He considers that each child creates it from a pooling of all the disparate pieces of information about government that he receives from many sources. Because children have only a vague image of what government is and of who the individuals are who constitute government, they assimilate all kinds of information about any of the tasks done in the remote world to their single conception of the governmental role.

As Connell points out, this indiscriminate assimilation produces what seems like an overestimation by children of the power of political figures. As government is seen as doing everything and responsible for everything, and as any political figure is assimilated into this encompassing role, children in effect attribute great powers to whatever particular political figures they talk about. This is what Connell sees as the true meaning of the oft-cited finding in American political socialization research that children see the President and other political figures as "benevolent." He says,

Explanations of this have usually been in terms of children's emotional need to see "authority" as benevolent. If we look back at Greenstein's celebrated article on the subject, we find that many of the statements he quotes are open-ended task descriptions of the kind we have just mentioned, or items from a general governmental task pool (F. I. Greenstein, "The Benevolent Leader"). If American children are like Australian ones in this, we may argue that the apparent benevolence of particular figures is in large part an effect of the undifferentiated task pool—that it has a cognitive, not an emotional, basis (28).

Connell's interpretation is, in effect, that political cognitions become progressively more refined and elaborated in the course of maturation and experience, serving at each point as the basis for assimilation and accommodation to incoming political information. It should be possible to identify other basic concepts, or schemas, such as that of the "task pool," on which political understanding builds and to then trace, for different individuals and different groups of individuals, the particular course that subsequent development takes in response to the specific political experiences of their interpersonal world and to the specific information provided them by the adult world. Variations in relation to such variables as social class, education, and subcultural identification would then be expected to reflect the differences in life experience and in the impact of the adult world that sociological variables shape or mediate.

CONCLUSIONS

What this chapter hopefully has contributed is a clarification of the nature of the child's encounters with political phenomena of all kinds in the course of development. For such a clarification, Piaget's formulation is crucial because it focuses one's attention on what the child is experiencing and doing as he goes about the business of adapting. This, it seems to me, is the main contribution to be derived from Piaget for an understanding of political learning: political learning occurs in the course of the child's spontaneous activities and interactions with other children, with adults and with the adult world, and it is in this context that the process and content of political learning must be understood.

However, Piaget's is a theory of intellectual development. It does not address itself to the development of affective, motivational, or behavioral phenomena. Accordingly, despite its considerable utility, a Piagetian approach is incomplete as a basis for a theory of political learning. To account for learning and development of other dimensions of political functioning beyond the cognitive, it is necessary to turn to other lines of theory and research and then to integrate the insights, hypotheses, and findings of these alternative approaches with the Piagetian into a coherent and empirically meaningful formulation of political learning and development. In particular, attention to classical conditioning, reinforcement, and observational learning is required.

The sequence which political learning takes can also be best understood partly in terms of possibilities and limits that Piaget and his followers have shown the child's developing capacities to involve. The behavioral consequences of other learning processes such as conditioning, reinforcement, and observational learning will be mediated by the child's cognitive abilities and thus shaped and limited by them as well. These additional processes must be invoked, however, because for a full exploration of the context of political learning and of its multiple consequences, Piaget's theory is in itself insufficient. The theoretical and empirical tasks of identifying the complex interrelationships that undoubtedly obtain among these processes lie ahead.

REFERENCES

Adelson, J. "The Political Imagination of the Young Adolescent," *Daedalus* 100 (1971), 1013–50.

————, J., and R. P. O'Neil. "Growth of Political Ideas in Adolescence: The Sense of Community," *Journal of Personality and Social Psychology* 4 (1966), 295–306.

————, .B. Green, and R. O'Neil. "Growth of the Idea of Law in Adolescence," *Developmental Psychology* 1 (1969), 327–32.

Alvik, T. "The Development of Views on Conflict, War, and Peace Among School Children," *Journal of Peace Research* (1968), 171–95.

Connell, R. W. *The Child's Construction of Politics* (Carlton, Victoria: Melbourne University Press, 1971).

Cooper, P. "The Development of the Concept of War," *Journal of Peace Research* (1965), 1–17.

Flavell, J. H. *The Development of Role-taking and Communication Skills in Children* (New York: Wiley, 1968).

————. *The Developmental Psychology of Jean Piaget* (New York: D. Van Nostrand Company, 1963).

Gallatin, J., and J. Adelson. "Legal Guarantees of Individual Freedom: A Cross-national Study of the Development of Political Thought," *Journal of Social Issues* 27 (1971), 93–108.

Greenstein, F. I. "The Benevolent Leader," *American Political Science Review* 54 (1960), 934–43.

Inhelder, B., and J. Piaget. *The Growth of Logical Thinking from Childhood to Adolescence* (New York: Basic Books, 1958).

————. *The Early Growth of Logic in the Child: Classification and Seriation* (London: Routledge and Kegan Paul, 1964).

Jahoda, G. "Development of Scottish Children's Ideas and Attitudes about Other Countries," *Journal of Social Psychology* 58 (1962), 91–108.

————. "The Development of Children's Ideas about Country and Nationality.

Part I: The Conceptual Framework," *British Journal of Educational Psychology* 33 (1963a), 47–60.

————. "The Development of Children's Ideas about Country and Nationality. Part II: National Symbols and Themes," *British Journal of Educational Psychology* 33 (1963b), 143–53.

————. "Children's Concepts of Nationality: A Critical Study of Piaget's Stages," *Child Development* 35 (1964), 1081–92.

Kohlberg, L. "The Development of Children's Orientations Toward a Moral Order. I. Sequence in the Development of Moral Thought," *Vita Humana* 6 (1963), 11–33.

————. "Development of Moral Character and Moral Ideology," in M. L. Hoffman and L. W. Hoffman (eds.), *Review of Child Development Research* (Volume 1) (New York: Russell Sage Foundation, 1964).

————. "Stage and Sequence: The Cognitive-developmental Approach to Socialization," in D. A. Goslin (ed.), *Handbook of Socialization Theory and Research* (Chicago: Rand McNally, 1969).

Merelman, R. M. "The Development of Political Ideology: A Framework for the Analysis of Political Socialization," *American Political Science Review* 63 (1969), 750–67.

————. "The Development of Policy Thinking in Adolescence," *American Political Science Review* 65 (1971a), 1033–47.

————. *Political Socialization and Educational Climates* (New York: Holt, Rinehart & Winston, Inc., 1971b).

————. "The Structure of Policy Thinking in Adolescence: A Research Note," *American Political Science Review* 67 (1973), 161–6.

Middleton, M. R., H. Tajfel, and N. B. Johnson. "Cognitive and Affective Aspects of Children's National Attitudes," *British Journal of Social and Clinical Psychology* 9 (1970), 122–34.

Piaget, J. *The Child's Conception of Number* (New York: Humanities Press, 1952a).

————. *The Language and Thought of the Child* (London: Routledge and Kegan Paul, 1952b).

————. *The Moral Judgment of the Child* (London: Routledge and Kegan Paul, 1932).

————. *Play, Dreams and Imitation in Childhood* (New York: W. W. Norton, 1951).

————. *The Origins of Intelligence in Children* (New York: International Universities Press, 1952c).

————. "Piaget's Theory," in P. H. Mussen (ed.), *Carmichael's Manual of Child Psychology I* (third edition) (New York: Wiley, 1970).

————. *The Psychology of Intelligence* (London: Routledge and Kegan Paul, 1950).

————, and B. Inhelder. *The Psychology of the Child* (New York: Basic Books, 1969).

————, and A. Weil. "The Development in Children of the Idea of the Homeland and of Relations with Other Countries," *International Social Science Bulletin* 3 (1951), 561–78.

Riegel, K. F. "Dialectic Operations: The Final Period of Cognitive Development," *Human Development* (1973), in press.

Targ, H. R. "Children's Developing Orientations to International Politics," *Journal of Peace Research* 2 (1970), 79–98.

Vaillancourt, P. "The Stability of Children's Political Orientations," paper presented at the Annual Meeting of the International Studies Association, Dallas, 1972.

Weinheimer, S. "Egocentrism and Social Influence in Children," *Child Development* 43 (1972), 567–78.

Chapter Seven

Patterns of Cynicism: Differential Political Socialization among Adolescents

Sandra Kenyon Schwartz

INTRODUCTION

Political science interest in the study of political socialization rests in large part on the premise that the conditions under which an attitude is acquired can have important implications for the stability of that attitude and for its future attitudinal and behavioral impact. It is this argument that has directed our attention to the origins of political attitudes in childhood—a period of life held to be of major importance in shaping attitudes and behavior in general (Greenstein, 1965; Hyman, 1959). It is also this argument which has prompted some scholars to call for greater effort at specifying the processes by which attitudes develop (Sigel, 1966; Dennis, 1968; Schonfeld, 1971).

Stated briefly, this position maintains that "process affects outplay" or, in other words, the way in which an attitude is acquired affects the meaning to the individual of that attitude and its consequences. If this is true, or more precisely, to the degree that it is true, studying adult attitudes after they are formed will neglect information that is important not only to the explanation of those attitudes but also to an assessment of their impact. We need to know more about the circumstances of attitude acquisition—timing, sequencing, causes, and patterns of reinforcement, for example—to specify later effects.

The approach taken in this chapter is to explore the influence of the timing of attitude acquisition on the development of an important political attitude, cynicism, in order to show that the circumstances under which an attitude develops can have important implications for both the causes and consequences of holding that attitude.[1] The study focuses on adolescents, who are in the period of life during which political cynicism under-

---

[1] An approach similar in some ways to the one taken here has been used by Engstrom, who found the basis for compliant attitudes toward police to vary by race (for whites, benevolence; for blacks, attributed power-punishment capacity). He suggests the

goes substantial development, and compares eighth-grade, tenth-grade, and twelfth-grade students.

I define political cynicism as the perception that political authorities and/or the regime generally and regularly violate prescriptive standards for their behavior.[2] In other words, the political system or aspects of it are perceived to behave *illegitimately*. Cynicism is an orientation of particular theoretical and empirical relevance to students of socialization. Political trust (the polar opposite of cynicism) has been identified in the literature with concepts of legitimacy and diffuse support (Easton, 1965; Easton and Dennis, 1969) and hence with system capacity to govern and system persistence (Gamson, 1968; Lipset, 1960, 64; Easton, 1965). Socialization research has described the "origins of legitimacy" and the widespread political trust found among young children (Easton and Dennis, 1969; Hess and Torney, 1967; Greenstein, 1965). But the virtual absence of cynicism among children[3] is not matched among adults.

A rapid increase in political cynicism occurs during adolescence (Kenyon, 1970; Lyons, 1970; Freeman, 1966) and a lesser increase with age continues through adulthood (Agger, Goldstein, and Pearl, 1961, 488). This post-childhood increase in cynicism (or decrease in trust) does not appear to be explained by the findings and interpretations of research with younger children.[4] Therefore, both from the point of view of "system relevance" (Dennis, 1968) and of the centrality of this and related concepts in the socialization literature, an examination of adolescent political cynicism would seem useful.

The variables examined here are those commonly found to be associated with political cynicism in adult populations. Thus, pessimism, political and personal inefficacy, and personal cynicism have been shown to be correlated with political cynicism among adults and interpreted as causing individuals to develop feelings of political cynicism (Horton and Thompson, 1962; Agger, Goldstein, and Pearl, 1961; Litt, 1963; Aberbach and Walker, 1970; Almond and Verba, 1963; Rosenberg, 1956; Finifter, 1970). Are these variables associated with political cynicism among adolescents,

---

basis for compliance among blacks may be less stable (Engstrom, 1970). Other fruitful approaches to a process-oriented study of political socialization include the application of learning theories and developmental psychology. See, for example, the chapters by Rohter and Rosenau in this volume.

[2] This usage is similar to Finifter's definition of political normlessness, conceptualized by her as a dimension of political alienation (Finifter, 1970).

[3] Exceptions occur in some subcultures. See, for example, Jaros, Hirsch and Fleron, 1968; Abramson, 1973.

[4] It should be noted that the measures used to tap childhood positive affect for and trust in the political system and those used to measure cynicism among adolescents and adults are quite different. Nonetheless, the benevolent, pro-system pattern of early learning does not seem, in itself, to account for the subsequent rise in negative evaluations of politics during adolescence.

and more particularly, do they account for the increase in political cynicism observed in this age group? Second, considered as the independent variable, political cynicism has been found to have some impact on the frequency and nature of political participation among adults (Agger, Goldstein, and Pearl, 1961; Schwartz, 1973; Aberbach, 1969; Stokes, 1962). Does political cynicism among adolescents have similar consequences?

The argument made here suggests that there are important differences in the causes and consequences of political cynicism associated with the age at which the attitude is acquired. Further, the pattern of attitude acquisition in this case is not one of continous, incremental movement towards the adult model as is postulated in so much of the socialization literature.

METHODS

The data consist of a cross-sectional survey conducted in the late spring of 1967 with a sample of eighth-grade, tenth-grade, and twelfth-grade students ($N = 897$). They were pupils in one high school and one junior high school, in the same school district in a major metropolitan Northeastern city. The schools were chosen purposively, based on the heterogeneity of their students' class, ethnic, and racial backgrounds. Within each grade, a random sample was drawn that was clustered by social studies classrooms and stratified by "track" (ability groupings).[5]

Questionnaires were self-administered in classrooms, except that the researcher read aloud the questions in those classes characterized by very low reading levels. In addition to receiving the usual pledges of confidentiality and disclaimers of its not being a test, students sealed their completed questionnaires in envelopes to protect the privacy of their responses. All questionnaires in each school were completed on the same day to avoid contamination of results from discussion among the students.

Basing the sample on adolescents in school means that those who drop out of school are not represented in the tenth and particularly the twelfth grades while future drop-outs are included in the eighth grade. Undoubtedly this introduces a bias into the results. However, it seems probable that this bias is not overly large. Absenteeism was higher in the lower grades, particularly in the eighth grade. An analysis of absentee records of those students actually in the sample shows that high absenteeism is related to considering dropping out of school. By inference, then, those who were actually absent on the date of the data collection would be disproportionately inclined to leave school later.

---

[5] In the senior year where there were some options in social studies courses, the sample was also stratified by course.

Political cynicism was measured by a seven-item scale scored by the summated ratings method and combined into three categories (low, medium, high) of approximately equal size. Three items were newly designed for the study, and four were adapted from the cynicism scale developed at the Survey Research Center at the University of Michigan and used by Jennings and his associates in their study of political socialization among seniors(Langton and Jennings, 1968, 856, n. 25). The test of critical ratios was applied (Edwards, 1957) and inter-item correlations computed; all items scaled.[6]

The items all tap perceptions of whether or not "government" or "the people running the government" abide by prescriptive standards.[7] They do not use the pejorative term "politician" and are reversed to present cynical alternatives first in three of the seven cases.

Political cynicism among adults has often been seen as an outgrowth of one or more of a cluster of other negative orientations toward the sociopolitical world and one's role in it.[8] It appears to be based in part on a sense of political inefficacy or felt inability to influence politics. (Agger, Goldstein, and Pearl, 1961; Litt, 1963; Aberbach and Walter, 1970; Almond and Verba, 1963, Ch. 9). Some scholars conceptualize these two attitudes

[6] Gamma Values

						Critical Ratios
						2.58
.49						2.85
.21	.37					7.82
.44	.53	.47				6.35
.33	.38	.10	.33			4.72
.19	.45	.36	.51	.42		7.34
.30	.32	.34	.44	.27	.44	6.26

[7] (1) * Over the years, how much attention do you feel the government pays to what the people think when it decides what to do—a good deal of attention, some attention, not much attention; (2) * Would you say the government is pretty much run by a few big interests looking out for themselves, or is it run for the benefit of all the people; (3) Do you think that almost all the people running the government treat people equally, or do you think that quite a few of them treat people unequally; (4) Would you say that you can trust the people in the government to tell the truth almost all the time, only sometimes, or almost never; (5) * Do you think that the people in the government waste a lot of the money paid in taxes, waste some of it, or don't waste very much of it; (6) * Would you say that quite a few of the people running the government are a little crooked, not very many are, or do you think that hardly any of them are; (7) Do you think that almost all of the people running the government work hard at their jobs, or do you think that quite a few of them do as little work as they can get away with? Items marked with an asterisk (*) are adapted from the S.R.C. scale.

[8] Some social correlates of political cynicism including race and class have also been reported in the literature, but the findings have been inconsistent (Agger, Goldstein, and Pearl, 1961; Litt, 1963; Aberbach and Walker, 1970; Abramson, 1973; Finifter, 1970). Among these adolescents, however, neither race nor class was related to political cynicism (Kenyon, 1970).

as dimensions of political alienation (Finifter, 1970; Aberbach, 1969) or, in their general, nonpolitical form, as dimensions of social alienation (Seeman, 1959). Political cynicism among adults is also associated with nonpolitical orientations. One of its strongest correlates is personal cynicism or low faith in people (Rosenberg, 1956; Agger, Goldstein, and Pearl, 1961; Finifter, 1970; Litt, 1963; Aberbach and Walker, 1970). Finally, it has been associated with a pessimistic outlook on life (Horton and Thompson, 1962). These variables, then, together with personal efficacy, defined as "feelings of mastery over the self and the environment" (Campbell et al., 1960, 517), an attitude bearing the same relationship to political efficacy as personal cynicism does to political cynicism, are the ones investigated here among adolescents.

All four independent variables were measured by three-item scales. Three were adapted for use among pre-adults from standard scales;[9] the fourth, the pessimism scale, was created for use in this study. The measure of political efficacy is based on Campbell's scale (Campbell et al., 1954, 787, 8); scale scores were dichotomized.[10] The personal efficacy scale adopted two items from the Survey Research Center's measure as used by Jennings and his associates (Codebook, 1971, 130) and added a third: Do you feel pretty sure that you will succeed at what you really put your mind to, or are there times when you're not sure you'll be successful?[11] Respondents were categorized as "low," "medium," or "high." The personal cynicism scale was created using three items from Rosenberg's faith in people scale (Rosenberg, 1956, 690) and analyzed in four roughly equal categories.[12] Pessimism was measured by three items tapping one's outlook on life in general, and scale scores were dichotomized.[13]

[9] The exact wording of items based on standard measures is available in Kenyon (1970, 61, 65, 67).

[10] Gamma Values

.32	
.24	.18

[11] Gamma Values

.41	
.36	.56

[12] Gamma Values

.44	
.60	.51

[13] The items read: Do you feel that somehow things usually turn out badly in life, or would you say things mostly turn out for the best; Would you say that, by and large, life is pretty good, or do you think life is generally unpleasant; Do you usually feel pretty optimistic about things, or do you often feel sort of gloomy.

Gamma Values

.78	
.50	.65

FINDINGS

In the sample over-all, the pattern of relationships reported among adults is not found among these adolescents. Although all the relationships are in the predicted direction, none of them are very strong. The strongest association is with personal cynicism (Gamma = .28). Pessimism, political efficacy, and personal efficacy are all essentially unrelated to political cynicism (Gammas = .19; − .16; − .12) and the latter relationship is not statistically significant even at $p \leq .05$.

Further, none of the independent variables shows any increase with grade, yet political cynicism does increase. Table 7–1 summarizes these data, showing the percentage of respondents who fell into the highest category of each variable (e.g., "most politically cynical") for each grade.

Table 7–1. Summary of Attitude Distributions by Grade

RESPONDENTS WHO ARE:	GRADE IN SCHOOL		
	EIGHTH	TENTH	TWELFTH
Most personally cynical	26.2%	30.1%	30.0%
Most pessimistic	40.3	44.5	43.9
Most politically efficacious	60.2	55.3	63.6
Most personally efficacious	24.6	17.9	24.9
Most politically cynical	22.7	32.4	40.1*

* Significant, p ≤ .001.

Examining changes in these patterns by grade permits us to make some inferences about the developmental process.[14] When the findings are compared across grades a different pattern emerges. Political cynicism appears to rest on different foundations among younger respondents than it does among older ones.

In the eighth grade where political trust is more common and cynicism correspondingly less frequent, those who are politically cynical tend also to be pessimistic, politically inefficacious, personally inefficacious, and, although this relationship is not significant, to have some tendency to be

---

[14] Although longitudinal data would provide a much better basis for determining developmental processes occurring over time, they are difficult to obtain. Cross-sectional comparisons are only a partially adequate substitute. Here, for example, we cannot separate those seniors who became cynical several years earlier from those whose cynicism is of more recent origin. There is also the danger of interpreting a generational change as a developmental process.

personally cynical or misanthropic. These relationships are modest in strength, but nonetheless much stronger than in the sample over-all. Controlling these independent variables for each other indicates their effects are independent of one another. Among the eighth graders, then, the pattern among these variables is similar to that found among adults.

By contrast, seniors who are politically cynical—and there are almost twice as many cynical seniors as there are cynical eighth-graders—do not fit this pattern. They are only trivially more inclined to be pessimistic than are trusting seniors. They are not at all more politically or personally inefficacious. However, they are high in personal cynicism, the variable that had the weakest relationship among eighth graders.

Sophomores occupy an intermediate position, sometimes resembling the younger respondents and sometimes more like the oldest group. Political efficacy is still related to political cynicism in the tenth grade, and the relationship with personal cynicism remains at a relatively weak level as is the case among eighth graders. But pessimism and personal efficacy are now completely unrelated to political cynicism, which resembles the twelfth-grade findings. Table 7–2 presents these data in the form of the values of gamma obtaining between the independent variables and political cynicism in each grade.

Table 7–2. Influences on Political Cynicism by Grade

	GRADE IN SCHOOL		
	EIGHTH	TENTH	TWELFTH
Pessimism	.31*	.07	.18*
Personal efficacy	−.27*	−.08	−.06
Political efficacy	−.27**	−.25*	−.05
Personal cynicism	.23	.24*	.34***

* Significant, p ≤ .05; ** p ≤ .01; *** p ≤ .001.

To summarize, the causes of political cynicism appear to differ as a function of the age at which the attitude develops. Among eighth-graders, cynicism depends (in part) on several related orientations to society and one's relationship with it. By contrast, among seniors, only one general orientation, personal cynicism, is associated with political cynicism. Further, the pattern is not one of a gradual move toward the model of associations among adult attitudes and even tends towards the reverse.

Eighth grade students are generally closer to the pattern displayed by adults than are twelfth graders.

Differences by grade in the apparent causes of political cynicism are matched by some differences in consequences. We investigated the impact of cynicism on a number of attitudes and behaviors related to political participation. While junior and senior high school students cannot participate in the full range of ways available to older citizens (and in 1967 of course the voting age was still twenty-one), still they can express political involvement in a sense of political interest,[15] in attention to political affairs in the media,[16] and in discussing politics with their families.[17] They can have anticipatory attitudes about voting[18] and adopt a party identification.[19] They also can engage in acts of political behavior such as wearing campaign buttons or working in a political campaign.[20]

Again, the data reveal some differences between younger and older adolescents, although in general political cynicism is not associated with reduced politicization in any of the groups. However, on those variables on which political cynicism did have an impact, the relationship does differ by grade. The effects of political cynicism seem to be slightly greater among those who became cynical at a relatively early age.

The impact of political cynicism on politicization is not to reduce political involvement in general. Political interest, attention to media, frequency of political discussions with parents, and participation were not lowered by feelings of political cynicism in any grade.[21]

However, the findings are different on the two measures of politicization of those available here which are most likely to reflect a supportive political stance. Highly cynical eighth graders are less likely than more

[15] Measured by a standard single-item indicator (Langton and Jennings, 1968, 855, 6, n. 19).

[16] Students were asked how often they read about politics and public affairs in newspapers, listen to political news on television, and watch political documentaries or discussion programs. Answers were summed, and scores categorized into four groups from "low" to "high."

[17] Measured by a single item: How often do you talk about politics and public affairs with your parents—almost never, a few times a month, several times a week?

[18] Students were asked whether they intended to vote regularly. "No" and "Don't know" responses were combined.

[19] Answer categories for the item on party preference included "As an Independent, not favoring any party" and "I really don't care."

[20] The items used were: wearing campaign buttons or displaying bumper stickers; attending political meetings; writing letters to government officials; and campaigning. Scores were combined to form categories of those who had engaged in no acts, one, or more than one.

[21] Finifter reports no association between "normlessness" and participation among adults (Finifter, 1970, 403).

trusting students in the same grade to express an intention to vote in the future. Also, they are less involved in the party system, being more likely to respond that they don't care about parties and slightly more likely to be Independents rather than partisans.[22]

Among seniors, political cynicism has no substantial effects on any of these variables. The direction of the relationships with vote intentions and party involvement do remain the same, but the associations are weak and insignificant. Tenth-grade students resemble seniors. Table 7–3 compares the gamma values on these two variables by grade.

Table 7–3. Consequences of Cynicism by Grade

| | GRADE IN SCHOOL | | |
	EIGHTH	TENTH	TWELFTH
Vote intention	.49*	.11	.19
Party involvement	.34**	.08	.17

* Significant, p ≤ .001; ** p ≤ .02.

To some degree, then, the consequences of cynicism are associated with age. Cynicism among younger respondents affects vote intentions and involvement in the party system. But among older respondents, political cynicism has no discernible effects on politicization as measured here. Thus the impact of being politically cynical may vary with the age at which the attitude is acquired.

The tendency for eighth-grade cynics to be less committed to voting and to be less involved with the party system without being generally less politically attentive and active raises the possibility that cynicism may reduce conventional and supportive political participation while increasing political dissent.

As the school system in which this research was carried out refused to permit any questions concerning protest participation and the like, no data are available here to test this possibility. However, this argument has been advanced in the literature (Stokes, 1967, 72; Aberbach and Walker, 1970, 1199; Finifter, 1970, 406, 7) and is supported by findings on adults that political cynicism predicted to voting for two unconventional political candidates: Goldwater in 1964 (Aberbach, 1969) and Wallace in 1968 (Converse, 1969). In addition Aberbach and Walker found that cynicism

[22] Stokes has reported a similar finding among adults (Stokes, 1962, 69).

was associated among blacks with being able to imagine a situation in which one could riot and among whites in casting a mock ballot for a "backlash candidate" (Aberbach and Walker, 1970, 1213). If the developmental inference made here is allowed, one would expect the incidence of these and similar behaviors by adult cynics to vary with the age by which their cynicism developed.

DISCUSSION AND IMPLICATIONS

Political cynicism, an attitude not commonly found among children but fairly frequent among adults, increases substantially during adolescence. However, this increase is not due to a corresponding increase in the independent variables that have been related to cynicism among adults. The causes and consequences of political cynicism appear to vary with the age at which the attitude develops.

In the youngest group in the sample, where cynicism is least common, being politically cynical is associated with four general orientations toward the sociopolitical world: pessimism, political inefficacy, personal inefficacy, and, to a lesser degree, personal cynicism. Thus it appears that political cynicism here is part of a generalized negative outlook, including negative views toward the self (inefficacy), other people (person cynicism), politics (political cynicism), and life in general (pessimism). It seems quite likely, therefore, that the political cynicism among these eighth graders tends to be derived from personality and to be relatively enduring.

By contrast, political cynicism among the seniors is not generally associated with these negative orientations. In three of four cases there is no relationship. The only case in which a general negative orientation is related to political cynicism in the twelfth grade is that of personal cynicism. Thus, it appears that political cynicism among seniors is less likely to derive from personality and personality-related variables.

Why should personal cynicism be the exception? I would hypothesize that the increasing tendency with grade to generalize from cynicism toward people in general to cynicism toward people in government may be related to the life cycle. Some scholars have suggested that young children may be motivated to respect and like authority because of their dependent and vulnerable position (Hess and Easton, 1960; Hess and Torney, 1967). Such a motivation might tend to depress negative political orientations in general but would particularly inhibit one's making a simple response generalization from general cynicism felt toward ordinary people to authority figures. However, adolescence is a period of life during which the individual strives to develop his own sense of identity (Erikson, 1968) and, in the course of this process, begins to assert his independence from authority. Such a development might progressively remove this inhibition "blocking" the response generalization from personal to political cynicism. Thus, while personal cynicism remains at a constant level over the grades, an increasing tendency to generalize from this view of people to the special case of "people in government" may explain the increase in political cynicism to some degree.

Differences by grade in the patterns observed extend not only to the apparent causes of cynicism but also to its impact. The eighth-grade students who are cynical tend to be less committed to regular voting and less involved in the party system, while cynical students in the twelfth grade are not differentiated from trusting students on any of the dependent variables. The somewhat greater impact of cynicism among eighth graders is not surprising if indeed their cynicism is more likely to arise out of personality. The greater coherence of the pattern among these younger respondents together with their resemblance to cynical adults suggests that those who develop feelings of political cynicism relatively early, when it is still rather unusual to do so, may constitute a "hard core" of cynics for whom the attitude has more centrality and stability.

The lack of fit between the patterns associated with cynicism among adults and seniors, the relative lack of association between general orientations and political cynicism, and the absence of any discernible consequences of cynicism among seniors on any of the dependent variables cast doubt on the significance of cynicism among people of that age. Political cynicism in this group, in contrast with the younger respondents, appears to occupy a more peripheral position in their attitude structures.

There are many questions about this process left unanswered here. Future research using data from a panel study would clearly be desirable as a method of tracing developmental patterns. Identifying the factors that account for the greater frequency of cynicism among older adolescents would help in interpreting the significance of this group's pattern. Possibly cynicism increases in adolescence because of a diffuse desire to sound more "sophisticated." Perhaps these older cynics are more likely to be expressing a political cliché, not a fundamental distrust. Or, increasing information about politics and the political process may alter perceptions of the political system. In this case, changed perceptions may or may not be accompanied by negative evaluations. (The cynicism scale used here measures perceptions of politics, not outrage.) If their new perceptions are negatively valued, this may stem from their comparison of an earlier-learned idealized model with "real world" politics (Hess and Torney, 1967, 58). Another hypothesis advanced by Easton and Dennis suggests the possibility of a "trough" (temporary decline) in support for authority in adolescence and early adulthood, of which political cynicism may be one manifestation (Easton and Dennis, 1969, 292–305). However, whatever the explanation of cynicism among seniors, the data presented here raise doubts about the centrality, the significance, and the stability of political cynicism among these older adolescents.

Perhaps indeed we should reexamine our assumption that late adolescence is a period of life during which political attitudes come to substantially resemble those of adulthood. A recent national study of political socialization among high school seniors found disappointingly few relationships explaining these students' political attitudes (Jennings and Niemi, 1968; Langton and Jennings, 1968). Merelman found slightly greater coherence in the structure of policy thinking among eighth-graders than among twelfth-graders (Merelman, 1971, 166). Late adolescence may be a time of life during which one is increasingly cognizant of political issues and terminology and hence more likely to verbalize political opinions found in the culture, but, being still in the process of developing a sense of identity and unsure as yet of one's own social location, older teenagers may be more likely to "try out" a variety of political positions than to form lasting and coherent attitude patterns at this time.

Whether such a general pattern should be found among older adolescents or not, the differences in the causes and consequences of political cynicism among eighth-graders, tenth-graders, and twelfth-graders observed here should alert us to the importance of studying the processes of political socialization. The analysis here indicates the limitations of assuming continuities in the processes that underlie incremental percentage change in attitude distributions from younger to older groups. Table 7–4 presents the frequency distribution of cynicism from eighth to

Table 7–4. Percentage Change in Political Cynicism

POLITICAL CYNICISM	EIGHTH-GRADERS	TENTH-GRADERS	TWELFTH-GRADERS	TEACHERS
Trusting	40.8%	29.4%	24.3%	19.6%
Neutral	36.5	38.2	35.6	26.1
Cynical	22.7	32.4	40.1	54.4
	(233)	(275)	(362)	(50)

twelfth grade and adds that of the social studies teachers in the two schools. Simply seeing this table, we—and I include myself—would probably be inclined to infer a regular, consistent developmental process, thereby missing the differences and discontinuities observed here. If process does affect outplay, as it appears to here, then we need to pay greater attention to unraveling the complex and various paths by which political attitudes are acquired.

REFERENCES

Aberbach, Joel D. "Alienation and Political Behavior," *American Political Science Review* 63 (1969), 86–99.

———, and Jack L. Walker. "Political Trust and Racial Ideology," *American Political Science Review* 64 (1970), 1199–219.

Abramson, Paul R. "Political Efficacy and Political Trust Among Black School-children: Two Explanations," *Journal of Politics* 34 (1972), 1243–75.

Agger, Robert E., Marshall N. Goldstein, and Stanley A. Pearl. "Political Cynicism: Measurement and Meaning," *Journal of Politics* 23 (1961), 477–506.

Almond, Gabriel, and Sidney Verba. *The Civic Culture* (Princeton: Princeton University Press, 1963).

Campbell, Angus, *et al. The American Voter* (New York: Wiley, 1960).

———, Gerald Gurin, and Warren Miller. *The Voter Decides* (Evanston, Illinois: Row, Peterson and Company, 1954).

Codebook of the Survey Research Center, Student-Parent Socialization Study (Ann Arbor: Inter-University Consortium for Political Research, 1971).

Converse, Philip E., *et al.* "Continuity and Change in American Politics: Parties and Issues in the 1968 Election," *American Political Science Review* 63 (1969), 1083–105.

Dennis, Jack. "Major Problems of Political Socialization Research," *Midwest Journal of Political Science* 12 (1968), 85–114.

Easton, David. *A Systems Analysis of Political Life* (New York: Wiley, 1965).

———, and Jack Dennis. *Children in the Political System: Origins of Political Legitimacy* (New York: McGraw-Hill, 1969).

Edwards, Allen L. *Techniques of Attitude Scale Construction* (New York: Appleton-Century-Crofts, 1957).

Engstrom, Richard L. "Race and Compliance: Differential Political Socialization," *Polity* 3 (1970), 100–11.

Erikson, Erik. *Identity, Youth and Crisis* (New York: W. W. Norton and Company, 1968).

Finifter, Ada W. "Dimensions of Political Alienation," *American Political Science Review* 64 (1970), 389–410.

Freeman, Caroline. "The Origins of Political Cynicism: A Study of the Development of Political Orientations in Adolescents," unpublished Ph.D. dissertation, Massachusetts Institute of Technology, 1966.

Gamson, William A. *Power and Discontent* (Homewood, Illinois: The Dorsey Press, 1968).

Greenstein, Fred I. *Children and Politics* (New Haven: Yale University Press, 1965).

Hess, Robert D., and David Easton. "The Child's Changing Image of the President," *Public Opinion Quarterly* 24 (1960), 632–44.

————, and Judith V. Torney. *The Development of Political Attitudes in Children* (Chicago: Aldine Publishing Company, 1967).

Horton, John E., and Wayne E. Thompson. "Powerlessness and Political Negativism: A Study of Defeated Local Referendums," *American Journal of Sociology* 67 (1962), 485–93.

Hyman, Herbert H. *Political Socialization* (New York: Free Press, 1959).

Jaros, Dean, Herbert Hirsch, and Frederic Fleron, Jr. "The Malevolent Leader: Political Socialization in an American Sub-Culture," *American Political Science Review* 62 (1968), 564–75.

Jennings, M. Kent, and Richard G. Niemi. "The Transmission of Political Values from Parent to Child," *American Political Science Review* 62 (1968), 169–84.

Kenyon, Sandra J. "The Development of Political Cynicism: A Study of Political Socialization," unpublished Ph.D. dissertation, Massachusetts Institute of Technology, 1970.

Langton, Kenneth P., and M. Kent Jennings. "Political Socialization and the High School Civics Curriculum in the United States," *American Political Science Review* 62 (1968), 852–67.

Lipset, Seymour Martin, *Political Man* (Garden City: Doubleday Anchor Books, 1960).

Litt, Edgar. "Political Cynicism and Political Futility," *Journal of Politics* 25 (1963), 312–23.

Lyons, Schley R. "The Political Socialization of Ghetto Children: Efficacy and Cynicism," *Journal of Politics* 32 (1970), 288–304.

Merelman, Richard M. "The Development of Policy Thinking in Adolescence," *American Political Science Review* 65 (1971), 1033–47.

Rosenberg, Morris. "Misanthropy and Political Ideology," *American Sociological Review* 21 (1956), 690–95.

Schonfeld, William R. "The Focus of Political Socialization Research: An Evaluation," *World Politics* 23 (1971), 544–78.

Schwartz, David C. *Political Alienation and Political Behavior* (Chicago: Aldine Publishing Co., 1973).

Seeman, Melvin. "On the Meaning of Alienation," *American Sociological Review* 24 (1959), 783–91.

Sigel, Roberta S. "Political Socialization: Some Reactions on Current Approaches and Conceptualization," paper delivered at the 1966 Annual Meeting of the American Political Science Association, New York.

Stokes, Donald E. "Popular Evaluations of Government: An Empirical Assessment," in Harlan Cleveland and Harold D. Lasswell (eds.), *Ethics and Bigness: Scientific, Academic, Religious, Political and Military* (New York: Harper, 1962), 61–73.

Chapter Eight

Early Socialization and Elite Behavior
John C. Pollock

INTRODUCTION

This study focuses on adult socialization in a situation experienced by many adults that is relatively continuous and enduring: a person's occupational environment. Such environments are often examined in order to measure their impact on individual efficiency and adjustment to work-role requirements (Roethilisberger and Dickson, 1939). Relatively little attention, however, has been given to the way occupational milieu affects political judgments. It might be expected that an activity filling a large proportion of an individual's life span, his occupation, would receive considerable attention from students of political attitude formation. Curiously, nevertheless, little is known or reported about the processes whereby occupational experiences influence political attitudes, beliefs, and orientations (Wahlke *et al.*, 1966; Barber, 1965; Janowitz, 1960; Johnson, 1962; Lane, 1971).

The importance to political socialization research of studies of occupational socialization lies partly in their assessment of adult learning generally. In the case of governmental and other political occupations (such as the urban housing bureaucrats examined here), there is in addition something to be learned about the factors that influence the formation and execution of political decisions. For most students of political socialization, however, the major theoretical significance of studies of adult occupational socialization rests in the light such studies may cast on the relative impact of early versus later learning. Questions about occupations and their influence on political opinions must be raised in order to understand to what degree attitudes are generally learned relatively early, prior to entering occupational structures, and to what degree occupational experience contributes significantly to the formation of political attitudes. This is the focus adopted here.

The literature on political socialization abounds with evidence that politically relevant attitudes are learned rather early and also that various kinds of political attitudes are formed and perhaps consolidated (solidified) during the years of schooling (Coleman, 1961; Langton, 1969; Hess and Torney, 1967; Prewitt, 1971). Studies of the political values of college students have pointed to considerable change in political dispositions over the course of four years of formal learning (Lipset, 1966; Lipset and Salari, 1967). But at this point students of political socialization typically leave "political man" to the vagaries of chance and circumstance. The presumption appears to be that *homo politicus* is fully formed and that little can be done to shake his essential political orientations.

Yet the individual continues to live and hold political opinions. Do his various roles as husband, father, resident, holder of a particular social status, and worker have no impact on his political beliefs? Most socialization studies seem to assume that what happens after formal education is completed is either of little consequence for political attitude formation or of little importance for the questions socialization scholars have traditionally asked, questions such as: At what age do individuals become aware of political individuals and institutions? How do individuals acquire feelings about a government's legitimacy and how can such feelings be fostered? What background factors correlate with higher levels of political interest or participation? What background variables predict the choice and intensity of political party allegiance? Such questions are asked about individuals until they graduate from college. Then they seem of little interest except to purveyors of political polls.

This essay is an effort to explore the nature and extent of adult learning about politics by focusing on a particular experience shared by many adults: occupational experience. What is the contribution of occupational experience to political attitude formation? More important, how can we compare the different impacts of pre-occupational and occupational experience on political learning? What does that comparison reveal about the relative influence of early learning on later learning about politics?[1] To begin answering these questions, this study examines the political case histories of elite bureaucrats charged with administering urban housing programs in Colombia.

Colombia's urban housing agencies and the elites who administer them

---

[1] This study measures only the influence of occupational characteristics of those who have already chosen their occupations (in this case, that of an elite bureaucrat). Inferences stemming from career recruitment choices (such as career self-selection or anticipatory socialization) may also be associated with political attitude formation. This investigation, however, is not a longitudinal study measuring attitudes at different points in time and relies only on recall data. The usual caveats about imprecision in remembering early influences are therefore necessary and worth considering.

are of interest for several reasons. One is that urban migration has increased since the 1930s in Colombia (the country boasting the highest birth rate in Latin America, 3.2 percent). As the demand for urban services has grown, the housing agencies are agreed the most successful in meeting demands (Dix, 1967, 148). Another reason Colombia's housing agencies are admired is that their performance record is considered superior to that of similar agencies in other Latin American countries, especially in the following areas: greatest average number of housing units per project; the most widespread use of prefabricated materials; the smallest time elapsed for the construction of each housing unit (except in comparison with Nicaragua); a larger number of self-help or mutual aid projects built; and a ratio of annual family income of dwellers to the average cost of a dwelling unit higher than all other countries except Venezuela, and approximately equal to that of Peru (Koth et al., 1964, 167–73).

A third reason Colombian housing agencies merit attention is that the bureaucrats who manage them have acquired substantial influence over housing decision-making. Low-income citizens have not organized to demand the low-income housing they so clearly need, and politicians have traditionally paid close attention not to the underclasses but to the demands of organized middle-income and upper-income citizens. The organizing impulse for low-income housing has come, rather, from elite (college-educated) housing bureaucrats themselves, together with some allies near the president. It was partly because of the ability of the bureaucrats and their carefully prepared plans that the U.S. Agency for International Development gave more funds for urban housing to Colombia than to any other Latin American country (Koth et al., 1964, 171). It was also in recognition of this ability and motivation that Colombia's major housing agency, the Institute of Territorial Credit, was selected by the United Nations to host a third-world conference on uncontrolled squatter settlements in Medellín, Colombia, in February, 1970.

Because elite housing bureaucrats are influential in promoting low-cost housing, it is useful to study their patterns of political learning. Why have the housing elites exercised so much concern for the marginal sectors of society? Why do some of the bureaucrats favor low-income housing more than others? What background and occupational experiences distinguish those who favor more low-income housing from those who do not? These questions help explore the origins of two distinct attitudes toward opportunity distribution in Colombia.

Despite the proliferation of institutes charged with new tasks, despite housing achievements, a major obstacle to the implementation of programs providing a wider distribution of benefits is a predisposition found in the culture of Colombian political elites generally, and among elite bureaucrats as well. It is the tendency to view change mostly in terms of its consequences for oneself or a small, nuclear group (Hirschman, 1963; Payne, 1969; Pollock, forthcoming). This focus on the "nuclear" consequences of change is essentially the opposite of a focus on the social or public consequences of change. In this study a predominant concern with the impact of distributive policies on a nuclear group will be called an "exclusive" attitude, a tendency to exclude others from one's perspective on distribution.

The contrary of exclusivity will be considered an "inclusive" attitude: a tendency to concern oneself with the public or social consequences of distributive policies. Both tendencies refer to views about the distribution of change. One is relatively narrow and personal, the other relatively broad and social (Pollock, 1973).

How do elites acquire exclusive and inclusive attitudes in Colombia? It is an assumption of this study that a partial answer to that question can be found by comparing pre-occupational and occupational experiences of elites. Are elites socialized toward inclusive or exclusive attitudes early in life? Or do significant changes occur in distributive attitudes after formal schooling has ended, produced by varied occupational situations? Before considering those questions, it is useful to know something about the pre-occupational and occupational experience of the bureaurats.

PROFILES OF BUREAUCRATS

About ninety bureaucrats in Colombia's three urban housing agencies[2] and five in the national budget Planning Office have college degrees, here considered the operational indicator of elite bureaucratic status. Eighty-two structured interviews with these individuals, almost the entire universe, were completed in early 1970. Each one lasted from one and one half to two hours, and generous use of openended questions provided numerous answers rich in detail. The background characteristics and occupational environments of respondents may help explain why housing functionaries have a reputation for inclusivity.

Several measures indicate that the bureaucrats are part of some elite group in Colombia. They are educationally advantaged, with college degrees mostly in architecture and some in engineering. About 50 percent have engaged in some kind of graduate work. By contrast, a 1964 study of Colombian youth revealed that, in the 20 to 24 age group, the youngest group capable of having completed an educational cycle in its totality, only 1.8 percent had entered a university, had entered and left, or had graduated (Departamento Administrativo Nacional de Estadística, 1964).

[2] Located in Colombia's capital, Bogotá, they are: Instituto de Credito Territorial (Institute of Territorial Credit), Banco Central Hipotecario (Central Lending Bank) and the Caja de la Vivienda Popular (Popular Housing Office).

Because college degrees are at a premium in Colombia, and as graduate work is an experience far rarer in Colombia than in the United States, the respondents rank among the most privileged of the university educated.

The respondents also rank themselves and their fathers high on three self-anchored scales of social, economic, and political influence,[3] where a score of "1" is no influence at all and "10" is maximum influence. Economic, political, and social ranking all reveal that the bureaucrats consider their family origins consistently more advantaged than other Colombians. On the 10-point scales, the average score given to fathers is 6.51, the average score given to sons, 6.24. In addition, interviewees generally perceive few differences between their own and their fathers' economic and political rankings. An examination of father and son social rankings, however, reveals a somewhat more noticeable difference. A comparison of mean rankings reveals that sons rank themselves lower than or equal to their fathers more consistently on the social influence dimension than on the other two. (The average social rank for fathers is 7.20, for sons, 6.54).

The respondents come from large families, a characteristic that does not clearly distinguish elite from non-elite families in Colombia, where large families are found in every social class. About 60 percent have four or more siblings, and at least 20 percent belong to families of nine or more children. Yet most respondents, about 55 percent, are either eldest or next to eldest children.

Most bureaucrats are also quite young: one half are 33 years old or younger. About two thirds have worked fewer than twelve years. Compared with other elites in Colombia the housing bureaucrats are younger, have spent a larger portion of their lives in the capital city, Bogota, display interest in only a few leisure activities, and limit leisure participation to noncontroversial (nonpolitical or nonreligious) activities in professional, cultural, and educational organizations.[4]

[3] Political influence or power is considered to refer not to political party involvement but to proximity to formal decision-making, in this case a proximity facilitated by positions as elite government functionaries. The occupation of government "technocrat" received new importance in the regime of President Carlos Lleras Restrepo (1966–1970), with the creation of a multitude of special government agencies to deal with the challenges of industrialization, finance, and the statistical organizations necessary to expand industrialization. New opportunities in the sixties therefore created an opportunity for a new political role, the technocrat, who promotes industrialization or tries to resolve politically relevant social dilemmas through the use of planning and technical skills.

[4] "Other" elites refers to a sample survey of over 1,000 Colombian elites in legislatures, bureaucracies, and intellectual activities carried out in 1966–67. The study, as yet unpublished, was undertaken by Colombia political scientist Samuel Yohai, a Ph.D. candidate in government at Harvard University.

Privileged origins apart, what are the characteristics of the occupational milieu surrounding the bureaucrats? Several questions help determine how "inclusive" that environment is: How open is the job recruitment process? What proportion of their colleagues do respondents consider motivated by "inclusive" or public-service goals? How collective or co-operative is the nature of daily work; and conversely, how isolated? Similarly, are the housing institutions relatively hierarchical in decision-making, or is decision-making more decentralized and more participatory and inclusive? Finally, how optimistic are the bureaucrats about agency performance now and in the future? Answers to the preceding questions can provide information on bureaucrats' perceptions of inclusivity in their occupational milieu.

Consider the first question: Do the respondents consider job recruitment relatively open or relatively closed? A large majority (about 73) proudly estimate that recruitment into their housing agencies is based largely on merit criteria such as competitive exams, experience, or accomplishment. But other estimates of occupational opportunity do not give much evidence of inclusive practices.

Despite their optimism about agency recruitment, a majority of respondents (about 55 percent) believe that contacts, personal recommendations, and ascriptive criteria generally are of primary importance in finding most jobs in the government. (As of this writing, Colombia does not have a civil service system requiring competitive exams for all who wish to enter government service.) A similar percentage (about 54 percent) believe that jobs are more difficult to find now than in the past. And about 55 percent believe that advancement within bureaus is more difficult now than in the past. In addition, the belief that achievement criteria are paramount in recruiting new housing bureaucrats is somewhat paradoxical in that only 24 respondents, or about 29 percent of them, reported that they obtained their own jobs through examination. By contrast, fifty-five, or about 69 percent of the respondents, reported they found their first positions in urban housing through friends either inside or outside the urban housing agency joined. About the same percentage report urban housing recruitment to be merit-based as report their own positions found through friendship ties.

Possibly bureaucrats believe present recruitment practices employ more merit criteria than did those in the past, when the respondents found their first positions in urban housing. Or perhaps respondents are evaluating goals rather than current practice when they evaluate recruitment in their housing agencies. Quite possibly, respondents think more about criteria for advancement than about criteria for recruitment when estimating housing recruitment as largely merit-based.

For example, large majorities report they believe that ambition, efficiency, and achievement criteria generally are crucial in promotions. When asked which factors contribute most to promotions, about two thirds of the respondents mentioned ambition and efficiency. Regardless of their estimates of government recruitment, in general, most bureaucrats believe that recruitment and promotion into their housing agencies are based largely on merit.

In contrast to the inclusive, "open" evaluations of recruitment and promotions, most bureaucrats believe that they themselves and other bureaucrats are motivated more by individual gain or accomplishment, "exclusive" goals, than by collective goals. When asked in open-ended questions to give their own reasons for preferring some previous positions more than others, about 84 percent of the respondents mentioned personal independence, initiative, or security, and personal professional growth. Only about 16 percent reported, when asked to list the characteristics of the positions they liked best, the opportunity to aid others.

A similar response pattern emerged when respondents were asked (using multiple choice questions) about motivations of other bureaucrats in government service. About 64 percent estimated that those who enter government service do so for reasons connected with financial and social security, personal independence and power, and the advancement of personal professional growth. Only about 36 percent believe people join the government primarily because it affords opportunities to aid others. Most respondents clearly consider themselves and most colleagues motivated primarily by "exclusive" criteria.

"Inclusivity" has been used to refer to the openness of the recruitment process and to the perceived collective or personal motivations of bureaucrats. In each of these instances, inclusivity refers to the extent to which collective rather than individual or personal considerations are given importance in a particular process or role. The same concept can be used in describing a bureaucrat's daily work and decision-making opportunities. Do most respondents interact with a relatively large number of people in their daily work? Is their work schedule, by that criterion, "inclusive"? And on decisions of some importance or controversy, are superiors' decisions automatically obeyed? Or are the bureaucrats able or likely to register objections and possibly, therefore, collectivize decision-making? Answers to these questions reveal degrees of inclusivity in working relationships.

A number of criteria indicate that the elite bureaucrats consider their work roles relatively isolated from frequent interaction with others. About 54 percent describe their work primarily in technical terms, involving designing and programming of housing and writing legal and financial advice. Further, in their estimates of how long a trainee for their work roles should spend outside their own sections in order to perform his job well, 50 percent of the respondents allow no time at all, while another

29 percent allowed between one and three days. Similarly, if respondents are asked to estimate the number and rank of people they would consult in the construction of a training program designed to help someone perform their tasks, about 60 percent mention two or fewer people, and another 20 percent would consult only three or four people. Such replies indicate that these bureaucrats consider themselves relatively isolated in their work.

They also seem aware of hierarchy. Regarding the same training program, respondents seem more apt to ask advice from superiors than from subordinates or colleagues. Ninety percent replied they would consult no one below them in occupational rank, and about 50 percent would consult no one of equal rank in forming a training program. Yet only 25 percent would consult no one of higher rank, and about 65 percent would consult one or two people of higher rank. These estimates indicate a consciousness of hierarchy, a conclusion reinforced somewhat by replies to imaginary questions about colleague reactions if they were asked by superiors to prepare a report which conflicted with their professional values. About 40 percent of the bureaucrats believe 50 percent or more of their colleagues would prepare the requested report. To be sure, most respondents believe that fewer than 50 percent would prepare a report conflicting with their professional values, but it is clear that a substantial number are believed capable of submitting to orders even in that extreme circumstance. The daily work roles of bureaucrats seem rather isolated and exclusive, and the decision-making power of superiors suggests that hierarchical roles are of at least moderate importance and that decision-making processes are moderately exclusive.

A final measure of inclusivity in a bureaucrat's work environment is his estimate of agency performance. Do most respondents believe their urban housing agencies are improving their performance (and thereby affecting more groups, becoming more inclusive), or are the agencies believed rather perfunctory? Most bureaucrats are clearly proud of the performance record of their agencies. For 1970, the time the questionnaire was administered, about 75 percent ranked their agencies at 7 or higher on a 10-point self-anchoring scale, where 1 is the worst performance possible and 10 is the best. Estimating performance levels five years in the future, in 1975, 80 percent believed that performance would rank at 8 or above, and about 46 percent placed the 1975 rank at 10, the best possible score. Most respondents believe their agencies rather inclusive.

WORK PERCEPTIONS AND INCLUSIVITY

The information on elite background profiles and perceptions of occupational milieu can be used to generate a number of hypotheses about inclusive attitudes. Consider first some propositions about the relation between work role perceptions, role performance, and inclusive attitudes. It is reasonable to expect that those who are surrounded by or who believe themselves imbedded in an inclusive work environment are more likely than others to exhibit inclusive attitudes. Inclusive environments should foster inclusive beliefs.[5] Given that assumption as a general umbrella hypothesis, a number of specific hypotheses can be derived from the data on occupational characteristics:

Role Perceptions

Fair Recruiting. Those who believe that the government generally, or their agencies in particular, use merit criteria in recruiting new bureaucrats are likely to exhibit inclusive attitudes. So it should also prove with:

Altruism. Those who believe themselves and other bureaucrats to be motivated primarily by a desire to aid others (rather than to promote individual monetary or professional gain) are likely to display inclusive attitudes.

Role Integration. Those whose daily work involves contact with relatively large numbers of people are more likely to reveal inclusive attitudes.

Role Integrity. Those who are likely to challenge authority and to promote collective decisions when a superior issues an order challenging professional values are likely to hold inclusive attitudes.

Performance Optimism. Those who are most optimistic about housing agency performance in the future are those most likely to favor inclusive housing policies.

Role Performance

Vertical Job Mobility. Those who report that they have held many positions ranking below their present one can be considered more occupationally mobile than those who list relatively few previous positions of lower rank. Those who consider themselves most upwardly mobile in this sense may be expected to exhibit inclusive attitudes.

---

[5] Perceiving oneself in an inclusive environment is not necessarily the same as actually performing in an inclusive environment. But in this study both role perceptions and role performance are considered components of role behavior. Although occupational role perceptions and role performance are distinct aspects of behavior, they are both related to the influence of occupational environment on inclusive attitudes and orientations. Both perceptions and performance inform the process of occupational role socialization. (For a brief discussion of this position, refer to Andrain, 1971.)

Rank. Those who have acquired high status and rank (as measured by income) within their agencies and who direct their agencies may be assumed to consider themselves and their agencies relatively inclusive, given the superior performance of the housing agencies to other urban service bureau in Colombia.

Experience. Similarly, those with more years of work experience in the housing field may be expected to know their colleagues and their agencies relatively well, to perceive them as benevolent as friendships grow, and to acquire inclusive attitudes. Both considerable work experience and age should be positively related to the possession of inclusive attitudes. The measurement of years of work experience, although not obtained from a longitudinal study, approximates a longitudinal measure of attitude change. If major learning occurs in one's occupational role, rather than prior to it, this indicator is the most likely to reveal it. As a key measure of occupational impact, work experience is an accurate gauge for estimating the relative influence of occupational learning and prior learning.

These hypotheses can be tested by constructing a definition of inclusivity appropriate for this study, namely, a preference for low-cost housing. Before testing these propositions, however, it is useful to ask what proportion of the elite housing bureaucrats, as a group, exhibits inclusive attitudes toward housing. If asked directly to choose between middle-class and lower-class housing, about 45 percent of the respondents prefer housing for the lower sectors, about 28 percent prefer middle-class housing, and an equal percentage don't know or don't care. A question forcing dichotomous choice between two housing types therefore yields a plurality for low-cost housing.

In order to diminish the number of responses labeled "indifferent" or "don't know," it is useful to allow respondents to register different degrees of support for different types of housing. Respondents were therefore asked to allocate an imaginary 100 pesos among four kinds of housing policies.[6] Two kinds, middle class and lower class, received the highest amount of

---

[6] The four policies presented were the following:

1. The relocation of housing settlements that prevent the growth of the city, so that it is worthwhile relocating them (relocation).
2. The improvement of existing housing settlements that are not self-sufficient and will deteriorate without aid and create serious problems in the future (improve existing squatter settlements).
3. The provision of housing to those who have insufficient incentive or resources to build by themselves and who are unable to grasp the alternatives currently available (low-cost housing).
4. The provision of housing to those with sufficient resources to acquire adequate housing by some means (middle-income housing).

funding. For each of these two housing types, responses were dichot-omized. Those who allocated 50 pesos (50 percent of the total budget) or more to one housing type were considered to favor that housing construction strongly. Some overlap occurred, in that some respondents allocated 50 pesos each to middle-class and lower-class housing. Some who have high scores on the low-cost housing preference scale therefore also have high scores on the middle-class housing preference scale, but such even distributions are rare. Using this measure, about 46 percent have high preferences for low-cost housing, and about 46 percent score high on the middle-class housing scale.

A test of the hypotheses provides initial confirmation of all but two. High role integration with colleagues and high role integrity are not associated positively or negatively with a preference for low-income housing. Some of the variables are more clearly associated than others with inclusive housing attitudes: more years of work experience, optimism about agency performance, and perception of colleagues as motivated by altruism (Gammas are .46, .38, and .56 respectively). Table 8–1 reveals the relation between these variables and inclusivity.

Table 8–1. Support for Low-Cost Housing, by Colleague Altruism, Occupation-al Experience, and Optimism About Agency Performance

		COLLEAGUE ALTRUISM		OCCUPATIONAL EXPERIENCE		PERFORMANCE OPTIMISM	
		LOW	HIGH	9 YEARS OR LESS	MORE THAN 9 YEARS	HIGH	HIGHEST
Support for Low-Cost Housing	High	29.4%	60.0%	34.1%	58.5%	37.2%	56.8%
	Low	70.6%	40.0%	65.9%	41.5%	62.8%	43.2%
Number of Cases		34	45	41	41	43	37
		($N = 79$)		($N = 82$)		($N = 80$)	
Column Percent of Total Sample		43%	57%	50%	50%	53.8%	36.2%
Gamma		.56		.46		.38	

The other hypothesized associations were also confirmed, at least in the sense that correlations, although not especially large, pointed in the predicted direction. A positive relationship was found between a preference for low-income housing and: a belief that the government bureaucracies use merit criteria in recruitment (Gamma .22); confidence in one's own occupational altruism (Gamma .32); high bureaucratic rank as measured by income (Gamma .33); vertical job mobility (Gamma .32); and age (Gamma .32). The broad assumption that inclusive occupational surroundings encourage inclusive housing attitudes seems confirmed. But are inclusive attitudes learned mostly on the job, or do individuals approach occupations with inclusive and exclusive attitudes already largely formed? One way to begin answering that question is to determine how strongly pre-occupational background characteristics are related to housing inclusivity.

EARLY INFLUENCES AND INCLUSIVE ATTITUDES

To study the contribution of pre-occupational experience to the formation of inclusive attitudes, it is useful to focus on the notion of relative privilege. Information gathered about bureaucrats' backgrounds indicates they are among the most privileged members of Colombian society. Among their own cohorts, however, some can be considered more or less privileged in various role situations, roles defined by the following variables: family size (total number of siblings); sibling birth order; amount of higher education; perceived economic, political, and social status in relation to other citizens; and perceived economic, political, and social status in relation to one's own father. Each variable defines a role situation in which a bureaucrat can be considered more or less privileged than siblings, age-cohorts, colleagues, or parents. In each role the individual may view himself as relatively privileged or underprivileged. Our task is to discover the contribution of these multiple "privilege" roles to the acquisition of political attitudes.

Does the possession of privilege correlate with inclusivity? It is expected that elite bureaucrats whose status, income, and position are relatively secure or established are likely to display inclusive attitudes. Conversely, those whose status or security is most questionable or tenuous may be expected to exhibit more exclusive attitudes. It is predicted that bureaucrats who are or who see themselves as relatively disadvantaged elites are more likely to "compensate" for this perception by becoming more "elitist" than their colleagues. Several specific hypotheses follow.

1. *Family Size.* In relatively large families, individuals are likely to experience less sibling rivalry (see, for example, Bossard and Bowl, 1956) and are likely to find a relatively large number of allies in conflicts either with the parents or with other siblings. The presence of many siblings

should enhance some kinds of personal security and therefore, inclusivity (Clausen, 1968).

2. *Birth Order.* First-born children are generally found to be more insecure than later arrivals (Sears, Macoby, and Levin, 1957). It is not unlikely that those with a relatively large number of older siblings are relatively secure and can be predicted to display inclusive attitudes.

3. *Schooling.* Those whose schooling is more advanced, who have spent time in specialized training or graduate school, and who have often engaged in advanced work abroad can be considered more advantaged than their colleagues who have not pursued special training beyond the initial college degree. Those whose training gives them special status may be expected to be relatively inclusive.

4. *Social, Economic, and Political Power Status.* Extending the concept of privilege further, those who perceive themselves and their fathers as members of a relatively high-ranking social, political, and economic elite are more likely to display inclusivity than those who rank themselves among the lower-status elites.

When these hypotheses are tested by asking the extent to which each measure of privilege is associated with a preference for low-cost housing, all hypotheses are confirmed. Calculations performed to test the hypotheses linking privilege and inclusive attitudes suggest that two different status categories may affect inclusivity differently. One seems to refer to respondents in their roles as members of society, the other in their roles as members of families. Measures of general social status include number of years of higher education achieved and self-anchored estimates of parental and respondent status ranks in relation to other citizens. Measures of family status include estimates of filial mobility indicated by differences between respondents' rankings of themselves and their fathers on the social, economic, and political scales (referred to here as "filial power status"); family size; and birth order. Consider social status first.

Social Status

University attendance for a large number of years is a reliable indicator of privileged status, and it is clear that elites who are educationally privileged are relatively inclusive. The greater number of years spent in the university, the more likely respondents are to allocate funds for low-cost housing (Gamma .64), and the less likely they are to support middle-income housing (Gamma − .33).

It is predicted that the higher an individual perceives his social, economic, and political status in relation to others in society, the more inclusive he will be. This hypothesis is disconfirmed. Respondents were asked to estimate their own and their fathers' status rankings along three dimensions, corresponding to social, economic, and political status. The higher the father's ranked economic, social, and especially political status, the less the respondent favors low-cost housing (Gammas are − .26 for father economic status; − .32 for father social status; and − .41 for father political status). Moreover, there is little positive or negative relation at all between a respondent ranking his own political, social, and economic status highly and a preference for low-cost housing. Table 8–2 reveals the relation between privileged education and high parental citizen status, on the one hand, and a preference for low-income housing on the other.

Table 8–2. Support for Low-Cost Housing, by Amount of Higher Education and Perceived Political Power Ranking of Father

		NUMBER OF YEARS IN A UNIVERSITY	
		5 OR LESS	6 OR MORE
Support for Low-Cost Housing	High	31%	68%
	Low	69%	32%
Number of Cases (N = 82)		48	34
Gamma .64			
		FATHER'S CITIZEN POWER RANK	
		LOW	HIGH
Support for Low-Cost Housing	High	57%	36%
	Low	43%	64%
Number of Cases (N = 81)		42	39
Gamma −.41			

Measures of association between privileged schooling, high social status of father and son, and inclusivity appear to yield contradictory results. The advantage of privileged schooling does predict a preference for low-cost housing, but a high ranking of father-and-son status does not. What explains this apparent inconsistency? Do the findings suggest that privileged schooling is an unsatisfactory measure of privilege, that other status measures predict low inclusivity, and that therefore the privilege-inclusivity hypothesis must be rejected? Or do advantaged schooling and measures of one's own and one's father's social status reflect quite different dimensions or concepts of privilege, compelling a modification but not a rejection of the privilege hypothesis? An examination of family status characteristics helps resolve these questions.

Family Status

It is expected that those with a large number of siblings, especially those with a large number of older siblings, are likely to be relatively secure and therefore inclusive. Both predictions are confirmed. The larger the family, the greater the tendency to support low-cost housing (Gamma .40). Similarly, those with a relatively large number of older siblings are somewhat more likely than others to support low-cost housing (the highest correlation is between a large number of older brothers and inclusivity, Gamma .30).

Number and birth order of siblings aside, respondents' perceptions of the status differences between themselves and their fathers prove strong predictors of inclusivity. For the association between father-and-son status vis-à-vis other citizens and inclusivity, the privilege hypothesis is disconfirmed. But the higher the respondent perceives his own status, especially his political power vis-à-vis his father (his filial "power" status), the more inclusive, generous and favorably disposed toward low-cost housing he is (Gammas are .20 for filial economic status; .35 for filial social status; and .49 for filial political status). Table 8–3 illustrates the

Table 8–3. Support for Low-Cost Housing, by Number of Siblings and Son's Filial Power Rank

		NUMBER OF SIBLINGS	
		FOUR OR FEWER	FIVE OR MORE
Support for Low-Cost Housing	High	38%	59%
	Low	62%	41%
Number of Cases (N = 79)		45	34
Gamma .40			

		SON'S FILIAL POWER RANK		
		LOWER THAN FATHER	SAME AS FATHER	HIGHER THAN FATHER
Support for Low-Cost Housing	High	32%	38%	70%
	Low	68%	62%	30%
Number of Cases (N = 81)		28	26	27
Gamma .49				

strong positive relation between family size, filial political rank, and support for low-income housing. Information on family background and perceptions, therefore, suggests that the more advantaged or upwardly mobile a respondent is in relation to his siblings or his father, the more inclusive he is likely to be.

CONCLUSION: THE IMPORTANCE OF EARLY LEARNING

This investigation reveals a number of factors associated with inclusivity. Several variables measuring workplace conditions and perceptions and several measuring pre-occupational privilege are related to attitudes on the desirability of low-cost housing. But which set of experiences is more important in predicting inclusivity: the pre-occupational or the occupational? Among all the variables, which are the very strongest predictors of inclusive attitudes toward housing clients? These two questions can be answered by isolating the impact of each variable on low-cost housing preferences through partial correlations. Partial correlations simply subtract interfering influences caused by other variables in calculations of relations between a single independent variable and a single dependent variable, in this case, a preference for low-cost housing (Nie *et al.*, 1970). The additional calculation of partial correlations for all the variables, one with another (and each with low-cost housing preferences), permits the reduction of salient variables to those shown in Table 8–4.

The Primacy of Early Learning

From Table 8–4, a ranking of variables can be made according to their predictive strength.

The ranking reveals that two of the three best predictors of inclusivity are experienced, learned, or initially acquired before occupations are

Table 8–4. Relative Priority of Influences on Policy Preferences

STRONG INFLUENCES	PARTIAL CORRELATIONS WITH A PREFERENCE FOR LOW-COST HOUSING
Colleague Altruism	.34
Privileged Schooling	.29
Filial Power Status	.25
Government Merit Recruitment	−.24
Family Size	.22

entered: filial power status and privileged schooling. The table thus underscores the substantial impact that early pre-occupational learning has on later, occupational learning (see also Reading, 1968). It also permits the generation of a number of propositions.

1. *Selective types of intergenerational mobility are potent predictors of inclusivity.* A respondent's perceptions of his political mobility in relation to his father correlate strongly with inclusive attitudes toward housing clients. They also seem strongly associated with privileged schooling, which in this study appears to indicate some kind of upward mobility as well. The lower a bureaucrat ranks his father's economic and political status, the more likely he is to have pursued advanced studies at the university (Gammas are + .43 between low economic ranking of father and years in the university, and + .42 between low political ranking of father and years in the university). And many years of university attendance correlate positively with filial political mobility (Gamma .41).[7]

2. *Perceptions of altruistic work motives in colleagues are clearly associated with inclusive attitudes.* Those who see themselves in a work environment that recruits or retains inclusive colleagues are likely to support funding for low-cost housing. Although it is not difficult to notice which relations are corroborated or included in Table 8–4, and Figure 8–1, it is also important to observe what is excluded, as described in propositions three and four.

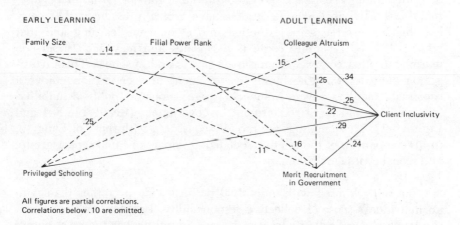

EARLY LEARNING   ADULT LEARNING

Family Size   Filial Power Rank   Colleague Altruism

All figures are partial correlations.
Correlations below .10 are omitted.

Privileged Schooling   Merit Recruitment
                                       in Government

Client Inclusivity

Figure 8–1. Client Inclusivity, by Early Learning and Adult Learning

[7] The evidence that postgraduate education is strongly associated with perceived upward mobility, especially filial power mobility, may suggest the importance of family—and not just general social status—in explaining political attitudes.

3. *Social status rankings of self and father are relatively weak predictors of inclusivity.* Respondent status ranking of self and father along social and political dimensions, despite their apearance of strong association with inclusivity and exclusivity, are not as potent as are measures of relative family advantage. Relative sibling security (the presence of many siblings) and relatively greater filial power or political status (than one's father) are both more consistently associated with inclusivity than are estimates of more general social status.

4. *Rank (measured by income), age, vertical mobility, and years of work experience are relatively weak predictors of inclusivity.* Initial gamma correlations between income, age, job mobility, years of work experience, and inclusivity suggested that older, more occupationally mobile, and more economically comfortable bureaucrats tend to favor low-cost housing. If one factors out the influences of filial power mobility, and perceptions of colleague altruism, however, these predictions assume less importance. More significant than job mobility, experience, or comfort are perceptions of personal power mobility and perceptions of altruistic, public service motivations among colleagues. It will be noted that the indicator most likely to reveal the impact of occupational socialization years of work experience, is not a significant predictor of inclusivity. As work experience bears little relation to distributive attitudes, the argument for the importance of occupational socialization is weakened; and the case for the primacy of early learning is hereby strengthened.

5. *Early sibling experience has a considerable impact on adult occupational attitudes.* Socialization studies have typically assumed that early learning has exerted some extended impact on later learning and that what is learned in family contexts permeates and may even supersede learning in other contexts, among peer groups and in school. This investigation indicates that the family as an agent of socialization enjoys a remarkable staying power, influencing perceptions of: political mobility, job mobility, and merit recruitment in government (See Table 8–4 and Figure 8–1). These findings are broadly consistent with those of Langton, in his comparison of the relative socializing impact of family, peer group, and school civics curriculum.

Concerning himself with individual political efficacy rather than with an individual's sense of collective responsibility, Langton concludes that the family (specifically its level of interest in politics) is the most potent predictor of political efficacy. He also cautions, however, that the family's political interest, though pervasive in impact, has a relatively low threshold of influence; that it can socialize individuals to exhibit a moderate interest in politics; but that other conditions and situations produce incremental jumps in political interest from moderate to intense (Langton, 1969, 158–159, 173–174). This investigation, an elite study, differs from the Langton investigation in that sibling number rather than parental political interest or relative authority of father and mother are considered salient predictors of political attitudes. Yet despite some differences, the two studies arrive at fundamentally similar conclusions. The Colombian elite study concerns itself with predicting inclusive attitudes, but like Langton's concludes that early family experience is pervasive in impact and that its threshold of influence on most other variables associated with inclusivity is low.

A Convergence of Two Modes of Learning

A close examination of Table 8–4 and Figure 8–1, together with the calculation of correlations relating several characteristics to the major independent variables, reveals the operation of two distinct learning paths or mechanisms.

1. The first mechanism is interpersonal transfer or diffusion. The transfer model of learning assumes that in relations with adults a child will establish "modes of interaction which are similar to those he has experienced with persons in his early life." (Adler and Harrington, 1970, 9). The transfer model expects that attitudes developed toward one person are transferred to apply to a new object or set of persons.

The influence pattern of sibling number and filial power mobility on inclusive attitudes resembles the transfer learning mode. The more siblings a respondent has and the more he considers himself politically mobile relative to his father, the more likely he is to believe himself vertically mobile occupationally (not shown in the tables) and to perceive government recruitment as basically fair and merit-inspired. In short, a respondent from a large family appears to view his occupational world as relatively generous, accommodating, and fair. This perception of a rather open occupational structure is clearly inclusive in its implication that interaction with occupationally significant others is basically beneficial. The world has treated the bureaucrat inclusively, and he, not unpredictably, views it in reciprocal fashion. What may have occurred in this learning process is a generalization of affect from early feelings of security (enjoying many siblings) to later feelings about the occupational recruitment and promotion process. Security in childhood may have been transferred to later beliefs about security or privilege in government employment; attitudes toward siblings appear transferred to other government employees, immediate colleagues, and housing clients in a diffuse, affective flow.

2. A second mechanism, identification, is apparent in Table 8–4 and Figure 8–1. This model stresses the individual's imitation of some significant other person—a parent, a teacher, or in this case, more experienced bureaucrat colleagues. In the transfer model, attitudes developed toward one person (or group of siblings) are transferred to apply to other objects. In the identification model, attitudes toward a given person or group may be acquired by direct imitation of the respected other. In this study, it is likely that attitudes toward clients may be acquired through direct imitation of the attitudes of other elite bureaucrats. Those who believe their colleagues motivated by a desire to aid others are those most likely to prefer low-income housing, as Table 8–4 indicates (partial correlation .34). It is likely that those who both perceive colleagues as inclusive and prefer low-cost housing do so because they identify with their housing colleagues.

A negative example will illustrate. It seems probable, given the negative relation between inclusivity and belief in merit recruitment in government (partial correlation − .24), that inclusive respondents identify less with government employees generally than with a special group of bureaucrats, elite functionaries, and within that group, those motivated by a wish to aid marginal people. In effect, the negative correlation suggests that those with inclusive attitudes toward housing clients view government employees generally as relatively underqualified and ascriptively recruited. The strong, close association between perceptions of colleague altruism or inclusivity and respondent inclusivity, therefore, is not necessarily the result of a diffuse benign accommodating outlook, but rather a special kind of relationship, perhaps the product of close identification of respondent with a few of his more inclusive colleagues.

The conclusion that some kind of identification process is at work is further reinforced when one notices that of all the pre-occupational and occupational variables tested, the variable associated most highly with a belief in colleague inclusivity is a belief in one's own inclusive motives (Gamma .54). Bureaucrats were asked questions about what they liked most and disliked most about their previous positions. The results were dichotomized into generally exclusive and generally inclusive motives. Those who describe their own motives as most inclusive (a wish to contribute something, to aid others) are those most likely to consider colleagues inclusive.

This identification, moreover, may have roots in a need to compensate for relatively inferior social status. The lower the respondent perceives his own social and political status, the more likely he is to view his colleagues as inclusive (Gammas are − .51 between high perceived social status and colleague inclusivity and − .30 between high perceived political status and colleague inclusivity or altruism). In addition, perceived social inferiority is associated with mobility. Privileged schooling seems related to mobility in that the lower a respondent ranks his father's economic and political status, the longer the time he has spent in universities (as privileged schooling is clearly related to filial political mobility, Gamma .41). That same privileged schooling is also clearly related to perceptions of housing colleagues as altruistic (partial correlation .15). Perhaps some learning process occurs in which those of perceived inferior social status compensate for their perceptions by identifying strongly with those colleagues they believe most superior, benevolent, and inclusive. For the relatively less privileged, perhaps, the acquisition of *noblesse oblige* is the essential characteristic of the comfortably privileged. In sum, the close relation between perceived colleague altruism and inclusivity, and the negative relation between perceptions of merit criteria used in the government generally and inclusivity, together with the observation that inclusivity is clearly acquired by many of those who are upwardly mobile, all suggest that some direct "upward" identification mechanism leads bureaucrats to acquire inclusive attitudes.

Essential Questions

Each of these learning models helps explain the discrete contributions of different pre-occupational and occupational experiences to the acquisition of inclusive attitudes. They are offered more as propositions for cross-national testing than as definite conclusions, because their generality may be circumscribed by a number of factors. First, this study is confined to elites and cannot be construed as measuring the general impact of class mobility on inclusive attitudes. Colombia's social system allows relatively little social mobility by Latin American standards, and the mobility registered in this sample is not interclass but intraclass, among elites.[8] Second, cross-national studies of the impact of intergenerational social mobility on political attitudes indicate that mobility may exert different influences in different national and class contexts (Thompson, 1971).

Third, the very importance of "occupation" in the social and political life-space of individuals may vary cross-nationally. "Occupation" as a variable predicting political attitudes may rank high or low in a rank ordering of potent attitude predictors according to the country studied.

[8] Although a high salary is positively related to filial political mobility, for most bureaucrats wealth seems to beget wealth (Gamma .27). Salary size is essentially unrelated to filial economic mobility (Gamma .05), but it is strongly correlated with father's economic rank (Gamma .61), and economic rankings of fathers correlate highly with economic ranking of sons (Gamma .45). By contrast, there is little correlation, positive or negative, between political power of father and political power of son.

Searing, for example, concludes that occupation is the most potent predictor of political attitudes in Venezuela, somewhat less important in France and Germany, and of relatively small importance in the United States and Israel (Searing, 1969).

Nevertheless, if we can assume that Almond and Verba are essentially correct in *The Civic Culture* when they conclude that, regarding political attitudes, elites in one country may resemble elites in other countries more than their own countrymen (Almond and Verba, 1963, 380–381), then findings about elites in Colombia may adumbrate something about learning patterns among elites elsewhere. Specifically, this study suggests that we examine how politically relevant attitudes and behavior are acquired in the process of learning three roles: sibling roles, filial power status roles, and occupational "purpose" or "motive" roles (or role expectations) with colleagues. At what point in an individual's life or learning experience do these roles become associated with politically relevant predispositions? How can that learning process be best described? How does political learning attached to one role become connected, if it is connected at all, with learning attached to other roles? These questions should help guide comparative investigations on the impact of pre-adult and adult experience on the acquisition of political attitudes.

REFERENCES

Almond, Gabriel, and Sidney Verba. *The Civic Culture* (Boston: Little, Brown, & Co., 1963).

Andrain, Charles F. *Children and Civic Awareness* (Columbus, Ohio: Charles Merrill Publishing Co., 1971).

Barber, James D. *The Lawmakers: Recruitment and Adaptation to Legislative Life* (New Haven: Yale University Press, 1965).

Bossard, James, and Eleanor Bowl. *The Large Family System* (Philadelphia: University of Pennsylvania Press, 1956).

Clausen, John. "Perspectives on Childhood Socialization," in John Clausen (ed.), *Socialization and Society* (Boston: Little, Brown, and Co., 1968).

Coleman, James S. *The Adolescent Society* (New York: The Free Press, 1961).

——— (ed.). *Education and Political Development* (Princeton: Princeton University Press, 1965).

Dawson, Richard, and Kenneth Prewitt. *Political Socialization* (Boston: Little, Brown, & Co., 1963).

Departamento Administrativo Nacional de Estadística (DANE) XIII Censo Nacional de Población (15 de julio 1964), Bogotá, 1967.

Dix, Robert. *Colombia: The Political Dimensions of Change* (New Haven: Yale University Press, 1967).

Hess, Robert D., and Judith V. Torney. *The Development of Political Attitudes in Children* (Chicago: Aldine Publishing Co., 1967).

Hirschman, Albert O. *Journeys Toward Progress* (New York: Twentieth Century Fund, 1963).

Janowitz, Morris. *The Professional Soldier: A Social and Political Portrait* (Glencoe, Ill.: The Free Press of Glencoe, 1960).

Johnson, John J. *The Role of the Military in Underdeveloped Countries* (Princeton: Princeton University Press, 1962).

Koth, Marica N., Julio G. Silva, and Albert G. H. Dietz. *Housing in Latin America* (Cambridge, Mass.: M.I.T. Press, 1965).

Lane, Mark. *Conversations with Americans* (New York: Simon & Schuster, 1971).

Langton, Kenneth. *Political Socialization* (New York: Oxford University Press, 1969).

Lipset, S. M. (ed.). *Comparative Education Review*, Vol. X (1966), entire issue.

———, and Aldo Solari (eds.). *Elites in Latin America* (New York: Oxford University Press, 1967).

Nie, Norman H., Dale H. Bent, and C. Hadlai Hull. *Statistical Package for the Social Sciences* (New York: McGraw-Hill, 1970).

Payne, James. *Patterns of Conflict in Colombia* (New Haven: Yale University Press, 1969).

Pollock, John. "How Violence and Politics are Linked: the Political Sociology of *La Violencia* in Colombia," *Studies in Comparative International Development*, Vol. VIII, forthcoming.

———. "Upper Class Benevolence: The 'Modern' Political Attitudes of Colombia's Elite Housing Bureaucrats," in Francine Rabinovitz and Felicity Trueblood (eds.), *Latin American Urban Research*, Vol. III (Beverly Hills: Sage Publications, 1973).

Prewitt, Kenneth. "Political Education and Political Socialization," in Roberta Sigel (ed.), *Learning About Politics—Studies in Political Socialization* (New York: Random House, 1971).

Reading, Reid. "Political Socialization in Colombia and the United States," *Midwest Journal of Political Science* 12 (1968), 352–81.

Roethlisberger, F. J., and William J. Dickson. *Management and the Worker* (Cambridge: Harvard University Press, 1939).

Searing, Donald R. "The Comparative Study of Elite Socialization," *Comparative Political Studies* 1 (1969), 471–500.

Sears, R. R., E. E. Maccoby, and H. Levin. *Patterns of Child Rearing* (Evanston, Ill.: Row, Peterson, 1957).

Thompson, Kenneth. "A Cross-National Analysis of Intergenerational Social Mobility and Political Orientations," in *Comparative Political Studies* 1 (1969), 471–500.

Wahlke, John C., *et al.* "The Role of Legislators in the Legislative Process," in Bruce J. Biddle and Edwin J. Thomas (eds.). *Role Theory: Concepts and Research* (New York: John Wiley, 1966).

————, Heinz Eulau, William Buchanan, and LeRoy C. Ferguson. *The Legislative System: Explorations in Legislative Behavior* (New York: John Wiley, 1962).

Part Four

Beyond the Traditional Age Groups and Agencies

Chapter Nine

Preschoolers and Politics

Sandra Kenyon Schwartz

INTRODUCTION

When does political socialization begin? What are the first political objects to enter the child's world? When does a youngster begin to locate himself in a broad sociopolitical space? These questions are clearly important for the study of political socialization because it is concerned with the origins of political attitudes, arguing that early political learning is important to later learning and behavior and that, even when attitudes change later in life, the first tentative orientations to politics provide a basis on which later, more sophisticated attitudes are built. A growing body of research has shown us that important political learning occurs between the ages of seven and thirteen (Greenstein, 1965; Hess and Torney, 1967; Easton and Dennis, 1969). It is the purpose of this chapter to show that some political learning takes place considerably earlier, between the ages of three and six, if not earlier, and to suggest some questions to be investigated in studying these earliest political orientations.

Before presenting some exploratory data, let us consider why preschoolers are an interesting age group to examine. It is common in the study of political socialization to borrow from psychologists the proposition that early learning and early childhood are particularly important, but when psychologists advance this argument they do not mean to begin studying child development at age seven or older. They include the very first years of life, years in which the human organism undergoes change more rapidly than ever again and years in which the individual's first and most basic interactions with the environment begin to shape fundamental personality (Freud, 1938; Erikson, 1950). Within these early years, the preschool period (from about age three to age six) is the period during which the child develops considerable symbolic skill (e.g., language) and begins to experience a variety of types of social interactions, including relationships with peers and others outside his immediate family. The

229

child becomes increasingly aware of a broader and more varied environment and seeks to explore it, assimilate it, and relate it to himself (Palmer, 1970, Ch. 4).

Among the social phenomena of which the child becomes aware are a variety of social identities. These include sex (Mischel, 1970; Kohlberg, 1966) and race (Goodman, 1964; Stevenson and Stewart, 1958), two social identities that have distinguishing physical (and hence concrete and visualized) features. Preschool children attach social meaning to these characteristics, often quite stereotyped, and sort themselves and others into these categories. But in addition to these proximate, visible social identities, children of this age also become aware, albeit hazily, of more abstract identities present in their cultures, such as religion. And, I suggest, they experience a dawning recognition of their political world.

The young child's impressions of and orientations towards politics may often be vague and inaccurate, making these first political images considerably different from those of an adult viewing the same objects. Indeed, Piaget has argued that the acquisition of logically correct and morally developed conceptions of such complex concepts as "nations" must await the development of cognitive capacities not yet present at the preschool age (Piaget and Weil, 1951). Nonetheless, early awareness of and attachment to political symbols may lay the foundation for later, more sophisticated learning.

Further, orientations toward political objects need not necessarily be logically correct to be important in political socialization. For example, to return to the concept "nation," Jahoda has shown that the development of some sense of nationality can occur in the absence of a prior sorting out of the spatial relationships between towns and countries (or parts and wholes) (Jahoda, 1964). The concern here, then, is not with the accuracy of the child's view of politics, but rather with the extent and the nature of his early awareness of and attachment to political symbols such as the political community.[1]

In addition, preschool children are old enough to encounter the presence of authority outside the home, from the policeman at the corner to the nursery school teacher. Does the young child become aware that his parents' authority is limited? Does he perceive political figures as authoritative and discriminate specifically political authority from other types?

Early childhood socialization relevant to politics is clearly not confined to specifically political attitudes. In addition to important personality development, this stage of the life cycle is also one in which children

---

[1] The political community salient in a given culture or subculture need not, of course, be national. One of the fascinating questions for comparative research is whether variations in the earliest learned definitions of political community account for many problems of political integration.

begin to learn what styles of interpersonal interactions are rewarded by adults and by peers. Thus, siblings are urged to share with each other, and mothers and nursery school teachers set up norms of behavior by saying "wait your turn" and "that's not fair." Experiences of this kind may lay a foundation not only for the development of personal morality (Piaget, 1965; Kohlberg, 1964) but for normative expectations of a political system. At least in those systems in which primary and secondary structures are relatively well integrated, notions of fairness on the play-ground may in part derive from and in turn provide support for standards of political justice, and standards of appropriate conduct in interpersonal relationships may be generalized to expectations about elite–mass inter-actions (Greenstein and Tarrow, 1971).

However, for the purposes of this chapter, I will confine myself to a discussion of the narrower, and perhaps more surprising, area of specifi-cally political learning among preschool children. What political symbols —heroes, rituals, authorities and the like—are perceived when children first begin to notice things political? What content, however vague, do these symbols convey, and what is their affective meaning? In what sequence do political symbols enter the child's perceptual field, and to what extent and in what ways does the child link them together as he gradually comes to recognize the existence of a political world? What feelings does the child develop toward these symbols, and when does he come to see them as linked to himself? Finally, what processes explain this early political learning?

I hypothesize that children move out of a prepolitical state, one in which they are unable to respond to political symbols, a stage where such symbols go unnoticed and unremembered even if present in the children's environment, to a precursive stage in which certain political symbols are "assimilatable," in Piaget's terminology (Baldwin, 1967). Here children may begin to learn simple political terminology and to recognize worlds and images as familiar when they encounter them. In this stage, they become ready to respond to political stimuli and sufficiently politically aware to begin to attach meaning to political symbols.

The information they then learn will necessarily be sketchy, vague, and not infrequently illogical and inaccurate from an adult point of view, but even very modest information transforms a word from a meaningless collection of sounds to a symbol evoking associations and having meaning to the child. Affect toward political symbols should await some minimum level of information and be particularly affected by perceived linkages between the symbol and the child. For example, "that is the American flag" and "that is *our* flag" should have very different implications for the affective response of the child.

Presumably proximate concrete and visible symbols will be perceived earliest, and more distant verbal and abstract ones later; but even young children are hypothesized to develop some diffuse notions about general organizing concepts such as "government" that can link symbols together in a set and differentiate that set from others. If easily comprehended and positively valued symbols are included in such a set, then the development of a broader attachment to the political community should be facilitated.

To illustrate that preschool children do undergo political socialization, I am presenting here some preliminary data from the first of several projected pilot studies. Although these data deal with a narrower array of variables than those I have suggested here, they may serve to indicate the utility of our directing research attention to the more broadly defined socialization topics just mentioned, so that we may come to understand the origins of political learning.

METHODS

The pilot data discussed here were collected from a population of 79 children attending seven nursery school classes in six different schools, who were interviewed in April, 1972. The schools were selected purposively to yield a student population of largely middle-class white children aged three to six. Seven different classes were included to minimize bias from any unusual teacher or class. Students participated on a volunteer basis; limitations on available time and personnel necessitated restricting the number of children interviewed to between ten and thirteen pupils per school or just over 50 percent of the total school population.

Interviews were conducted in privacy and tape-recorded. The study design called for each child to receive two interviews of approximately ten minutes in length at intervals of about a week. However, fifteen children interviewed in the first wave were absent for the second interview, reducing the N for that material to 64.[2] The interviews contained a set of structured open-ended and closed-ended items, supplemented by pictures where possible. Interviewers were instructed to probe extensively and to follow up any topics opened up by the child.

The population contains 77 white children and two black children. The youngest child is two years eleven months and the oldest five years seven months. Twenty of the children are under four and a half, with six of these being younger than four. Twenty-eight of the children are between four and a half and five, and 27 are five. (No data on age were available in four cases.) The group is evenly divided by sex, but five of the youngest six children are male.

[2] A comparison of the marginals from the first interview obtained with the full 79 with those obtained with the reduced N of 64 shows them to be virtually identical.

A brief word on the nature of interviewing children of this age about politics is in order to help assess the validity of the data. First, because their language skill levels are low and their knowledge often rudimentary, a child may not be able to respond to a question worded one way and yet be able to answer a question on the same topic phrased differently. Pictures and other nonverbal measures help reduce this problem, but interviewer probing is essential. Second, the children tended to volunteer very brief answers to questions and stop, but after probing they often revealed a considerably broader knowledge. It is probable that these patterns tended to depress our estimates of their political awareness to some degree.

Third, on closed-ended items such as answering yes or no or pointing to a picture, some children (especially the youngest) appear to have a tendency to guess when it seems from other evidence that they should say they don't know. It is therefore necessary to keep in mind what the distributions would be like by chance alone. Where departures from chance distributions occur and where coherent patterns emerge, one can be more confident of the validity of the responses.

One problem I had anticipated did not emerge. Although generally positive in outlook, the children were not inveterate yea sayers. They said "no," and they objected when they wished. For example, if an interviewer misheard an answer and repeated it inaccurately to the child, they did not hesitate to correct the interviewer and insist upon their original answer.

The symbols used in this study include several that have been studied among elementary school children. A substantial portion of the interview is devoted to measuring early awareness of authority figures, symbols which—being personal—may be crucial to the development of the young child's awareness of the broader political world. Political authority figures studied include the policeman and the President, the "head and tail" of the system discussed by Easton and Dennis (1969), Presidents here being represented by Richard Nixon, George Washington, and Abraham Lincoln. The children were also asked about the mailman and, for a nonpolitical comparison, the milkman. Because of the confusion elementary school children make between politics and religion (Hess and Torney, 1967) and because of an interest in comparing political to religious identity, they were asked about God. Finally, some questions involved choosing which authority figure "helps the most" and the like, and here the choices were made from among the father, the teacher, the policeman, and the President (Easton and Dennis, 1969).

A development of a sense of attachment to the political community obviously requires more than orientations toward discrete authority figures. Therefore, the children were asked various questions about "America" as a more direct indicator of the development of their political identity (Piaget and Weil, 1951; Jahoda, 1963a and 1963b). Several studies have been done with elementary school children on children's preference for their national flag as an indicator of patriotism or nationality (Horowitz, 1940; Weinstein, 1957; Lawson, 1963). Here children were asked to choose their favorite flag from among a group of flags and to point to the American flag.

Finally, as some general political concept is crucial to linking a variety of symbols together, in addition to being asked about America, a few questions were included about "government." Although certainly distant and abstract from the child's perspective, and less well linked than "America" to such visible symbols as the flag, the concept of government is not unfamiliar to the elementary school child. Only about one quarter of the second graders in Easton and Dennis's study said they felt unsure about its meaning (Easton and Dennis, 1969, 113).

FINDINGS

Authority Figures

Are preschool children at all aware of political authority figures? Is their awareness simply a recognition of familiar-sounding words, or do they possess some information about these authority figures? Do they draw any meaningful distinctions between political and nonpolitical authority figures? Do awareness, information, and ability to discriminate increase with age, i.e., are there indications that political orientations undergo development during the preschool years? This section presents our findings on these questions.

The political authorities emphasized here are the policeman and the President. The policeman, although not perhaps a very crucial political symbol for adults, is emphasized here because he combines an authoritative political role with high visibility to the child. He is a government employee who is likely to be directly encountered fairly frequently. The policeman possesses power, power which he exercises over a broader arena than authorities such as the father and power to enforce a system of laws. This combination of visibility and political authority makes the role of policeman a likely vehicle for introducing the young child to politics and a potentially important link to the political system.

The role of the President is of interest because of the prominent position, both real and symbolic, it occupies in our national political system. Furthermore, studies of elementary school age children have found the President to loom very large in the relatively young child's political world —perhaps in part because, being a person, the President is easier to understand and relate to than institutions such as Congress or abstract principles such as the rule of law (Greenstein, 1965; Hess and Torney, 1967).

It is hypothesized here that simple recognition of political authorities will be widespread, particularly in the cases of the more proximate and visible figures such as the policeman. It is further hypothesized that many of these preschoolers will have some rudimentary information about these authorities, but that information on the more familiar, less distant figure of the policeman will be more extensive than information on Presidents. Third, I suggest that the father will not dominate all other authority figures regardless of the quality being rated, but that political authorities will tend to be perceived as more important and powerful and the father will be selected most often on affective dimensions. However, between the political figures, the policeman should be preferred on affective dimensions more often than the President as a function of the children's greater familiarity with and information about him. Finally, I hypothesize that age will be directly associated with increases in recognition, information, and discrimination among authorities.

An overview of the data indicates that these hypotheses are generally borne out. These preschool children recognized and reacted to political symbols to a not inconsiderable degree. Some are still prepolitical, and some have only a vague sense that they have heard of these authority figures before. But others are aware of an array of symbols and are acquiring rudimentary information to go with them. In general, familiarity with and knowledge about the policeman is considerably more extensive than for Presidents, who remain rather shadowy and nonsalient for these children. The children do tend to discriminate political from nonpolitical authorities, and over-all the older children are more politically knowledgeable than the younger. The specific findings to be described here deal first with simple recognition, second with the children's information, third with choices among authorities, and finally with age trends.

Virtually all of the children correctly identified "the man in the picture" when shown drawings of the policeman, mailman, and milkman (90, 89, and 90 percent respectively). Recognition of Richard Nixon occurred less often but was still quite frequent. When asked if they had ever heard of President Nixon, 60 percent said they had. Indeed, this simplest form of familiarity with these authority figures tended to be rather common; when asked about Washington, Lincoln, and God (for whom no pictures were used), most children believed they had heard of them (Washington 72 percent, Lincoln 53, and God 84). Very few children said they had not heard of any president (11 percent) and a third "recognized" all three of them (37 percent).

Not surprisingly, very few children recognized a photograph of Nixon. Unlike the drawings depicting the policeman, the mailman, and the milkman, which contained identifying clues such as uniform ānd mailbags, the photograph of Nixon was simply a facial closeup. Six children did correctly identify him, however, and two others came very close with "He's America" and "Is he a government?" The other children either said they didn't know or commented in ways like the little boy who said, "He looks like my daddy's daddy."

Before describing what these children think and feel about these figures, it behooves us to note that simply remembering that one had heard of a political symbol, while certainly a minimal level of awareness, is a step above total nonrecognition. It has been suggested in the Introduction that prepolitical children will not remember political symbols even if they have been exposed to them. Although this study does not include a measure of the frequency or vividness of nursery school teaching, teachers were asked to complete a questionnaire including information on their classroom use of the political symbols studied. Five of the seven teachers responded, and in all these cases the policeman, "President," and Nixon's name had been mentioned in class, usually in terms such as "the leader of our country." Four of the five had also discussed Washington and Lincoln and shown pictures of them as well. Out of the 56 children whose teachers responded, fully 30 claimed to have heard of fewer Presidents than their teachers say they discussed. Undoubtedly some of these children were absent during these discussions, but it seems clear that political information, even when deliberately taught, does not necessarily enter the child's mind. Simple familiarity with these terms, although fairly common, is less widespread than exposure.

Is familiarity with these figures confined to a vague recollection of having heard of them, or do the children make cognitive associations with these terms? The richness of the cognitive meaning of these authority figures to the children varies as expected with the proximate and visible nature of the symbol. These preschool children are a good deal more aware of the policeman's role than of the President's. Three quarters of the children were able to name correctly at least one thing that policemen do, and 38 percent gave two or three answers, other than such vague replies as "He goes in the car." These findings are in contrast to those reported in a study of preschoolers which included a few directly political items. Goodman found the policeman to be "a shadowy figure on no more than the periphery of perception for some forty-five percent of the [four-year-olds studied]" (Goodman, 1970, 16).

The answers given by these children depict the policeman as regulating traffic, helping lost children, and catching "bad people." The majority of the answers cite a service policeman perform for children—helping them cross the street or find their way home.[3] But in addition many of these children perceive the policeman in what Easton and Dennis have called his prohibitive and punitive roles (Easton and Dennis, 1969, 223). For example, one four-year-old boy commented, "The policeman can make people stop by raising his hand up like this," and a five-year-old girl said, "He puts people in jail for doing bad things . . . drives after the people going too fast and give lots of tickets." A less articulate child simply answered "he shots bad people."

Altogether, over a third of the sample responded that the policeman helps lost children, nearly half mentioned traffic regulations (usually in conjunction with children crossing the street), and a third gave some response having to do with the policeman's role as law enforcer. The policeman, then, appears often in a benevolent, child-centered light. In addition to the proximity and high visibility of the policeman, it may be that adult stress on basic safety education is responsible for this child-oriented, benevolent view of the policeman's role.

Cognitive meaning of the term "President" is less well developed. Only a handful of children gave specifically political answers to "What does President Nixon do?" and even these were inaccurate. The one exception was a five-year-old boy who consistently displayed a political sophistication far beyond that of his peers and whose favorite television program was the news; he replied, apparently not disapprovingly, "He did war." One child placed the President in "the court," one said "He talks about news," and one identified him as a soldier. Several other children responded more vaguely that "He does very important business" or "He flies to country to country." Just what the President's role is is a mystery to these children.

They are, however, somewhat more likely to know what "President Nixon is president of," and here, even when their answers are incorrect, many indicate an association among political symbols.[4] Fifteen children knew that Nixon is President of America (or the United States), and an additional twelve connected him with some other political symbol ranging from "George Washington" and "North America" to the response of one little girl that he is President "of liberty and peace." Thus, while about a third of the children made some political connection, over-all the cognitive meaning of the symbol "President" is often entirely lacking or when present in rudimentary form is extremely hazy. The person of the Presi-

---

[3] The picture used may have increased the relative frequency of these responses, as it depicted a uniformed policeman looking at two children.

[4] Sometimes the children's wrong answers hint at interesting associations and patterns of salience. A black boy, for example, who knew nothing about any of the three Presidents, volunteered "I saw Martin Luther King on television and he got put in jail," when asked if he had heard of President Nixon (to which he replied "no").

dent, who looms so large in the mental set of the second grader (Easton and Dennis, 1969, Ch. 6) is here a pallid image, while the policeman is a much clearer and more familiar figure. The fact that these data were collected during a Presidential primary campaign underscores this conclusion.

Notions about George Washington and Abraham Lincoln are sometimes more colorful, reflecting political myths and occasionally the ritual of a birthday celebration, an event likely to be appealing to a young child. One unusually well-informed girl told us her teacher had told her about Washington, and she went on, "He died a long time ago and now . . . that's why . . . um . . . the other one is President Nixon. On Valentine's Day we tell about him. He used to be a soldier, but he died because he was a very old man. He helped people a lot." A boy said of Lincoln, "I know he got shot by a person. I know the story of that. His wife and Abraham Lincoln [were] watching a movie and then some kind of cowboy came in . . . then he sneaked up . . . ." Answers such as these are atypical, but they suggest the possibility that folk anecdotes, personal details, and ritual celebrations can—where present—capture the young child's attention somewhat more vividly than less storylike explanations.

Do these children discriminate among authority figures? Several of the dimensions used by Easton and Dennis to assess the elementary school child's rating of authority figures were selected for study here (Easton and Dennis, 1969, Ch. 8). However, rather than asking the children to rate each figure separately, the procedure forced the child to choose among four authority figures: the President, the policeman, the father, and the teacher. Each figure was represented by a picture to which the child pointed in answering. Unfortunately, although this format permits an assessment of the child's own choices among these authority figures, it also encourages guessing. Still, the over-all pattern of responses does form a sensible whole. The questions were of the format, "Who helps you the most?" The dimensions include some affectively loaded and some more cognitive. Table 9–1 presents these data.

Not surprisingly, these children tend to choose their father on the three affective dimensions. However, contrary to my hypothesis, he also tends to be chosen as the one who punishes. Nonetheless, the father does not override all the other figures regardless of the dimensions. The President is seldom chosen. There is some tendency for him to be seen as important, as hypothesized, but not as powerful. These young children do not feel strong affect for him; on all three affectively loaded dimensions, the President is very seldom chosen. Perhaps the most interesting results are those on the policeman. The policeman rivals the father on two of the affective items and is considerably more likely than the father to be perceived as important.

Table 9–1. Choices among Authority Figures (N = 79), in Percent*

	PRESIDENT	POLICEMAN	DADDY	TEACHER	DK/NA†
Helps the most	6	35	33	20	5
Friendliest	11	35	40	10	3
Like the best of all	9	24	51	14	2
Punishes lots of people	10	14	47	19	10
Makes people do things	18	20	22	34	6
Knows more than anyone	20	32	28	16	4
Is the most important	32	34	18	13	4

* Percentages add to 100 horizontally.
† Don't know/No answer.

This pattern appears more clearly when authority choices are cross-tabulated with measures of knowledge, a procedure that helps to separate those children who are simply choosing a picture at random from those whose choices are based on knowledge about the various authority figures. To illustrate, Table 9–2 presents the relationship between knowing that a policeman does and choosing him from among the other figures. The children have been combined into those who gave no answer or only one answer and those who gave two or three answers to the question on what policeman do.[5] Percentages in the table represent the frequency with which the policeman was chosen for each of the seven dimensions.

Table 9–2. Percent Choosing Policeman by Knowledge of Police

CHOICE OF POLICEMAN AS:	NO ANSWERS OR ONE (N = 49)	TWO OR THREE ANSWERS (N = 30)
Helps the most	20%	60%
Friendliest	20	60
Like the best of all	20	30
Punishes lots of people	12	17
Makes people do things	20	20
Knows more than anyone	22	47
Is the most important	18	60

[5] Although cell sizes are extremely small when the number of answers is left uncollapsed, the same pattern consistently appears.

Among those with more knowledge of his role, we see a stronger tendency for the policeman to emerge as a figure both benevolent and authoritative. Children with some knowledge of his role-related activities tend to prefer the policeman to the President, father, and teacher on a number of dimensions, namely being helpful, friendly, knowledgeable, and important.

It is also interesting to note that the coercive power of the policeman is least likely to be perceived. Nearly two thirds of the most knowledgeable children select either the father or the teacher on the two ratings of coercive power. Apparently the direct experience with the father's and the teacher's discipline leads these young children to choose them rather than political figures as those who can "make lots of people do things" and are able to "punish lots of people." Easton and Dennis have reported that second-graders, by contrast, are quite aware of the ability of the policeman to make people do things (Easton and Dennis, 1969, 221–7). These pilot data suggest, then, that young children may first perceive a benevolent and helpful policeman, a man with stature in a broader world than the family, and only subsequently attach an awareness of his coercive powers to his kindly and prestigious image.

These findings should be viewed tentatively, but this pattern is very suggestive. It appears that some preschool children have already learned that their fathers are not the preeminent authorities in the broader world. The President is recognized as important (and among the more knowledgeable children, he is also more likely to be chosen as knowing the most), but this perception rests on a mysterious and dimly perceived basis and is not accompanied by strong benevolent images. It is the policeman who seems to be the crucial figure in the political socialization of the preschool child. He is seen positively and he conveys authority. This pattern, taken together with the high visibility of the policeman and his role and the positive, specific services he is seen as rendering to children, indicate that the policeman may indeed provide an important link to the development of a more generalized benevolent image of government among young children such as Easton and Dennis suggest (1968, Ch. 11).

An examination of the relationships between age and knowledge about authority figures allows us to make some developmental inferences. Which political authorities become increasingly obvious to preschool children, and which images remain the same? For this analysis, the children were divided into those under four and a half (N = 20), those between four and a half and five (N = 28), and those over five (N = 27).[6] In general, these children appear to learn more about the policeman than Presidents. Three quarters of the youngest children and virtually all of those in the two older groups can identify the policeman's picture, while only a handful of children of any age recognize the photograph of President Nixon.

[6] No data on age are available in four cases.

Claims that they have heard of the three Presidents do increase with age, but even this hazy familiarity starts at lower levels and remains somewhat lower than for the policeman; about two thirds of the oldest children have heard of Nixon and Lincoln and 85 percent of Washington.

Differences by age in information acquisition about these two political roles are greater than simple recognition. For example, 85 percent of the youngest children can name no aspect of a policeman's duties while half of the five-year-olds name three. By contrast relevant answers to questions about who George Washington and Abraham Lincoln are or what the President does are not only nonexistent among the youngest group (with the exception of one child), but infrequent as well among the oldest. Washington is the best known, but even here only a third of the five-year-olds can give any information about him. It appears, then, that information about the policeman is somewhat easier for preschool children to learn. Both the person and the role of the policeman are increasingly cognized, but "President," while vaguely familiar, remains largely a content-free symbol.

An interesting indication of further differences between the preschool child's developing image of these two political roles is found in the changes with age in their ratings of the President and the policeman on the various dimensions of authority examined here. As cell sizes are very small, data should be regarded extremely tentatively, but there is some indication that what changes most with age with regard to the policeman is affective response. There is an increase in choosing the policeman on all three of the affectively loaded dimensions. On the other hand, affective response to the President remains constant, while perceptions of him as powerful, knowledgeable, and important increase somewhat. To illustrate, one quarter of the youngest group say the policeman is the friendliest, while nearly half of the oldest children do so. At the same time, the policeman is chosen as the person who can make people do things by approximately 15 percent of both groups. In the case of the President, approximately equal percentages of the youngest and oldest children selected him as the friendliest (10 and 15 percent respectively), but choosing him as the one who can make people do things increases from 5 to 26 percent. It should be recalled that as the question format calls for a forced choice among the four figures rather than among the dimensions, the implication is not that these children are saying the President is powerful and important rather than benevolent. But it may be that the perceptually salient dimensions of these two roles differ.

Political Community

Is the preschool child's political awareness confined to persons, or does he also perceive other political symbols including concrete and visible ones such as the flag and abstract terms such as "America," symbols which may be more directly relevant than authority figures to a developing orientation toward the political community? More importantly, do the children perceive those political symbols of which they are aware merely as a series of unconnected objects, or are they capable of making appropriate linkages among these symbols and of differentiating political from unpolitical ones? Finally, do preschool children begin to link themselves to the political community?

In general, it is expected that orientations toward the political community will be less well developed than those toward authority figures but that nonetheless there will be some awareness of the existence and meaning of impersonal political symbols. Awareness of the flag, which is concrete and visible to the child, should be higher than of "America." Even though I anticipate confusion over the meaning of "America" due to its cognitive complexity, I hypothesize that, not only will the term be widely recognized, but that a majority of these children will attach sufficient meaning to "America" (and to "government") to link these terms with other political symbols and to differentiate them from nonpolitical ones. I hypothesize further that some of these children will recognize the link between themselves and America and identify themselves as Americans, but that this more sophisticated political awareness should be less common than perceiving linkages among various political symbols themselves. Finally, I suggest that the older children should have more information (although still be confused as to the exact meaning of "America"), be better at sorting political from unpolitical symbols, and be somewhat more likely to see themselves as American than the younger children.

In general, the results tend to confirm these hypotheses. The flag is widely known (and liked). The term "America," while familiar, is not well cognized. Nonetheless, most children, expecially the older ones, do link "America" (and "government") with other political symbols and not with nonpolitical symbols. (The exception here is an interesting one: The church tends to be perceived as political.) Identification of oneself as American is quite infrequent and, contrary to my hypothesis, does not increase as expected with age. The detailed description of these findings which follows discusses the results concerning the flag first, recognition of and information about America second, patterns in sorting the symbols third, identifying oneself as American next, and age trends last.

Flags are colorful, concrete, and frequently displayed. As such they would appear to be among the most prominently visible national political symbols to young children. This has led researchers to investigate the development of preferences for one's national flag over others as an indication of early attachment to the nation. An early study conducted among elementary school children found that first-grade children tended to choose flags with animals and the like as among the five best looking with only 27 percent choosing the American flag (Horowitz, 1940). However, a similar although not identical study conducted twenty-five years later found that about 70 percent of all children in grades K–12 placed the United States flag in the top five (Lawson, 1963). These preschoolers resemble the elementary school children of the more recent study.

These children were shown a picture containing nine flags including both the American and the Liberian flag, which closely resembles the American one. Almost all the children recognized them as flags. Rather than being asked to identify the top group, they were asked "Which flag do you like best of all?" Over-all, 60 percent (38)[7] chose the American flag, 19 percent (12) picked the Liberian one—sometimes after vacillating between these two—and 20 percent chose a different flag.

More children were able to identify correctly the American flag when asked than had previously chosen it as their favorite. (Possibly this is because there is a time lag between the first recognition of a symbol and the subsequent development of affect for it.) Fifty-three children (83 percent) pointed to the right flag, including a few who had previously picked the Liberian one as their favorite and a few who had chosen an entirely different flag. Six of the remaining eleven children incorrectly pointed to the Liberian flag. These figures compare favorably to the 42 percent of the middle-class Scottish six-and seven-year-olds who could name the Union Jack (Jahoda, 1963b, 146).[8] Over-all, then, these preschool children recognize and prefer their country's flag, a concrete, visual and familiar symbol, and one verbally linked through its name to the nation.

The flag is concrete, and the policeman and the President are both people and as such perhaps easier for the child to orient toward than more abstract concepts such as "America" (Easton and Dennis, 1969). Not only are people familiar to the child; the child's own perspective on the world at this stage is an egocentric one in which motivations such as he himself experiences may be projected onto inanimate objects (Piaget, 1955; Merelman, 1969, 297). Furthermore, the child's cognitive ability to comprehend rather complicated spatial relationships such as "the town is in the state is in the country" does not develop until considerably later (Piaget and Weil, 1951; Jahoda, 1963a). Indeed, even the term "country"

[7] Questions concerning the variables reported in this section were contained in the second interview, for which the total N is 64. As noted above, a comparison of responses on the first interview between the full sample of 79 and the smaller group who received both interviews reveals an extremely close distribution of responses.

[8] Only 29 percent of the Scottish working-class children of this age could name this flag, a class difference quite typically found within the study.

may be misleading; informal pretesting before undertaking this pilot study indicated that "our country" may mean cows and meadows to the preschool child. Earlier research on the development of a sense of nationality in children has located the acquisition of a firm and accurate sense of the basic meaning of the nation at approximately age ten. (See Davies, 1973, for a review of this literature.)

These same studies have shown, however, that children as young as six and seven have some awareness that place names are geographical and that they may be able to locate themselves within their town or country. Jahoda, studying the development of nationality in Scotland, found that six-and seven-year-olds had at least a hazy awareness that Glasgow was a place name, while 21 of the 48 children in this group knew they lived there (Jahoda, 1963a, 51). A study in Australia found the nation's name more familiar to six-and seven-year-olds than their city's name (reported by Davies, 1973). Thus, even before a comprehensive or accurate sense of the spatial relationships among political units develops, children may acquire a rudimentary awareness of these terms and may begin, however diffusely, to identify themselves with them (Jahoda, 1964, 1086–9). Furthermore, symbols such as "America" occur in conjunction with other nongeographical symbols such as the flag and even the President. Thus, young children may orient to the term "America" in other than a geographic sense.

Three quarters or 48 of these children have heard of America, but only 28 percent or 18 of them can give any relevant answer when asked to tell the interviewer "what America is." Note that this question is open-ended and therefore more difficult than one which presents the child with options. Some of these eighteen children simply responded with other political symbols, such as naming it "the United States of America" or referring to the flag. Others made vague references to a "state." A number of the children who gave wrong responses described it as a place—the little boy who commented "We're going there at a Bar Mitzvah," the girl who said "America is at my brother's school," and the boy who responded "Men work there—it's next to Washington." Thus, although cognitive understanding of America is low, some political and some geographical associations are occasionally made.

These children may lack a logically correct and clear understanding of America (and the literature cited on the cognitive development of children would seem to explain why), yet still possess some important, if more diffuse, notions as to its meaning. For example, the child may be unable to comprehend the logic of parts and wholes involved in specifying the relationship between his town and his country and yet be aware that the nation's name somehow fits with other political symbols and not with nonpolitical symbols. The ability to link political symbols with each other and to discriminate between them and nonpolitical ones is a crucial step in the development of orientations toward politics. It represents both a rudimentary awareness of a distinctly political arena and the potential capability of generalizing information and affect from one more readily comprehended symbol to another more difficult one.

Accordingly, these children were shown pictures of political and non-political persons and objects and asked "Which of these things goes together with America; does the house belong with America, or not," and similar questions. The political symbols used include the flag, President Nixon, and the policeman. Nonpolitical symbols were the church, the milkman, the teacher, and the house. A parallel set of questions was asked concerning "government," another general, cognitively difficult term but one familiar to second-graders (Easton and Dennis, 1969, 113).

The general pattern of responses indicates a fairly high sense of the appropriate linkages among symbols by these children. Approximately 70 percent of the children associate the flag and President Nixon with America and with government. Just under two thirds see the house, the nursery school teacher, and the milkman as nonpolitical. Apparently, the policeman and the church are more confusing; both are linked with America and government about half the time.

This study does not permit a test of why these two symbols should be more ambiguous. One can speculate, however, that the policeman lags behind the other two political figures because, being a local official, he is not often verbally linked by adults to the term "America." The church (and God?) may tend to be politically linked more often than other non-political symbols because they may be perceived as partaking of the same broad prestige and authority as that associated with political figures.

In any case, the over-all pattern is fairly clear. About two thirds of these children correctly discriminate between political and nonpolitical symbols on five of the seven symbols studied.

Linking political symbols with each other may be easier for young children than perceiving a general connection between themselves and the political community. On the one hand, political authority figures and other symbols may seem distant, adult prerogatives inappropriate to childhood. On the other, there will be cognitive confusion over the meaning of an invisible political community; something one is part of but can neither see nor touch is a complex concept to grasp. Therefore, identifying themselves as Americans should occur less frequently among these children than making connections among political symbols themselves. However, in light of the beginnings of racial, sexual, and religious identities among preschoolers referred to in the Introduction, I have hypothesized that some children will identify themselves as American despite this cognitive confusion.

The children were asked, "Are you an American or not?" Only 20 of the 64 children said they were. Those who did were also likely to answer that their parents were American, and sometimes to volunteer that their brothers and sisters were too. Several of the children who denied they were American were quite emphatic about it. One three-year-old boy told the interviewer "Little boys don't do things like this." Several children referred to their street address or town, denying that they could live both there and in America. Such answers indicate the children may indeed be having the type of difficulties suggested.

Further evidence that cognitive confusion may be a barrier to identifying oneself as American comes from the fact that these denials were made despite efforts by all five of the nursery school teachers on whom data are available to teach this concept to the children. The teachers report that they explained that "all the states are in America" or that "it is our country and we all live here." The children don't appear to believe it. Possibly teaching that did not stress the geographic aspect of being American would be more successful.

Those children who do say they are American, however, are typically among the more knowledgeable children. It appears likely, then, that at least for most of these self-identified Americans their response is not just a random guess. To test this possibility further, the children were also asked if they were French. Five of the 20 children who had said they were American also said they were French as did six of the 40 who denied being American. Over-all, 25 percent (or 16) of the children classified themselves as American only, 8 percent (5) thought they were both, 9 percent (6) said they were French only, and over half (37) denied being either. Thus, few of the children seem to have a clear sense of national identity.

Although the older children tend to have some greater political awareness, there is less change with age regarding this set of variables than there was in the case of political authorities.[9] The American flag is preferred among the older children more often than among younger ones, as a result of increasing discrimination between the American flag and the visually similar Liberian one. Thirty percent (6 of the youngest group) chose the Liberian flag, only 21 percent (or 5) of the middle group, and only one child among the 18 five-year-olds. At all ages, however, approximately one fifth chose an entirely different flag as their favorite.

There is little relationship between age and knowledge of America. Most of the children in all age groups have heard of America, but the group least familiar with the term is the middle group. There is some

[9] Of the 64 children who were given the second interview, 20 are under four and a half years old, 24 are between four and a half and five, and eighteen are five or more. No data on age are available in two cases.

increase in being able to give relevant answers describing what America is among the five-year-olds, but not among the middle group. Twenty-one percent of the youngest children, 25 percent of the four and a half to five-year-olds, and 44 percent of the five-year-olds gave some relevant though not necessarily specific answer.

Contrary to my hypothesis, identifying oneself as American does not increase with age. Denying one is American does decline slightly with age (from 68 percent to 50), but increasing identification does not occur. Rather, the older children occasionally say they don't know. Denying one is French, however, increases with age (from 63 to 83 percent). Putting these two trends together, one might hypothesize that the five-year-olds are hovering on the brink of sorting out their national identity in verbal terms. However, among these children, it seems clear that recognition of their being American (or being placed in America?) escapes all but a few of them.

The most important age-related finding here has to do with discriminating between political and nonpolitical symbols. In general, the older children do a more accurate job of sorting. They associate political symbols with government and America more often and private symbols less often. Cell size is very small, but the pattern is quite consistent.

An exception to the general tendency for age to be associated with greater accuracy is sorting these symbols in the case of the church. There is some tendency for the church to be politically linked more frequently by the older children (a pattern also observed among the more politically informed children). This may well be a consequence of confusing the authority of the church and God with the authority of politics. Table 9–3 presents these data, giving the percentage saying the symbol in question does belong with America and government.

Table 9–3. Linkages among Symbols by Age

| | GOVERNMENT | | | AMERICA | | |
	UNDER 4½ (N=20)	4–4½ (N=24)	5 (N=18)	UNDER 4½ (N=20)	4–4½ (N=24)	5 (N=18)
Flag	58%	79	78	63%	88	83
President Nixon	58	79	78	42	75	83
Policeman	26	58	61	53	67	50
Church	42	67	56	32	50	61
Milkman	53	33	28	42	38	33
Teacher	37	42	17	32	54	28
House	26	33	33	26	38	28

I do not interpret these findings to mean that three- to five-year-old children have an elaborated notion of either the interrelationships among political symbols or the boundaries between the political and nonpolitical worlds. Presumably, their images are much hazier and more diffuse than that. Nonetheless, it appears that these children are developing sufficient political awareness to begin to think of one political symbol in mental connection with another. In this way, affect and respect for one symbol may spill over onto others.

The fairly good performance of these children on sorting the various symbols with respect to America and their preference for the American flag stands in contrast to their inability to define America when asked an open-ended question and their reluctance to call themselves Americans. The latter two cases appear to be related to each other and to stem from cognitive difficulties with the concept "America," difficulties which are not overcome until later ages. But the early development of recognition of and affect for the flag and the emerging awareness of linkages among political symbols may prove to lay the groundwork for a deeper and firmer attachment to the nation among older children.

Affect

This discussion has touched on a few affective feelings toward politics in connection with choices among authority figures and preference for the American flag. But is there any other indication that preschool children might be developing the positive affect toward politics found among most elementary school children (Greenstein, 1965; Hess and Torney, 1967; Easton and Dennis, 1969)? I hypothesize that positive affect will tend to be stronger when the symbol in question is most familiar. I am not suggesting that detailed and copious information is a precondition of affective feelings, but that simple recognition of and familiarity with symbols as well perhaps as some rudimentary information concerning them is necessary before the child will develop a positive affective response.

After the information questions on each authority figure and America had been asked, the children were then asked questions of the format: "Do you like the policeman, or don't you like him," followed by "Do you like/not like him a lot, or do you like/not like him a little?" It is apparent that most of the children lean toward a positive response. Many more children said they liked the various figures than said they disliked them. Accordingly, answers were combined so as to yield three categories: like a lot, like a little, and dislike.

While the children do tend to give positive answers to all these symbols, their responses are differentiated in ways that suggest they are not simply naive or indiscriminately positive (see Table 9–4). First, affect for well-known figures such as the mailman is higher than for more remote and unfamiliar figures such as the President. Second, as a test of whether generalized positive affect might really be naiveté or acquiescence, an index was created summing the number of times each child replied most strongly positive. The least positive children tend to be younger and less knowledgeable, while the most positive tend to be the reverse.

The most often liked figures are the mailman and the milkman (the most familiar people) and the least often liked are President Nixon and America (the least familiar). Note that a minority of the children express negative affect for political symbols, unlike elementary school children who are more uniformly positive (Greenstein, 1965).

Table 9–4. Affect for Authority Figures, in Percent*

	LIKE A LOT	LIKE A LITTLE	DISLIKE	N
Mailman	77	19	4	79
Milkman	67	23	8	77
God	67	16	12	61
Policeman	57	23	15	74
President Nixon	52	13	28	73
America	44	25	25	60

* Percentages add to 100 horizontally.

The percentage liking these figures is roughly stable with age in the cases of the mailman and the milkman, who start high and maintain this position, and President Nixon and America, who are less often liked and register only minor gains among the older children. However, affect for both the policeman and God is more frequent among the older children. In the youngest group, 45 percent say they like the policeman a lot and 58 percent like God a lot; in the oldest group, these percentages are 74 and 78, respectively. A parallel decline occurs in the percentage of dislike responses, from 30 percent to zero for the policeman and from 21 to 5 percent for God. Once again, the policeman emerges as a crucial political symbol, one to whom these preschool children relate in both a cognitive and an affective manner.

The strong positive affective orientation to the policeman is also seen in that, asked to choose the one they like the best of all from among the policeman, mailman, and milkman, 45 children out of 75 responding choose the policeman. This choice is not common among the youngest children, where only 35 percent pick the policeman, but is very frequent among the five-year-olds, 70 percent of whom prefer him to the others.

CONCLUDING NOTE

The data presented here are exploratory and based on a small population of preschool children selected purposively. It is not my intention to argue that the patterns described here are representative of preschool children in general or even that this preliminary study has definitively mapped the political orientations of these children. What I have tried to demonstrate is that children as young as three to six do undergo a substantial amount of political socialization and that those of us with an interest in early political learning would therefore do well to study young children. In the judgment of this researcher, it seems that, considering their age, the extent of these children's recognition of and information about political symbols is fairly high.

Beyond this, I have described the emergent patterns obtaining in this population with the view of identifying some important variables and suggesting that early political socialization has an internal coherence and over-all structure related to theories of child development and to the findings of other researchers on elementary school children. Consistent with this, the political orientations of these children have been found to vary with the concreteness, visibility, and proximate nature of the symbols.

Perhaps the most noteworthy of the substantive findings observed in this population are those concerning the role of the policeman and the capacity of many of these children to discriminate between political and nonpolitical authority figures and other symbols. The policeman is familiar, relatively well cognized, well liked, perceived as important, and fairly often linked with government and America. Attitudes toward this figure are considerably more vague and less affectively tinged among those children under four and a half, but appear to become more developed both cognitively and affectively during the next several months. For these children, it seems that this personal, proximate political authority figure constitutes the most important point of contact they have with the political system from among the various symbols examine here.

The recognition on the part of many of these children that the general prestige and importance of as salient a figure as their father is less than that of political authorities and their increasing ability to sort political symbols from nonpolitical ones suggests a dawning awareness of a broad political world of some importance and a developing capacity to assimilate new political cues.

In addition to the limitations on the data base available here, the variables examined are limited. Future research should include a wider array of topics. Additional political symbols should be investigated. For example, one study by psychologists including some political data on 45 children aged two to five found them more aware of war than of the President and suggests we examine the impact of salient political topics on children's introduction to politics (Rebelsky, Conover, and Chafetz, 1969). The impact of Watergate comes strongly to mind in this connection.

Orientations that are politically relevant but not governmental constitute a broad and important area of study. General orientations toward authority, interpersonal trust or distrust, and developing norms of fairness are three illustrations of this type of socialization.

Children from different backgrounds and different cultures should be compared, and the impact of various socializing agencies should be assessed. Here, for example, one should look at the influence of daily experiences in the family and with peers and compare children at home with those in day care centers and nursery schools. The role of television in preschoolers' political learning may be particularly important.

Finally, I would hope that the processes that explain varieties of early political learning will be examined. A thorough consideration of these processes would include attention to theories of child development and measurement of the political stimuli and reinforcement schedules to which preschool children are exposed. Combining developmental concepts of the capacity of children to learn with observations of the learning situations in which they actually find themselves should yield a more comprehensive and accurate explanation of why they learn what they learn and assist us to evaluate the significance of early political socialization for later learning and behavior.

REFERENCES

Baldwin, Alfred L. *Theories of Child Development* (New York: John Wiley and Sons, 1967), 171–300.

Davies, A. F. "The Child's Discovery of Nationality," in Jack Dennis (ed.), *Socialization to Politics* (New York: John Wiley and Sons, 1973), 105–29.

Easton, David, and Jack Dennis. *Children in the Political System: Origins of Political Legitimacy* (New York: McGraw-Hill, 1969).

Erikson, Erik H. *Childhood and Society* (New York: Norton, 1950).

Freud, Sigmund. *The Basic Writings of Sigmund Freud* (New York: Random House, 1938).

Goodman, Mary Ellen. "Emergent Citizenship: A Study of Relevant Values in Four-Year-Olds," in Roberta S. Sigel (ed.), *Learning About Politics* (New York: Random House, 1970), 15–17.

————. *Race Awareness in Young Children,* 2nd ed. (London: Collier-Macmillan, 1964).

Greenstein, Fred I. *Children and Politics* (New Haven: Yale University Press, 1965).

————, and Sidney Tarrow. "Political Orientations of Children: The Use of a Semi-Projective Technique in Three Nations," *Sage Professional Papers in Comparative Politics,* No. 01–009, 1971.

Hess, Robert D., and Judith V. Torney. *The Development of Political Attitudes in Children* (Chicago: Aldine, 1967).

Horowitz, Eugene L. "Some Aspects of the Development of Patriotism in Children," *Sociometry* 3 (1940), 329–41.

Jahoda, Gustav. "The Development of Children's Ideas About Country and Nationality, Part I: The Conceptual Framework," *British Journal of Educational Psychology* 33 (1963a), 47–60.

————. "The Development of Children's Ideas About Country and Nationality, Part II: National Symbols and Themes," *British Journal of Educational Psychology* 33, Part 2 (1963b), 143–53.

————. "Children's Concepts of Nationality: A Critical Study of Piaget's Stages," *Child Development* 35 (1964), 1081–92.

Kohlberg, Lawrence. "A Cognitive-Developmental Analysis of Children's Sex Role Concepts and Attitudes," in Eleanor E. Maccoby (ed.), *The Development of Sex Differences* (Stanford: Stanford University Press, 1966), 82–173.

————. "The Development of Moral Character and Ideology," in M. Hoffman and L. Hoffman (eds.), *Review of Child Development Research,* Vol. 1 (New York: Russell Sage, 1964), 383–431.

Lawson, Edwin D. "Development of Patriotism in Children—A Second Look," *Journal of Psychology* 55 (1963), 279–86.

Merelman, Richard M. "The Development of Political Ideology: A Framework for the Analysis of Political Socialization," *American Political Science Review* 63 (1969), 750–67.

Mischel, Walter. "Sex-Typing and Socialization," in Paul H. Mussen (ed.), *Carmichael's Manual of Child Psychology,* 3rd ed., Vol. 2 (New York: John Wiley and Sons, 1970), 3–72.

Palmer, James O. *The Psychological Assessment of Children* (New York: John Wiley and Sons, 1970).

Piaget, Jean. *The Language and Thought of the Child* (Cleveland and New York: Meridian Books, 1955).

————. *The Moral Development of the Child* (New York: Free Press of Glencoe, 1965).

————, and Anne-Marie Weil. "The Development in Children of the Idea of the Homeland and of Relations with Other Countries," *International Social Science Bulletin* 3 (1951), 561–78.

Rebelsky, Freda, Cheryl Conover, and Patricia Chafetz. "The Development of Political Attitudes in Young Children," *Journal of Psychology* 73, second half (1969), 141–6.

Stevenson, Harold W., and Edward C. Stewart. "A Developmental Study of Racial Awareness in Young Children," *Child Development* 29 (1958), 399–409.

Weinstein, Eugene A. "The Development of the Concept of the Flag and the Sense of National Identity," *Child Development* 28 (1957), 167–74.

Chapter Ten

Toward a Generational Conception of Political Socialization

_____ *Neal E. Cutler*

INTRODUCTION

The purpose of this chapter is to suggest a substantial reorientation in the way political socialization is investigated. More specifically, its position is that, whatever else is included in the concept of socialization, investigators of the phenomenon should consider the generational context in which political socialization takes place.

A review of socialization studies in several of the social sciences, as well as a "review of reviews" of the recently expanding political socialization literature, yields the following conclusion: Despite the growing professional attention being paid to political socialization, generational factors in the genesis of individual political orientations and their maintenance throughout the life cycle have been largely overlooked.

In his review of relatively early political socialization studies, Hyman (1959) discounts the possibility of intergenerational discontinuities in patterns of political orientations mainly because his observation of parent–child correlations indicated substantial areas of intrafamily agreement on selected attitudes. He did not, however, review actual cross-generational studies but only intrafamily studies. Although survey research techniques have allowed social scientists to investigate patterns and sources of political orientations for about three decades, Lipset (1960, 281) observed that "unfortunately there has been no attempt to study systematically the effects of generation experiences with modern survey research techniques." In what is one of the most comprehensive reviews of survey research in political studies (McClosky, 1967), only two pages of 80 are descriptive of studies of political trends in general, and McClosky's prognosis for the future of political survey research makes no mention of the study of generations. In his review of political socialization literature for the *International Encyclopedia of the Social Sciences,* Greenstein (1968) outlines what he believes to be the major agencies of socialization, but makes no mention of any research in which the concept of generation is employed to further understanding of either the process or content of political stcialization. Similarly, see Andrain (1971), Dawson (1966), and Dawson and Prewitt (1969). Rintala's brief review article on "Political Generations" (1968) concluded that significant empirical studies of political generations are yet to be done. Finally, we should mention the broad political socialization review conducted by Dennis (1967, 1968), which was based on a literature search as well as a questionnaire interrogation of hundreds of social scientists who had, in one way or another, demonstrated an interest in the general subject; the review cites over 300 political socialization studies. In describing the generational dimensions of political socialization, Dennis was able to cite only two empirical studies; he concluded that "this is one of the areas of political socialization research where least is known."

The emphasis in political socialization studies has been most often on the agencies of socialization. The main agency of political socialization to receive scholarly attention has been the family, as it is in the family context that the child spends his early formative years. Emphasis upon the family is perhaps a "natural" one, given the evidence of personality formation within the family context, the lessons of Freudian psychology at their most general level, and the results of the early parent–child studies summarized by Hyman (1959). The interest of early learning for political scientists, however, lies not in the development of a "political psychology of adolescence"; rather, there is theoretical interest in childhood orientations as the possible explanatory gcnesis of adult political attitudes.

Thus the study of political socialization produces something of a contradiction. Theoretical interest is based on the proposition, or belief, that orientations socialized in childhood or adolescence are the bases of adult orientations, with the latter being important for the operation, and thus for the understanding, of the political system (Dawson, 1966, 4). On the empirical side, however, there has been little research tracing the orientations of adults to their socialization origins. In other words, although students of political socialization assume a linkage between childhood experiences and adult political orientations, there has been little evidence of this link.

The establishment of a theoretical basis for the childhood–adult linkage is particularly important because virtually all the modern studies of political socialization leave considerable unexplained variance on almost every political orientation, which suggests appreciable limitations on the socialization impact of families, schools, peer groups, and the like. A recent reexamination of American family political socialization studies (Connell, 1972) reviewed 50 studies based on comparisons in which data from parents and children in the same family were present. Although there was some parent–child similarity in most of the studies, Connell observed that the similarity was "in parallel" rather than "in series," concluding: "To sum up: it appears from a substantial body of evidence that processes within the family have been largely irrelevant to the formation of specific opinions" (330). Of course, many socialization studies do recognize that even the family operates in a larger sociopolitical context, a context which can and does change dramatically over time, making political generations potentially quite different. Yet, there has been little systematic inquiry into the influence of generations as a force either for the genesis of individual political orientations or of their maintenance throughout the life cycle.

This chapter argues that the linkage between childhood experiences and adult orientations will become verifiable when political socialization is conceptualized in a political generations framework. If we can identify successive generational groups of citizens who have undergone substantially different sets of experiences in their formative years, and if these generational groups can be empirically seen to maintain sets of political orientations grounded in these experiences, then it can be more authoritatively claimed that processes of political socialization are important for understanding adult political orientations and consequently for understanding the operation of a political system.

The sections of this chapter explore some basic issues relevant to the argument that there is a significant generational basis to political socialization. The next section proposes two perspectives. The thrust of this discussion is that the political socialization process, even within the family, does not take place in a vacuum but in the content of the wider social and political environment. The content of what is socialized, the orientations of the participants in the socialization process, and the very nature of parent–child interactions are all affected by the wider environment of the political system. The two basic conceptual approaches explored are called the "Psychohistorical Approach" and "Socialization as Intergenerational Negotiation." To the latter we have added a corollary, the notion of "Critical Life-Stages."

The subsequent section presents a case study in the generational analysis of political orientations. In particular, this discussion focuses upon a sequence of published studies investigating the existence of generational trends in American political party identification. Although other political behavior variables might be proposed for an examination of generational political socialization, this subject is useful because it represents a controversy in which several social scientists have directly confronted one another's explanations and analytic procedures. Varieties of techniques and data are brought to bear on the issue of generational trends such that these studies as a group clearly indicate the substance of, and some of the approaches to, a generational investigation of political socialization. The concluding remarks indicate the potential for further generational investigations of political socialization.

TWO CONCEPTUAL BASES FOR A GENERATIONS APPROACH

The agencies of political socialization clearly operate within a larger social and political environment, the impact of which can be felt in at least two ways: The political content of what is socialized will vary from historical time to historical time, and the very nature of the socialization process within the family and related agencies may be affected by the nature of the times. In this section we will suggest and review two conceptual bases for considering the proposition that the historical times do interact with socialization in such a way that identifiable patterns of generational political socialization should be expected. These conceptual bases are not considered mutually exclusive; to the contrary, they overlap in the kinds of explanations they seek and to some extent may be considered alternative paths to the same general theoretical goal.

The Psychohistorical Approach

The thesis that the individual-level aspects of political socialization substantially interact with the larger political events of the (macro) environment has been recognized by historians whose goal has been to analyze the individual development of particular historical elite figures. The emphasis of political socialization studies within political science has definitely not been on the socialization and psychological development of particular identifiable individuals. Yet, the conceptual argument in the area of psychohistory, when combined with some well-known areas of attitude theory, make this approach useful for understanding the generational bases of political socialization.

In general, as Mazlish (1972) has recently stated in his analysis of Richard Nixon, the psychohistorian is interested in examining psychoanalytic concepts in juxtaposition with historical events. "For example, while all children presumably experience an Oedipal conflict of sorts— it is a universal constant in this sense—the particular way it is experienced and its intensity vary enormously in different times and cultures" (151). In the Nixon case, Mazlish argues, Quaker religion and a rural California culture are not by themselves enough to explain the subject's development; it must be understood in light of the process of maturation in twentieth-century American society (152).

What Mazlish describes as being important in the analysis and understanding of a single individual is directly germane to the thesis that political socialization in general should be approached from a generational perspective:

> . . . we can think of developments in the mature individual corresponding with developments in the political or economic area surrounding him. His psyche, developed in terms of earlier . . . processes, will lead him to perceive events around him in a certain way, thus affecting the events themselves (especially if he is a leader). The political and economic developments will in turn affect the further development of his psyche, for such changes continue into maturity, though rooted in earlier, infantile processes (157).

Certainly the same kinds of processes that can be reconstructed from the biographical and behavioral data of well-known political figures operate similarly for members of the mass public. It is only that in the latter case we do not have the wealth of data, nor are we particularly interested in such a meticulous psychoanalytic reconstruction.

The basic point which Mazlish makes, however, is important in political socialization: the more political the subject, the more it is imperative for the analyst to consider the wider social and political environment in which maturation takes place (157). Similarly, in the present context, the more political the area of individual learning and development which is being considered, as in the study of political socialization, the more it is incumbent upon analysts to consider the wider environment in which the individual matures politically.

The basic thesis of Mazlish's psychohistorical approach may become clearer when seen in relationship to the functional approach to the analysis of attitudes as found in social psychology. A final example from the study of Nixon will serve to illustrate this point. Mazlish noted in reviewing Nixon's autobiographical *Six Crises* that Nixon used the term "bums" to refer to his political opponents in particular situations and noted also that Nixon used the term again in referring to student demonstrators in more recent campaigns. Mazlish concludes, "What I was 'predicting' was that 'bums' meant something special in Nixon's psychic economy, and that under certain special conditions it was likely to appear as a term of opprobrium" (162). Transposed into the area of political socialization, the example suggests that for different individuals, members of different generations, raised in different social and historical periods, certain political attitudes and symbols can have special meanings, perhaps quite different from the meaning attached by members of other political generations.

Indeed, the functional theory of attitude formation argues in part that the holding of a particular attitude by an individual performs a variety of personal or psychological functions. Katz (1960), for example, describes four different functions that attitudes may serve for an individual: an adjustment or utilitarian function, an ego defensive function, a value-expressive function, and a knowledge function. In different generational and historical contexts, sets of social–psychological "meanings" attached to political objects may serve different functions (Shibutani, 1961, 97–118); or, different attitudes might serve the same function for members of different political generations.

The value-expressive function in Katz's discussion, for example, helps give expression to basic and central values. The individual may hold attitudes toward particular political programs and policies because such attitudes are felt to be in consonance with the image of the kind of person the individual aspires to be. The knowledge function, to take another example, is served when the attitudes help to provide general or specific frames of reference by which the individual can make some order out of the diverse universe of political stimuli present in the environment. In a political context, for example, Smith, Bruner, and White (1956) employed the functional approach to attitudes as a way of understanding the genesis of an individual's attitudes toward Russia.

In the context of the present discussion it may be argued that the meaning attached to objects in the political world or the function that such attitudes serve will be different depending upon the wider political context in which the individual is socialized. The family and school, for example, may effectively teach the same positive value of political participation and citizen obligation in democratic processes to two generations; yet, the meaning and scope of such terms as "participation" and "obligation" may be quite different in the early 1950s and early 1970s.

This kind of socialization dynamic is forcefully demonstrated in Inglehart's (1971) recent cross-national study of Western Europe. During the 1968 political crisis in France there was initially an alliance between the student left and the labor unions in their joint dissatisfaction with the policies of President De Gaulle. But there seemed to be a dramatic parting of the ways when the students went beyond marching and protesting and began to overturn cars and set them afire. In Inglehart's reconstruction of the situation, automobiles were symbols of acquisition, of "making it" economically to the older union members. To the students the cars were also symbolic of the acquisition process but in a quite negative way: Cars were the symbols of the overconsumerized society, of pollution, of big corporations. It did not bother them at all to destroy this detested symbolic artifact.

Inglehart's attitudinal analysis of French and other Western European respondents focused on the political value hierarchies of the respondents. His substantive hypothesis was that the attitudes and values concerning the imperatives of economic security were not felt among the younger cohorts who have been socialized in the midst of the postwar "miracle" of economic recovery. Inglehart identified two basic clusters of political values, the "Acquisitive" and the "Post-Bourgeois." In the context of the present discussion, the important point of Inglehart's findings is that endorsement of these two attitude clusters was strongly related to generational location. In five of the six Western European nations the youngest cohorts, socialized during the European economic recovery after 1945, were 20 percentage points more Post-Bourgeois in their orientations than were the historically prior cohorts. The one exception, interestingly enough, were the British respondents. As Great Britain is the country that least benefited from the general European economic recovery, it is, perhaps, the exception that proves the rule.

Inglehart's other major findings provide further support for the importance of generational analysis. The Acquisitive respondents, for example, were more concerned with problems of rising prices and the maintenance of public order, while the Post-Bourgeois respondents were more interested in the protection of free speech and the extension of popular political participation. In the area of foreign policy, Inglehart found that the younger cohort Post-Bourgeois respondents were twice as much in favor of supranational European integration than the older generation Acquisitive respondents. In much of these data, the largest differences were between the youngest cohort, aged 16–24 years, and the older cohorts. Inglehart recognizes the generational socialization element of this pattern in observing that this youngest cohort is the only one entirely born and raised in Europe's postwar economic boom.

Patterns of political socialization, therefore, can be seen to be related to the events and conditions of the wider social and political environment. The "psychohistory" notion is a shorthand way of indicating that the individual development, within the family and other childhood agencies, is strongly affected by this wider environment. Childhood agencies of socialization may "transmit" some political orientations, but these often are given meaning, and perhaps psychologically functional importance, by the political factors external to the family and other agencies. In this context, then, we can see that the content of political socialization may be expected to vary from generation to generation.

As Talcott Parsons (1955, 35) noted almost two decades ago:

> But we must not forget that the nuclear family is *never*, most certainly not in the American case, an independent society, but a small and highly differentiated subsystem of a society. This fact is crucially relevant to our interests at two points. First, the parents, as socializing agents, occupy not merely their familial roles, but these articulate, i.e., interpenetrate, with their roles in other struc-

tures of the society, and this fact is a necessary condition, as we hope to show, of their functioning effectively as socializing agents, i.e., as parents at all. Secondly, the child is never socialized only for and into his family of orientation, but into structures which extend beyond this family, though interpenetrating with it.

It is highly plausible, therefore, to expect that the nature of political socialization even within the family can be affected by the external political environment, and it is to a consideration of this that we now turn.

Socialization as Intergenerational Negotiation

Although the conceptual base that we have referred to as the Psycho-historical approach focuses attention on the interaction of external events and the development of the individual being socialized, the wider external environment can also act upon the relationships between the individual being socialized and the agencies of socialization. A basic point of this conceptual approach is that in the family it is not only the child who is undergoing developmental processes. The parents also are developing human beings, undergoing various forms of adult development and socialization (Brim, 1966). The fact that the parents' developmental agenda may be quite different from that of the child should nonetheless be considered when the environment in which political socialization takes place is discussed.

Although the political socialization literature has paid some attention to intrafamily factors that might enhance or detract from "effective transmission" of parental values (e.g., Jennings and Niemi, 1968; McClosky and Dahlgren, 1959), there has been virtually no attention paid to the parents as representing changing "clusters of variables" and therefore representing a varying set of orientations, life views, and so on. This latter point is important, for, if parents as well as children are seen to have developing sets of orientations, then we can better explain situations in which parents and their children hold quite different views on similar sets of issues. These issues are not only political ones but also basic life-views, including, perhaps, the nature of the socialization process. Furthermore, if such life-views or global orientations are divergent between generations within the family, then the process of socialization in general and political socialization in particular is affected by the ways in which these differences are reconciled (or fail to be reconciled).

This point of view has been comprehensively elaborated by Bengtson and Black (1973), who conceive of socialization itself as a confrontation between generations, a confrontation which not only takes place in the context of microlevel intrafamily events but is also affected by macrolevel environmental and historical events.

> First, consideration of the larger social structure is necessary to a comprehensive view of socialization and interpersonal generational relations. The nature of the relationship between representatives of different generations within the family is, to a significant extent, determined by events, experiences and attributes acquired by each generation as a result of membership in a particular set of age peers. Consequently, the relationship of family members to large social and cultural elements within a historical time frame—the macro-perspective—forms an important context for the generational socialization relationship (p. 30).

In the context of political socialization, this confrontation between parents and children is much broader than the mere supposition of political rebellion on the part of adolescents. Where attempts have been made to discuss political socialization as the consequence of such youthful rebellion, the results have been quite mixed, indicating that a simple model of parent-child disagreement on political matters is not a very powerful one (e.g., Lane, 1959; Maccoby *et al.*, 1954; Middleton and Putney, 1963; Jennings and Niemi, 1968). At a much more inclusive level, however, the observation that parents and children are at different stages in their respective life cycles and thus have different agendas based on their developmental problems can be seen as quite germane to the process of political socialization. When we consider that this process of intrafamily, intergenerational negotiation takes place in the wider context of salient historical and politically relevant events, the explanatory potential of a political generations conception for political socialization is enhanced.

To be more specific about the different developmental agenda that intrafamily generations possess, Bengtson and Black (1973, 27 ff.) cite five ways in which age differences can be viewed as a function of what they call "developmental time." The following discussion builds on their suggestions.

1. Cognitive development. The degree to which parents and their children can assimilate and understand both life cycle events and political events will affect the way that they view each other as well as the way they view the external world.

2. Differentiation of social reality. Maturation brings the cognitive skills by which the social and political worlds are viewed in terms of increasing complexity, with parents able to see more gray between the black and white than is seen by their children. Varieties of differentiation in perception of social reality will affect the way the two generations view external events, and these perceptual differences will have import for the family socialization process itself.

3. *Orientation toward future time.* Studies by psychologists and gerontologists have shown that age is strongly related to an individual's future time perspective. This time perspective, in turn, is strongly related to attitudes toward a variety of personal and social, as well as political, attitudes (Reichenbach and Mathers, 1959; Kastenbaum, 1961, 1963, 1964). In the political realm, for example, Back and Gergen (1963a, 1963b) and Gergen and Back (1965) have demonstrated that among other public-policy attitudes, orientations toward solutions to problems in the sphere of international politics are substantially related to one's perception of personal future time. More generally, Rokeach and Bonier (1960) have related future time perspective to dogmatism. In childhood the dominant perception is that time is limitless; early adulthood brings the realization that time is in fact finite and should be allocated as a scarce resource; and middle age and advancing years lead to the perception that time is not only finite but is becoming seriously limited so that the individual has to allocate life choices accordingly (Kuhlen, 1956). Such differences in time orientation between parents and children, in the context of varying historical contexts, will surely affect the nature, process, and outcomes of political socialization.

4. *Differences in social positions between the parent and child generations.* Parents, of course, occupy much more differentiated social role structures as a consequence of their adult statuses, with accompanying differences in their various responsibilities. Yet this can also vary in its personal impact according to the wider context of historical events. Adult generational cohorts differ in size, in levels of educational attainment, in fertility, economic prospects, and so on (Bogue, 1969, 152–153). Thus the pressures on individuals within successive generational cohorts, given by the varying kinds of social and economic pressures precipitated by the intersection of their cohort characteristics and the historical context, can have differential effects upon the way they participate in processes of political socialization. Sheatsly (1949), for example, found that there are definite attitudinal patterns involved in negative expectations emanating from the sociopolitical environment in terms of both wars and depressions; and Cutler (1968, Ch. 7) found that there have been definite generational patterns of such negative expectations.

5. *Differences in intercohort perceptions of generational solidarity.* There are two manifestations of this kind of differential perception. First, successive generations may differ in the way they view what might be called "cohort solidarity." To use Ryder's phrase, "a cohort may be defined as the aggregate of individuals . . . who experience the same event within the same time interval. In almost all cohort research to date the defining event has been birth" (Ryder, 1965, 845). In this discussion we have been using the terms "cohort" and "generation" interchangeably, although coming from the field of demography "cohort" can be used in empirical research with more specificity than the more generic term "generation." Nonetheless, although a cohort can be assumed to conceptually "exist" by nature of the coincidence of the birth of its members, every cohort does not have to have similar "cohort consciousness" or cohort self-identity as a distinct generational group. In this sense, the concept of a generational cohort is analogous to the concept of social class. Social scientists can classify individuals "objectively" into different social strata by a variety of measurement indicators, but the social and political significance of such groupings become enhanced by the self-identification and the consequent behavioral predispositions of individuals within social classes. In turn, such class consciousness is variable over time, as are the behavioral consequences which can flow from such consciousness. It is the same with cohort consciousness (Mannheim, 1952, 289; Riley, 1971). At different times in history, parental cohorts as well as child or student cohorts can have different levels of generational consciousness and different personal, social, and political agendas based on that consciousness.

A second aspect of differential intercohort perceptions of generational solidarity or consciousness concerns the way the cohorts view each other. Again, the wider environment in which socialization takes place has an effect upon the way in which the parent and child generations negotiate the socialization relationship. The parental generation may see in their children a continuation of themselves, of their values, of the creation of "social heirs." The younger generation, on the other hand, may not have this kind of concern, but has its own agenda of developmental priorities which might be perceived as being hindered by the values and subsequent behaviors of the parents (Bengtson and Black, 1973, 335).

In a series of studies, Bengtson has provided interesting evidence of differential cohort perceptions on the part of successive generations. In a study design that included a sample of three-generation families, the children, parents, and grandparents in the same family were asked to rate the closeness of relationships between the three generational groups. Interestingly, the question was posed both for the respondents' own family and again for the society as a whole. In both instances the youngest of the three generational groups had the highest level of perceived "generation gap." More interesting, however, is the contrast between perceptions of the "family's generation gap" and perceptions of "society's generation gap." In the former, the perceived gap was not too different across the three cohorts of perceivers; for the society as a whole, however, the cohort differences were rather pronounced. The two distributions together indicate a response that may say "Yes, there are substantial generational gaps, but not so much in my family." Bengtson concludes: "This is in keeping with the 'developmental stake' theory: in attempting to emphasize individuality, the younger generation perceives differences which may not be there; the older generations, attending to issues of family continuity and perpetuation, tend to underemphasize potential differences."

Another study illustrates that the different generational groups have different bases for perceived intergenerational differences. Parents and their children were asked to indicate what kind of issues separated them from each other. In an item which asked the respondents to define the generation "gap," more than four times as many youngsters as their parents chose politics and social relations, although this response was not the first choice of either group. In another item, which asked the respondents to name the area of most disagreement with the "other" generation, almost twice as many youngsters chose the politics and social relations response (Bengtson and Kuypers, 1971, Tables 2–3).

In summary, it may be seen that parents as well as children are affected by a series of developmental events and that parents can have their own evolving agenda for personal and social behavior based upon such events. Equally critical is the fact that parents may find themselves in crucial developmental periods at the very time when they are called upon to act as "agencies of socialization." Perhaps one of the most dramatic examples of the fact that parents are undergoing development themselves is briefly to note the life-stage event of the onset of parenthood itself as it may affect the new parents.

The fact that parenthood can be a traumatic developmental event has often been noted by sociologists; Martinson, for example, noted that "young couples in our society are apparently ill prepared to face the realities of having babies and living with children" (1963, 379). LeMasters (1957), in a study titled "Parenthood as Crisis," found that 83 percent of the couples interviewed "reported extensive or severe crisis in adjusting to the first child." This crisis was not due to unplanned or undesired pregnancies but rather to being unprepared for the reception of a new baby into the marital dyad. In a follow-up study, Dyer (1963) found similar "crisis perceptions" on the part of new parents. In an additional pair of studies, however, Hobbs (1965, 1968) felt that the term "crisis" was a bit strong: "On the basis of the present investigation it would seem more accurate to view the addition of the first child to the marriage as a period of transition which is somewhat stressful than to conceptualize beginning parenthood as a crisis" (1968, 417).

Recognizing this general problem Rossi (1968) has indicated that much significant recent research in the sociology of the family has finally recognized that the focus within socialization research need not be solely upon the child. The understanding of the socialization milieu requires, as Benedek (1959) has pointed out, that parenthood be considered as an important developmental phase. Four factors have been cited as contributing to the dislocative aspect of parenthood: (1) the paucity of preparation for parenthood in formal educational channels, (2) the lack of pregnancy-period learning opportunities, (3) the abruptness of change in incurring responsibilities of parenthood, and (4) the lack of general guidelines as to the meaning of successful parenthood (Rossi, 1968, 35). Jacoby (1969) also eschews the label "crisis" in attempting to evaluate the problems associated with new parenthood, but notes that parenthood is a "disruptive life cycle developmental event" for the parents. Parental attitudes may vary in evaluation of this disruption, and these variations may be related to social class, to the age of the parents, to marital adjustment, and the like. Thus, various responses may be expected to the parenthood event, and these must be mapped in order to understand the influence of this developmental event upon the socialization process.

Rossi takes this discussion more directly into the area of generational trends in noting that the major societal change in marriage in the past few decades has been the widespread use of contraception and subsequent choices in the direction of delaying first pregnancies. Thus, in past years when parenthood came soon after marriage, it was the marriage which was the major "transition point" in the life cycle. With delayed parenthood, however, the first pregnancy becomes a much more distinct event. Rossi concludes that "the transition point is increasingly the first pregnancy rather than the marriage" (31).

According to a variety of studies and points of view, therefore, parenthood itself is an adult life-cycle developmental event that ranges from "severe crisis" to "distressful disruption." Furthermore, the nature and consequences of the disruption or crisis has been seen to be linked with generational phenomena. What this brief discussion of parenthood has sought to illustrate is the more general proposition that parents as well as children are involved in developmental events and that the socialization relationship is negotiated in the context of the differing agendas based upon the different developmental tasks. More generally, the developmental events that the several parties to the socialization process are involved in take place in an historical context. Thus, the nature of the socialization is itself affected by the wider social and political environment. The position of Parsons, quoted earlier, is also relevant here: The family is not an independent society, but a subsystem of the wider society, and it exists in a relationship of interpretation with that wide society. As Bengtson and Black (1973, 26) summarize this position,

> the generational relationship should be viewed as one of bilateral negotiation in which the issues negotiated are based in several important contextual elements. First, each lineage member belongs to an age cohort, a membership that has implications for behavior, both as independent individuals and with respect to one another. Second, the relationship exists within a context of variable historical time, such that the issues negotiated on a personal level may have as well cultural and historical consequences. Third, each lineage member is a developing individual; within the relationship, each represents a unique set of concerns in working out those problems that face him as a result of his own personal development experiences.

Critical Life Stages: A Corollary

The notion of socialization as a bilateral negotiation process between generations located at different places in the developmental continuum leads to a corollary that may be called "Critical Life-Stages," which is certainly not unknown to students of human developmental processes. There has been substantial work, especially by psychologists, on various stages of cognitive and emotional development of children. Although it is recognized that socialization is a life-long process, there are identifiable stages at which certain skills, orientations, and problems develop and which thus can be referred to as critical lifestages in the socialization process. There are, of course, differences of opinion as to the specific ages in the developmental life-process in which these critical stages occur, as well as disagreement concerning their relevance for the development of particular political orientations.

In the context of the present discussion, we will only note that critical life-stages do occur both for children and adults, and that the intersection of these critical stages and the social and political events of the external environment can precipitate substantial political differences between the generations. In his classic essay on the sociology of generations, Mannheim (1952) suggests that the critical generation-forming life-stage is the period from about 17 to 25 years of age. More recently, Lambert (1971) has reviewed a variety of psychological findings to provide the justification for this definition of critical life-stages, which Mannheim did not elaborate.

Lambert considers discussions of staging in intellectual development (Inhelder and Piaget, 1958), moral development (Maccoby, 1968), and socio-emotional development (Erikson, 1950, 1968). His conclusion is that children in their early years do not have the ability to formulate important political orientations but that such abilities are present in the later years of adolescence. He writes: "It would seem, in conclusion, that the foregoing discussion of research and theory in human development supports the idea of a critical period for the emergence of political–cultural consciousness typically during the stage of Youth (17–25)" (23–34). In an empirical example of generational research, Bobrow and Cutler (1967) mapped the foreign policy orientations of three generational cohorts, which were labelled the "World War I" cohort, the "World War II" cohort, and the "Nuclear Era" cohort. These cohorts were identified as those individuals who were about 20 years old at the time of the event in question. Although the choice of matching labels and cohort definitions was arbitrary rather than based on an empirical process, it was nonetheless found that the three cohorts did have identifiably different foreign policy orientations on a number of separate dimensions spanning the 1946–1966 period. An analogous study of foreign policy attitudes in Finland found that generational cohorts identified by events taking place at age fifteen provided useful and interesting explanations of the attitude patterns (Cutler and Heiskanen, 1973; Cutler, 1973).

It should not be thought, however, that the notion of critical life-stages is appropriate only for adolescents and youth. The discussion of socialization as intergenerational negotiation warrants the observation that we should be attentive to critical adult life-stages as well. At the older end of the life span we know that there are important processes of "disengagement" that can affect a variety of social and political orientations (Cumming and Henry, 1961; Back and Gergen, 1966; Glenn, 1969). More important in the context of political socialization, however, are the critical life-stages that parents experience. As is often noted in the sociological literature, the passing of an individual from adolescent to adult roles represents a critical life-stage, given the pressures and responsibilities of entering the labor force, marriage, and setting up a home. Indeed, as has been noted, the arrival of parenthood and the responsibilities of "becoming an agency of socialization" is itself a critical life-stage.

Parental cohorts arrive at their critical life-stages in differing sets of social and political circumstances compared to their children. Thus, the nature of the job and housing markets are influenced by the aggregate size and educational levels of the cohorts. The response of the political and economic systems to these demographic differences in cohort profiles and the pressures they create contribute to the way successive parental cohorts react to their own critical life-stages. Research has shown, for example, that "children of the Depression" or" children of the New Deal" have quite different sets of social and political orientations than generational cohorts coming before them, e.g., their own parents. Centers (1950, 325) has dramatically summarized this position.

These are children of the New Deal. Born in depression, reared in unemployment and insecurity, constantly exposed to the ideology of three Roosevelt administrations, witnessing the dramatic victories of welfare legislation, T.V.A., etc., and probably in numerous instances personally and tangibly and perceptibly benefitting from welfare measures, could one expect a result other than just what we have in these youth?

The notion of critical life-stages, thus, complements and enhances the notion of socialization as negotiation between two generational groups, each at its own stage in the life-long developmental process. We not only have the observation that the socialization process itself takes place in the context of the political and social events of the wider environment but that the participants in this process may be experiencing varieties of critical life-stages. In some instances, the effects of the external environment may be to harmonize and synchronize the developmental agenda of the participants. Yet, in other historical contexts, these external factors may serve to heighten intergenerational differences and to crystallize generational consciousness of one or both of the generational groups involved. In these latter times, especially, we would expect strong generational bases of political socialization.

GENERATIONAL POLITICAL SOCIALIZATION: THE EXAMPLE OF PARTY IDENTIFICATION IN THE UNITED STATES

In this section we will review a sequence of studies that have more or less built upon one another, centering upon the empirical identification of generational trends in party identification in the American electorate. Other areas of study could be used to demonstrate the impact of generational political socialization, but this topic has been the subject of a "debate" in the professional journals and thus has had extended exposure. This topic is especially useful in clarifying the main conceptual and methodological issues involved in the investigation of generational socialization.

By now it is clear that the investigation of generational socialization is dependent upon data sets in which the association or correlation between age and the political orientation under study can be observed. Yet, as has been discussed extensively elsewhere, the age of an individual simultaneously represents not only the time of birth or the generational milieu of significant political socialization, but also the maturation life-stage of the individual (Cutler, 1968, 1971a, 1974). Thus, there is an ambiguity in interpreting observed age correlations, especially when the data under scrutiny are from a single cross-sectional study of attitudes. In his early study of attitudes toward tolerance and civil liberties, for example, Stouffer found that the younger respondents were more tolerant than older respondents. He noted that cross-sectional data could not be used to explain whether younger people were just basically more tolerant than older people in general or whether the newer generation was socialized to greater tolerance than earlier generations (Stouffer, 1955, 89).

It is the same with the question of party identification. Some have argued, mainly on the basis of cross-sectional evidence, that as people get older they change in the direction of the Republican party as part of a more general tendency, supported in part by gerontological evidence, of increasing conservatism on the part of older persons. On the other hand, patterns of party identification analyzed within the context of generational political socialization, with appropriate generational cohort analytic methods and data, have resulted in support for a generational rather than a maturational interpretation of observed associations between age and party identification.

Recent evidence of family political socialization (Jennings and Niemi, 1968) has demonstrated that the family transmission of party identification is not an overwhelming explanation of this political orientation. Thus, the investigation of the generational sources of political party identification becomes a useful test case for the establishment of the importance of generational political socialization.

In 1960, the authors of *The American Voter* interpreted cross-sectional data on party identification as providing evidence of generational political socialization, at least with respect to the influence of the American Depression and New Deal period. Looking at the percentage of Democratic party identifiers in their national sample of the 1956 electorate they concluded on the basis of an age analysis that those who "came of age" in the 1920s had a much lower proportion of Democratic identifiers than any of the age groups who came of age in years during and subsequent to the Depression. They argued, for example, that if aging rather than generational socialization were the operative force then there would not be so many Democrats in the 1956 sample. They concluded, therefore, in favor of the generational explanation:

> Despite all these considerations the evidence seems to justify our
> conclusion that the Great Depression swung a heavy proportion of
> the *young* electors toward the Democratic party and gave that party
> a hold on *that generation* which it has never fully relinquished
> (Campbell *et al.*, 1960, 154–155, emphasis added).

Using somewhat more animated language, Lubell (1956, 63) also explained current patterns of party identification in terms of generational socialization.

> The essential difference between the Republican-rooted middle class and the newer Democratically-inclined middle class . . . is the factor of timing—of when each arrived at the state of middle-class blessedness. The newer middle class, having achieved their gains in a period of expanding governmental activity, are not as hostile to "big government" as are the older middle-class elements.

These conclusions favoring a generational socialization interpretation of the observed data, however, were based on indirect inference from cross-sectional data. Although they are intuitively appealing, it takes longitudinal data to actually distinguish a generational from a maturational interpretation. In 1962 Crittenden published a study that presented longitudinal data but strongly argued against a generational interpretation of changes in party identification. Rather, Crittenden argued quite the opposite, saying that it was aging that brought about a conversion to the Republican party. Data were presented from surveys taken at four-year intervals from 1946 to 1958; the percentage of Republican identifiers in each survey, sorted into four-year age groups, were presented. Crittenden compared the four youngest age groups with the four oldest age groups in each of the four national surveys. He did this separately for both high and low education respondents, thus yielding 128 separate comparisons, and observing that "in only five of these 128 observations is the older group not more Republican than the younger" (Crittenden, 1962, 650–651). The conclusion was that the conversion from Democratic identification to Republican was a linear function of aging and that a generational interpretation of party identification was therefore to be dismissed.

In a more recent study Cutler applied formal cohort analysis to Crittenden's data (Cutler, 1969). A major methodological difference between the two analyses of the same data was that while Crittenden looked at each of his four national surveys as separate cross-sectional replications, Cutler observed the age groups as representing successive samples, over time, of the *same* generational cohorts. Thus, for example, where Crittenden compared the 21–24 age group in 1946 with the 61–64 age group in the same 1946 sample, Cutler compared this 21–24 age group with the 25–28 age group in the 1950 sample. The latter approach is the essence of cohort analysis, in which the analyst longitudinally examines a number of surveys in order to see how samples of the same cohort appear as that cohort ages. The application of the cohort analysis procedure to all cohorts in the Crittenden data that were fully represented in the 1946–1958 data matrix revealed that a generational rather than a maturational explanation was warranted.

In his published "Reply to Cutler," Crittenden's rebuttal focused on the issue of his correction for trend in the electorate as a whole (Crittenden,

1969). He agreed that Cutler's analysis of his data did not provide evidence of increasing Republicanism with aging when the data were examined on a cohort-by-cohort basis. Rather, he argued that his conclusion concerning the clarity of the Republican conversion phenomena was based upon the "relative" increases in Republicanism on the part of the older age groups when compared with the electorate as a whole in the 1946–1958 period. Thus, for example, if an age group actually had the same percentage of Republicans in two time periods but in that interval the whole electorate had a decrease in Republicanism, by comparison, the age group had "changed" in a more Republican direction relative to the electorate. Crittenden even observed that a change of one percentage point in the Democratic direction by an age group, if compared to a pro-Democratic change of three percentage points in the electorate as a whole, would be scored in his statistical procedure as a relative change in the Republican direction. On the basis of these kinds of empirical observations and interpretations, corrected for national trend, Crittenden concluded that aging is accompanied by increasing conservatism, by shifts on the part of older persons to the Republican party.

When dealing with the question of generational political socialization and the kinds of evidence which might be brought to bear on the question, corrections for trend are, of course, quite important. Yet, such corrections must be considered in light of the analytic and theoretical goals of any particular analysis. If the goal of the analysis is to determine the relative position of a given life-stage age group or generational cohort group vis-à-vis the whole electorate, such as to estimate the potential for intergenerational conflict, then some kind of correction for relative trends might be appropriate. On the other hand, if the goal of the analysis is to say something about individual behavioral processes as in the case of the conservatism issue which seeks to link aging processes with individual behavioral decisions, then such trend corrections can be quite misleading.

In this regard, it can be seen that Crittenden's analysis contains two rather serious errors. The first concerns the meaning of "correction for trend." Relative measures that contain a trend correction require two components: the measure of the age group and the measure of the national electorate. We may conceive of the age structure of a national electorate as a system (or population pyramid) that is open at two ends; new cohorts are entering the electorate at the "bottom end," while historically prior cohorts are literally dying out at the "top end." If there are generational processes that are changing the party identification structure of the electorate and if the results of the generational socialization are at least temporarily linear, then each new generation might contain increasingly larger proportions of non-Republicans (Democrats or Independents). At the same time, as the non-Republican generational cohort enters this population system, a heavily Republican cohort is leaving the system. As a result the proportion of Republicans in the total electorate will be smaller. If, then, one observes the *relative* proportion of Republicanism in an older cohort that has not yet left the electorate, that cohort will *appear* to be getting more and more Republican. Even if that generational cohort has remained absolutely fixed in its proportional mix of Republicans and Democrats, when compared to an increasingly Democratic electorate the cohort will statistically appear to be getting more Republican as it gets older. Correction for national trend, which at first blush would seem a useful addition to longitudinal analyses, can in fact produce erroneous results when the goal of the analysis is to understand individual behavioral patterns. Thus, in the first instance, the original conclusions about the "linear" relationship between aging and Republicanism seem the result of statistical artifact.

An equally significant error can be made in the generalization of age group trends to individual behavior, an error similar to the fallacy of ecological correlation that has been known in the social science literature for at least two decades (Robinson, 1950). It is, of course, possible and even likely that a cohort will change in composition as it ages. Different rates of human mortality as well as sample survey mortality may be associated with socioeconomic factors that are at the same time related to political behavior variables. It is not implausible, for example, that in the later stages of its aggregate life history a given generational cohort will have a much higher proportion of rich Republican females than it had during most of its life course. Thus, in terms of demographic processes, the cohort, as contrasted with individuals in the cohort, may in fact become more Republican.

This point is given an even more dramatic example in Riley's (1973) useful discussion of cohort analysis fallacies. Referring to this problem as the "compositional fallacy," Riley notes that "certain characteristics which are irreversible with respect to the individual are reversible with respect to the cohort." Thus, individuals within a cohort afflicted with a given incurable disease may die fairly young; once these persons have died, the death rates from this disease within the aggregate cohort will decrease. "This could scarcely lead to the inference that aging decreases a person's risk of death from this incurable disease!" (11). The fallacy, as already mentioned, is in generalizing from a cohort process to an individual behavioral process.

Thus, Crittenden's conclusion that aging brings about a conversion to conservatism and to the Republican party appears to be based on a statistical artifact and an interpretive fallacy. In the reanalysis of the Crittenden argument based upon a cohort analysis that did not employ the "correction for trend," however, Cutler did not go beyond a reanalysis of the data already presented by Crittenden. Thus, although Cutler reached a conclusion favoring a generational political socialization interpretation, in accord with the earlier conclusion in *The American Voter*, it was not until later analyses, with different data, that the generational conclusion was verified.

In 1971 Klecka presented a paper, the main emphasis of which was a methodological investigation of the aging versus generational interpretations of political behavior data. Klecka designed a series of computer algorithms to empirically locate the "boundaries" of generational cohorts. These statistical techniques were based on an analysis of variance model and sought to inductively identify cohort groups on the basis of minimizing variance within the groups and maximizing the variance between them. In entering the Crittenden–Cutler controversy, Klecka first reanalyzed the original data from the Crittenden article and found that the empirical patterns were "slightly in favor of a generational interpretation. This is congruent with Cutler's finding" (Klecka, 1971*b*, 18). He then went further and examined party identification data from a series of eight national election surveys carried out by the University of Michigan Survey Research Center. Comparing the SRC data with Crittenden's Gallup data Klecka concluded "in neither instance is there substantial evidence to support the hypothesis that Republicanism increases as generations age" (18–19).

Klecka's analysis, while mildly supporting the conclusion that a generational socialization interpretation appears more substantiated than the maturational aging interpretation, was still not the last word on this issue. His analysis was mainly methodological, and as his techniques are somewhat complex and can be employed only upon access to his particular set of computer programs, they have not been applied by other scholars. Therefore, the publication of a new cohort analysis study of party identification by Glenn and Hefner was a welcome addition to the literature. Glenn and Hefner (1972) assembled a data base representing surveys taken every four years between 1945 and 1959. Except for 1945, each point in their longitudinal analysis was represented by an aggregation of three, four, or five different national Gallup surveys. They included in their cohort analyses controls for sex and educational influences and corrected their data for the underrepresentation of lower-class respondents found in the earlier Gallup surveys. Thus, their analysis brings to the question of generational political socialization a new and expansive data base as well as a sophistication and experience with secondary analysis in general and cohort analysis problems in particular (Glenn and Grimes, 1968; Glenn and Zody, 1970).

Their analysis begins by noting that the Crittenden data do not provide evidence of increasing Republicanism associated with aging. In their own data they also compute the ratio of cohort Republicanism to Republicanism in the total electorate, only to find that if this "corrected" evidence alone were available, it would appear that aging was strongly related to increasing Republicanism. An analysis of the party identification percentage data quite apart from ratios and corrected scores brings another rejection of the aging hypothesis.

> This study should rather conclusively lay to rest the once prevalent belief that the aging process has been an important influence for Republicanism in the United States. Aging cohorts have become more Republican in a relative sense as a result of a secular trend away from Republicanism in the total adult population. However, this trend has grown to a large extent out of the dying off of the older, more Republican cohorts (those least affected by the massive defections from the Republican party during the Great Depression), and therefore the failure of aging cohorts fully to conform to it in no sense implies that aging exerts influence toward Republicanism (47).

But what of the "other end" of this discussion; that is, is there evidence of generational socialization and is there evidence that generational cohorts as compared with maturational life-stages exhibit homogeneity with respect to their partisanship? To test the generational hypothesis, Glenn and Hefner compared the cohort trends with the trend for the youngest life-stage group in their data, the 21–29 age group. They argue that if there are any substantial change-oriented influences in the political environment (e.g., presidential election campaigns), then the change would be reflected most in the youngest life-stage. While the cohort estimates are based upon successive samples of the same cohort, the life-stage estimates represent the orientations of unrelated samples of, in this case, the newer entrants to the electoral system.

Glenn and Hefner then looked at the "Republican" years of 1953, 1957, and 1969, each representing the immediate post-election years of Republican victors, and also looked at the Democratic years of 1949, 1961, and 1965. Their analysis revealed no evidence of substantial reorientations of the generational cohorts as compared with the youngest life-stage.

In each of the Republican years, in comparison with the previous sampling point, the youngest life-stage did indicate an increase in Republicanism; this increase was, with one exception, larger than the average cohort increase in Republicanism. In looking at the Democratic years, the youngest life-stage, as expected, showed a decrease in Republicanism, but this change or fluctuation was greater than the average change for the cohorts. *Thus this analysis demonstrates the impact of substantial generational political socialization, as the generational cohorts maintained stable partisan alignments in the face of national political fluctuations.*

The one notable exception to the pattern of cohort stability concerned the change recorded subsequent to the Republican Presidential victory of 1968. For this comparison the average cohort Republican increase was greater than that of the 21–29 life-stage. Although this might at first seem evidence of substantial generational cohort fluctuation when compared to the newer members of the electorate, Glenn and Hefner hastened to point out that this represents the possible emergence of a new generational trend signalled by the youngest voters in the most recent survey, that of a general movement away from identification with either party. "Almost 90 per cent of the Democratic loss in the 21–29 life-stage was to independence" (43). Indeed, for the youngest cohort group in the analysis (born 1936–45), the 1965–69 increase in "Independent" as a party affiliation was 6.4 percent, while the increase in "Republican" identification after the Republican victory of 1968 was only 3.3 percent (Table 1, 36). This trend was also signalled in the 1965 study of high school seniors and their parents cited earlier. That study revealed that there were 12 percent more Independent party identifiers among the students than among their parents (Jennings and Niemi, 1968, Table 1, 173). The generational cohort represented by these high school seniors is included, interestingly enough, in the youngest life-stage group of the Glenn and Hefner study. Further evidence of this trend toward independence from strong party identification is given in a recent study of electoral "ticket splitting." DeVries and Tarrance (1972, 60) report on the basis of a national Gallup survey that the newer generation of voters is more disposed toward this form of independence than older voters.

Therefore, the one exception to greater cohort stability does itself appear to be the beginning of a different kind of generational trend, one in which the influence of the external political environment in the process of socialization is one of diminishing importance of strong party identification. The general conclusion is one which supports the thesis of generational political socialization. Although Glenn and Hefner do not rule out the possibility of future large-scale cohort shifts in response to major political events, the data they have presented "which are traced through all seven dates attest to the greater stability of the cohorts, which generally changed less than the life stage regardless of the direction of the change" (42).

The evidence in the area of party identification has demonstrated the explanatory power of a generational conception of political socialization. It is also possible to demonstrate, which will be done so here only briefly, that the social processes that may be responsible for generational trends in political orientations are themselves potentially generational in nature. Perhaps one of the most basic of generational trends in recent American (if not worldwide) history is the basic demographic fact of life expectancy. Each successive generation has a greater average life expectancy. For example, data from United States Public Health Service Reports indicate that the age-specific number of deaths per 1000 population for the age 65–74 was 56.4 in 1900, 48.0 in 1940, and 37.8 in 1964 (Bogue, 1969, 593). That it is the age-specific mortality rate that has been declining is evidence of a trend that is generational in nature.

From basic demographic trends indicating generational or cohort patterns, it is not difficult to move into the area of politics. Another recent demographic trend with lasting political importance is the dramatic change in fertility patterns in the United States (Bogue 1969, 152–153), which has affected the demand structure for social benefits. The period of very low fertility in the 1930s yielded a relatively small cohort of high school children in the 1940s, of college students in the 1950s, and of professors and enginers in the 1960s. By dramatic contrast, the 1940s represented such a large increase in American fertility as to become known as a "Baby Boom." Facilities (e.g., schools), which had not expanded due to the small size of the preceding cohort, were overcrowded and understaffed as the Baby Boom generation passed through the successive ages of the life cycle. The political system thus was faced with increasing demand by sheer force of generational demographic change, and the political implications of this kind of "generational crowding" may provide intriguing hypotheses about mass politics in the 1960s and the 1970s. One should not think that the interaction of politics and demographic generations is limited only to crowded educational facilities. One need only note that the Baby Boom of the 1940s is destined to become the Gerontology Boom of the 2010s, with subsequent demands of a different nature but nonetheless legitimate upon the resources of the polity and society.

Finally, we may return to the issue of political party identification in the United States. The evidence reviewed in this section has demonstrated the explanatory value of a generational political socialization conception of party identification. In a recent study, however, Abramson (1972) has taken the investigation a step further by concentrating on one important mechanism in the selection of party identification, that of social class. His starting point was that much of party identification in recent years was based on a correlation or association with social class—the working-class Democratic identification and the middle-class Republican identification.

On the basis of a generational cohort analysis of the six SRC presidential studies in 1948–1968, Abramson concluded that there has been a marked attenuation in the association between class and party. In more recent generational cohorts, there are greater proportions of middle-class Democrats and working-class Republicans. As Lubell was quoted earlier as saying, it is a matter of timing, of when in history a generational group attains the state of so-called "middle-class blessedness."

Thus this discussion comes full circle. It has been seen that there does appear to be evidence of a generational basis to the political socialization in which party identifications and attachments are formed. Yet, the very underlying demographic, sociological, and political processes that may account for the formation of generations in even recent political history are themselves processes subject to generational change. As was said in the Introduction, whatever else is considered to be included in the concept of political socialization, investigators of the subject would do well to analyze and understand the generational context—which has been seen here to include demographic and sociological as well as political and historical components—in which the content and processes of political socialization develop.

CONCLUDING REMARKS

The previous section attempted to demonstrate the utility of a political generations conception of political socialization, based upon a sequence of empirical studies undertaken in a common area. American party identification is, of course, not the only relevant variable in political behavior, and other studies of the impact of generational socialization could have been cited, e.g., Klecka's (1971a) analyses of domestic policy attitudes and Cutler's (1970) analysis of foreign policy attitudes. Yet, this area is perhaps the most widely researched area of political behavior. More significantly, for the present discussion, the notion of party identification has been the focus of an interesting and enduring empirical debate on the very question of the generational basis of political learning and socialization. Claims and counterclaims have been clearly stated in professional journals, and a substantial number of analysts have occupied themselves, both theoretically and empirically, with the issues. The results are illustrative and supportive of a political generations conception of political socialization.

This sequence of empirical studies has also illustrated another point critical to the pursuit of generational analysis of political socialization, that of the growing availability of both longitudinal data bases and analytic techniques. The original analyses by Crittenden, Klecka, Glenn and Hefner, and Abramson were all based upon data bases which included time-series of comparable items from successive annual or periodic national samples. While these studies have focused on American political behavior, cross-national longitudinal data bases are also becoming established.

Abramson (1971, 1972), for example, has undertaken the kinds of generational analyses described in the preceding section in the context of several Western European countries. Inglehart has similarly amassed a cross-national data base for the study of generational trends (1967, 1971). Barnes (1970) has demonstrated the utility of generational analysis for the case of Italy, as have Cutler (1971) and Cutler and Heiskanen (1973) for the case of Finland and Butler and Stokes (1971) for England. More generally, Cutler and Cutler (1974) have described the generational analysis potentials of their "Macro-Survey" data base of Western Europe data encompassing tens of thousands of respondents over the years 1957–1969. A series of reviews edited by Rokkan (1966) has demonstrated the increasing potential for cross-national trend studies. In general, increasing numbers of social scientists are becoming aware of the products of the "data bank movement" begun in the late 1950s and early 1960s. Discussion by Deutsch (1966), Nasitir (1968), Bisco (1970), and Hyman (1972) all attest to the growing potential for trend analysis and generational analysis based upon the increasingly growing and available data archives of such institutions as the University of Michigan, the Roper Center for Public Opinion Research at Williams College, and the International Data Library at Berkeley.

Paralleling the growth in available data resources has been a growth in the attention being paid to the various analytic techniques that can be called upon in the empirical investigation of generational phenomena. Evan (1959) initially demonstrated the feasibility of deriving generational cohort inferences from successive cross-sectional surveys. In the years following, varieties of cohort analytic studies have appeared, many of which have been noted in this chapter. More recently, however, there have begun to appear more methodological treatments of generational analysis. Cutler (1968) and Glenn (1970) have discussed the problems and prospects of assembling time-series of comparable items from the thousands of items stored in archives of survey data. Glenn and Zody (1970) have discussed correction procedures in comparing recent surveys with earlier surveys that underrepresented the lower educational strata. Klecka (1970, 1971a) has developed the "Automatic Generation Detector," a series of computer routines that uses an analysis of variance criterion for the selection of "optimal" age intervals for cohort analysis and Mason et al. (1973) have presented alternative regression models of the basic cohort analysis problem in which the relative weight of the aging effect and the generational effect can be mathematically determined.

Two recent efforts, however, stand out as comprehensive and sophisticated treatments of the potentials and difficulties of generational analysis. As part of a larger effort, Riley (1973) has outlined a number of analytic problems and fallacies that must be faced by anyone using archival data in the study of age-related phenomena. Understanding of such problems as the "compositional fallacy" and the "fallacy of proportional representation" will go a long way in facilitating meaningful generational analyses. In the third volume of a massive study of "Aging and Society," Riley, Johnson, and Foner (1972) have included several discussions of the methodological and analytic problems of age and generational analysis. Their discussions of "Interpretation of Research on Age," "The Succession of Cohorts," and "Some Problems of Research on Age" have clarified and enhanced the potential for future research.

Finally, and by no means least, Hyman's recent book on secondary analysis of sample surveys (1972) has filled an important gap in the literature of social science. Hyman reviews the secondary analysis procedures available to confront a large variety of research questions in political science, sociology, and related fields. His exposition, with numerous examples, covers both cross-sectional analysis and trend analysis. Included in the latter is a significant discussion of age and generational analysis, in both American and cross-national contexts. Hyman's conclusions are quite optimistic with respect to the future of generational cohort analysis. There are problems, to be sure, but there are also increasing numbers of scholars who are attempting to come to grips with those problems. As Hyman observes, the task of cohort analysts "is made progressively easier by each cohort analyst who has preceded them. He has already located for them a pool of trend surveys, where the age codes are flexible and suited to the design, and which treat some domain of variables that can be further explored" (286–287).

Given the development of large-scale data bases and the growing attention to the techniques of generational analysis, a generationally based conception of political socialization can be applied to a rather large set of questions. Perhaps the most straightforward approach concerns a single dependent variable, as illustrated in the preceding section, in which generational patterns in party identification were explored. This direct approach could be applied to more specific kinds of public policy attitudes in both domestic and foreign policy areas. General indicators of satisfaction with the political system could also be analyzed in the context of generational patterns.

It is possible, of course, to go beyond single-variable analyses and look at multivariate complexes of social and political orientations within successive generational cohorts. One might ask if successive generations possess more inclusive or more fragmented political ideologies encompassing many or few discrete policy orientations. The relationship of class and party affiliation has undergone a generational change, as Abramson's analyses demonstrated. Expanding this approach we may ask, for example, whether the nature of various occupational roles in relationship to political orientations is affected by generational socialization or whether educational and residential patterns have different political implications for successive generational groups. A generational analysis of mass media habits, for example, would surely identify different "media generations"; however, the political orientations of several successive television generations are yet to be explored. Still another aspect of this multivariate approach would look at generational patterns in sex differences and the social–psychological nature of sex-role orientations as they might have an impact on levels and directions of political participation (e.g., Starr and Cutler, 1972).

An interest in the macro-analysis of the political system could well build upon the empirical parameters of generationally based political socialization. Estimates of future system states with respect to political behavior should not be based upon simple extrapolations of current patterns; rather, such extrapolations must consider the demographic processes of fertility, mortality, and differential cohort composition as affecting the flow of political generations through the system (Grauman, 1959; Shryock and Sigel, 1971, Ch. 23). Carlsson and Karlsson (1970), for example, have proposed a learning–decay model of generational analysis in which the propensity for attitude change within a cohort decreases as the cohort ages. The size of new cohorts as compared to aging cohorts, therefore, will provide some estimate of the "political elasticity" of the system in future years. A suggestive application of this kind of approach was made by Butler and Stokes (1971, 143), who used a generational cohort technique in estimating the size of Labour Party support in Great Britain through the year 2015 based upon the party distribution of the 1963–1966 electorate. Given the empirical verification of generational patterns of political socialization, one of the most exciting prospects within interdisciplinary social sciences may be the growth of a field called "political demography."

Of course, the notion of generational socialization can apply to subgroups within a society as well as to a society as a whole. It should not be expected that the social–psychological meaning and interpretation of the features of the external political environment will be identical for all social groups within the population. As Glenn (1967) discovered in a trend study of massification and differentiation of social and political orientations within the United States, many such orientations continue to be diversified on regional, religious, ethnic, and racial grounds. In fact, a generationally based investigation of differences in political orientation would help in monitoring and understanding the divergent attitudes of various social groups. It is important to know, for example, if the calendar-defined birth cohort of individuals raised in a given historical milieu does in fact contain several distinctive generational groups from the point of view of class and racial differences. The lack of generational synchronization within a large birth cohort may be an indicator of potentially severe strains within the political system.

As a final example of future research we may return to the question of the family's role in the socialization process. It has not been the aim of this paper to suggest that the family and related childhood socialization agencies have no impact upon the political socialization process. Rather, we have attempted to demonstrate that the child, the parents, and the family unit are all affected by the larger political environment. In what ways, it should be asked, does the family respond to the larger political and social environment in terms of the political socialization process? How does a politically based "generation gap" affect the parent-child negotiations that are part of the socialization process? Are there generational variations in the influence that the family and other childhood socialization agencies have upon adolescents; for example, are there generational differences in the residual or sustaining impact of childhood experiences upon adult political orientations?

In sum, it has been the position of this paper that it is both imperative and possible to investigate political behavior from a political generations conception of political socialization. The nature of the external environment affects not only the content of socialization but the very processes of socialization as well. The understanding of the generational genesis of political orientations not only is important for its own scientific purposes but, as illustrated in these concluding remarks, is contributory to a large variety of investigations. As Mannheim (1952, 287) has stated:

> The problem of generations is important enough to merit serious consideration. It is one of the indispensable guides to an understanding of the structure of social and intellectual movements. Its practical importance becomes clear as soon as one tries to obtain a more exact understanding of the accelerated pace of social change characteristic of our time. It would be regrettable if extra-scientific methods were to conceal elements of the problem capable of immediate investigation.

REFERENCES

Abramson, P. R. "Social Class and Political Change in Western Europe: A Cross-National Longitudinal Analysis," *Comparative Political Studies* 4 (1971), 131–55.

————. "Intergenerational Social Mobility and Partisan Choice," *American Political Science Review* 66 (1972a), 1291–94.

————. "Generational Change in Britain and Italy: A Cohort Analysis of Social Class and Partisan Choice," paper prepared for the Annual Meeting of the International Studies Association (Dallas, 1972b).

Andrain, C. F. *Children and Civic Awareness* (Columbus: Charles E. Merrill, 1971).

Back, K. W., and K. J. Gergen. "Apocalyptic and Serial Time Orientations and the Structure of Opinions," *Public Opinion Quarterly* 27 (1963a), 427–42.

————. "Individual Orientations, Public Opinion and the Study of International Relations," *Social Problems* 11 (1963b), 77–87.

Barnes, S. H. *The Legacy of Fascism: Generational Differences in Italian Political Attitudes and Behavior,* Institute of Social Research, University of Michigan, 1970.

Benedek, T. "Parenthood as a Developmental Phase," *Journal of the American Psychological Association* 7 (1959), 389–417.

Bengtson, V. L. "Inter-age Perceptions and the Generation Gap," *The Gerontologist* 11 (Part 2) (1971), 85–89.

————, and K. D. Black. "Intergenerational Relations and Continuities in Socialization," in K. Schaie and P. Baltes (eds.), *Personality and Socialization* (New York: Academic Press, 1973), 207–34.

————, and J. A. Kuypers. "Generational Difference and the Developmental Stake," *Aging and Human Development* 2 (1971), 249–60.

Bisco, R. L. *Data Bases, Computers, and the Social Sciences* (New York: Wiley, 1970).

Bobrow, D. B., and N. E. Cutler. "Time-Oriented Explanations of National Security Beliefs: Cohort, Life-Stage and Situation," *Peace Research Society (International) Papers* 8 (1967), 31–57.

Bogue, D. J. *Principles of Demography* (New York: Wiley, 1969).

Brim, O. G. "Socialization through the Life Cycle," in O. G. Brim and S. W. Wheeler, *Socialization After Childhood: Two Essays* (New York: Wiley, 1966).

Butler, D. E., and D. E. Stokes. *Political Change in Britain* (New York: St. Martin's, 1971).

Campbell, A., P. E. Converse, W. E. Miller, and D. E. Stokes. *The American Voter* (New York: Wiley, 1960).

Carlsson, G., and K. Karlsson. "Age, Cohorts and the Generation of Generations," *American Sociological Review* 35 (1970), 710–18.

Centers, R. "Children of the New Deal: Social Stratification and Adolescent Attitudes," *International Journal of Opinion and Attitude Research* 4 (1950), 315–35.

Connell, R. W. "Political Socialization in the American Family: The Evidence Re-examined," *Public Opinion Quarterly* 36 (1972), 321–33.

Crittenden, J. "Aging and Party Affiliation," *Public Opinion Quarterly* 26 (1962), 648–57.

————. "Reply to Cutler," *Public Opinion Quarterly* 33 (1969), 589–91.

Cumming, E., and W. Henry. *Growing Old* (New York: Basic Books, 1961).

Cutler, N. E. *The Alternative Effects of Generations and Aging upon Political Behavior* (Oak Ridge: Oak Ridge National Laboratory, 1968).

————. "Generation, Maturation, and Party Affiliation: A Cohort Analysis," *Public Opinion Quarterly* 33 (1969), 583–88.

————. "Generational Succession as a Source of Foreign Policy Attitudes: A Cohort Analysis of American Opinion, 1946–1966," *Journal of Peace Research* 6 (1970), 33–47.

————. "Generational Analysis in Political Science," paper prepared for the Annual Meeting of the American Political Science Association (Chicago: 1971a).

————. "Generational Cohort Analysis: Applications to Finnish Politics," paper prepared for the Annual Meeting of the Society for the Advancement of Scandinavian Study (Lexington, 1971b).

————. "Aging and Generations in Politics: The Conflict of Explanations and Inference," in A. R. Wilcox (ed.), *Public Opinion and Political Attitudes: A Reader* (New York: Wiley, 1974).

————, and E. S. Cutler. "The Western European USIA Macro-Survey: A Tool for Cross-time/Cross-national Comparative Analysis," in N. E. Cutler (ed.), *Emerging Data Sources for Comparative and International Studies* (Beverly Hills: Sage, forthcoming).

————, and I. Heiskanen. "Foreign Policy Orientations in Finland, 1964 and 1971: An Example of Generational Political Socialization," University of Helsinki, Institute of Political Science, *Research Reports*, 30 (1973).

Dawson, R. E. "Political Socialization," in J. A. Robinson (ed.), *Political Science Annual, Volume I* (Indianapolis: Bobbs-Merrill, 1966), 1–84.

————, and K. Prewitt. *Political Socialization* (Boston: Little, Brown 1969).

Dennis, J. "A Survey and Bibliography of Contemporary Research on Political Learning and Socialization" (University of Wisconsin, Research and Development Center for Cognitive Learning, Occasional Paper Number 8, 1967).

————. "Major Problems of Political Socialization Research," *Midwest Journal of Political Science* 12 (1968), 85–114.

Deutsch, K. W. "Information Needs of Political Science," in International Federation for Documentation, *Proceedings of the 1965 Congress, Volume III* (Washington, D.C.: Spartan Books, 1966), 199–203.

DeVries, W., and V. L. Tarrance. *The Ticket-Splitter: A New Force in American Politics* (Grand Rapids: William B. Erdmans, 1972).

Dyer, E. D. "Parenthood as Crisis: A Re-study," *Journal of Marriage and the Family* 25 (1963), 196–201.

Erikson, E. H. *Childhood and Society* (New York: Norton, 1950).

————. *Identity: Youth and Crisis* (New York: Norton, 1968).

Evan, W. M. "Cohort Analysis of Survey Data: A Procedure for Studying Long-Term Opinion Change," *Public Opinion Quarterly* 23 (1959), 63–72.

Gergen, K. J., and K. W. Back. "Aging, Time Perspective, and Preferred Solutions to International Conflicts," *Journal of Conflict Resolution* 9 (1965), 177–86.

————. "Communication on the Interview and the Disengaged Respondent," *Public Opinion Quarterly* 30 (1966), 385–98.

Glenn, N. D. "Massification versus Differentiation: Some Trend Data from National Surveys," *Social Forces* 46 (1967), 172–80.

————. "Aging, Disengagement, and Opinionation," *Public Opinion Quarterly* 33 (1969), 17–33.

————. "Problems of Comparability in Trend Studies with Opinion Poll Data," *Public Opinion Quarterly* 34 (1970), 82–91.

————, and M. Grimes. "Aging, Voting and Political Interest," *American Sociological Review* 33 (1968), 563–75.

————, and T. Hefner. "Further Evidence on Aging and Party Identication," *Public Opinion Quarterly* 36 (1972), 31–47.

————, and R. E. Zody. "Cohort Analysis with National Survey Data," *The Gerontologist* 10 (1970), 233–40.

Grauman, J. "Population Estimates and Projections," in P. M. Hauser and O. D. Duncan (eds.), *The Study of Population: An Inventory and Appraisal* (Chicago: University of Chicago Press, 1959), 544–75.

Greenstein, F. I. "Political Socialization," *International Encyclopedia of the Social Sciences* Volume XIV (New York: The Free Press, 1968), 551–55.

Hobbs, D. F. "Parenthood as Crisis: A Third Study," *Journal of Marriage and the Family* 27 (1965), 367–72.

————. "Transition to Parenthood: A Replication and Extension," *Journal of Marriage and the Family* 30 (1968), 413–7.

Hyman, H. H. *Political Socialization: A Study in the Psychology of Political Behavior* (New York: The Free Press, 1959).

————. *Secondary Analysis of Sample Surveys: Principles, Procedures, and Potentialities* (New York: Wiley, 1972).

Inglehart, R. "An End to European Integration?" *American Political Science Review* 61 (1967), 91–105.

————. "The Silent Revolution in Europe: Intergenerational Change in Post-Industrial Societies," *American Political Science Review* 65 (1971), 991–1017.

Inhelder, B. and J. Piaget. *The Growth of Logical Thinking from Childhood to Adolescence* (New York: Basic Books, 1958).

Jaccoby, A. P. "Transition to Parenthood: A Reassessment," *Journal of Marriage and the Family* 31 (1969), 720–7.

Jennings, M. K., and R. G. Niemi. "The Transmission of Political Values from Parent to Child," *American Political Science Review* 62 (1968), 169–84.

Kastenbaum, R. "The Dimensions of Future Time Perspective: An Experimental Analysis," *Journal of General Psychology* 65 (1961), 203–18.

———. "Cognitive and Personal Futurity in Later Life," *Journal of Individual Psychology* 19 (1963), 216–22.

———. "The Structure and Function of Time Perspectives," *Journal of Psychological Research* 8 (1964), 97–107.

Katz, D. "The Functional Approach to the Study of Attitudes," *Public Opinion Quarterly* 24 (1960), 163–204.

Klecka, W. R. "Political Generations and Political Behavior," unpublished Ph.D. Dissertation, University of Illinois at Champaign-Urbana, 1970.

———. "Applying Political Generations to the Study of Political Behavior: A Cohort Analysis," *Public Opinion Quarterly* 35 (1971a), 358–73.

———. "Distinguishing Life-Cycle and Generation Effects in a Cohort Analysis," paper prepared for the Annual Meeting of the American Political Science Association (Chicago, 1971b).

Kuhlen, R. G. "Changing Personal Adjustment During Adult Years," in J. Anderson (ed.), *Psychological Aspects of Aging* (New York: American Psychological Association, 1956), 21–35.

Lambert, T. A. "Generational Factors in Political-Cultural Consciousness," paper prepared for the Annual Meeting of the American Political Science Association (Chicago, 1971).

Lane, R. E. "Fathers and Sons: Foundations of Political Beliefs," *American Sociological Review* 24 (1959), 502–11.

LeMasters, E. E. "Parenthood as Crisis," *Marriage and Family Living* 19 (1957), 352–5.

Lipset, S. M. *Political Man* (New York: Basic Books, 1960).

Lubell, S. *The Future of American Politics*, second ed. (New York: Anchor Books, 1956).

Maccoby, E. E. "The Development of Moral Values and Behavior in Children," in J. A. Clausen (ed.), *Socialization and Society* (Boston: Little, Brown, 1968), 227–69.

———, R. Mathews, and A. Morton. "Youth and Social Change," *Public Opinion Quarterly* 18 (1954), 23–9.

Mannheim, K. "The Problem of Generations," in *Essays on the Sociology of Knowledge* [1928] (translated and edited by P. Kecskemeti) (London: Routledge and Kegan Paul, 1952), 276–332.

Martinson, F. M. *Marriage and the American Ideal* (New York: Dodd, Mead, 1963).

Mason, K., H. Winsborough, W. Mason, and W. Poole. "Some Methodological Issues in Cohort Analysis of Archival Data," *American Sociological Review* 38 (1973), 242–58.

Mazlish, B. *In Search of Nixon: A Psychohistorical Inquiry* (New York: Basic Books, 1972).

McClosky, H. "Survey Research in Political Science," in C. Y. Glock (ed.), *Survey Research in the Social Sciences* (New York: Russell Sage, 1967), 63–143.

―――, and H. E. Dahlgren. "Primary Group Influence on Party Loyalty," *American Political Science Review* 53 (1959), 757–76.

Middleton, R., and S. Putney. "Political Expresison of Adolescent Rebellion," *American Journal of Sociology* 68 (1963), 527–35.

Nasitir, D. "The International Data Library and Reference Service," *Public Opinion Quarterly* 32 (1968), 688–90.

Parsons, T. "Family Structure and the Socialization of the Child," in T. Parsons and R. F. Bales, *Family, Socialization and Interaction Process* (Glencoe: Free Press, 1955), 35–131.

Reichenbach, M., and R. A. Mathers. "The Place of Time and Aging in the Natural Sciences and Scientific Philosophy," in J. E. Birren (ed.), *Handbook of Aging and the Individual* (Chicago: University of Chicago Press, 1959), 797–851.

Riley, M. W. "Social Gerontology and the Age Stratification of Society," *The Gerontologist* 11 (Part 1) (1971), 79–87.

―――. "Aging and Cohort Succession: Interpretations and Misinterpretations," *Public Opinion Quarterly* 37, (1973), 35–49.

―――, M. Johnson and A. Foner. *Aging and Society, Volume Three: A Sociology of Age Stratification* (New York: Russell Sage, 1972).

Rintala, M. "Political Generations," *International Encyclopedia of the Social Sciences*, Volume VI (New York: The Free Press, 1968), 92–6.

Robinson, W. S. "Ecological Correlations and the Behavior of Individuals," *American Sociological Review* 15 (1950), 351–7.

Rokeach, M., and R. Bonier. "Time Perspective, Dogmatism, and Anxiety," in M. Rokeach, *The Open and Closed Mind* (New York: Basic Books, 1960), 366–75.

Rokkan, S. *Data Archives for the Social Sciences* (Paris: Mouton, 1966).

Rossi, A. S. "Transition to Parenthood," *Journal of Marriage and the Family* 30 (1968), 26–39.

Ryder, N. B. "The Cohort as a Concept in the Study of Social Change," *American Sociological Review* 30 (1965), 843–61.

Sheatsley, P. B. "Expectations of War and Depression," *Public Opinion Quarterly* 13 (1949), 685–6.

Shibutani, T. *Society and Personality* (Englewood Cliffs: Prentice-Hall, 1961).

Shryock, H., and J. S. Siegel. *The Materials and Methods of Demography* (Washington: United States Government Printing Office, 1971).

Smith, M. B., J. S. Bruner, and R. W. White. *Opinions and Personality* (New York: Wiley, 1956).

Starr, J., and N. E. Cutler. "Sex Role and Attitudes Toward Institutional Violence Among College Youth: The Impact of Sex-Role Identification, Parental Socialization, and Socio-Cultural Milieu," paper presented for the Annual Meeting of the American Sociological Association (New Orleans, 1972).

Stouffer, S. *Communism, Conformism, and Civil Liberties* (New York: Doubleday, 1955).

Chapter Eleven _____

Popular Music as an Agency of Political Socialization: A Study in Popular Culture and Politics

_____ *David C. Schwartz and Charles J. Mannella*

INTRODUCTION

The elements of popular culture—popular music, television, literature, drama, humor, rumor, cinema—and the resultant heroes, myths, and moods that popular culture can create are widely recognized as potentially important agencies of socialization in most of the social sciences. In cultural anthropology and social history, for example, emphasis is placed on the potential socialization impacts of popular culture. In these disciplines, popular culture is treated as an expression of a people's or group's salient concerns, attitudes, and values—an expression which may be representative of the prevailing culture or of an alternative to that culture but which, in either case, is very likely to be influential in socialization processes (Abrahams and Bauman, 1971; Lystad, 1960; Silverman, 1971; DePillis, 1967; Finnegan, 1970; Halpern, 1961; Breckenridge and Vincent, 1965). In the fields of child development, psychology, educational research, and the sociology of mass communications, greater emphasis is placed on the direct socialization processes whereby popular culture influences the attitudes and behaviors learned by people in a given society or social stratum. Recent studies in these disciplines suggest the importance of such popular culture elements as television, movies, and children's literature in influencing American children's perceptions of self, appropriate sex roles, aggressive behavior, and other important behaviors (Stearns, 1970; Witty and Kinsella, 1958; Hirsch, 1972; Tuchman, 1972; Gekas, 1972; Gans, 1972; Weitzman *et al.*, 1972; McClelland, 1961).

The study of political socialization, however, seems to have ignored popular culture quite completely. The major books and anthologies reporting research in political socialization contain virtually no mention of popular music, movies, novels, advertising, drama, political humor, or rumor; they contain only a very few, brief, and generally nonsubstantive references to the possible socializing influences of television or other mass communications media (Dawson and Prewitt, 1969; Dennis, 1973; Green-stein, 1965; Hess and Torney, 1967; Hyman, 1959; Jaros, 1973). If people learn anything about politics, or relevant to politics, from the songs they listen to and sing, the books and magazines they read, the movies and television they watch, the jokes they laugh at, the rumors they hear and spread—if the stimuli of everyday life have any significant effect on people's politics—we do not seem to know very much about it or to care very much about it in the study of political socialization.

In this almost total deemphasis on popular culture, the study of political socialization parallels political science generally. A recent review of the articles published in seven major political science journals between 1960 and 1970 revealed no articles that focused centrally on the political impacts of television, radio, drama, rumor, humor, or underground media and only a relative handful of articles that focused on the political impact of newspapers or on literature (Schwartz, 1974). We may suspect that national anthems, protest songs, and patriotic music express profoundly felt political values and can function to integrate or divide a people; we may hypothesize that rumors are quite important elements in the onset of riots; we may be aware that much of today's theatre is intensely political and that both elite and folk drama have been major techniques of political conflict in many nations; we may reason, or guess, that all that television watching is having some political consequences. We may suspect, hypo-thesize, reason, and guess about all these matters—but we cannot know very much about them because we do not study them.

This relative neglect of popular culture seems particularly unfortunate for the study of political socialization in our time and place, when several popular culture media—especially music and television—have probably become relatively important agencies of political socialization (at least for significant numbers of young people). We suggest that popular American music (and television) have become significant agencies of American political socialization because: (1) they are of very high and increasing salience in American youth and adolescent cultures; (2) the political content of these popular culture media has expanded significantly of late; and (3) the political concerns, attitudes, and values expressed in popular music (and probably on television) seem to be somewhat incongruent with those expressed in most family and school socialization. This incon-gruence implies that youngsters learning political attitudes and values during periods of high politicization and salience of the popular culture may experience significantly greater discontinuities, inconsistencies, and cross-pressures in their set of political learning experiences than youngsters socialized when the popular culture is less salient, less politicized, and less incongruent.

There is extensive documentation available elsewhere to show that popular music and television have become increasingly salient and politicized. There is even some evidence suggesting divergence between the political values expressed in today's popular music and school socialization patterns. Therefore we need merely note the following few major pieces of evidence here.

The Salience of Popular Music and Television

Involvement with popular music and television-watching are both at an all time high among American teenagers, each having increased significantly in recent years. American teenagers spent more than $1.75 *billion* on records and tapes in 1971, a figure which excludes all costs for the equipment on which to play the records and tapes, all costs for live concerts, record magazines and all the posters, books, "T" shirts and other novelty items depicting popular musicians as the heroes they have become (Dougherty, 1969; Recording Industry of America release, 1972). Reliable national data on the number of hours spent listening to popular music by teenagers are hard to come by, but in the study reported below:

1. The modal respondent spent 19–29 hours per week listening to popular music.

2. About half of this time was spent in uninterrupted concentration on the music, not doing anything else like studying or working while listening.

3. About one fifth of our sample reported themselves as listening to more than 50 hours of music per week.

Even if these figures are somewhat higher than is true for the nation as a whole, multiplying anything like these figures by the sheer numbers of youngsters in the music-receiving audience yields quite a staggering number.

The figures on the extent of television-watching among American young people are also staggering. It is estimated that by the time an American child born in the television era reaches 18 years of age, he or she has spent some 20,000 hours watching television. This is more time than the combined amount of time which that child has spent in school and in talking with parents (Frank, 1973). Television is a credible source of information, too. Television news, for example, is now the most widely used news medium in the nation and, among those who watch it, is also the source of news information most believed (Frank, 1973a).

The Politicization of Popular Music and Television

The politicization of popular music, defined as the significantly increasing number of songs on the national popularity charts that contain political themes (as identified by the investigator or a team of coders), has been well documented over the decade of the 1960s (Rodnitzky, 1969; Denisoff and Peterson, 1972). Indeed, researchers have not only shown the increased politicization of popular music as a whole but have demonstrated that several specific genres of popular music—folk, rock, soul, and country-and-western—have also become increasingly politicized (Lund, 1972; Rodnitzky, 1969). More detailed content-analytic treatment of the political themes in popular music, which would allow us to measure politicization of popular music in a more refined manner, is only now getting under way.

The increased politicization of American television programming over, say, the past five years is also documentable. The number of hours devoted by the networks to public affairs programming and the political content of television drama seem to have expanded significantly (Frank, 1973b).

Incongruities Between Popular Culture and Other Socialization Agencies

There can be little doubt that the degree of incongruity between the values expressed in today's popular music and those of parents, teachers, and government leaders is what lies behind much of the recent interest in research on the effectiveness of popular music as a socialization agency. Content analysts have shown that the songs of the late 1960s contained significantly more references to alienation themes (themes chronicling various dysfunctions in American society and politics, themes calling for revolution) and, at the same time, extolled the merits of experimentation with drugs and freer sexual behavior. Social scientists and politicians have seen in these themes evocations of "a new 'social ethic,' a 'new order' " (Denisoff and Peterson, 1972). In *The Sounds of Social Change* (1972), Denisoff and Peterson indicate some of the dimensions on which parents, politicians, and commentators perceive incongruities between today's pop music and traditional values. Research on hypothesized incongruities between the values most frequently expressed in television programming and that of other socialization agencies is also in progress (Frank, 1974).

In sum, we have ample evidence to suggest that popular music is a very salient and increasingly important American popular culture medium, one that is especially appealing to young Americans during a highly politicizable period in their lives, their teen years. There is evidence too, that popular music is increasingly political in content and that that political content is perceived to be quite incongruent with the political values held by most parents and teachers (quite incongruent indeed, with all those political socialization agencies—like textbooks—that tend to be influenced by parents and teachers). We also know that popular culture media, like popular music, are considered to be important agencies of socialization in the other social sciences.

All of this gives us strong reason to hypothesize that popular music in America today does function as a significant agency of political socialization for an appreciable number of young people. The study reported below is a research report on a preliminary effort to test this typothesis.

IS POPULAR MUSIC AN AGENCY OF POLITICAL SOCIALIZATION? TWO BASIC APPROACHES TO THE QUESTION

Although the degree of popular music's influence on young people's political attitudes has been hotly debated in speculative and interpretive commentary, it has thus far been the subject of relatively little empirical research. The few published studies on this topic, however, are united by a common approach and highly compatible findings. Here we present the basic research design and findings of the major available studies, in order to critique that design and to challenge those findings. Thereafter, we present an alternative approach.

The Previous Approach

In the major published studies, Denisoff (1970), Denisoff and Levine (1972), and Robinson and Hirsh (1972) use a rather indirect approach in attempting to assess the impact of music on people's political views. In each of these studies, student respondents were asked to interpret the meaning of one to four popular songs which the investigators considered to have sociopolitical message content. The percentage of respondents giving "correct," "partially correct," and "incorrect" interpretations (as judged by the investigators and/or their coders) was computed and cross-tabulated against the percentage of respondents who had previously heard the songs and/or who expressed "liking" for the songs. The respondents' liking for the song was then cross-tabulated against a measure of the degree to which respondents oriented to the lyrics (rather than just the music or sound) of the song.

These studies revealed that only 10 to 30 percent of the respondents gave sufficiently "correct" interpretations of the sociopolitical themes as to be coded as having "understood the theme" but 65–85 percent either "understood" or "partially understood" the theme. There was a significant tendency for respondents who had heard the song or who were lyrics-oriented to correctly "understand" the theme. Respondents who were lyrics-oriented tended significantly more often to like the songs than did sound-oriented respondents, but no significant relationships were reported between liking a song and "understanding" its sociopolitical themes. Finally, most of the respondents were more attracted to a song for its sound than for its lyric. As might be expected, these findings did not encourage the investigators to take a particularly strong position one way or the other as to the relative importance of popular music as an agency of political socialization.

A Brief Critique of the Previous Approach

We think that the approach taken in these previous studies yields some very interesting information but that it is too indirect and too restricted to tell us whether or not popular music is now a relatively important agency of political socialization and, if so, for whom. More specifically, we think that the assumptions made and the methodology used in the previous studies were questionable and, further, that some of the most important variables relevant to music's influence on people's political attitudes were left out of the studies. *Basically these studies do not tell us whether or not teenagers regularly learn political attitudes, values, or behaviors from the popular music they listen to (or from a peer group or social setting that centrally includes listening to popular music); they tell us only that teenagers imperfectly understood highly specific messages in a very few unsystematically selected songs.* Also these investigators apparently:

1. Did not control for the frequency with which the respondents had been exposed to the songs.

2. Did not ask the respondents how important music (or these songs) were to them.

3. Made little or no effort to gauge the respondent's affect for popular music performers.

4. Included no measures on the role of music in the respondent's peer group life (or of the peer group's or the respondent's relationship to popular music).

5. *Made no effort to measure any of the respondent's political concerns, attitudes, values, or characteristic behavior.*

We think that these are not unimportant weaknesses in the previously published studies, weaknesses which should be briefly examined here.

The major, if implicit, assumption underlying these studies seems to be that popular music cannot be a relatively important agency of political socialization for a given set of people unless those people understand rather specific, cognitive, sociopolitical meanings in specific, isolated songs. We think this assumption is quite questionable on several grounds. First, people can learn from music important general political attitudes and persistent moods toward politics, without necessarily learning more specific themes or sub-attitudes in a given song. One can recognize and even adopt the attitudes of political alienation, cynicism, and skepticism in today's music without being able to note that a particular song attacks a particular political institution, process, outcome, or personality.

Second, the assumption that people cannot be politically influenced by music if they do not understand the theme of one or a small number of "political" songs seems dubious. People are likely to be influenced by the music they like best and listen to most often. They are most likely to be influenced by a whole repertoire of music with which they are familiar, not by one or two isolated songs.

The songs employed in these studies are not an adequate sample of songs with sociopolitical themes, let alone songs with themes broad enough to be easily generalized to politics. The fact that a group of teenagers cannot verbally report the theme of a given song tells us nothing about their ability to recognize sociopolitical themes in other music unless the song was selected on some basis which allows such generalization. In the previous studies there was virtually no discussion of this matter at all , but obviously if the songs used in these studies significantly differ from most of today's political music on important dimensions (such as lyric complexity or music structure) the findings in the previous studies are of restricted utility.

The songs presented to the respondents were of uncertain salience and familiarity to the respondents. The investigators report only whether or not respondents had ever heard a given song prior to the study (i.e., they do *not* report controlling for the frequency with which the respondent had listened to the song). As the frequency of exposure to a stimulus is a major variable in almost every learning theory, this also seems a weakness in the early studies.

More substantively, as the earlier studies seem to have deemphasized the social and psychological contexts in which teenagers listen and react to popular music, these studies cannot tell us how music functions to socialize even those respondents who did understand the theme. We think that the respondent's relationship to popular music is critical in determining whether or not anything will be learned from the music, what will be learned, how it will be learned, and how durable (stable) the learned attitude or behavior is. More specifically, we think, that teenagers who typically listen to music in a group are likely to learn different amounts and different things than those who listen alone. Furthermore, people who feel that music is a basic characteristic defining their peer group will probably react to music differently than those for whom music is less central to peer group processes. Respondents who feel high positive affect (even hero worship) for popular music performers will almost certainly learn more and different things from music than will respondents who are emotionally neutral or negative toward performers. People who are highly involved in popular music will react differently to the political content of the music than people who are less involved. The type of popular music should also be important. People whose musical preference runs to, say, folk-rock will learn different things from popular music than those whose preference is for jazz, blues, or country-and-western music. Listeners who perceive their favorite music (and musicians) as political will differ significantly in what political things they learn from music from people who see the music they like as nonpolitical.

Most of these variables were left out of the previous studies. In so doing, the respondent's frame of reference is deemphasized. The early studies asked, essentially: "Did you learn what we think (or what the media say) this particular song is about?" We are more interested in asking "What do you think the music you listen to is about?" and "Do you think that it is political?"

Most importantly of all, we believe that the influence of popular music on listener's sociopolitical attitudes and behaviors cannot be assessed if the respondent's sociopolitical attitudes and behaviors are not studied. Are teenagers who think their favorite music is political more interested in politics and/or more politically alienated? Are kids who are most involved in today's popular music also most attentive to politics? The previous studies deemphasized such questions and tended to exclude such variables as political interest, political alienation, and attentiveness to politics. These variables, however, are central to the approach we have used in assessing the importance of popular music as an agency of political socialization.

A More Direct and More Comprehensive Approach

If popular music functions as an agency of policital socialization we would minimally expect the amount and type of music that people listen to, its importance and function in their lives and the social setting in which they listen, to be significantly associated with:

1. their perception of the music as containing political statements;
2. their level of agreement with these statements; and,
3. the pattern of their political interests, attitudes, and involvement.

More broadly, one might wish to explore interrelationships among the following five types of variables.

Independent variables:

1. Musical involvement variables (e.g., amount of musical involvement, type of music preferred, perceived importance of popular music).

2. Variables describing the social setting in which music is listened to (e.g., the degree to which respondents typically listen alone or in a group, the degree to which respondents perceive common musical preferences to be a basic factor defining salient peer groups).

Intervening variables:

3. Variables linking music to politics (e.g., the extent to which respondents perceive political statements in their favorite music; the extent to which they perceive popular musicians as social critics or seeking political change).

Dependent variables:

4. Political variables (e.g., respondent's level of political interest, alienation, attentiveness to politics, agreement with perceived political statements in music).

5. Complementary, reinforcing and competing socialization influences (e.g., respondent's perception of the degree to which parents, teachers, and peers agree with the perceived political statements in music). In some senses, social class, age and sex can be treated as summary variables which describe alternative socialization experiences.

All the listed variables were included in our study (as were several others to be discussed in the next section of this chapter). Accordingly, we were able to explore the following seven basic questions about popular music as an agency of political socialization.

1. Do a sizeable proportion of teenagers perceive that their favorite music contains political statements or ideas? This is an important question because there is a great deal of theory and evidence in psychology to suggest that people's reactions to a stimulus are very much influenced by the labels they place on it, the context in which they see it, the things they think the stimulus relevant to (Schachter and Singer, 1962). We are not saying that people who are involved in popular music but who do not perceive the music as political cannot or do not learn anything political from the music. We expect, however, that people who do see political content in music will have their politics very much more influenced by music than people who do not.

2. Does a respondent's level of musical involvement and/or the social setting in which he listens to music influence the likelihood that he views music as political? What other factors (age, sex) influence this perception? In short, what kinds of teenagers see their music as political?

3. Do respondents who perceive their favorite music as political differ significantly in their political attitudes and behaviors from respondents who do not?

4. If so, is there any evidence that it is the music or their relationship to the music that causes those who perceive political content in music to have different political attitudes from those who do not? This question is important because it speaks to the causal patterns linking teenagers' musical experiences to their political attitudes. Thus far, the questions we have asked derive from the hypothesis that teenagers who are most exposed to popular music are most likely to perceive the political statements in today's music and that this combination of high exposure plus recognition of the political content of music leads to political learning. But it is entirely possible, of course, for the reverse causal pattern to operate, such that teenagers who are most interested in politics or who have strong political views come to perceive the political statements in music as a result of their prior political socialization. To the extent that this pattern obtains, popular music would usualy act more as a reinforcer of previously learned political interests and views than as an agency teaching new political attitudes.

5. What processes of a personal, peer group, or familial nature contribute to the link between perceiving music as political and adopting distinctive political attitudes and behaviors?

6. Does popular music function as an agency of political socialization primarily by teaching (influencing) values or primarily by stimulating individuals to political interest and activity, activity in conformity with attitudes and values learned in other contexts?

7. Does popular music function as an agency of political socialization in the same way that other agencies do and/or in the same way that socialization theorists have posited mass media in general function?

PROCEDURES

Respondent Population

We explored these questions in a respondent population of 610 suburban New Jersey high school students who were surveyed in February, 1972. These students were sophomores, juniors, and seniors from a suburban high school in southern New Jersey that was purposively selected as the research site because of the access and cooperation provided by the school and because of the interesting diversity of the student body. The following demographic characteristics of our respondent population indicate that diversity.

Year in School: Sophomore 37%; Junior 26%; Senior 37%

Sex: Male 49%; Female 51%

Social Class: Upper Middle Class 23%; Middle Class 16%; Working
                           Class 32%

                           Not Ascertained 29%

The respondent population was primarily white (84%).

These students participated in our study on an entirely voluntary basis
—the 610 constitute a response rate of 81 percent—by completing, in
class, a self-administered questionnaire on the variables of interest. The
questionnaire was a three-page, 56-item instrument composed largely of
closed-ended items in a Likert-type format (agree strongly, agree, don't
know, disagree, disagree strongly). Open-ended items were used to inquire about the students' favorite songs and artists and the political statements, if any, the respondent perceived to be associated with those songs
and artists.

Measures

The variables of interest were, of course, operationally defined in terms of
the items on the questionnaire. Most of the variables were defined as
multi-item indexes constructed by aggregating the scores on each indicator
(item) in the index. A few of the variables—especially the demographics
—were defined as single-item indicators.

Here we provide a list of the variables of interest. The items comprising
each index, and the inter-item correlations for each index by which we
assured ourselves of some appropriate degree of index homogeneity, are
reported in a brief Methods Appendix at the end of this chapter.

Musical Involvement Variables

1. Level of musical involvement (e.g., time spent listening to
   music).

2. Types of music preferred (e.g., folk, ballads, opera, rock).

3. Affect toward popular musicians (e.g., approval vs. disapproval).

4. Perceived importance of music to respondent.

5. Degree of attention to lyrics.

Variables Describing the Social Setting of Listening to Music

6. Typically listens to music in groups vs. listens alone.

7. Degree to which musical preference defines respondent's peer group.

Variables Linking Music to Politics

8. Perception of music as political (e.g., perception of political statements in favorite music).

9. Time at which respondent became aware of political statements in music (before, during, or after initial exposure to Artist's work).

10. Degree of respondent's agreement with political statements in music.

Political Variables

11. Political interest.

12. Attentiveness to politics in mass media.

13. Political alienation.

Complementary and Reinforcing Socialization Influences

14-17. Perceived agreement of parents, teachers, friends, and government leaders with political statements in music.

18. Demographic indicators (age, sex, race, and social class).

FINDINGS

Question 1: Do a sizeable proportion of teenagers perceive that their favorite music contains political statements or ideas?

In our respondent population, the answer to this question clearly appears to be yes. It will be recalled that we asked our respondents whether they perceived the existence of political statements in the music of their favorite recording artists and in their favorite music as a whole. Fifty-two percent of our respondents perceived political statements in at least one of these categories. Interestingly, only 26 percent of our respondents perceived political statements in both categories, but even this smaller number exceeds the 23 percent who perceived neither the music of their favorite artists nor their favorite music in general as political. Table 11–1 illustrates the patterns of findings on this point:

Question 2. Does a respondent's level of musical involvement and/or the social setting in which he listens to music influence the likelihood that he views music as political? What other factors (age, sex, and the like) influence this perception? In short, what kinds of teenagers see their music as political?

Table 11–1. Percent of Respondents Perceiving Music as Political

MUSIC OF FAVORITE ARTISTS	FAVORITE MUSIC IN GENERAL		
	PERCEIVED AS POLITICAL	DON'T KNOW	PERCEIVED AS NONPOLITICAL
Perceived as Political	28.5	2.8	3.4
Don't Know	8.7	15.6	3.2
Perceived as Nonpolitical	12.0	5.8	22.6

$r = .49$; sig. $= .001$.

This is obviously an important set of questions in assessing whether or not popular music functions as an agency of socialization for, if those people who are most extensively exposed to popular music and/or most intensely involved with music do not perceive the increasingly political content of today's music, then the argument for popular music as a socializer is weakened. Similarly, if the tendency to perceive music as political is restricted primarily to one social class, age group, or sex, then the effects of popular music as a socializer are likely to be restricted (to that class, age group, or sex).

In our respondent population, however, the people who perceive music as political do tend to be slightly more extensively and emotionally involved with popular music. Specifically, there is a significant and positive association between "perceiving music as political" and:

level of musical involvement

level of perceived positive affect for performers

preference for folk music

preference for rock music

listening to music in a group rather than alone.

The fact that these relationships are in the predicted direction and do achieve statistical significance tends to provide some support for the idea that today's popular music functions as an agency of political socialization. However, the strength of these relationships, expressed in Table 11–2, tends to be quite modest, a fact which suggests caution in their interpretation.

Table 11–2 also indicates that the tendency to perceive one's favorite music as political is not restricted to a single social class or age group or sex.

Table 11–2. The Relationship Between Perceiving Music as Political, Musical Involvement, and Demographic Variables

	GAMMA VALUE	LEVEL OF SIGNIFICANCE
Preference for rock music	.38	.005
Level of positive affect for performers	.21	.01
Listening to music in a group	.19	.10
Preference for folk music	.17	.04
Level of musical involvement	.15	.02
Perceived importance of music	.22	.16
Attention to lyrics	0	N.S.
Perception of music as defining peer groups	−.06	N.S.
Age	−.08	N.S.
SES	.09	N.S.
Sex	.11	N.S.

N.S. = Not significant

Question 3. Do respondents who perceive their favorite music as political differ significantly in their political attitudes and behaviors from respondents who do not?

Given the framework we are developing here, this is clearly a rather crucial matter bearing on the question of music as a socialization agency. If people who perceive their favorite music as political, who have already forged a conscious cognitive link between the music and politics, do not differ in their political attitudes from those who think their music is nonpolitical, we believe that popular music will not be found to have much influence on politics. To be sure, it is conceivable that music (or any other pattern of stimuli) can have an influence on people's political attitudes without being consciously labelled as political and without being seen as relevant to politics. We believe in general, however, that variables perceived relevant to politics will have more influence on people's political attitudes and behaviors than those variables that people do not consciously perceive as politically relevant.

In our respondent population, teenagers who perceive their favorite music as political do differ significantly in their political attitudes and behaviors from those who see their music as nonpolitical. Indeed, perceiving music as political bears significant association with every political attitude or behavior dimension we studied. Specifically, perceiving music as political is significantly and positively related to political interest and attentiveness to politics in mass media, while significantly and negatively associated with political alienation. Our respondents exhibit a modest tendency not to agree with the political statements they heard in the music and a strong tendency to perceive their parents, teachers, and friends as disagreeing with such statements. The strength of these relationships are presented in Table 11–3.

Table 11–3. The Relationship Between "Perceiving Music as Political" and Political Attitudes and Behavior

	GAMMA VALUE	SIGNIFICANCE LEVEL
Political interest	.34	.01
Attentiveness to politics in mass media	.18	.01
Political alienation	−.23	.05
Respondent's agreement with political statements in music	−.26	.002
Respondent's perception of the degree to which parents, teachers, friends, and government leaders would agree with political statements	−.56	.05

Thus far we have found that a substantial proportion of our teenage respondents perceive that their favorite music contains political statements and that there is some tendency for these teenagers to be those who are most extensively and affectively involved in popular music. Further, those who believe music to have political content tend to have significantly different political attitudes and behavior patterns from people who do not. The former tend to be significantly more politically interested and more attentive to politics in the mass media but significantly less politically alienated than others.[1]

This pattern of findings is certainly quite consistent with the proposition that popular music functions as a significant agency of political socialization among these young people. Before we are entitled to conclude that

[1] Given the prevalence of alienation themes in the rock music these teenagers preferred and the fact that involvement in music does bear a modestly positive relationship to alienation (.15, sig. = .10), this finding seems somewhat surprising. As we will indicate, what seems to be happening here is that teenagers who perceive political statements in music with which they tend to have moderate disagreement, become more interested in politics. Exposure to, and recognition of, alienation themes in music clearly did not teach these students to become alienated (which might have been evidence for one kind of socialization impact).

our data actually support that proposition, however, we must ask our next set of questions.

Question 4. Is there any evidence that it is the music or their relationship to the music that causes those who perceive political content in music to have different political attitudes from those who do not?

We have been hypothesizing that the answer to this question would be in the affirmative, that the combination of high exposure to today's music plus a recognition of the political content of that music will lead teenagers to higher levels of interest in politics (and, possibly, to different political views) than belongs to those who have been less exposed and are less aware of today's musical content. We have also recognized, however, that the causal pattern might be quite the contrary—that youngsters who are already politically interested might be sensitized by that interest to perceive political statements in the music. To the degree that this latter process is operative, popular music's impact on political socialization might be to reinforce extant political interests.

Clearly, this study—based as it is on a single survey—cannot definitively document any causal relationships because such relationships involve matters of temporal precedence that ideally require observations made at two or more points in time.

The analytic introduction of third variables, which can provide useful information as to the directions of likely causal impact, however, is feasible with cross-sectional survey data of the type we are considering here; we have performed several analyses on our data that are suggestive. More specifically, we examined the strength of association between perceiving music as political and political interest, controlling for several music-related and political variables. We reasoned that, if the relationship between perceiving music as political and political interest was significantly stronger at high levels of musical involvement and/or among respondents with distinctive musical preferences, then the importance of music as a political socialization agency would be indicated because:

1. one could interpret the findings as suggesting that exposure to, plus recognition of, political themes in music had led to increased political interest; or, at the very least,

2. one could assert that increased exposure to, and involvement in, popular music leads politically interested teenagers to perceive the political content of music (which may be a prerequisite for the impact of music on political attitudes). We reasoned, further, that if the linkage between perceiving music as political and political interest was significantly stronger at high levels of media attention to politics, this could be interpreted to mean that people who are already sufficiently interested in

politics to attend to political events in nonmusical media are generally those most likely to perceive political statements in music. For such people, the political statements in music might well reinforce their political interests and views (but the basic process characterizing these people would be that political interest leads to recognizing the political content of music).

The results of these analyses are reported in Table 11–4. It will be observed that the relationship between perceiving music as political and political interest is significantly stronger among respondents who are most heavily involved in music, who tend to use musical preferences to define their peer group, and whose taste runs to rock music than it is among teenagers less involved, less centrally oriented to music. From contextual knowledge, we interpret these findings to mean that for many of our respondents, exposure to, plus recognition of, political themes in music lead to increased political interest. Relevant contextual knowledge, here, includes the fact that music was far more salient to most of our respondents than were political events and processes and the fact that a significant proportion of our respondents became aware of political statement in music only after repeatedly listening to given artists and songs. The data reported here do not permit us to differentiate unambiguously between those respondents for whom this interpretation is correct and those already politically interested respondents for whom increased exposure to music led to a recognition of politics in the music. The data do permit us to conclude, tentatively, that music-related variables are important in forging a cognitive link between perceiving music as political and political interest. We think that this finding does suggest that popular music was a significant agency of political socialization for our respondents. We think, too, that the one unpredicted, contrary indication reported in Table 11–4— namely, that respondents who perceived music to be especially important in their lives behaved quite differently from other respondents—should be taken into account in interpreting our findings.

Table 11–4 also provides some support for the alternative notion that it is political interest that leads to perceiving music as political rather than the other way around. This can be seen in the fact that the link between political interest and recognizing political statements in music is stronger among people who are most attentive and moderately attentive to politics in nonmusical media. The people whose experiences are reflected in this relationship may be led to recognize political statements in music because they have been sensitized to political statements in other media. We would guess that, for these people, the political statements in their favorite music reinforces political interests and views more than they teach new levels of interest and/or new political views.

Table 11–4. The Relationship Between "Perceiving Music as Political" and Political Interest, Controlling for Selected Musical and Political Variables (significance level in parentheses)

CONTROL VARIABLE	ASSOCIATION AT HIGHEST VALUES OF CONTROL VARIABLES	ASSOCIATION AT MODERATE VALUES OF CONTROL VARIABLES	ASSOCIATION AT LOWEST VALUES OF CONTROL VARIABLES
Musical involvement	.47(.03)	.30(.02)	.26(N.S.)
Preference for rock music	.39(.01)	.19(N.S.)	−.04(N.S.)
Using music to define peer groups	.50(.01)	.42(.001)	.31(.01)
Importance of music to respondent	.17(N.S.)	.34(.02)	.52(.02)
Attention to politics in nonmusic media	.35(.01)	.43(.001)	.04(.01)

N.S. = not significant

Question 5. What processes of a personal, peer group, or familiar nature contribute to the link between "perceiving music as political" and adopting distinctive political attitudes and behaviors?

Thus far we have, naturally, stressed music-related variables in this study. We explicitly recognize, however, that teen-agers listen to and react to popular music in a social context—a context provided by peers, family, and social roles.

If the data presented above provide some tentative indication that teen-agers' experiences with music do lead those who see political content in their favorite music to become more politically interested, this is all the more reason to explore the social context in which musical experiences take place. Accordingly, we were led to inquire whether the political views of a teenager's parents and friends, as well as his own sex-role and political views, have important influence on the relationship between perceiving music as political and political interest.

In our data, a consistent set of relationships obtain: the relationship between perceiving music as political and political interest is significant among respondents whose parents', friends', and own political views are ambiguously related to the political statements seen in the music; respondents who see music as political and who strongly agree or disagree with the political statements they see in the music and/or whose parents and friends strongly agree or disagree with these statements do not tend to become particularly interested in politics (Table 11–5).

To us, these findings make sense. We think it very reasonable for people who are relatively ambivalent about the political statements they hear in music to be encouraged to think about politics and to follow political events more closely in order to reduce their ambivalence, to decide whether they really agree or disagree with those statements. People in whom the political content of music creates no ambivalence or dissonance, because they already have strong opinions about politics, should not be motivated to follow politics more closely. Similarly, strong parental and peer pressures against the political ideas heard in the music appears to inhibit one from becoming politically interested, perhaps through anticipatory conflict-reduction or dissonance-reduction processes, whereas strong parental and peer agreement with the political content seems to make further politicization unnecessary. Again, however, a moderate amount of ambivalence, dissonance, or uncertainty appears to motivate people who perceive political content in their favorite music to become more interested in politics.

Table 11–5 also indicates that the significant positive relationship between perceiving music as political and political interest tends to be predominantly a male phenomenon.

It will be recalled that perceiving the political content of popular music bears a most modest but positive and statistically significant relationship to attention paid to politics in nonmusical media (.18, sig. = .01). We found that this relationship was not significantly intermediated by any of

Table 11–5. The Relationship Between "Perceiving Music as Political" and Political Interest, Controlling for Selected Variables (significance level in parentheses)

CONTROL VARIABLE	ASSOCIATION AT HIGHEST VALUE OF CONTROL VARIABLES	ASSOCIATION AT MODERATE VALUE OF CONTROL VARIABLE	ASSOCIATION AT LOWEST VALUE OF CONTROL VARIABLE
Respondent's agreement with political music	.11(N.S.)	.39(.02)	.08(N.S.)
Perceived agreement of parents with political music	.41(N.S.)	.49(.03)	.19(.10)
Perceived agreement of "people your age" with political music	−.06(N.S.)	.40(.02)	−.11(N.S.)
Sex Male:	.44(.0004)	Female:	.19(.07)

N.S. = Not significant

our musical, peer, or familial variables. It was, however, significantly intermediated by age and sex, and in a most intriguing fashion. It was among girls and younger teenagers, the very groups that were least likely to be attentive to politics in nonmusical media, that the relationship between perceiving music as political and attentiveness to politics was strongest (Table 11–6). These findings may be consistent with those just reported if we interpret them to mean that the influence of perceiving political content in music is strongest (most apparent) among those for whom competing politicizing influences are weakest.

Table 11–6. The Relationship Between "Perceiving Music as Political" and "Attentiveness to Media," Controlling for Selected Variables (significance level in parentheses)

CONTROL VARIABLE	ASSOCIATION AT HIGHEST VALUES OF CONTROL VARIABLE	ASSOCIATION AT MODERATE VALUES OF CONTROL VARIABLE	ASSOCIATION AT LOWEST VALUES OF CONTROL VARIABLE
Sex	MALE	FEMALE	
	.10(.07)		
Age	15 YEARS	16 YEARS	17 YEARS
	.30(.05)	.20(N.S.)	.09(N.S.)

N.S. = Not significant

Question 6. Does popular music function as an agency of political socialization primarily by teaching (influencing) values or primarily by stimulating individuals to political interest and activity?

We really studied only one basic political value, the value which our respondents placed on the American political system itself. We investigated this value by our questions about political alienation, for alienation involves a fundamental negative evaluation of the political system.

A fair proportion of the political themes expressed in today's popular music appear to be alienation themes, but in our data only a quite small amount of the variation in political alienation seems attributable to music-related variables. Popular music does not seem to directly socialize very many of our respondents to very much alienation.

But, as reported, our respondents perceived the alienation (and other) political themes in popular music to be inconsistent with the views of parents, teachers, and peers; and the resulting ambivalences, dissonances, and conflicts led some portion of our respondents to increased political interest.

Insofar as our data enable us to answer the question we have posed, insofar as our data are at all representative, it would seem to us that popular music may tend to function more to stimulate teenagers' interest in politics than to teach basic political values directly.

Question 7. Does popular music function as an agency of political socialization in the same way that other agencies do and/or in the way that socialization theorists have posited mass media in general function?

In our judgment, popular music functions as an agency of political socialization but does so somewhat differently from the ways in which other agencies operate and somewhat differently from the ways in which socialization theorists have posited mass media to function. We think that popular music influences teenagers' political attitudes differently from the ways in which parents, teachers, and friends do because: the politics in popular music is vicariously experienced; popular music is essentially nonreactive (i.e., the music or musician does not react to the behavior of the individual as an individual); and popular music is avoidable; whereas in contrast parents, teachers, and friends do interact nonvicariously with teenagers, do react to the teenager's questions, comments, and behaviors, and are more or less unavoidable. In most life circumstances, of course, parents, teachers, and friends are far more salient sources of information too.

These differences affect the amount and type of influence which popular music exerts on young people's political attitudes in complex ways. On the one hand, it seems clear that popular music is restricted in its influence compared to that of other socialization agencies, for relationships which are personal, face-to-face, continuing, habitual, and unavoidable are likely to be far more influential than those which are essentially vicarious, avoidable, and not necessarily continuing. On the other hand, popular music can derive important socialization influence precisely because it is extraordinary and vicarious. Today's leading popular musicians are subcultural heroes; they may be of enormous short-term salience to the teenager. They are not habitual or mundane but rather glamorous figures who can and do challenge the attitudes, mores, and morals of more traditional socialization agencies. Because the teenager's relationships to the music, the musician, and the politics of both are salient but vicarious, he is encouraged to reexamine the political attitudes and values with which he grew up and can safely "try on" new attitudes.

As the music and musician do not, of course, react directly to the teenager as an individual, popular music is probably more effective in creating moods and challenging old values than in the more individual-specific task of teaching new values. Similarly, music seems better able to critique our politics and to arouse political interest than it is to influence the specific directions that political behavior might take.

But the differences between popular music as an agency of political socialization and other socialization agencies must not be overstated. The teenagers' contacts with popular music may be as regular, frequent, and salient as his contacts with friends, where the peer group centrally involves listening to and talking about popular music. In this sense, popular music may be as unavoidable as other socialization agencies. Teenagers can also try mightily to personalize their relationships to popular musicians—as by fan clubs or magazines. The differences between a teenager's relationships with music and his relationships to parents and teachers are real, strong, and enormously significant; we are merely noting here that there are some similarities, too, similarities which may have consequences for music's capability to influence teenager's politics.

WHY THE TRADITIONAL INTERPRETATIONS OF MASS MEDIA AS SOCIALIZATION AGENCIES DON'T EXPLAIN MUSIC'S SOCIALIZATION IMPACT

Students of political socialization have tended to ignore the mass media as agencies of political socialization. In the most extensive rationale for this deemphasis of the mass media, Dawson and Prewitt (1969) gave four basic reasons that, they believe, limit the importance of mass media as socialization agencies. Simply stated, these are:

1. The media tend to be merely transmitters, not originators, of attitudes, values, and information.

2. The media reinforce extant values rather than challenge such values or create new ones, partly because people most attend to media that agree with their extant values.

3. The effects of media tend to be so strongly influenced by opinion leaders (i.e., peer group leaders) who interpret the media, that it is the socialization influence of these leaders, not the media, which should be emphasized.

4. Mass media messages are received and interpreted in a given social setting, a social setting that is likely to have more important impact on people's attitudes than any given set of messages or message-styles (within the social setting).

We think that this reasoning is far from persuasive with reference to most mass media today; here we can argue it to be largely inapplicable to the socialization influence of contemporary popular music.

First, popular musicians are largely and increasingly the originators of the attitudes, values, and themes they transmit. A sizeable proportion of today's pop songs are written by the artists who introduce them. Performers are increasingly expected to believe in and care about the things they are singing.

Second, it should be obvious that today's popular music does not tend merely to reinforce extant values. To the contrary, the political themes in contemporary popular music tend to be alienation themes. Our respondents found the political content of their favorite music to be inconsistent with their own previously held political views, and even more of them found the politics in their favorite music to be inconsistent with the political attitudes of parents, teachers, and peers. Popular music need not reinforce extant values! Even more important, in the study of socialization, the young influencee may not have a given extant value for music to reinforce. When the question is "What do a given class of people learn about X from agency Y?" the response "Nothing, because agency Y only reinforces (makes stronger) a previous attitude," is a nonanswer on its face (as well as an assumption that should be tested, not relied upon without evidence).

Third, the influence of popular music (or any other media) on teenagers' political attitudes does not seem to be rendered unworthy of study even if that influence is mediated in part by peer-group or opinion-leader influence. In our data, 65 percent of our respondents typically listened to popular music alone, not in a group—a fact which suggests that at least some of music's influence is likely to be unmediated by peers. On the other hand, we are certainly willing to admit that peers do exert influence on young people's politics, as there was a .61 gamma value (sig. $\lessapprox$ .001) between respondent's degree of agreement with political statements in music and their perception of their peers' agreement.

Finally, we agree that popular music (like any mass media or other element of popular culture) transmits messages that are received and interpreted within a sociopolitical setting. We agree that the social and political setting influences what people learn from music and how they learn it. We point out, however, that the concerns, attitudes, values, and behaviors expressed in popular music also affect sociopolitical systems, challenging or supporting them. Music can have these important effects only because it is an agency of political socialization.

SUMMARY

The following distributions and relationships obtained in our data.

1. A sizeable proportion of teenagers perceived their favorite music to contain political statements: Some 52 percent of our respondents perceived political statements in the music of their favorite musicians, their favorite music as a whole, or both.

2. There was a significant tendency for those respondents who perceived political statements in music also to be those who were:

    a. most heavily involved in popular music,

    b. most highly positive in affect for popular musicians,

    c. strong in a preference for rock and/or folk music,

    d. more likely to listen to music in a group than alone.

3. The predisposition to see music as political is not restricted to a single age grouping, social class, or sex.

4. Respondents who perceive popular music as political tend significantly to have some distinctive political attitudes and behaviors compared to those who do not. Specifically, people who perceived music as political were significantly more interested in politics and more attentive to politics in nonmusical media.

5. The relationship between "perceiving music as political" and these political attitudes tends to be significantly affected by both music-related variables and political factors.

6. The relationship between perceiving music as political and political interest is also significantly intermediated by several personal, peer-group, and familial variables. We believe that respondents with less definite opinions about the political statements in music are most likely to become more politically interested, especially under the condition that their parents, peers, and general previous political socialization have not had such strong influence as to inhibit the influence of music.

7. Popular music, then, does appear to function as a significant agency of political socialization for a sizeable proportion of our respondents. It functions, however, in a manner somewhat different from other agencies of political socialization and different, too, from the ways in which socialization theorists have expected communications media to operate.

METHODS APPENDIX

Here we provide the exact wording of each item comprising the indexes we developed to measure the variables of interest. Inter-item correlations are given in parentheses.

Musical involvement variables:

    1. Level of musical involvement: Number of hours spent per week listening to music during the last year; total number of records bought in the last year ($r = .23$; sig. $< .001$).

2. Types of music preferred: Respondents ranked each of the following genres of music from most to least liked—rhythm and blues, country-and-western, hard to acid rock, folk music, soul music, classical music, jazz, ballads, opera.

3. Perceived affect for popular musicians: "When I think of the popular recording artists that I enjoy most, I think of them with respect and admiration," "Today's popular musicians are important social critics, prophets, and seekers of social change." (r = .20; sig. ≤ .001).

4. Perceived importance of music: "How important has music been in your life?" "How important would you say music has been in your parent's home?" (r = .28; sig. < .001).

5. Attention to lyrics: A single-item indicator in which respondents were asked what they noticed first when listening to a rock song—the music, the lyrics, or the artist. Respondents who answered "lyrics" were distinguished from respondents giving any other answer.

Variables describing the social setting of listening to music:

6. Typically listens in groups vs. Typically listens alone. A single-item indicator.

7. Perception of music as a defining characteristic of peer group: "Music sets people of my age apart from older people." "The people I meet who like the same kind of music that I do generally also agree with me about politics." "My friends like the same kind of music that I do." (r averaged .12; sig. ≤ .006).

Variables linking music to politics:

8. Perception of music as political: "Do you think that there are political statements or ideas in your favorite artist's or group's music?" "Now please answer the following questions about your favorite music as a whole, not thinking about the five artists or groups you named—do you think that your favorite music contains political statements or ideas." (r = .49; sig. ≤ .006).

9. Timing of respondent's recognition of music as political: A single-item indicator asking respondent to recall when he became aware of the political statements in his favorite artist's music—before he had heard them, at the same time, or after he had heard them.

Political variables:

10. Political interest: "I try to follow closely what goes on in American politics"; "I think and talk a lot about American politics." (r = .55; sig. ≤ .001).

11. Attentiveness to politics (in media): "I watch TV programs about politics a lot;" "I listen to radio programs about politics a lot." "I read (books, newspapers, and so on.) about politics a lot." ($r = .55 \ll .001$).

12. Alienation: "When I think about politics and government, I feel like an outsider." "I approve of most of the politics and programs of the American government." "I feel that I can influence the policies of the American government." (Index was constructed on theoretical grounds.)

13. Degree of agreement with political statements in music: A two-item indicator asking respondent the extent of his agreement with the political statements in his favorite music as a whole and in the music of his favorite recording artists and groups. ($r = .46; \ll .001$).

Complementary, reinforcing, and competing socialization influences:

14. Perceived agreement of parents with political statements in music: A two-item index as in #13 ($r = .58$; sig. $\ll .001$).

15. Perceived agreement of teachers with political statements in music: A two item index as in #13. ($r = .50$; sig. $\ll .001$).

16. Perceived agreement of friends with political statements in music. A two-item index as in #13. ($r = .43$; sig. $\ll .001$).

17. Perceived agreement of government-leaders with political statements in music: A two-item index as in #13. ($r = .52$; sig. $< .001$).

18. Perceived agreement of family, teacher, friends, and government leaders with political statements in music: Various combinations of variables 14–17 were constructed.

19. Age, sex, race and social class: Single-item indicators. Social class was defined by the occupational status of the respondent's father's occupation (professional = upper middle class; white-collar nonprofessional = middle class, blue-collar = working class).

REFERENCES

Abrahams, Roger D., and Richard Bauman. "Sense and Nonsense in St. Vincent: Speech Behavior and Decorum in a Caribbean Community," *American Anthropologist* 23 (1971), 762–72.

Breckenridge, Mariane, and E. Lee Vincent. *Child Development* (Philadelphia: W. B. Saunders and Co., 1965).

Dawson, Richard, and Kenneth Prewitt. *Political Socialization* (Boston: Little, Brown and Co., 1969).

Dennis, Jack. *Socialization to Politics* (New York: John Wiley and Sons, 1973).

Denisoff, R. Serge. "Protest Songs," *American Quarterly* 22 (1970), 807–823.

———, and Mark H. Levine. "Brainwashing or Background Noise: The Popular Protest Song," in R. Serge Denisoff and Richard A. Peterson (eds.), *The Sounds of Social Change* (Chicago: Rand McNally and Co., 1972).

———, and Richard A. Peterson. *The Sounds of Social Change* (Chicago: Rand McNally and Co., 1972).

DePillis, Mario S., "Trends in American Social History and the Possibilities of Behavioral Approaches," *Journal of Social History* 1 (1967), 38–60

Dougherty, Philip. Signed Column in *New York Times* (December 21, 1969).

Finnegan, Ruth. "A Note on Oral Tradition and Historical Evidence," *History and Theory* 9 (1970), 1955.

Frank, Robert Shelby. *Message Dimensions of Television News* (Boston: D. C. Heath, 1973a).

———. Personal Communication with Senior Author, 1973b.

———. *A Longitudinal Analysis of the Relative Effects of Television and Classroom Educational Materials upon the Political Education and Socialization of Primary Grade Children* (Philadelphia: Foreign Policy Research Institute, 1974).

Gans, Herbert J. "The Famine in American Mass-Communications Research," *American Journal of Sociology* 77 (1972), 697–705.

Gekas, Viktor. "Motive and Aggressive Acts in Popular Culture," *American Journal of Sociology* 77 (1972), 680–96.

Greenstein, Fred I. *Children and Politics* (New Haven: Yale University Press, 1965).

Halpern, Ben. "Myth and Ideology in Modern Usage," *History and Theory* 1 (1961), 129–149.

Hess, Robert D., and Judith V. Torney. *The Development of Political Attitudes in Children* (Chicago: Aldine Publishing Co., 1967).

Hirsch, Paul M. "Processing Fads and Fashions," *American Journal of Sociology* 77 (1972, 639–59).

Hyman, Herbert H. *Political Socialization* (New York: The Free Press, 1959).

Jaros, Dean. *Socialization to Politics* (New York: Praeger Publishers, Inc., 1973).

Lund, Jens. "Country Music Goes to War," *Popular Music and Society* 1 (1972), 210–230.

Lystad, Mary H. "Adolescent Social Attitudes in South Africa and Swaziland," *American Anthropologist* 22 (1960), 1389–1397.

McClelland, David C. *The Achieving Society* (New York: The Free Press, 1961).

Recording Industry Association of America, Inc., press release, May 8, 1972.

Robinson, John P., and Paul M. Hirsch. "Teenage Response to Rock and Roll Protest Songs," in R. Serge Denisoff and Richard H. Peterson (eds.), *The Sounds of Social Change* (Chicago: Rand McNally and Co., 1972).

Rodnitzky, Jerome C. "The Evolution of the American Protest Song," *Journal of Popular Culture* 3 (1969), 35–45.

Schachter, S., and J. E. Singer. "Cognitive, Social and Psychological Determinants of Emotional State," *Psychological Review* 69 (1962), 379–99.

Schwartz, David C. "Toward a More Relevant and Rigorous Political Science," *Journal of Politics* (forthcoming, 1974).

Silverman, Martin G. "A Review of Natural Symbols," *American Anthropologist* 23 (1971), 1293.

Stearns, Peter S. "National Character and European Labor History," *Journal of Social History* 4 (1970), 95–125.

Tuchman, Gaye. "Objectivity as Strategic Ritual," *American Journal of Sociology* 77 (1972), 660–79.

Weitzman, Lenore J., *et al.* "Sex Role Socialization in Picture Books for Preschool Children," *American Journal of Sociology* 77 (1972), 1125–1150.

Witty, Paul, and Paul Kinsella. "Children and TV—A Ninth Report," *Elementary English* 31 (1958), 450–56.

Chapter Twelve

When Soldiers Return: Combat and Political Alienation among White Vietnam Veterans

John C. Pollock, Dan White, and Frank Gold

INTRODUCTION

The study of political socialization has tended to neglect the socializing effects of actual political experience. Wartime military service is a political experience of particular interest. Actual involvement tends to be relatively prolonged, all-encompassing, and above all, intense, especially in contrast with other forms of political activity. Further, the discontinuities between civilian and military role expectations are severe, raising the possibility that one effect of wartime service may be the resocialization of the individuals involved.

These subjects have acquired special importance now that our Vietnam veterans have returned home. Questions about the impact of war on returning servicemen have always been important issues (Stauffer *et al.*, 1949), but they have become especially significant as the United States diminishes its official military role in Vietnam. To be sure, the Vietnam veteran, like the veteran of many other wars, is faced with a difficult though traditional task: to transform his reactions from those instilled to protect him in a relatively hostile environment to ones appropriate for a somewhat more tranquil domestic milieu. But the Vietnam veteran is additionally confronted with another task, also difficult but less traditional, a task produced by this particular war, namely: how to evaluate the worth of his own military role in Vietnam and how to judge the political leaders and the political system which sent him there, all in the context of having served in a war that is manifestly unpopular with many of his fellow Americans. In *No Victory Parades: The Return of the Vietnam Veteran* (1971), Murray Polner notes that not one of the veterans, whether they were hawk or dove, was entirely free of doubt about the nature of the war and the American role in it. Polner and others warn that never before have so many questioned, as much as these veterans have, the essential

317

rightness of what they were forced to do (Hersh, 1970; Jones, 1972; Lifton 1972; Lane, 1970).

It is suggested that one reaction of returning Vietnam veterans is to become alienated from both their military role and the civic role of citizen. Civilian or civic role alienation may be evident in cynicism toward the uses of military force by the United States and toward politicians, political parties, and voting. It may also extend to a belief that violence is perhaps the only or most effective way for groups either to protect themselves and their allies or to accomplish serious social and political change.

It is contended, moreover, that the likelihood of such alienation is related to the nature of one's military experience. Specifically, it is assumed that differing *intensities* of military experience, in which an individual is required to adhere to his military role more or less rigidly, directly affect the adjustment of servicemen to civilian roles. We may expect that the supply clerk stationed in Saigon will have significantly divergent views of the military from those of a combat infantryman having served 24 months on an advisory team assigned to some firebase. Obviously, it is not location but the intensity of the military experience that distinguishes between the clerk and the combat soldier. The man located in Saigon will not face situations calling for either the time or the emotional involvement confronting the Military Assistance Command Vietnam advisor. In particular, those who have killed can be assumed to have undergone more intense military role experiences than those who have not. The central question of this study, then, is: Does the intensity of a veteran's military role experience (which is assumed to vary with proximity to combat) predict critical or alienated attitudes toward his civic and military roles when he returns home?

A corollary of this proposition is that maximum distance in time from combat roles or combat conditions is also associated with military and civic attitudes. Specifically, those returned veterans who have been in the United States a relatively long time since serving in Vietnam can be expected to exhibit attitudes different from those who have returned only recently.

This assumption predicts that those who returned long ago will have more opportunities to become "resocialized" into nonalienated citizen roles. As the multiple benefits and cross-pressures of living in America have had more time to affect the long-returned veteran than his recently returned peer, it is reasonable to assume that those with more post-Vietnam exposure to the American environment are relatively likely to exhibit supportive rather than alienated attitudes toward military and civic issues. Therefore, we suggest that the more time passed since his re-entry, the more the Vietnam veteran will display supportive, nonalienated attitudes toward the American political system, becoming "resocialized" into mainstream beliefs and values suitable for harmonious living in the United States.

The twin assumptions that combat experience is related to alienation and that maximum resocialization time is related to supportive attitudes allow us to ask a number of pertinent questions. Does the act of killing affect substantially the way Vietnam veterans view the war and their country? Does the amount of time spent in Vietnam significantly affect veteran attitudes? Does amount of return time affect veteran attitudes? To the extent it does, are combat and noncombat servicemen affected in similar or dissimilar ways? At least partial answers to these questions can be provided by examining the information which follows.

A STUDY OF RETURNING VETERANS

Procedures, Demographics, and General Attitudes

To examine the preceding questions, a survey of veterans enrolled in a large state university in the western United States was undertaken in January and early February of 1972, when students were registering for the spring semester. After registering, veterans go to a veterans' office on campus to show eligibility for educational benefits. At the office at least 50 percent of the total of approximately three thousand veteran students were asked to fill out the survey questionnaire. To determine which 50 percent of the group would be exposed to the survey, a cluster sample was taken. All the hours of student registration were listed in one-hour segments, and half were chosen at random using a table of random numbers. During the selected hours, participation in the study was requested on a voluntary basis. Three hundred and eighty-three questionnaires, representing over 10 percent of the university's veteran population, were completed. Of those, 163 were veterans who had served in or immediately offshore from Vietnam. Fifty-four can clearly be considered combat veterans in that they report having killed people. The remainder, including veterans of the Navy who served with the fleet off Vietnam, can be considered noncombat veterans. In this study we shall only consider the attitudes of actual Vietnam veterans, not those of all veterans who were servicemen during the war in Vietnam.

The sample is limited to veterans who are college students, and the conclusions offered cannot therefore be taken to represent the views of veterans not in college. The sample also consists almost entirely of white males (not surprisingly, since relatively few nonwhites are enrolled at the university research site). We feel that a measure of minority group military and civic role alienation would have been desirable. Nonetheless, it seems likely that the results can be generalized to a sizeable portion of the college-age Vietnam veterans in the United States.

The sample is quite homogeneous. About two thirds were born and reared in cities of 20,000 inhabitants or more, and about one third come from cities containing one half million or more. About 60 percent are married. Of those, about half have children, almost always between one and three. About 60 percent entered the service at age twenty or younger, although the sampled respondents consider their parents privileged economically, about 80 percent ranking their parents above-average or higher. Over 40 percent report combined parental incomes of $15,000 or more.

Profile data on Vietnam college veterans after their return suggest that they remain, as a group, relatively homogeneous and register academic progress and perceived increments in political interest and awareness. The veteran students are strikingly homogeneous with respect to age. About 60 percent are between 25 and 27 years old, about 20 percent are younger, and about 20 percent are older. Scholastic progress is also evident. In contrast to preservice levels of education firmly in the 12- to 14-year bracket (high school diploma or a couple of years of college), about 60 percent have now completed four or more years of college, and about 35 percent of the sample is in graduate school. Similarly, in contrast to the less than 45 percent with a higher than C plus average prior to their Vietnam experience, today over 50 percent earn averages of 3.0 (B) or better. In great contrast with the majority's lukewarm interest or in awareness of politics prior to Vietnam, after returning about 84 percent report themselves interested or very interested in politics, and about 80 percent now consider themselves aware or very aware of politics. Over 60 percent of the respondents call themselves Democrats, while about 25 percent identify with the Republican Party.

Regarding experience in the service, about 60 percent of the veterans spent three years or less in the service, and another 27 percent spent four years. Most served a relatively short time. The highest rank two thirds of them obtained was that of E–4 or E–5, noncommissioned officer status.[1] Only one of the respondents was given a dishonorable discharge. About one fourth spent six months or less in Vietnam; about one half spent between seven and twelve months there; and another fourth were in Vietnam between thirteen and eighteen months. The variation in respondents' ages when they went to Vietnam is quite great, rather evenly distributed between ages 20 to 25 or older, the highest frequencies in the 20- and 21-

[1] The distribution of respondents by branch of service was: Air Force = 8%; Navy = 32%; Army = 43%; Marine Corps = 17%.

year age bracket. But over 50 percent of the veterans were sent to Vietnam after their 21st birthday.

About 40 percent spent most of their time at a firebase, and about half of the veterans are proud or extremely proud of their units. While only about 25 percent of the veterans report heavy casualties in their units, almost half report losing an exceptionally close friend or buddy. Fewer respondents, however (about one third), of the Vietnam veterans, say they have killed or believe they have killed Vietnamese.

Biographical profiles apart, most Vietnam veterans seem to exhibit a wide range of attitudes toward politics and the use of violence domestically that can be described as "ambivalent" about existing institutional arrangements and practices.

Regarding the use of violence, most of the veterans, between 52 to 59 percent, do not believe violence is necessary or the only way to accomplish political change, and about 70 percent disagree that private groups should have guns or train citizens in gun use because the government is unreliable as a protector. Rejection of violence and even civil disobedience extends to its disavowal even if the government were to do something severely jeopardizing the civil liberties of a specific group: blacks. When asked what they would do if the government had just arrested and imprisoned many of the Negroes in their communities even though there had been no trouble, about 64 percent replied they would try to free blacks through conventional political means. Only about 27 percent would become involved in protest movements possibly involving civil disobedience, and only 4 percent would resort to some sort of armed action.

About 45 percent of the respondents do not consider black and brown power movements a new and dangerous form of racism (with about 23 percent undecided), and about 55 percent agree that minority peoples in the United States have been systematically excluded from the benefits of the American political system.

Most of the respondents feel some sort of personal political efficacy, believing that they make some difference as individuals, although most also suspect that voting as a means of political expression is not the main thing deciding policy in the United States. And most of the veterans, typically about 60 percent, also exhibit considerable mistrust of "politicians," viewing most of them as self-serving, manipulative, and "removed" from the expression of popular will. (Presumably, however, if those same "politicians" are given specific titles such as "Senator" or "President," many veterans, like many Americans, would want their children to become one.) Attitudes toward political parties are ambiguous, about half the veterans considering them important in the political process, the other half believing them useless.

The extent of national agreement with such attitudes is hard to assess. The over-all pattern appears to be fundamentally supportive, however, in that although politicians may be mistrusted, individuals view themselves as politically "efficacious," able to "get by," and unready to consider violence as useful or necessary for social change.

Attitudes toward the use of military force reveal serious doubts about the propriety of the world military role of the United States. To be sure, most respondents disagree or are undecided in reacting to the statement that "our government is too ready to use military force in dealing with other countries." About 60 percent of the Vietnam veterans agree with the statement that "the men in Lt. Calley's platoon probably were not responsible for what they did at My Lai because they were acting under the orders of their platoon leader."

Other evidence nevertheless suggests some alienation from our war-making role. Over 50 percent of the veterans disagree that our government is always hesitant in using the military power at its disposal in dealing with other countries. About 60 percent agree that they sometimes feel ashamed of what our military forces have done in Vietnam. And, responding to the statement, "most of the killing done by the U.S. forces in Vietnam is justified," only 36 percent agree, 18 percent are undecided, and 46 percent disagree. Furthermore, in contrast to specific sympathy for Calley's companions, about 69 percent believe that, in principle, individuals should be made to account for their actions. What they do is not the responsibility of their officers. About 52 percent of the veterans (with 15 percent undecided) disagree that Lt. Calley was probably justified in doing what he did at My Lai. It is not clear to what extent these opinions are shared nationally, but they reveal some measure of discontent with our military behavior in Vietnam.

Combat Experience and Alienation

In the Vietnam war, because it is so controversial, because combat experience is intense relative to the experience of noncombat personnel, and because in it an individual suffers high risk of death both for himself and friends, combat soldiers may become more alienated from military and civic roles than noncombat soldiers. A combat soldier is defined as someone who reports that he has killed or thinks he has killed individuals.[2] Three related hypotheses can be advanced regarding attitudes toward the use of military force; parties, politicians, and voting; and violence and change:

1. The closer to combat a serviceman is, the more he will be alienated from U.S. military actions.

[2] Combat soldiers = 54.

2. The closer to combat a serviceman is, the more alienation he will experience from U.S. parties, politicians, and the voting process and the less political efficacy he will display.

3. The closer to combat a serviceman is, the more alienated he will be from incremental change and the more likely to perceive some violence as necessary to accomplish significant change.

These hypotheses were tested using a number of Likert scale items, and the highest Gamma correlations (those above .25) were recorded. All but two of the sixteen relatively significant correlations confirmed the hypotheses in the predicted direction, as the list of items in Table 12–1 demonstrates.

Only two of the significant correlations disconfirm the hypotheses, suggesting that combat soldiers do not condemn the actions of U.S. troops generally at My Lai and that they prefer to think that politicians care what they think (Gamma − .31). But they also believe even more strongly that as individuals they have little say about what the government does (Gamma .55). The prediction that those who have killed in combat are likely to be alienated from shows of military force and to believe that violence may be necessary for significant change is confirmed, but what is confirmed most strongly is the association between combat experience and alienation from the American political system.

Of all the variables associated with service in Vietnam, combat experience probably exhibits the greatest predictive power. Time spent in Vietnam also predicts stateside alienation. The longer a veteran was in Vietnam, the more likely he is to believe he has no say in government (.45), to believe that one cannot really influence what happens in society at large (.36), and to think that the way people vote is not the main thing that decides how things are run in this country (.35). Similarly, the lower the highest rank someone attained in the service, the more likely he is to register several kinds of alienation: to feel ashamed sometimes of what the U.S. has done in Vietnam (.30), to believe public officials do not care what people like him think (.30), to resort to civil disobedience or guerrilla warfare if blacks are arbitrarily incarcerated without justification (.30), and to think that one of the best reasons for people to have guns is to make sure that the government doesn't get too much power (.28).

While time in Vietnam and low rank are associated with alienation, the act of killing itself predicts a far broader range of variables associated with alienation than these variables or indeed than any other measure of experience in Vietnam. It is also probably the most valid measure of experience in Vietnam. For example, lack of pride in one's unit's performance in Vietnam predicts to a range of variables connected with alienation at home and predicts them more strongly than combat experience. In particular, the less proud a veteran is of his unit's conduct in

Table 12–1. Combat Experience and Alienation

VIETNAM COMBAT VETERANS ARE LIKELY TO:	GAMMA*
A. REGARDING U.S. MILITARY FORCE:	
1. Condemn actions of U.S. troops at My Lai.	−.26
2. Agree that the U.S. is seldom justified in using military force.	.29
3. Agree that our government is too ready to use military force in dealing with other countries.	.25
B. REGARDING PARTIES, POLITICIANS, AND VOTING:	
1. Disagree that parties are means by which citizens make their opinion felt on the government.	.26
2. Agree that American political parties are so similar that a vote for either one results in the same thing.	.46
3. Disagree that politicians represent the general interest.	.38
4. Agree that in America, only mediocre candidates run for office.	.49
5. Agree that a large number of city and county politicians are political hacks.	.33
6. Disagree that the way people vote is the main thing that decides how things are run in this country.	.38
7. Agree that public officials don't care much what people like him think.	−.31
8. Agree that people like him don't have much say about what the government does.	.55
C. REGARDING VIOLENCE AND CHANGE:	
1. Agree that there will always be wars because, for one thing, there will always be races who ruthlessly try to grab more than their share.	.29
2. Disagree that the American political system provides so many opportunities for change that violence is unnecessary.	.25
3. Agree that the American political system is so stacked against some people that the only way they can make changes is through the use of violence.	.32
4. Agree that if the government had just arrested and imprisoned many of the Negroes in the community even if there had been no trouble, appropriate reactions would include civil disobedience and even, in some cases, guerilla warfare.	.36

* A positive Gamma value indicates confirmation of the combat-alienation proposition; a negative value disconfirms it.

N.B. The phrasing of the items in the tables reflects the responses of veterans to the original test items, which in the questionnaire were carefully balanced for negative and positive connotations and phrasing.

Vietnam, the more likely he is to consider the U.S. as too ready to use military force abroad (.58), to believe that most of the killing accomplished by the U.S. in Vietnam has been unnecessary (.60), and to feel ashamed of our actions there (.33). At the same time, the individual with little pride in his unit feels little sense of efficacy in his ability to influence government (.38), and he also believes that violence may be necessary (.40) and perhaps the only way (.46) for many people to bring about change in the United States.

In this study, nevertheless, lack of unit pride may not be a wholly satisfactory measure of experience *in Vietnam,* experience which in turn predicts subsequent experience or attitudes in the United States. To be sure, whether a veteran is proud of his unit or not has virtually no relation at all (Gamma − .02) to whether he killed anyone. But those already alienated prior to serving in Vietnam may have simply retained their alienation through their Vietnam experience and perhaps considered service in their units as alienating as other experiences associated with American life. Or perhaps subsequent, post-Vietnam views of the war and one's own role there modified perceptions of unit performance. In either case, unit pride or its lack may not be largely generated by experiences specifically undergone in Vietnam. Alienation from unit performance may not *predict* stateside alienation in a causal sense, but rather may be simply another element in a larger pattern of alienation from American public life. Combat experience, on the other hand, specifically the act of killing, definitely did occur inside Vietnam and can be considered a valid predictor of the attitudes of returned veterans.

Some variables associated with experience in Vietnam predict support for rather than alienation from the U.S. politico–military system. The older a veteran was when he went to Vietnam, in fact the older a veteran is generally, the more likely he is to feel politically efficacious, to do less for blacks who are jailed without cause, and to reject violence as necessary for change in America. Similarly, if a veteran spent five years or more in the service, he is more likely to support prevailing notions about our political and military system, to believe especially in his own efficacy, and to reject the use of violence as a means for change in the United States. Only 15 percent of the veterans served in the armed forces for five years or more, however, and for the majority (those serving two years or less, three years, and four years), amount of time spent in the service has little relation to political alienation.

To discover that U.S. soldiers who killed in Vietnam are alienated compared with those who did not kill is perhaps not especially surprising. The act of killing may lead a serviceman to consider in sharp relief his own and his country's reasons for combat participation and, to the extent he has doubts about his combat role, to doubt also the purposes of those who created it. It is more surprising, however, to learn that although killing *per se* predicts alienation, those who have killed a rather large number of people are the very opposite of alienated; they support U.S. institutions and actions completely.

Regarding U.S. military behavior, those who killed six or more people in Vietnam are much more likely to support our activities there than those who killed five or fewer.[3] Soldiers who killed often, comprising 39 percent of the combat soldiers, are more supportive than those who killed occasionally, comprising 61 percent of the combat soldiers. The men who have often killed are likely to disagree that the U.S. is seldom justified in using force in dealing with other countries (.51), to believe that most of the killing done by U.S. forces in Vietnam is justified (.50), and to feel no shame about what the U.S. has done in Southeast Asia (.33). Similarly, they are more confident than those who killed occasionally that our political party and voting systems are meaningful and display far more personal political efficacy. The frequent killers believe that they have a considerable say in government affairs (.42), that what happens to them is largely their own doing (.73), that the two parties offer genuine alternatives (.43), and that politicians do not spend most of their time getting reelected or reappointed (.53). These men, furthermore, are apt to believe private groups do not have the right to train members in marksmanship and underground warfare tactics to help put down any conspiracies that might occur in this country (.30) and to believe individuals do not need guns to prevent the government from gaining too much power (.48).

Soldiers who have often killed seem different from occasional killers in other respects. In Vietnam more of their buddies were killed (.42), and they exhibit far more pride in their units (.62). They consistently have achieved higher rank (high noncommissioned officer and low beginning officer ranks) than occasionals (.62). They also consider their present economic rank relatively low (− .55).[4]

---

[3] Respondents who reported killing a specific number of Vietnamese = 46. Most of these (61%) reported killing 2–5 persons; 13% reported killing 6–19 persons; 26% reported killing 20 or more persons.

[4] It should be noted that the experience of killing in combat was only weakly associated with time spent in Vietnam (.21) or years in service (.26). It is possible, therefore, that experience in Vietnam or the service did not socialize these respondents to new orientations. Instead, they may have begun their military training with a thorough acceptance of both their civic and military roles, thus becoming more efficient soldiers and remaining supportive citizens. These respondents may have entered the service with general "role-accepting" orientations, disposed to perform well in whatever role society cast them at a particular time. The postulation of a preservice "role-accepting" disposition may help explain why those who attained high rank, showed great pride in their units, and killed many Vietnamese seem highly supportive of U.S. military activity and the legitimacy of the U.S. political system. Yet killing many Vietnamese predicts system support far more strongly than the other two variables (high rank and unit pride), suggesting that battlefield experience may contribute substantially to the formation of alienated or supportive attitudes, regardless of prior dispositions. The resolution of this issue will depend on further research.

A threshold effect is therefore apparent in measurements of the impact of killing on alienation. In general, those who have killed at all are relatively alienated compared to those who have not. Among killers, however, those who have killed a large number strongly support the use of military force and the party and voting systems and reject the use of violence in domestic politics.

Resocialization and Alienation

Do attitudes change after Vietnam veterans have been reacclimated to American life for some time, or does prolonged exposure to the United States have little impact? To what extent are veterans who returned several years ago "resocialized" into legitimate, nonalienated, supportive political attitudes?

A majority of veterans studied had been back in the United States less than 36 months, as Table 12–2 reveals.

Table 12–2. Return Time: Number of Months Passed since Vietnam Veterans Returned

NUMBER OF MONTHS	FREQUENCY	PERCENT	CUMULATIVE PERCENT
6 or less	6	3.7	3.7
6–12	3	1.8	5.5
12–18	19	11.7	17.2
18–24	20	12.3	29.4
24–36	45	27.6	57.1
36 or more	70	42.9	100.0
Total	163	100.0	100.0

If noncombat and combat soldiers are considered together, it is clear that number of months of reexposure to the United States has virtually no impact on political attitudes. Those who returned home many months ago are no more likely or unlikely to be alienated from the political system than are recent returnees. The single notable exception to that observation is that long-returned veterans are more likely than recent arrivals to believe one of the best reasons for people to have guns is to make sure that the government doesn't get too much power (Gamma .43).

It may be thought, nevertheless, that other factors affecting returned veterans may also influence their political attitudes, two of which are self-ranked economic status and educational achievement. In general differentials in veteran economic status, like different return times, have little relation to political attitudes. On the only three items showing significant correlations, those who rank their present economic status as average, above average, or high (about 55 percent) are likely to consider U.S. military policies justified (one item) and violence unnecessary for change (two items). But little can be concluded from such meager evidence.

Educational achievement after reentry, by contrast with time since reentry and economic status, appears to affect all Vietnam veterans. Those with some formal education beyond the bachelor's degree (about 34 percent of the sample), compared with those exhibiting less education, are somewhat more likely to consider individuals responsible for actions in combat, regardless of officers' orders; to believe that voting is not the main thing that decides how things are run in this country; and to reject the notion that one of the best reasons for people to have guns is to make sure that the government doesn't get too much power. For all Vietnam veterans considered together, time passed since reentry and high economic status exert little impact on political attitudes, although high educational achievement clearly does.

If the veterans are divided into two groups of nonkillers and killers, however, very different tendencies are evident. Those very factors expected to "resocialize" veterans into supportive attitudes—time, economic and educational success—do as predicted for nonkillers. Integrative factors are related to politically supportive attitudes for nonkillers. For soldiers who have killed, however, precisely the opposite occurs. The passing of time and the acquisition of economic and educational success are related to increased alienation from the U.S. political system.

Nonkillers and killers alike who have been back a relatively long time believe that people should have guns to ensure the government doesn't acquire too much power (Gammas are .42 and .52, respectively). But nonkiller attitudes toward military force, parties, and voting do not vary with time. For those who killed in Vietnam, however, as the years since reentry pass, attitudes toward military and political procedures become markedly alienated, as shown in Table 12–3.

Post-Vietnam educational achievement does not seem to affect noncombat and combat veterans in such strikingly different ways as do time back and economic status. Nevertheless, the over-all trend is again confirmed. Highly educated killers are likely to be more alienated than highly educated nonkillers. Table 12–4 reveals that, although well-educated nonkillers are somewhat alienated from the political system, well-educated killers are even more so. The major exception to the trend is that both combatants and noncombatants disagree with arming the populace in the United States, and killers additionally believe that violence is not neces-

Table 12–3. Political Alienation of Combat Soldiers, by Time since Re-entry and Post-Vietnam Economic Status

	GAMMA
I. **LONG-RETURNED KILLERS ARE LIKELY:**	
A. REGARDING MILITARY FORCE:	
1. to feel ashamed of something that we did in Vietnam;	.34
2. to feel most of the killing was unnecessary;	.31
3. to believe individuals cannot escape personal responsibility for following orders;	.55
4. to consider the men in Lt. Calley's platoon responsible for their actions; and	.36
5. to believe Lt. Calley unjustified in doing what he did to My Lai.	.34
B. REGARDING PARTIES, POLITICIANS, AND POLITICAL EFFICACY:	
1. to believe political parties so similar in America that it doesn't matter which one you vote for—they'll both do the same thing;	.38
2. to believe that politicians often manipulate people; and	.42
3. to believe that what happens to oneself is not largely one's own doing	.60
II. **HIGH-STATUS KILLERS ARE LIKELY:**	
A. REGARDING PARTIES AND SELF-EFFICACY:	
1. to believe that political parties are *not* the means through which a citizen makes his opinion felt on the government; and	.40
2. to believe that "what happens to me" is *not* "largely my own doing."	.53
B. REGARDING INTERNAL OPPRESSION:	
1. to believe that minority peoples in the U.S. have been systematically excluded from the benefits of the American political system; and	.36
2. to consider one of the best reasons for people to have guns is to make sure that the government doesn't get too much power.	.38

sary for change in the American political system.[5] Only one small inconsistency appears. Well-educated combat soldiers appear more disposed to believe that parties express the political will of citizens than do noncombatants.

[5] It should be noted that education may not be a major means of social mobility for combat veterans since, among them, education varies inversely with parental income $(-.44)$ and self-ranked economic status $(-.54)$.

Table 12–4. Political Alienation of Veterans by High Post-Vietnam Level of Education

	NON-KILLERS*	KILLERS*
A. REGARDING U.S. MILITARY FORCE:		
1. Individuals are responsible for their actions, regardless of officers' order.	.30	.31
2. The men in Lt. Calley's platoon were responsible for what they did.	—	.66
3. Calley was unjustified in doing what he did.	.38	—
4. Lack of pride in one's unit.	—	.48
B. REGARDING VOTES, PARTIES, AND POLITICIANS:		
1. The way people vote is not the main thing that decides how things are run in this country.	.36	.70
2. Political parties are not the major means of political expression for citizens.	.36	−.52
3. Politicians represent special interests more than the general interest.	—	.39
4. Politicians spend most of their time getting reappointed or reelected.	—	.59
5. I don't think public officials care much what people like me think.	−.33	.72
C. REGARDING INTERNAL VIOLENCE:		
1. One of the best reasons for people to have guns is to make sure that the government doesn't get too much power.	−.47	−.75
2. The American political system provides so few opportunities for change that violence is unnecessary.	—	.29

CONCLUSION: THE DESOCIALIZED COMBAT VETERAN

This study of 163 Vietnam veterans in college yields a number of conclusions suitable for testing on the Vietnam veteran population as a whole. They include the following:

1. Vietnam veterans in general support the notion that violence is unnecessary for some groups to improve their social and economic position; register ambivalence about politicians, party, and voting systems; demonstrate high levels of personal efficacy and self-confidence; and reject much of what the U.S. military has done in Vietnam.

2. Veterans who engaged in active combat (those who killed people) in Vietnam display political attitudes markedly different from those held by noncombat veterans (those who did not kill anyone).

3. Combat veterans are relatively likely to exhibit alienation from what U.S. military forces have done in Vietnam, and from parties, politicians, and voting. They are also more likely than noncombat veterans to exhibit little confidence that they matter or to believe in their own ability to control their own destinies, and they are relatively likely to view violence as necessary for certain groups in their efforts to achieve social change.

4. An exception to the proposition that combat experience is linked to alienation is the finding that the more people a combat soldier has killed, the less alienated he is likely to be and the more supportive of existing military and political behavior.

5. Reentry into the United States has little effect on the political attitudes of Vietnam veterans as a group. Length of time since reentry and economic status have relatively little impact on the attitudes of returned servicemen, although high education levels are associated with political alienation.

6. Reentry and return to civilian life, however, have an impact on combat soldier attitudes different from their impact on noncombatant attitudes.

7. Combat veterans who returned many months ago and who enjoy privileged economic status are likely to display high levels of political alienation whereas noncombat servicemen who reentered the United States a long time ago and who are privileged economically hold political attitudes supporting current military and political arrangements.

8. Although all highly educated veterans are likely to display political alienation, combat soldiers who display a high level of education after reentry are likely to show far more alienation than noncombat personnel.

9. Factors assumed to be associated with reintegration into civilian life— a relatively large amount of time elapsed since reentry and economic and scholastic success—do not reduce the political alienation suffered by combat soldiers. On the contrary, time, monetary success, and educational achievement all *increase* the political alienation of those who killed people in Vietnam. For the soldier engaged in combat in the Vietnam war, a war fraught with controversy, the trauma of high risk and killing do not diminish with the passing months. Time does not heal the combat soldier's psychic wounds. Nor does success. Instead, time and success increase his alienation from both political and military systems and reduce his confidence in his capacity to control the direction of his life.

What best explains these findings? Why does alienation increase after reentry into the United States? Is it temporary, likely to pass as official U.S. military involvement in Southeast Asia diminishes? Or is the alienation likely to endure, even grow? Clearly further study is required to explain what seems an exceedingly complex phenomenon (Fendrick and Person, 1970). One conclusion about resocialization can be reached, however, which our data, although limited to white, middle-class college students, allow us to answer in a tentative way.

The evidence presented here suggests that the alienation will persist. Not only are combat soldiers alienated from the military, and especially the political system, but they also appear alienated from themselves. They manifest disbelief in their own efficacy, a lack of confidence in their ability to have much control over the direction of their own lives. Because alienation is apparent at both political and personal or psychological levels, it is likely that combat participation induces both political and psychological trauma.

No precombat study of servicemen attitudes toward politics was made, testing degrees of support and alienation prior to military service, and as a result no definitive conclusions can be offered about attitude change. Nevertheless, combat soldiers in Vietnam can be considered likely to have undergone a "desocialization" experience, in which supportive attitudes toward the polity and self, nurtured by a variety of factors through the years of childhood and adolescence, are probably ruptured. Combat soldiers in the war in Vietnam are further desocialized when they return, and time and success do not diminish but rather augment the alienation from politics and self. Indeed, this desocialization may constitute a disability as severe as the physical disabilities suffered by servicemen.

The disintegration of old political roles and the formation of new ones by Vietnam veterans have been described masterfully by Robert Jay Lifton in *Home From the War: Vietnam Veterans: Neither Victims nor Executioners* (Simon and Schuster, 1973). Describing the process of role transformation undergone by a specific group of Vietnam veterans, Vietnam Veterans Against the War, Professor Lifton isolates three discrete steps: confrontation, reordering, and renewal (Gray, 1973). The third stage refers to the self's attainment of a form for its newly won integrity. The study described here does not focus on Vietnam Veterans Against the War (VVAW) but on a representative sample of veterans in a large university. It agrees that college combat veterans generally have undergone civic role confrontation and perhaps reordering, but the evidence for "renewal" is less clear. Rather, the alienation from roles calling for self-efficacy and political efficacy evident in our study suggests more about disintegration than it does about reintegration or renewal. The VVAW have a special role identified by Lifton as a "survivor mission" to expose to civilians the guilt, evil, and absurdity of this war. Yet most veterans are not active politically but struggle silently. Most college combat veterans and combat veterans generally may lack that "mission," may feel not only the loss of old roles but the absence of new ones. Our study indicates that the political role disintegration of combat veterans is thorough, enduring, and cumulative, a civic tragedy of considerable dimension. Unless these veterans are able to locate or forge new civic roles appropriate to the experiences they have undergone, the consequences both for them and for society could be shattering.

REFERENCES

Fendrick, J. M., and Michael A. Person. "Black Veterans Return," *TransAction* (March 7, 1970), 32–7.

Gray, J. Glenn. "Black," *The New York Review of Books* XX:II (June 28, 1973), 22–4.

Hersh, Seymour M. "My Lai 4: A Report on the Massacre and its Aftermath," *Harper's Magazine* (May, 1970), 53–84.

Jones, Tony. "The Invisible Army," *Harper's Magazine* (August, 1972), 10–18.

Lane, Mark. *Conversations with Americans* (New York: Simon and Schuster, 1970).

Lifton, Robert Jay. "Home From the War—the Psychology of Survival," *The Atlantic Monthly* (November, 1972), 56–72.

———. *Home From the War: Vietnam Veterans: Neither Victims Nor Executioners* (New York: Simon and Schuster, 1973).

Polner, Murray. *No Victory Parades: The Return of the Vietnam Veteran* (New York: Holt, Rinehart, and Winston, 1971).

Stouffer, Samuel, *et al. The American Soldier:* Vol. I *(Adjustment During Army Life)* and Vol. II *(Combat and its Aftermath)* (Princeton: Princeton University Press, 1949).

Index